D1527589

The Critical Response to Mark Twain's *Huckleberry Finn*

The Critical Response to Mark Twain's *Huckleberry Finn*

EDITED BY
Laurie Champion

Critical Responses in Arts and Letters, Number 1
Cameron Northouse, Series Adviser

GREENWOOD PRESS
New York • Westport, Connecticut • London

Library of Congress Cataloging-in-Publication Data

The Critical response to Mark Twain's Huckleberry Finn / edited by
Laurie Champion.
     p. cm.—(Critical responses in arts and letters, ISSN 1057-0993
; no. 1)
   Includes bibliographical references and index.
   ISBN 0-313-27575-0 (alk. paper)
   1. Twain, Mark, 1835-1910. Adventures of Huckleberry Finn.
I. Champion, Laurie.   II. Series.
PS1305.C75   1991
813'.4—dc20   91-25255

British Library Cataloguing in Publication Data is available.

Library of Congress Catalog Card Number: 91-25255
ISBN: 0-313-27575-0
ISSN: 1057-0993

First published in 1991

Greenwood Press, 88 Post Road West, Westport, CT 06881
An imprint of Greenwood Publishing Group, Inc.

Printed in the United States of America

The paper used in this book complies with the
Permanent Paper Standard issued by the National
Information Standards Organization (Z39.48-1984).

10 9 8 7 6 5 4 3 2 1

Copyright Acknowledgments

The editor and publisher gratefully acknowledge the following for permission to use copyrighted materials:

"Twain to Webster—4 April 1885," *Mark Twain's Letters to His Publisher, 1867-1894*, ed. Hamlin Hill (Berkeley: University of California Press, 1967), 187-188. Copyright © 1967, the Mark Twain Company.

"Twain's Journal Entries," *Mark Twain's Notebooks & Journals. Volume III*, ed. Robert Pack Browning, Michael B. Frank, and Lin Salamo (Berkeley: University of California Press, 1979), 132, 134, 135-136, 356. Copyright © 1980.

Asa Don Dickinson, "Huckleberry Finn is Fifty Years Old—Yes; But is He Respectable?" *Wilson Bulletin for Librarians*, X (Nov. 1935), 180-185.

V. S. Pritchett, "Books in General," *New Statesman and Nation*, XXII (2 August 1941), 113. Reproduced with permission of *New Statesman and Society*.

Leslie Fiedler, "Come Back to the Raft Ag'in, Huck Honey!" first appeared in *Partisan Review*, 15, No. 6 (June 1948), 664-671. Reprinted with permission of Leslie Fiedler.

T. S. Eliot, "Introduction," *Adventures of Huckleberry Finn*, New York: Chanticleer Press, 1950, vii-xvi. Reprinted by permission of Faber and Faber, Ltd.

Leo Marx, "Mr. Eliot, Mr. Trilling, and *Huckleberry Finn*," *The American Scholar*, 22, No. 4 (Autumn 1953), 423-440. Reprinted with permission of Leo Marx.

Henry Nash Smith, "A Sound Heart and a Deformed Conscience," *Mark Twain: The Development of a Writer*, Cambridge, Massachusetts: The Belknap Press of Harvard University Press, 1962, pp. 113-137. Reprinted by permission of the publishers from *Mark Twain: The Development of a Writer* by Henry Nash Smith, Cambridge, MA: The Belknap Press of Harvard University Press, Copyright © 1962 by the President and Fellows of Harvard College.

Peter G. Beidler, "The Raft Episode in *Huckleberry Finn*," *Modern Fiction Studies*, XIV (Spring 1968), 11-20. *Modern Fiction Studies*, Copyright 1968, by Purdue Research Foundation, West Lafayette, Indiana 47907. Reprinted with permission.

Alan Trachtenberg, "The Form of Freedom in *Adventures of Huckleberry Finn*," *Southern Review*, VI (October 1970), 954-971. Reprinted with permission of the author.

Neil Schmitz, "The Paradox of Liberation in *Huckleberry Finn*," *Texas Studies in Literature and Language*, 13 (1971), 125-136. Reprinted from *Texas Studies in Literature and Language* by permission of the author and the University of Texas Press. Copyright © 1971 by the University of Texas Press.

Walter Blair, "Was *Huckleberry Finn* Written?" *Mark Twain Journal*, 19, No. 4 (1979), 1-3. Reprinted by permission of *Mark Twain Journal*.

Harold H. Kolb, Jr. "Mark Twain, Huck Finn, and Jacob Blivens: Gilt-Edged, Tree-Calf Morality in *The Adventures of Huckleberry Finn*," *Virginia Quarterly Review*, 55 (Autumn 1979), 653-669. Reprinted by permission of *Virginia Quarterly Review*.

David Carkeet, "The Dialects in *Huckleberry Finn*," *American Literature*, 51 (1979). Reprinted by permission of Duke University Press.

Barry A. Marks, "The Making of a Humorist: The Narrative Strategy of *Huckleberry Finn*," first published in *The Journal of Narrative Technique*, 12 (1982), 139-145.

To Bill, Brooke, and Billy Bob

Contents

Contents

Foreword

Critical Responses in Arts and Letters is designed to present a documentary history of highlights in the critical reception to the body of work of writers and artists and to individual works that are generally considered to be of major importance. The focus of each volume in this series is basically historical. The introductions to each volume are themselves brief histories of the critical response an author, artist, or individual work has received. This response is then further illustrated by reprinting a strong representation of the major critical reviews and articles that have collectively produced the author's, artist's, or work's critical reputation.

The scope of *Critical Responses in Arts and Letters* knows no chronological or geographical boundaries. Volumes under preparation include studies of individuals from around the world and in both contemporary and historical periods.

Each volume is the work of an individual editor, who surveys the entire body of criticism on a single author, artist, or work. The editor then selects the best material to depict the critical response received by an author or artist over his/her entire career. Documents produced by the author or artist may also be included when the editor finds that they are necessary to a full understanding of the materials at hand. In circumstances where previous, isolated volumes of criticism on a particular individual or work exist, the editor carefully selects material that better reflects the nature and directions of the critical response over time.

In addition to the introduction and the documentary section, the editor of each volume is free to solicit new essays on areas that may not have been adequately dealt with in previous criticism. Also, for volumes on living writers and artists, new interviews may be included, again at the discretion of the volume's editor. The volumes also provide a supplementary bibliography and are fully indexed.

While each volume in *Critical Responses to Arts and Letters* is unique, it is also hoped that in combination they form a useful, documentary history of the critical response to the arts, and one that can be easily and profitably employed by students and scholars.

Cameron Northouse

Introduction

Mark Twain began *Adventures of Huckleberry Finn* in 1876 and completed it in 1883. In the introduction to the definitive text published in 1988 as a volume in the Mark Twain Project of the Bancroft Library by the University of California Press and edited by Walter Blair and Victor Fischer, Blair provides a thoroughly documented account of Twain's progress in the novel.

After completing the novel, Twain insisted it was not to be released until 40,000 copies had been ordered under what was known as the subscription method, the sales procedure Twain used. Since Charles L. Webster, his nephew, was in charge of publication, Twain had control over promotion and publication. The book was first published in England in late 1884, but during the publication of the first American edition one of the drawings was marred, giving the illustration, especially with the caption, obscene overtones. Publication was therefore delayed in America until February 1885.

The illustrations were an important attribute of the first edition. Because of the door-to-door manner of the subscription method, potential buyers were allowed to examine the book. Edward Windsor Kemble drew the illustrations for the first edition, working mostly from the revised typescript Twain sent him. Douglas Anderson contributes an excellent study of the illustrations in *Adventures of Huckleberry Finn* in his essay "Reading the Pictures in *Huckleberry Finn*," *Arizona Quarterly*, 42 (Summer 1986), 101-20, discussing the influence of the illustrations on interpretations of the text.

When *Adventures of Huckleberry Finn* was first reviewed, it was often compared to *The Adventures of Tom Sawyer*, which is not surprising since it was promoted as its companion piece. It was because of its relation to *The Adventures of Tom Sawyer* that Webster persuaded Twain to remove the "Raft Passage." Webster thought it necessary for the two adventure books to be symmetric. Twain also feared readers would recognize the passage from *Life on the Mississippi*. When Webster suggested he omit the passage, Twain replied,

"Yes, I think the raft chapter can be left wholly out, by heaving in a paragraph to say Huck visited the raft to find out how far it might be to Cairo, but got no satisfaction. Even *this* is not necessary unless that raft-visit is referred to later in the book. I think it is, but am not certain."[1]

The definitive text includes the raft passage, but critics still debate over Twain's intentions concerning this issue. Peter Beidler's "The Raft Episode in *Huckleberry Finn*," included in this collection, depicts some strong arguments for the inclusion of the "raft episode" in the book.

Early Response

Early critical comments to *Adventures of Huckleberry Finn* are extraordinarily contradictory, ranging from high praise to condemnation. Until recently, critics thought *Adventures of Huckleberry Finn* had not initially received much attention from reviewers; however, Victor Fischer demonstrates that this is not the case, citing at least twenty reviews and over a hundred comments that appeared in American newspapers and magazines between 1885 and 1897. This detailed overview of the initial response to the book is in Victor Fischer's "Huck Finn Reviewed: The Reception of *Huckleberry Finn* in the United States, 1885-1897," *American Literary Realism*, 16, No.1 (Spring 1983), 1-57. He cites references from newspapers across the country and provides brief quotes as well as entire reviews to present a thorough representation of the initial response to *Huckleberry Finn*.

Fischer also dismisses the previously held assumption that the negative criticism was due to bad publicity, disapproval of subscription publishing, and the Concord Library banning that occurred shortly after the book was first published. He points out that bad publicity mainly affected critical reaction in Massachusetts. Although the disapproval of the book by critics in Boston and New York somewhat influenced national criticism, Fischer cites reviews that praise the book from critics in New York, Connecticut, Georgia, California, and even some in Massachusetts. He also demonstrates that the Concord Library ban, while bringing negative reactions to the book, also brought positive reviews and defenders of the book.

Fischer outlines several events that did, however, bring public attention to *Adventures of Huckleberry Finn*: the Estes & Lauriat lawsuit, the altered illustration, and, of course, the Concord Library banning. Another less important factor was that specific chapters of the book had been exposed before the actual publication, thus leading to some premature judgments of the book. *Century* magazine published three chapters in subsequent issues: "An Adventure of Huckleberry Finn: With an account of the Famous Grangerford-Shepherdson Feud," 29 (December 1884), 268-278, "Jim's Investments, and King Soller-mun," 29 (January 1885), 456-458, and "Royalty on the Mississippi," 29 (February 1885), 544-567.

Another essay that deals with the initial response to the book is Henry Nash Smith's "The Publication of *Huckleberry Finn*: A Centennial Retrospect," *Bulletin of the American Academy of Arts and Sciences*, 37 (February 1984), 18-40. Smith draws from Fischer's essay but focuses specifically on "the relation of Mark Twain's *Adventures of Huckleberry Finn* to American Society at the time of its publication in 1885."

Until 1920, the criticism centered mostly around general comments. Well-established critics such as William Archer, Barrett Wendell, Andrew Lang, Fred Lewis Pattee, Brander Matthews, H. L. Mencken, Sir Walter Besant, and Robert Louis Stevenson had ranked *Huckleberry Finn* as not only Mark Twain's masterpiece but as one of the greatest American novels.

In his essay "My Favorite Novelist and His Best Book," *Munsey's*, 17 (February 1898), 659-664, Besant commends the novel for the humor created by Huck's inability to see his book as comic. He says Twain's comic talent rests on his humorous treatment of a very serious subject matter, and Twain's genius is that the suggestions and meanings of the book go further than Twain intended. He praises the book for its ability to seize people of all ages yet convey different meanings to each age group.

H. L. Mencken proclaimed *Adventures of Huckleberry Finn* a national classic. Mencken, co-editor of *The Smart Set* magazine, brought the book attention as a masterpiece and is partially credited for shifting critical attention away from examining the book as a children's book and sequel to *The Adventures of Tom Sawyer*. In his essay "The Burden of Humor," he gives the reasons for prejudice against humor and says, "the average man is far too stupid to make a joke." Mencken continues with praise for Twain and says humor is misunderstood and thought to be unintellectual; the lack of appreciation for Twain's works stems from this misunderstanding. He says, "Mark [Twain] was the noblest literary artist who ever set pen to paper on American soil, and not only the noblest artist, but also one of the most profound and sagacious philosophers." Mencken also praises *Adventures of Huckleberry Finn* specifically: "I believe that *Huckleberry Finn* is one of the great masterpieces of the world. . . ."[2]

In 1920, Van Wyck Brooks' *The Ordeal of Mark Twain* offended many Twain critics with his thesis that Twain's move to the East prevented him from reaching his potential as a fully developed artist. Van Wyck Brooks agrees with Arnold Bennett that even though *Huckleberry Finn* and *Tom Sawyer* are "episodically magnificent, as complete works of art they are of quite inferior quality."[3]

The Ordeal of Mark Twain brought a rage of critical reaction, often identified with Bernard DeVoto as representative of those who considered *Huckleberry Finn* a masterpiece. DeVoto defended Twain in his book *Mark Twain's America*:

But more truly with *Huckleberry Finn* than with any other book, inquiry may satisfy itself: here is America. . . . The book has the fecundity, the multiplicity of genius. . . .[4]It is a passage through the structure of a nation. . . . It is an exploration of the human race. . . .

In 1941, Van Wyck Brooks retracted his statement about Twain's artistic abilities concerning *Huckleberry Finn*. In the introduction to "Letters to Van Wyck Brooks," he admits that after *The Ordeal of Mark Twain* was published, Sherwood Anderson "showed me clearly where my study had fallen short. I had failed to write the most important chapter, in which I should have praised *Huckleberry Finn*."[5]

Criticism 1930-1959

In 1935, Hemingway made his often quoted statement that praises *Adventures of Huckleberry Finn*: "All modern American literature comes from one book by Mark Twain called *Huckleberry Finn*. . . . All American writing comes from that."[6]

In Lionel Trilling's often anthologized introduction to the Rinehart edition (1948), he calls *Adventures of Huckleberry Finn*, "One of the world's great books and one of the central documents of American culture." He adds that its "greatness" lies "in its power of telling the truth." His essay also deals with the book's structure. He says, "in form and style *Huckleberry Finn* is an almost perfect work." He defends prior attacks against the ending, yet he admits the end is "Too long . . . a falling off, as almost anything would have to be, from the incidents of the river. Yet it has a certain formal aptness. . . . Some device is needed to permit Huck to return to his anonymity, to give up the role of hero. . . ."

T. S. Eliot's introduction to the Chanticleer (1950) edition is another landmark essay of this time period. He says, "It is Huck who gives the book style. The River gives the book its form." Eliot says the river dictates the journey, and we are always aware of the presence of the river, the "only natural force that can wholly determine the course of human peregrination. . . . We come to understand the River by seeing it through the eyes of the Boy. . . . the River makes the book a great book." Eliot, even more strongly than Trilling, defends the ending:

For Huckleberry Finn, neither a tragic nor a happy ending would be suitable. . . . Huck Finn must come from nowhere and be bound for nowhere. . . . He has no beginning and no end. Hence, he can only disappear; and his disappearance can only be accomplished by bringing forward another performer to obscure the disappearance in a cloud of whimsicalities. . . . And it is as impossible for Huck as for the River to have a beginning or end. . . . the book has the right, the only possible concluding sentence.

In 1953, Leo Marx wrote "Mr. Eliot, Mr. Trilling, and *Huckleberry Finn*," which, among other things, refutes the justification for the ending both Trilling and Eliot provide. He objects to the ending on the grounds that "It jeopardizes the significance of the entire novel. To take seriously what happens at the Phelps farm is to take lightly the entire downstream journey." He adds, "The most obvious thing wrong with the end, then, is the flimsy contrivance by which Clemens frees Jim."

James M. Cox's "Remarks on the Sad Initiation of Huckleberry Finn," *Sewanee Review*, 62 (July-September 1954), 389-405, debates Marx and defends the ending of the book on the grounds that the major theme is an adolescent boy's development. He says that Huck's development is illustrated through patterns of death and rebirth that become completely clear only in the end.

This period also produced Leslie Fiedler's "Come Back to the Raft Ag'in, Huck Honey!" It became an important and somewhat controversial essay due to Fiedler's implication that Huck and Jim are latent homosexuals.

Ralph Ellison's "Change the Joke and Slip the Yoke," *Partisan Review*, 25 (Spring 1958), 45-59, is another essay written during this period. In this essay, Ellison says, "Twain fitted Jim into the outlines of the minstrel tradition, and it is from behind this stereotype mask that we see Jim's dignity and human capacity—and Twain's complexity—emerge." He argues that Twain portrays the relationship between Jim and Huck as the friendship between two boys rather than as a relationship between a man and a boy.

Criticism 1960-1985

Walter Blair wrote *Mark Twain and Huck Finn* (Berkeley: University of California Press) in 1960. Twain scholars consider it an essential work for any serious scholar who pursues a study of *Adventures of Huckleberry Finn*. Carl Dolmetsch asked fifteen major American Twain scholars to name "two or three most important works about *Huck Finn*," and Blair's book was the unanimous choice for the most important work.[7] Blair describes "the forces which gave *Adventures of Huckleberry Finn* its substance and form." He studies factors that influenced the novel, such as Twain's wife, his friends, his readings, and his thoughts between 1874 to 1884.

Henry Nash Smith's book *Mark Twain: the Development of a Writer* (Cambridge: Harvard University Press, 1962) is another book that is vital to any serious Twain scholar. He essentially states that Twain's struggles as a writer resulted from "a conflict between the dominant culture of his day [the gentility cult] and an emergent attitude associated with the vernacular language of the native American humorists." He traces the effects of this conflict through individual works by Twain, and chapter 6, "A Sound Heart and a Deformed Conscience," represents his analysis of *Huckleberry Finn* in relation to his discussion of each work wherein he considers "problems of style and structure."

Peter Beidler wrote "The Raft Episode in *Huckleberry Finn*" in 1968. Beidler, now a chaired English professor at Lehigh University, wrote this article when he was a graduate student. It has been widely influential in encouraging modern editors of *Huckleberry Finn* to publish the novel with the raft episode restored to its original position in Chapter 16.

Two articles by Neil Schmitz in 1971 represent significant studies of *Huckleberry Finn*. One of these essays, "The Paradox of Liberation in Huckleberry Finn," is included in this collection. Schmitz's other essay is "Twain, *Huckleberry Finn*, and the Reconstruction," *American Studies*, 12 (Spring 1971), 59-67. In this essay, Schmitz argues that "Jim's situation at the end of *Huckleberry Finn* reflects the Negro in the Reconstruction, free at last and thoroughly impotent, the object of devious schemes and a hapless victim of constant brutality." Judith Fetterley's "Disenchantment: Tom Sawyer in *Huckleberry Finn*," *Publications of the Modern Language Association*, 87 (January 1972), 69-74, examines Tom's role in *Adventures of Huckleberry Finn*.

Harold Beaver's "Run, Nigger, Run: *Adventures of Huckleberry Finn* as a Fugitive Slave Narrative," *Journal of American Studies*, (December 1974), 339-61, is one of the most provocative essays written about *Huckleberry Finn* during this time period. Beaver's thesis is that Jim manipulates Huck in order to get Huck to help him escape. Louis Budd called David Carkeet's "The Dialects in *Huckleberry Finn*" the major contribution to *Adventures of Huckleberry Finn* scholarship in 1979.[8] Carkeet outlines nine dialects and cites some inconsistencies that are due to the seven-year span of the composition of the manuscript.

Centennial Celebration

1985 marked the hundredth anniversary of the publication of *Adventures of Huckleberry Finn*, the 150th anniversary of Twain's birth, and the 75th anniversary of his death and brought on a tremendous wave of centennial celebration. On April 25, 1985 the production of the musical "Big River," written by Roger Miller, opened at the Eugene O'Neill Theater in New York. PBS's American Playhouse version of *Huckleberry Finn*, directed by Peter H. Hunt and adapted by Guy Gallo, premiered in the Spring of 1986. Hamlin Hill edited a centennial edition of the book (New York: Harper & Row, 1987), a facsimile of the first edition. A group of scholars acclaimed Huck's centennial at Elmira College. Scholars held a symposium on *Huckleberry Finn* at the University of Missouri at Columbia; the readings are represented in *One*

Hundred Years of "Huckleberry Finn": The Boy, His Book and American Culture (Columbia: University of Missouri Press, 1985). John C. Gerber's excellent introduction to this anthology, "The Continuing Adventures of *Huckleberry Finn*," provides an overview of the first one hundred years of criticism. He gives both an overall perspective of individual time periods and assesses specific essays and works that deal with *Adventures of Huckleberry Finn*.

M. Thomas Inge edited *Huck Finn among the Critics: A Centennial Selection* (Frederick, MD: University Publications of America, 1985). The book consists of some reviews from the initial response and reprinted essays. He includes one new essay, Perry Frank's "Adventures of Huckleberry Finn on Film" (pp. 293-313). Frank gives an excellent discussion of the film adaptations and provides an overview of the initial critical response to each of these films.

Thomas A. Tenney's "An Annotated Checklist of Criticism on *Adventures of Huckleberry Finn*" is included in Inge's collection. Tenney's bibliography is the most complete bibliography on *Adventures of Huckleberry Finn*. Many of these references were taken from his book *Mark Twain: A Reference Guide* (Boston: G.K. Hall, 1977) with annual supplements in *American Literary Realism*. Tenney provides the most complete and in-depth bibliography of Mark Twain's writings and is a must for anyone who seriously desires to study Mark Twain. In my bibliography, I list other bibliographies that provide helpful extensions to Tenney's work.

Another in-depth survey of the first one hundred years of scholarship on *Adventures of Huckleberry Finn* is Carl Dolmetsch's "*Huck Finn's* First Century: A Bibliographical Survey," *American Studies International*, 22, No. 2 (October 1984), 79-121. He gives an excellent overview of the first one hundred years of criticism and discusses the various thematic interpretations, as well as the major books and articles. The checklist is conveniently categorized according to subjects.

The 1984 MLA Conference held a special session to celebrate Huck's hundredth birthday. The session was lead by Robert Sattelmeyer and J. Donald Crowley, the editors of the centennial collection. Three prominent Twain scholars presented papers at the special session entitled "*Adventures of Huckleberry Finn*: Centenary Perspectives." Jay Martin presented "The Genie in the Bottle: Huckleberry Finn in Mark Twain's Life"; John Gerber read "The Continuing Adventures of *Huckleberry Finn*," the introduction to the centennial collection mentioned earlier; and James M. Cox presented "*Huckleberry Finn*: A Hard Book to Take," which is reprinted in this collection.

Thomas A. Tenney celebrated Huck's birthday with a special issue of the *Mark Twain Journal*, Thadious M. Davis, guest ed., 22, No. 2 (1984) entitled "Black Writers on *Adventures of Huckleberry Finn*: One Hundred Years Later." It represents a collection of essays written by black scholars.

Louis J. Budd summarizes the centennial celebration in his essay "Huck at 100. How Old is *Huckleberry Finn*?," *Dictionary of Literary Biography 1985*, Jean W. Ross, ed. (Detroit: Gale, 1986), 12-23. In "Huck and Jim Begin Their Next 100 Years of Rafting Through the American Psyche," *The Chronicle of Higher Education*, 29 (February 13, 1985), 5-6, Angus Paul lists the events scheduled to celebrate Huck's birthday. He also outlines some contemporary critical response to *Huckleberry Finn*.

Contemporary Criticism

Contemporary criticism continues to debate the issues that have always been topics for studies of Twain's most critically acclaimed book. Huck has been examined from attitudes involved in all schools of literary thought. New trends in literary theory have produced new approaches to the novel such as the reliability of the text and readers' responses to the text. Huck has been analyzed from the new critical approach, psychoanalyzed, deconstructed, reconstructed, examined from feminist views, and mythologized.

Contemporary debates over the banning or removal of the book from required reading lists are as heated as ever before. A recent study cites *Adventures of Huckleberry Finn* as the fifth most commonly challenged book in the nation between the years 1982-1990. It is challenged because of accusations that it is "racist, frequently uses racial slurs."[9]

Henry B. Rule provides a short survey of the bannings of *Huck* in "A Brief History of the Censorship of *The Adventures of Huckleberry Finn*," *Lamar Journal of the Humanities*, 12 (1986), 9-18, focusing on the 1957 New York City banning and the 1982 Fairfax County, Virginia outrage against *Adventures of Huckleberry Finn*.

Attempts to ban or take *Adventures of Huckleberry Finn* off required reading lists continue. One of the most recent attempts to remove Huck from the required reading lists occurred in Texas in the late fall of 1990. Huck made the front page of both *The Dallas Morning News* and *The Dallas Times Herald*, which reported City Councilman David Perry's recommendation to take both *The Adventures of Tom Sawyer* and *Adventures of Huckleberry Finn* off the Plano Independent School District's required reading list. Perry claims *Huckleberry Finn* "uses the word *nigger* so many times it's pathetic. Any writer that's supposed to be a great writer would not fill his pages with this kind of negative word."[10] In the press reports, Jocelyn Chadwick-Joshua was the major defender for keeping Twain's novels on the reading lists. Chadwick-Joshua instructs teachers to present the novel in a manner that manifests Twain's message. Her essay in this collection represents her response to this particular attempt and her insights concerning the role of the teacher in presenting *Adventures of Huckleberry Finn* to students.

On February 4, 1985, the ABC News program "Nightline" featured "*Huckleberry Finn*: Literature or Racist Trash." This debate reflects contemporary opinions and issues involved in attempts to ban the novel. The program's anchor, Ted Koppel, and Jeff Greenfield interviewed Meshach Taylor, John Wallace, and Nat Hentoff. Taylor was the actor playing Jim in a Chicago theater performance of *Adventures of Huckleberry Finn*, John Wallace was involved in attempts to ban *Huckleberry Finn* from required school reading lists, and Nat Hentoff appeared as the author of *The Day They Came to Arrest the Book*, a novel concerning a high school controversy that arose in response to attempts to ban *Huckleberry Finn*.

Harold Bloom's collection of essays *Mark Twain* (Chelsea House, 1986) includes one new essay about *Huckleberry Finn*, Cleo McNelly Kearn's "The Limits of Semiotics in *Huckleberry Finn*" (pp. 207-22). Kearn examines the connection between signs and "Money, prediction, and textual interpretation."

Harold Beaver's *Huckleberry Finn* (London: Unwin Hyman, 1987) is an excellent book-length treatment of the novel. He provides many insights about the ambiguity and the paradoxes in the novel. Chapter 6, "Run, Nigger, Run," is a revised version of his 1974 essay "Run, Nigger, Run: *Adventures of Huckleberry Finn* as a Fugitive Slave Narrative."

In his essay "The Recomposition of *Adventures of Huckleberry Finn*," *Missouri Review*, 10 (1987), 113-29, Louis Budd outlines the effects of various factors such as adaptations, attempts to ban the book, and translations on contemporary interpretations of the book. He considers when, how, and why *Huckleberry Finn* was proclaimed a classic and the influences of its inclusion in the canon on modern readings of the novel.

In his prefatory "Notice," Mark Twain warns, "Persons attempting to find a motive in this narrative will be prosecuted; persons attempting to find a moral in it will be banished; persons attempting to find a plot in it will be shot." Far from keeping anyone from analyzing the book, scholars have and will continue to study Twain's masterpiece. John Gerber lists some of the many themes the novel has to offer:

alienation, conscience, death, disguise, faith in human goodness, fear, freedom, mock superstition, theft, setting a free man free, and of course, the damned human race. Some see the theme in oppositions: accommodation versus transcendence, black magic versus white, fantasy versus reality, appearance versus reality, imagination versus reality, imagination versus common sense, freedom versus slavery, the individual versus society, power versus love, Miss Watson's Providence versus the Widow Douglas's Providence, wish versus belief, and two favorites—head versus heart, and a sound heart versus a deformed conscience.[11]

Many sources for references to works on Mark Twain are available. As mentioned earlier, the best reference is Tenney's *Mark Twain: A Reference Guide* with annual supplements in *American Literary Realism*. There are also *The Mark Twain Journal* and the *Mark Twain Circular*, a publication of the Mark Twain Circle of America.

Another major source for Mark Twain articles is *American Literary Scholarship: An Annual* (Durham: Duke University Press, 1963-). The editors of each chapter provide overviews of the essays written on a particular subject for each particular year. The Mark Twain chapter is edited by prominent Twain scholars and represents their evaluations of the annual critical works on Mark Twain: John Gerber (1963-68), Hamlin Hill (1969-75), Louis Budd (1976-85), and Hamlin Hill (1986-).

James S. Leonard, Thomas A. Tenney, and Thadious M. Davis recently compiled a collection of essays published by Duke University Press. The anthology is an extension of Tenney's special centennial issue of the *Mark Twain Journal* that represents a collection of essays by African-American writers on *Huckleberry Finn*. Tenney is also busy preparing a second volume to his *Mark Twain: A Reference Guide*, to be published by G. K. Hall.

In late 1990, the manuscript of the first half of *Adventures of Huckleberry Finn* was discovered in a Los Angeles attic. It had been lost since the 1880s, when a New York man acquired it from Twain for donation to the Buffalo and Erie County Library in Buffalo, N. Y. The other half of the manuscript has been in the Buffalo and Erie County Library since 1887, and the owners of the newly discovered text presently are considering uniting the two manuscripts. The manuscript reveals many corrections in Twain's handwriting, showing, for example, that Twain changed the opening lines three times. It also portrays at least one long expurgated passage. The manuscript reveals that Twain incorporated the "Raftmen's Passage" as part of the original text, which proves Peter Beidler's assertion that the episode was orginally drafted as a segment of

Adventures of Huckleberry Finn. The discovery will provide scholars with evidence of Twain's creative process and will probably offer insights leading to interpretations based on textual criticism.

With the possible exception of Hawthorne's *The Scarlet Letter* or Melville's *Moby Dick,* Twain's *Adventures of Huckleberry Finn* has received more critical attention than any American novel. Many critics regard Twain's masterpiece as the greatest American novel and as one of the greatest novels in the world. It is established firmly in both the American and world literary canons as a classic work of art.

NOTES

1. Samuel Charles Webster, ed., *Mark Twain Business Man* (Boston, 1946), pp. 249-250.

2. H. L. Mencken, "The Burden of Humor," *The Smart Set,* XXXCIII (February 1913), 151-54.

3. Van Wyck Brooks, *The Ordeal of Mark Twain* (New York: Dutton, 1933), p. 29.

4. Bernard DeVoto, *Mark Twain's America* (Boston: Little Brown & Company, 1932), p. 314.

5. Sherwood Anderson, "Letters to Van Wyck Brooks," *Story,* 19 (Sept.-Oct. 1941), 42-43.

6. Ernest Hemingway, *Green Hills of Africa* (New York: Charles Scribner's Sons, 1979), p. 22.

7. Carl Dolmetsch, "*Huck Finn's* First Century: A Bibliographical Survey," *American Studies International,* 22, No. 2 (Oct. 1984), 94-95.

8. James Woodress, ed., *American Literary Scholarship: An Annual/1979* (Durham: Duke University Press, 1981), p. 89.

9. Stacey Freedenthal, "African-American Twain Scholar Backs Book," *The Dallas Morning News,* 18 Nov. 1990, p. 26A.

10. Freedenthal, "Scholar Backs Book," p. 26A.

11. John Gerber, "The Continuing Adventures of *Huckleberry Finn,*" in *One Hundred Years of Huckleberry Finn: The Boy, His Book and American Culture,* ed. Robert Sattelmeyer and J. Donald Crowley (Columbia: University of Missouri Press, 1985), p. 11.

EARLY RESPONSE

MARK TWAIN IN A DILEMMA—A VICTIM OF A JOKE HE THINKS THE MOST UNKINDEST CUT OF ALL

Huckleberry Finn, Mark Twain's new book, was complete last March, but owing to complications and differences with his publishers, it has not yet appeared, although it has been extensively announced—a prospectus of the story sent out and the opening chapters recently published in the *Century.* . . . In order to properly embellish the book, the services of a leading metropolitan engraver were secured, and from this comes all the trouble into which Hartford's popular author is now plunged. The engravings, after having been cut on the plates, were sent to the electrotyper. One of the plates represented a man with a downcast head, standing in the foreground of a particularly striking illustration. In front of him was a ragged urchin with a look of dismay overspreading his countenance. In the background, and standing behind the boy, was an attractive-looking young girl, whose face was enlivened with a broad grin. Something which the boy or man had said or done evidently amused her highly. The title of the cut was, "In a Dilemma; What Shall I do?"

When the plate was sent to the electrotyper, a wicked spirit must have possessed him. The title was suggestive. A mere stroke of the awl would suffice to give the cut an indecent character never intended by the author or engraver. It would make no difference in the surface of the plate that would be visible to the naked eye, but when printed would add to the engraving a characteristic which would be repudiated not only by the author, but by all respectable people of the country into whose hands the volume should fall. The work of the engraver was successful. It passed the eye of the inspector and was approved. A proof was taken and submitted. If the alteration of the plate was manifested in the proof it was evidently attributed to a defect in the press and paper, which would be remedied when the volume was sent to the press. Now the work was ready for printing.

In issuing books to be sold by "subscription only" the publishers first strike off a large number of prospectuses, which are to be used by the agents when soliciting subscribers to the work. Some 3,000 of these prospectuses, with the defective cut, were presented and distributed to the different agents throughout the country. The entire work had passed the eyes of the various readers and inspectors, and the glaring indecency of the cut had not been discovered. Throughout the country were hundreds of agents displaying the merits of the work and elaborating on the artistic work of the engravings. It was remarkable that, while the defects were so palpable, none of the other agents noticed it, or if he did so, he failed to report it to the publishers. Possibly they might have considered the alteration intentional, as the title to the illustration was now doubly suggestive.

At last a letter came from the Chicago agent calling attention to the cut. Then there was consternation in the offices of the publishers. Copies of the prospectus were hauled from the shelf and critically examined. Then for the first time it dawned on the publishers that such an illustration would condemn the work. Immediately all the agents were telegraphed to, and the prospectuses called in. The page containing the cut was torn from the book, a new and perfect illustration being substituted. Agents were supplied with the improved volumes and are now happy in canvassing for a work to which there can be no objection, while they smile at the prospects of heavy commissions. But the story leaked out. Several opposition publishers got hold of copies of the cut, however, and these now adorn their respective offices.

New York World, 27 Nov. 1884, p. 4.

ESTES & LAURIAT LAWSUIT

An interesting lawsuit has just been decided in Boston. It was brought by Mark Twain against the well-known publishing house of Estes & Lauriat, and was decided in favor of the defendants, the court refusing the injunction asked for by the plaintiff. The main points of the case are thus given in the *Advertiser*:

Estes and Lauriat are a firm of booksellers and publishers located in Boston. In their last holiday catalog appeared an advertisement in which a new work entitled *Huckleberry Finn*, written by the plaintiff under the name Mark Twain, was offered for sale at a price reduced from $2.75 to $2.25. The book is sold on what is known as the subscription plan, and the regular subscription price is $2.75. The canvass for the book has been in progress for some months. The advertisement to sell the work for less than the subscription price is working great injury to the regular sales by subscription. The book is not yet published, and will not be before February. On December 3, 1884, the title of the work was deposited with the librarian of Congress to secure a copyright. Charles L. Webster and Co., of New York are the general managers and authorized agents of the plaintiff in the publication and sale of the book. Numerous canvassing agents are appointed in different parts of the country. These agents purchase the books, but bind themselves by contract to sell only to subscribers, and not to the trade, and for the full retail price. Prior to the time the catalogue was issued, several persons called at the place of business of Estes & Lauriat, and offered them the book at such prices that they could afford to sell it at $2.25, and still make a fair profit. Dummies of the book were left for examination. Two of the persons who had called had previously sold Estes and Lauriat other works of the author. Estes and Lauriat contracted with these persons to take one hundred or more copies of the book, and then inserted in their holiday catalogue about to be published, the advertisement referred to. Up to this time, about thirty orders for the book have been received by them. They had no knowledge of the terms of contract between the plaintiff, or his publishers and their canvassing agents. They say the prior works of the author published by subscription have been freely offered to them at large discounts. As soon as suit was brought, they cut out the page from the catalogue containing the advertisement, and they have not since, and do not propose to distribute any more catalogues containing the advertisement.

Quoted by the *Literary World*, 21 Feb. 1885, p. 66.
Boston Daily Advertiser, 7 January 1885, p. 8.

THE CONCORD LIBRARY COMMITTEE'S BANNING OF *HUCKLEBERRY FINN*

Huckleberry Finn Barred Out

The Concord (Mass.) Public Library committee has decided to exclude Mark Twain's latest book from the library. One member of the committee says that, while he does not wish to call it immoral, he thinks it contains but little humor, and that of a very coarse type. He regards it as the veriest trash. The librarian and the other members of the committee entertain similar views, characterizing it as rough, coarse and inelegant, dealing with a series of experiences not elevating, the whole book being more suited to the slums than to intelligent, respectable people.

Boston Evening Transcript, 17 March 1885, p. 6.

Mark Twain's Last Book Excluded from a Public Library

The Concord Library Committee has unanimously decided to exclude from the shelves of that institution Mark Twain's new book, *Huckleberry Finn*. Said one member of the committee: "While I do not wish to state it as my opinion that the book is absolutely immoral in its tone, still it seems to me that it contains but very little humor, and that little is of a very coarse type. If it were not for the author's reputation the book would undoubtedly meet with severe criticism. I regard it as the veriest trash." Another member says: "I have examined the book and my objections to it are these: It deals with a series of adventures of a very low grade of morality; it is couched in the language of a rough, ignorant dialect, and all through its pages there is a systematic use of bad grammar and an employment of rough, coarse inelegant expressions. It is also very irreverent. To sum up, the book is flippant and irreverent in its style. It deals with a series of experiences that are certainly not elevating. The whole book is of a class that is more profitable for the slums than it is for respectable people, and it is trash of the veriest sort."

St. Louis *Globe-Democrat*, 17 March 1885, p. 1.

[Concord Library Draws the Line on Literature]

Members of the Concord public library committee have drawn the line on literature, and pronounced Mark Twain's *Huckleberry Finn* too "coarse" for a place among the classic tomes that educate and edify the people. They do not pick out any particular passage, but just sit on the book in general. When Mark writes another book he should think of the Concord School of Philosophy and put a little more whenceness of the hereafter among his nowness of the here.

Boston Daily Globe, 17 March 1885, p. 2.

[Concord Library Committee Concludes *Huckleberry Finn* Trashy]

The Concord public library committee deserve well of the public by their action in banishing Mark Twain's new book, *Huckleberry Finn*, on the ground that it is trashy and vicious. It is time that this influential pseudonym should cease to carry into homes and libraries unworthy productions. Mr. Clemens is a genuine and powerful humorist, with a bitter vein of satire on the weaknesses of humanity which is sometimes wholesome, sometimes only grotesque, but in certain of his works degenerates into a gross trifling with ever fine feeling. The trouble with Mr. Clemens is that he has no reliable sense of propriety. His notorious speech at an *Atlantic* dinner, marshaling Longfellow and Emerson and Whittier in vulgar parodies in a western miner's cabin, illustrated this; but not in much more relief than the *Adventures of Tom Sawyer* did, or than these Huckleberry Finn stories do. The advertising samples of this book, which have disfigured the *Century* magazine, are enough to tell any reader how offensive the whole thing must be. They are no better in tone than the dime novels which flood the blood-and-thunder reading population; Mr. Clemens has made them smarter, for he has an inexhaustible fund of "quips and cranks and wanton wiles," and his literary skill is of course superior, but their moral level is low, and their perusal cannot be anything less than harmful.

Springfield Daily Republican, 17 March 1885, p. 4.

Huckleberry Finn in Concord

The sage censors of the Concord public library have unanimously reached the conclusion that *Huckleberry Finn* is not the sort of reading matter for the knowledge seekers of a town which boasts the only "summer school of philosophy" in the universe. They have accordingly banished it from the shelves of that institution.

The reasons which moved them to this action are weighty and to the point. One of the Library Committee, while not prepared to hazard the point that the book is "absolutely immoral in its tone," does not hesitate to declare that to him "it seems to contain but very little humor." Another committee-man perused the volume with great care and discovered that it was "couched in the language of a rough, ignorant dialect" and that "all through its pages there is a systematic use of bad grammar and an employment of inelegant expressions." The third member voted the book "flippant" and "trash of the veriest sort." They all united in the verdict that "it deals with a series of experiences that are certainly not elevating," and voted that it could not be tolerated in the public library.

The committee very considerately explain the mystery of how this unworthy production happened to find its way into the collection under their charge. "Knowing the author's reputation," and presumably being familiar with the philosophic pages of *The Innocents Abroad, Roughing It, The Adventures of Tom Sawyer,* "The Jumping Frog," & c., they deemed it "totally unnecessary to make a very careful examination of *Huckleberry Finn* before sending it to Concord." But the learned librarian, probably seizing upon it on its arrival to peruse it with eager zest, "was not particularly pleased with it." He promptly communicated his feelings to the committee, who at once proceeded to enter upon a critical reading of the suspected volume, with the results that are now laid before the public.

New York Herald, 18 March 1885, p. 6.

Twain to Webster—18 March 1885

DEAR CHARLEY,—The committee of the Public Library of Concord, Mass., have given us a rattling tip-top puff which will go into every paper in the country. They have expelled Huck from their library as "trash and suitable only for the slums." That will sell 25,000 copies for us, sure.

Mark Twain's Letters, Vol II, ed. Albert Bigelow Paine (New York: Harper and Brothers, 1917), pp. 452-453.

[Twain Laughs in His Sleeves]

The Concord Library managers have pronounced *Huckleberry Finn* (Mark Twain's latest book) as trivial, of a low wit, immoral, and all that, and have withdrawn it from circulation. But why don't these good people do all this quietly, without getting into the newspapers with their disapprobation? We venture to say every boy and girl in Concord will make a point to get that book and read it. They will want to know if it is indeed an improper book. As for Twain himself, he is probably laughing in his sleeves at the advertisement his book has received in Concord, with every newspaper referring to it. There are some things best accomplished by quiet suppression, and a bad book is one of them.

Boston Commonwealth, 21 March 1885, p. 3.

[Concord Makes Amends]

Concord has made a sort of amends to Mark Twain, whose *Huckleberry Finn* it lately refused a place on its library shelves, by making him a member of its Free Trade Club. If the school of philosophy will now come forward with an honorary membership in its faculty for Mr. Twain, all, we have no doubt, will be forgiven.

Boston Daily Advertiser, 25 March 1885, p. 4.

Mark Twain and Massachusetts

He Presents His Acknowledgments to the state in General and Concord in Particular.
Concord, April 1—At a recent meeting of the Concord Free Trade Club, Mr. S.L. Clemens (Mark Twain) was elected an honorary member of the club. A certificate of his election was sent Mr. Clemens in due course, and the following acknowledgment of the same has just been received:—

Hartford, March 28, 1885.
Frank A. Nichols, Esq., Secretary Concord Free Trade Club—

Dear Sir,—I am in receipt of your favor of the 24th instant, conveying the gratifying intelligence that I have been made an honorary member of the Free Trade Club of Concord, Massachusetts, and I desire to express to the club, through you, my grateful sense of the high compliment thus paid me. It does look as if Massachusetts were in a fair way to embarrass me with kindnesses this year. In the first place, a Massachusetts judge has just decided in open court that a Boston publisher may sell, not only his own property in a free and unfettered way, but also may as freely sell property which does not belong to him but to me; property which he has not bought and which I have not sold. Under this ruling I am now advertising that judge's homestead for sale, and, if I make as good a sum out of it as I expect, I shall go on and sell out the rest of his property.

In the next place, a committee of the public library of your town have condemned and excommunicated my last book and doubled its sale. This generous action of theirs must necessarily benefit me in one or two additional ways. For instance, it will deter other libraries from buying the book; and you are doubtless aware that one book in a public library prevents the sale of a sure ten and a possible hundred of its mates. And, secondly, it will cause the purchasers of the book to read it, out of curiosity, instead of merely intending to do so, after the usual way of the world and library committees; and then they will discover, to my great advantage and their own indignant disappointment, that there is nothing objectionable in the book after all.

And finally, the Free Trade Club of Concord comes forward and adds to the splendid burden of obligations already conferred upon me by the Commonwealth of Massachusetts, an honorary membership which is worth more than all the rest, just at this juncture, since it indorses me as worthy to associate with certain gentlemen whom even the moral icebergs of the Concord library committee are bound to respect.

May the great Commonwealth of Massachusetts endure forever, is the heartfelt prayer of one who, long a recipient of her mere general good will, is proud to realize that he is at last become her pet.

    Thanking you again, dear sir, and gentlemen,
    I remain,
    Your obliged servant,

    S. L. Clemens.
(Known to the Concord Winter School of Philosophy as "Mark Twain.")

Boston Daily Advertiser, 2 April 1885, p. 2.

The Tide Turning

There is something very suggestive in the eagerness and unanimity with which library committees and newspapers throughout the country have followed the precedent established by the Concord library in condemning Mark Twain's last book, *Huckleberry Finn*. Great weight, no doubt, is ascribed to the action of the Concord men in this respect: the town in which the Concord "philosophers" summer and in which Emerson lived and died, is probably permeated with literature to such an extent that the boy who fetches the mail and the old woman who sweeps out the library are frequent contributors to the periodicals of the day. In fact, unless we are greatly deceived, we distinctly recognized the venerable hand of the library charwoman in a recent review of the biography of a former resident in that classic town. Nevertheless the general condemnation of *Huckleberry Finn* evidently proceeds from something more than mere deference to Concord authority.

It is an indication that in matters of humor the tide has turned at last, and that the old school of coarse, flippant and irreverent joke makers is going out, to return no more. *Huckleberry Finn* is little, if at all, worse than earlier works by the same author; but the public taste has improved, and the opportunity to revolt from the Mark Twains who have ruled so long has been seized with avidity. We have always had in this country, or at least we have had for many years, what may be called professional humorists, but their style has changed from time to time. The essentially American trait in them all has been exaggeration,—the boldness of their conceits; and this characteristic of our humor has frequently been cited by European critics as being the single respect in which the size of our country and the freshness of our civilization have produced a corresponding result in our literature.

Artemus Ward introduced the new feature of misspelling, which has been carried to such a dismal excess by Nasby and others, but which, neither by Ward nor by his imitators, was ever practised with any approach to the skill or delicacy of Thackeray in the Yellowplush Papers. Ward often went far afield for his jokes, but he had a geniality and a touch of pathos which saved him from vulgarity. Mark Twain and his followers have added to that exaggeration which is the normal trait in American humor the corroding element of burlesque. Nothing has been sacred with them, and over subjects dignified by age, tragedy and romance they have cast the slimy trail of the vulgar humorist.

The habit of mind which takes pleasure in reducing everything to the level of a jest is said by an eminent writer to be peculiar to the present time, and on the stage it has found its expression in the burlesque, which is perhaps the most vulgar, if not the most degrading form of theatrical representation known to history. That, too, has had its day, and even the comic opera which succeeded it, poor though it be, is a step in advance. The burlesque of the stage and the burlesque in literature, have their common root in that spirit of irreverence, which, as we are often and truly told, is the great fault in American character. In the cultivation of that spirit Mark Twain has shown talents and industry, which, now that his last effort has failed so ignominiously, we trust he will employ in some manner more creditable to himself and more beneficent to his country. We say failed, for we are unwilling to believe that his impudent intimations that a larger sale and larger profits are a satisfactory recompense to him for the unfavorable judgment of honest critics, is a true indication of the standard by which he measures success in literature.

Boston Daily Advertiser, 2 April 1885, p. 4.

[Twain to Reap Benefits]

The original and only Mark Twain has written to the Concord Free Trade club an ironic letter in acknowledgment of his election to an honorary membership. The letter must be given almost entire, as an illumination of Mr. Clemens, who carefully avoids defending himself from the criticism justly made upon his latest book, and simply rejoices in the fact that he is going to make money out of it. Mr. Clemens has found that vulgarity pays, and he proposes to reap the benefits of his discovery,—that is the essence of his letter. He ought to be ashamed of *Huckleberry Finn*, but he boastfully declares that he is not in this extraordinary communication.
[Quotes Twain's letter to Concord Free Trade club]

Springfield Republican, 3 April 1885, p. 4.

Twain to Webster—4 April 1885

Dear Charley—
The *Advertiser* and the *Republican* still go for me daily. All right, we may as well get the benefit of such advertising as can be drawn from it.

So, if the idea seems good to you, add this new page—this "Prefatory Remark," and insert it right after the copyright page in all future editions [of *Huck Finn*]. I would bind up a . . . few copies immediately and send to all the New York and Boston papers, and to a scattering few western ones—and don't *mark* them; but when you are ready to ship them get W. McKay [Mackay] Laffan (go to see him at Harper & Bros.) to drop the Prefatory Remark into the *Sun*, with a mere quiet editorial comment to the effect that we are inserting this in deference to a generally expressed curiosity on the part of the public to know whether Huck is a real or imaginary character.

You might bring a proof of the P.R. and hand it to Laffan for publication *immediately* (before Gen Grant dies and absorbs all newspaper interest,) without waiting to bind up and send off the books.

Ys
S L C

Prefatory Remark

Huckleberry Finn is not an imaginary person. He still lives; or rather *they* still live; for Huckleberry Finn is two persons in one—namely, the author's two uncles, the present editors of the Boston *Advertiser* and the Springfield *Republican*. In character, language, clothing, education, instinct, and origin, he is the painstakingly and truthfully drawn photograph and counterpart of these two gentlemen as they were in the time of their boyhood, forty years ago. The work has been most carefully and conscientiously done, and is exactly true to the originals, in even the minutest particulars, with but one exception, and that a trifling one: this boy's language has been toned down and softened, here and there, in deference to the taste of a more modern and fastidious day.

Mark Twain's Letters to His Publishers, ed. Hamlin Hill. (Berkeley: University of California Press, 1967), pp. 187-188.

Mark Twain in Massachusetts

The *Boston Advertiser* attacks Mark Twain as venomously and persistently as if his recent suit against a Boston publishing-house had been brought against itself; and it ventures into declarations which it would have hard work to prove. For example, it says that there is "something very suggestive in the eagerness and unanimity with which library committees and newspapers throughout the country have followed the precedent established by the Concord library in condemning Mark Twain's last book," but it omits to mention the libraries or to list the newspapers.

Indeed, some of the leading newspapers of the country have taken the liberty to laugh at the Concord folks for their conduct, and the libraries that have rejected the volume are, we venture to say, few and far between. They must all be of the class that the Concord library belongs to; for one of the trustees of that library, when interviewed on this matter, said that no fiction was permitted on the Concord shelves. Of course, *Huckleberry Finn* isn't a true story. It is fiction, and so it is barred by this Concord limitation. The discovery that they had bought a biography in good faith and had got something that was not true may be the cause of the discontent, although the Life of Huck Finn is not the only biography that partakes of the nature of fiction, and the Concord library would be further depleted if all biographies that are not true were cast out from it.

The Concord trustees, however, have a right to do as they choose and so have the trustees of other libraries. The question really is whether the rest have followed the Concord lead. To prove it, one must have something more than a newspaper assertion. Readers of the *Century* have been immeasurably entertained by the extracts from *Huck Finn* published there, and the book, now that it is on the market, is having a very large sale and getting no end of advertising from this episode. That is one effect of such an attack; but to charge, as the *Advertiser* does, that newspapers and libraries all over the

country are uniting in condemning the volume is to go as much beyond
advertising as it is beyond the facts. . . .
[Quotes Twain's letter to the Concord Free Trade club]

Hartford Courant—4 April 1885, p. 2.

[Twain's Journal Entries About Two Editors]

The severest censor has been the Boston Advertiser. I am sorry to impute
personal motives to him, but I must. He is merely taking what he imagines is
legitimate revenge upon me for what was simply & solely an accident. I had
the misfortune to catch him in a situation which will not bear {telling.}
describing. He probably think[s] I have told that thing all around. It is an error.
I have never told it, except to one man, & he came so near absolutely dying
with laughter that I judged it best to take no more chances with that narrative
(pp. 135-136).

The accident in a sitz-bath with a steel-trap to the editor of the Springfield
Republican . . . (p. 132).

Tell Smith how the Boston Ad man got his — caught in the steel trap (p. 234).

How the editor of the Springfield Republican got his Nüsse [nuts] caught in
the steel trap (p. 356).

Mark Twain's Notebooks & Journals, Vol. 3, ed. Robert Pack Browning,
Michael B. Frank, and Lin Salamo (Berkeley: University of California Press,
1979).

[Victor Fischer points out in his essay "Huck Finn Reviewed: The Reception
of *Huckleberry Finn* in the United States, 1885-1897," *American Literary
Realism*, 16 (Spring 1983), 48: "If such an accident occurred, it is not clear
whether it happened to the editor of the Boston *Advertiser* or to the editor of
the Springfield *Republican*, nor is it clear how or when Mark Twain happened
to be a witness to it."]

THE ADVENTURES OF HUCKLEBERRY FINN

[ATTRIBUTED TO WILLIAM ERNEST HENLEY]

For some time past Mr. Clemens has been carried away by the ambition of seriousness and fine writing. In *Huckleberry Finn* he returns to his right mind, and is again the Mark Twain of old time. It is such a book as he, and he only, could have written. It is meant for boys; but there are few men (we should hope) who, once they take it up, will not delight in it. It forms a companion, or sequel, to *Tom Sawyer*. Huckleberry Finn, as everybody knows, is one of Tom's closest friends; and the present volume is a record of the adventures which befell him soon after the event which made him a person of property and brought Tom Sawyer's story to a becoming conclusion. They are of the most surprising and delightful kind imaginable, and in the course of them we fall in with a number of types of character of singular freshness and novelty, besides being schooled in half a dozen extraordinary dialects—the Pike County dialect in all its forms, the dialect of the Missouri negro, and "the extremest form of the backwoods South-Western dialect," to wit. Huckleberry, it may be noted, is stolen by his disreputable father, to escape from whom he contrives an appearance of robbery and murder in the paternal hut, goes off in a canoe, watches from afar the townsfolk hunting for his dead body, and encounters a runaway negro—Miss Watson's Jim—an old particular friend of Tom Sawyer and himself. With Jim he goes south down the river, and is the hero of such scrapes and experiences as make your mouth water (if you have ever been a boy) to read of them. We do not purpose to tell a single one; it would be unfair to author and reader alike. We shall content ourselves with repeating that the book is Mark Twain at his best, and remarking that Jim and Huckleberry are real creations, and the worthy peers of the illustrious Tom Sawyer.

Athenaeum, 27 December 1884, p. 855.

HUCKLEBERRY FINN

[ATTRIBUTED TO BRANDER MATTHEWS]

The boy of to-day is fortunate indeed, and of a truth, he is to be congratulated. While the boy of yesterday had to stay his stomach with the unconscious humour of *Sanford and Merlon*, the boy of to-day may get his fill of fun and of romance and of adventures in *Treasure Island* and in *Tom Brown* and in *Tom Sawyer*, and now in a sequel to *Tom Sawyer*, wherein Tom himself appears in the very nick of time, like a young god from the machine. Sequels of stories which have been widely popular are not a little risky. *Huckleberry Finn* is a sharp exception to this general rule. Although it is a sequel, it is quite as worthy of wide popularity as *Tom Sawyer*. An American critic once neatly declared that the late G.P.R. James hit the bull's-eye of success with his first shot, and that for ever thereafter he went on firing through the same hole. Now this is just what Mark Twain has not done. *Huckleberry Finn* is not an attempt to do *Tom Sawyer* over again. It is a story quite as unlike its predecessor as it is like. Although Huck Finn appeared first in the earlier book, and although Tom Sawyer reappears in the later, the scenes and the characters are otherwise wholly different. Above all, the atmosphere of the story is different. *Tom Sawyer* was a tale of boyish adventure in a village in Missouri, on the Mississippi river, and it was told by the author. *Huckleberry Finn* is autobiographic; it is a tale of boyish adventure along the Mississippi river told as it appeared to Huck Finn. There is not in *Huckleberry Finn* any one scene quite as funny as those in which Tom Sawyer gets his friends to whitewash the fence for him, and then uses the spoils thereby acquired to attain the highest situation of the Sunday school the next morning. Nor is there any distinction quite as thrilling as that awful moment in the cave when the boy and the girl are lost in the darkness, and when Tom Sawyer suddenly sees a human hand bearing a light, and then finds that the hand is the hand of Indian Joe, his one mortal enemy; we have always thought that the vision of the hand in the cave in *Tom Sawyer* is one of the very finest things in the literature of adventure since Robinson Crusoe first saw a single footprint in the sand of the seashore. But though *Huckleberry Finn* may not quite reach these two highest points of *Tom Sawyer*, we incline to the opinion that the general level of the later story is perhaps higher than that of the earlier. For one thing, the skill with which the character of Huck Finn is maintained is marvellous. We see everything through his eyes—and they are his eyes and not a pair of Mark Twain's spectacles. And the comments on what he sees are his comments—the comments of an ignorant, superstitious, sharp, healthy boy, brought up as Huck Finn had been brought up; they are not speeches put into his mouth by the author. One of the most artistic things in the book—and that Mark Twain is a literary artist of a very high order all who have considered his later writings critically cannot but confess—one of the most artistic things in *Huckleberry Finn* is the sober self-restraint with which Mr. Clemens lets Huck Finn set down, without any comment at all, scenes which would have afforded the ordinary writer matter for endless moral and political and sociological disquisition. We refer particularly to the account of the Grangerford-Shepherdson feud, and of the shooting of Boggs by Colonel Sherburn. Here are two incidents of the rough old life of the South-Western States, and of the Mississippi Valley forty or fifty years ago, of the old life which is now rapidly passing away under the influence of advancing civilization and increasing commercial prosperity, but which has not wholly disappeared even yet, although a slow revolution in public sentiment is taking place. The Grangerford-Shepherdson feud is a vendetta as deadly as any Corsican could wish, yet the parties to it were honest, brave, sincere, good Christian people, probably people of deep religious sentiment. Not the less we see them taking their guns to church, and, when occasion serves, joining in what is little better than a general massacre. The killing of Boggs by Colonel Sherburn is told with equal sobriety and truth; and the later scene in which Colonel Sherburn cows and lashes the mob which has set out to lynch him is one of the most vigorous bits of writing Mark Twain has done.

In *Tom Sawyer* we saw Huckleberry Finn from the outside; in the present volume we see him from the inside. He is almost as much a delight to any one who has been a boy as was Tom Sawyer. But only he or she who has been a boy can truly enjoy this record of his adventures, and of his sentiments and of his sayings. Old maids of either sex will wholly fail to understand him or to like him, or to see his significance and his value. Like Tom Sawyer, Huck Finn is a genuine boy; he is neither a girl in boy's clothes like many of the modern heroes of juvenile fiction, nor is he a "little man," a full-grown man cut down; he is a boy, just a boy, only a boy. And his ways and modes of thought are boyish. As Mr. F. Anstey understands the English boy, and especially the English boy of the middle classes, so Mark Twain understands the American boy, and especially the American boy of the Mississippi Valley of forty or fifty years ago. The contrast between Tom Sawyer, who is the child of respectable parents, decently brought up, and Huckleberry Finn, who is the child of the town drunkard, not brought up at all, is made distinct by a hundred artistic touches, not the least natural of which is Huck's constant reference to Tom as his ideal of what a boy should be. When Huck escapes for the cabin where his drunken and worthless father had confined him, carefully manufacturing a mass of very circumstantial evidence to prove his own murder by robbers, he cannot help saying, "I did wish Tom Sawyer was there, I knowed he would take an interest in this kind of business, and throw in the fancy touches. Nobody could spread himself like Tom Sawyer in such a thing as that." Both boys have their full share of boyish imagination; and Tom Sawyer, being given to books, lets his imagination run on robbers and pirates and genies, with a perfect understanding with himself that, if you want to get fun out of this life, you must never hesitate to make believe very hard; and, with Tom's youth and health, he never finds it hard to make believe and to be a pirate at will, or to summon an attendant spirit, or to rescue a prisoner from the deepest dungeon 'neath the castle moat. But in Huck this imagination has turned to superstition; he is a walking repository of the juvenile folklore of the Mississippi Valley—a folklore partly traditional among the white settlers but largely influenced by intimate association with the negroes. When Huck was in his room at night all by himself waiting for the signal Tom Sawyer was to give him at midnight, he felt so lonesome he wished he was dead:

The stars was shining and the leaves rustled in the woods ever so mournful; and I heard an owl, away off, who-whooing about somebody that was dead, and a whippowill and a dog crying about somebody that was going to die; and the wind was trying to whisper something to me, and I couldn't make out what it was, and so it made the cold shivers run over me. Then away out in the woods I heard that kind of a sound that a ghost makes when it wants to tell about something that's on its mind and can't make itself understood, and so can't rest easy in its grave, and has to go about that way every night grieving. I got so downhearted and scared I did wish I had some company. Pretty soon a spider went crawling up my shoulders, and I flipped it off and it lit in the candle; and before I could budge it was all shrivelled up. I didn't need anybody to tell me that that was an awful bad sign and would fetch me some bad luck, so I was scared and most shook the clothes off me. I got up and turned around in my tracks three times and crossed my breast every time; and then I tied up a little lock of my hair with a thread to keep witches away. But I hadn't no confidence. You do that when you've lost a horse-shoe that you've found, instead of nailing it up over the door, but I hadn't ever heard anybody say it was any way to keep off bad luck when you'd killed a spider.

. . . . The romantic side of Tom Sawyer is shown in most delightfully humorous fashion in the account of his difficult devices to aid in the easy escape of Jim, a runaway negro. Jim is an admirably drawn character. There have been not a few fine and firm portraits of negroes in recent American fiction, of which Mr. Cable's Bras-Coupé in the *Grandissimes* is perhaps the most vigorous, and Mr. Harris's Mingo and Uncle Remus and Blue Dave are the most gentle. Jim is worthy to rank with these; and the essential simplicity and kindliness and generosity of the Southern negro have never been better shown than here by Mark Twain. Nor are Tom Sawyer and Huck Finn and Jim the only fresh and original figures in Mr. Clemens's new book; on the contrary, there is scarcely a character of the many introduced who does not impress the reader at once as true to life—and therefore as new, for life is so varied that a portrait from life is sure to be as good as new. That Mr. Clemens draws from life, and yet lifts his work from the domain of the photograph to the region of art, is evident to any one who will give his work the honest attention which it deserves. Mr. John T. Raymond, the American comedian, who performs the character of Colonel Sellers to perfection, is wont to say that there is scarcely a town in the West and South-West where some man did not claim to be the original of the character. And as Mark Twain made Colonel Sellers, so has he made the chief players in the present drama of boyish adventure; they are taken from life, no doubt, but they are so aptly chosen and so broadly drawn that they are quite as typical as they are actual. They have one great charm, all of them—they are not written about and about; they are not described and dissected and analysed; they appear and play their parts and disappear; and yet they leave a sharp impression of indubitable vitality and individuality. No one, we venture to say, who reads this book will readily forget the Duke and the King, a pair of as pleasant "confidence operators" as one may meet in a day's journey, who leave the story in the most appropriate fashion, being clothed in tar and feathers and ridden on a rail. Of the more broadly humorous passages—and they abound—we have not left ourselves space to speak; they are to the full as funny as in any of Mark Twain's other books; and, perhaps, in no other book has the humorist shown so much artistic restraint, for there is in *Huckleberry Finn* no mere "comic copy," no straining after effect; one might almost say that there is no waste word in it. Nor have we left ourselves room to do more than say a good word for the illustrations, which, although slight and unpretending, are far better than those to be found in most of Mark Twain's books. For one thing, they actually illustrate—and this is a rare quality in illustrations nowadays. They give the reader a distinct idea of the Duke and the King, of Jim and of Colonel Sherburn, of the Shepherdsons and the Grangerfords. They are all by one artist, Mr. E. W. Kemble, hitherto known to us only as the illustrator of the *Thompson Street Poker Club*, an amusing romance of highly-coloured life in New York.

London Saturday Review, 31 January 1885, pp. 153-54.

HUCKLEBERRY FINN

In his latest story, *Huckleberry Finn* (Tom Sawyer's Comrade), by Mark Twain, Mr. Clemens has made a very distinct literary advance over *Tom Sawyer*, as an interpreter of human nature and a contributor to our stock of original pictures of American life. Still adhering to his plan of narrating the adventures of boys, with a primeval and Robin Hood freshness, he has broadened his canvas and given us a picture of a people, of a geographical region, of a life that is new in the world. The scene of his romance is the Mississippi river. Mr. Clemens has written of this river before specifically, but he has not before presented it to the imagination so distinctly nor so powerfully. Huck Finn's voyage down the Mississippi with the run away Jim, and with occasionally other companions, is an adventure fascinating in itself as any of the classic out law stories, but in order that the reader may know what the author has done for him, let him notice the impression left on his mind of this lawless, mysterious, wonderful Mississippi, when he has closed the book. But it is not alone the river that is indelibly impressed upon the mind, the life that went up and down it and went on along its banks [is] projected with extraordinary power. Incidentally, and with a true artistic instinct, the villages, the cabins, the people of his river become startlingly real. The beauty of this is that it is apparently done without effort. Huck floating down the river happens to see these things and to encounter the people and the characters that made the river famous forty years ago—that is all. They do not have the air of being invented, but of being found. And the dialects of the people, white and black—what a study are they; and yet nobody talks for the sake of exhibiting a dialect. It is not necessary to believe the surprising adventures that Huck engages in but no one will have a moment's doubt of the reality of the country and the people he meets.

Another thing to be marked in the story is the dramatic power. Take the story of the Southern Vendetta—a marvelous piece of work in a purely literary point of view—and the episode of the duke and king, with its pictures of Mississippi communities, both of which our readers probably saw in the *Century* magazine. They are equalled in dramatic force by nothing recently in literature.

We are not in this notice telling the story or quoting from a book that nearly everybody is surely to read, but it is proper to say that Mr. Clemens strikes in a very amusing way certain psychological problems. What, for instance, in the case of Huck, the son of the town drunkard, perverted from the time of his birth, is conscience, and how does it work? Most amusing is the struggle Huck has with his conscience in regard to slavery. His conscience tells him, the way it has been instructed, that to help the runaway, nigger Jim to escape—to aid in stealing the property of Miss Watson, who has never injured him, is an enormous offense that will no doubt carry him to the bad place; but his affection for Jim finally induces him to violate his conscience and risk eternal punishment in helping Jim to escape. The whole study of Huck's moral nature is as serious as it is amusing, his confusion of wrong as right and his abnormal mendacity, traceable to his training from infancy, is a singular contribution to the investigation of human nature.

These considerations, however, do not interfere with the fun of the story, which has all the comicality, all the odd way of looking at life, all the whimsical turns of thought and expressions that have given the author his wide fame and made him *sui generis*. The story is so interesting[,] so full of life and dramatic force, that the reader will be carried along irresistibly, and the time he loses in laughing he will make up in diligence to hurry along and find out how things come out.

The book is a small quarto, handsomely printed and bound, and illustrated by 174 drawings which enter fully into the spirit of the book and really help to set forth the characters. (Published by Charles L. Webster & Company: New York. Sold by subscription only)

The Hartford Daily Courant, 20 February 1885, p. 2.

MODERN COMIC LITERATURE

[ATTRIBUTED TO ANDREW LANG]

No doubt in some books of "American Humour" colossal exaggeration makes part of the fun. No doubt there is a plentiful lack of good taste in *The Innocents Abroad*. But no critic worthy of the name can deny to Mark Twain at his best the essential qualities of wit and humour. He has, when quite himself, a lower kind of Sydney Smith's wonderful airy high spirits which lift him buoyantly into a kind of Laputa, a place whence he sees all the mad humours of men. He has, when he likes, tenderness and melancholy, and an extraordinary sense of human limitations and contradictions. The struggles of conscience of Huckleberry Finn about betraying the runaway negro have poetry and pathos blent in their humour. Only a great humorist could have made Huck give his own unvarnished account of the splendour and terror of a night of storm on the Mississippi, and of the coming of dawn. A mere buffoon could not have imagined the passage, a less finished humorist would have made Huck "talk fine" like Mr. Clark Russell's sailors in their high flown descriptive tootle. In Mark Twain the world has a humorist at once wild and tender, a humorist who is yearly ripening and mellowing. But our Australian censor calls him "the burlesquing and painfully artificial Mark Twain." Yes, there are men so great that nothing can please them, not even the miraculous observation, sympathy, and wit of the passage on the credulous blue jay, or the high spirits of the philological remarks on the German language, or the unrivalled adventure of the Celebrated Mexican Plug, or the story of editing an agricultural newspaper by a literary amateur.

Saturday Review, Volume 59, 7 March 1885, p. 301.

MARK TWAIN

T[HOMAS] S[ERGEANT] PERRY

Mark Twain's *Tom Sawyer* is an interesting record of boyish adventure; but, amusing as it is, it may yet be fair to ask whether its most marked fault is not too strong adherence to conventional literary models? A glance at the book certainly does not confirm this opinion, but those who recall the precocious affection of Tom Sawyer, at the age when he is losing his first teeth, for a little girl whom he has seen once or twice, will confess that the modern novel exercises a very great influence. What is best in the book, what one remembers, is the light we get into the boy's heart. The romantic devotion to the little girl, the terrible adventures with murderers and in huge caves, have the air of concessions to jaded readers. But when Tom gives the cat Pain-Killer, is restless in church, and is recklessly and eternally deceiving his aunt, we are on firm ground—the author is doing sincere work.

This later book, *Huckleberry Finn*, has the great advantage of being written in autobiographical form. This secures a unity in the narration that is most valuable; every scene is given, not described; and the result is a vivid picture of Western life forty or fifty years ago. While *Tom Sawyer* is scarcely more than an apparently fortuitous collection of incidents, and its thread is one that has to do with murders, this story has a more intelligible plot. Huckleberry, its immortal hero, runs away from his worthless father, and floats down the Mississippi on a raft, in company with Jim, a runaway negro. This plot gives great opportunity for varying incidents. The travelers spend some time on an island; they outwit every one they meet; they acquire full knowledge of the hideous fringe of civilization that then adorned that valley; and the book is a most valuable record of an important part of our motley American civilization.

What makes it valuable is the evident truthfulness of the narrative, and where this is lacking and its place is taken by ingenious invention, the book suffers. What is inimitable, however, is the reflection of the whole varied series of adventures in the mind of the young scapegrace of a hero. His undying fertility of invention, his courage, his manliness in every trial, are an incarnation of the better side of the ruffianism that is one result of the independence of Americans, just as hypocrisy is one result of the English respect for civilization. The total absence of morbidness in the book—for the *mal du siècle* has not yet reached Arkansas—gives it a genuine charm; and it is interesting to notice the art with which this is brought out. The best instance is perhaps to be found in the account of the feud between the Shepherdsons and the Grangerfords, which is described only as it would appear to a semi-civilized boy of fourteen, without the slightest condemnation or surprise,—either of which would be bad art,—and yet nothing more vivid can be imagined. That is the way that a story is best told, by telling it, and letting it go to the reader unaccompanied by sign-posts or directions how he shall understand it and profit by it. Life teaches its lessons by implication, not by didactic preaching; and literature is at its best when it is an imitation of life and not an excuse for instruction.

As to the humor of Mark Twain, it is scarcely necessary to speak. It lends vividness to every page. The little touch in *Tom Sawyer*, page 105, where, after the murder of which Tom was an eye-witness, it seemed "that his school-mates would never get done holding inquests on dead cats and thus keeping the trouble present to his mind," and that in the account of the spidery six-armed girl of Emmeline's picture in *Huckleberry Finn*, are in the author's happiest vein. Another admirable instance is to be seen in Huckleberry Finn's mixed feelings about rescuing Jim, the negro, from slavery. His perverted views regarding the unholiness of his actions are most instructive and amusing. It is possible to feel, however, that the fun in the long account of Tom Sawyer's artificial imitation of escapes from prison is somewhat forced; everywhere simplicity is a good rule, and while the account of the Southern *vendetta* is a masterpiece, the caricature of books of adventure leaves us cold. In one we have a bit of life; in the other Mark Twain is demolishing something that has no place in the book.

Yet the story is capital reading, and the reason of its great superiority to *Tom Sawyer* is that it is, for the most part, a consistent whole. If Mark Twain would follow his hero through manhood, he would condense a side of American life that, in a few years, will have to be delved out of newspapers, government reports, county histories, and misleading traditions by unsympathetic sociologists.

Century, 30 (May 1885), pp. 171-172.

CRITICISM 1930–1959

HUCKLEBERRY FINN IS FIFTY YEARS OLD—YES; BUT IS HE RESPECTABLE?

ASA DON DICKINSON

Fifty years ago Mark Twain published his masterpiece, *Huckleberry Finn*. Well worthy of commemoration is this anniversary for oftener than any rival save *The Scarlet Letter* has his Odyssey of the Mississippi been hailed as the Great American novel.

The book was begun in 1876 at Quarry Farm near Elmira, N. Y., when the author was in the flower of his age and at the height of his literary productivity. But with half the story written he could only say, "I like it only tolerably well, as far as I have gone, and may possibly pigeonhole or burn the manuscript when it is done." The time was not ripe; his inspiration failed entirely and the tale was put aside for years. The writing of *The Prince and the Pauper* and *A Tramp Abroad* engrossed him till 1880 when Huck once more unsuccessfully claimed his attention. It was a real steamboat voyage in 1882, preliminary to writing *Life on the Mississippi*, that brought Clemens's mind back to the glamorous river and revived in him the youthful enthusiasm of his pilot days.

In 1883 he resumed work on the old manuscript and now at last found himself writing with unexampled zest. In a letter to Howells (August 22, 1883) he says, "I have written eight or nine hundred manuscript pages in such a brief space of time that I mustn't name the number of days; I shouldn't believe it myself, and of course couldn't expect you to. I used to restrict myself to four or five hours a day and five days in the week, but this time I have wrought from breakfast to 5:15 P.M. six days in the week, and once or twice I smouched a Sunday when the boss wasn't looking. Nothing is half so good as literature hooked on Sunday, on the sly."

By the spring of 1884 the book was finished and Mark again wrote Howells: "My days are given to cursings, both loud and deep, for I am reading the Huck Finn proofs. They don't make a very great many mistakes, but those that do occur are of a nature to make a man swear his teeth loose." Howells offered to help with the proofs for the fun of reading the story. Clemens was equally astonished and delighted. "If you *mean* it, old man—if you are in *earnest*—proceed in God's name. . . . I can't conceive of a rational man deliberately piling such an atrocious job upon himself. But if there be such a man and you be that man, *pile it on*. The proof-reading of *The Prince and the Pauper* cost me the last shreds of my religion."

Huck Finn is of course a sequel to his former success, *Tom Sawyer*. Its hero, the town drunkard's son, is one of the principal characters in the earlier book. If we had had no Tom Sawyer we should have had no Huckleberry Finn. But during the years between the two stories the creator of Tom and Huck had grown older and wiser and mellower. He had watched and loved his own children growing up and around him. Tom Sawyer is the more exciting tale and remains the boys' favorite. Externally, Huck is just as lazy and ignorant and untruthful and uncouth in the later story as in the earlier one. But it is in the later yarn that we are for the first time made to recognize and to love him for the essential sincerity and integrity and faithfulness that underlie all his surface "orneriness."

Consider that time of soul-searching towards the end of the story—it is no irreverence to call it Huck's Gethsemane—after he finally makes up his mind that it is his plain Christian duty to betray his old comrade Jim and to inform his owner of his whereabouts:

It was astonishing, the way I felt as light as a feather, right straight off, and my troubles all gone. So I got a piece of paper and a pencil, all glad and excited, and set down and wrote:
Miss Watson your runaway nigger Jim is down here two mile below Pikesville and Mr. Phelps has got him and he will give him up for the reward if you send. Huck Finn.
I felt good and all washed clean of sin for the first time I had ever felt so in my life, and I knowed I could pray now. But I didn't do it straight off, but laid the paper down and set there thinking—thinking how good it was all this happened so, and how near I come to being lost and going to hell. And went on thinking. And got to thinking over our trip down the river; and I see Jim before me, all the time, in the day, and in the night-time, sometimes moonlight, sometimes storms, and we floating along, talking, and singing, and laughing. But somehow I couldn't seem to strike no places to harden me against him, but only the other kind. I'd see him standing my watch on top of his'n, stead of calling me, so I could go on sleeping; and see him how glad he was when I come back out of the fog; and when I come to him again in the swamp, up there where the feud was; and such-like times; and would always call me honey, and pet me, and do everything he could think of for me, and how good he always was; and at last I struck the time I saved him by telling the men we had smallpox aboard, and he was so grateful, and said I was the best friend old Jim ever had in the world, and the *only* one he's got now; and then I happened to look around and see that paper.
It was a close place. I took it up, and held it in my hand. I was a trembling, because I'd got to decide, forever, betwixt two things, and I knowed it. I studied a minute, sort of holding my breath, and then says to myself:
"All right, then, I'll *go* to hell"—and tore it up.

The honor of being the original Huck has been claimed for more than one of Sam Clemens' boyhood friends in Hannibal, Missouri. But Mark has explicitly stated that Huck is an exact portrait of Tom Blankenship, son of the Hannibal town drunkard. "He was ignorant, unwashed, insufficiently fed; but he had as good a heart as ever any boy had. . . . He was the only really independent person—boy or man—in the community, and by consequence he was tranquilly and continuously happy and was envied by all the rest of us." It may be noted that in later life Blankenship became a respected citizen of Montana and a justice of the peace. What would Miss Watson say to that?

From his fourth to his twelfth year little Sam Clemens spent his summers at the farm of his uncle, John A. Quarles, near Florida, Missouri. This became the Phelps farm in *Huckleberry Finn*. "I moved it down to Arkansas," he tells us. "It was all of six hundred miles, but it was no trouble; it was not a very large farm—five hundred acres perhaps—but I could have done it if it had been twice as large. And as for the morality of it, I cared nothing for that; I would move a state if the exigencies of literature required it."

On this farm Mark made the acquaintance of "Uncle Dan'l," the original of Jim. He was "a middle-aged slave whose head was the best one in the Negro quarters, whose sympathies were wide and warm, and whose heart was honest and simple and knew no guile."

There can be no doubt that Clemens wrote the stories of Huck and Tom not primarily for the edification of youth, but rather to please himself, and incidentally to earn a living. At the same time he was a good wholesome man, a lover of children, and the father of a family. When squeamish librarians, as they did now and then, saw in him a corrupter of youth, and excluded his books from their children's collections, Mark did not like it. His feelings were hurt. Were not his books much less outrageous than this gentle wild man would naturally have written them? Had he not, raging but dutiful, always submitted them to the home censor? Listen to his little daughter, Susy:

Ever since papa and mama were married papa has written his books and then taken them to mama in manuscript, and she has expergated [sic] them. Papa read *Huckleberry Finn* to us. . . . He would leave parts of it with mama to expergate, while he went off to the study to work, and sometimes Clara and I would be sitting with mama while she was looking the manuscript over, and I remember so well, with what pangs of regret we used to see her turn down the leaves of the pages, which meant that some delightfully terrible part must be scratched out.

Poor Mark! Was ever roaring lion so forced to content himself with a diet of prunes and prisms?

The Banishment of Huck

In 1905 I attended a meeting of children's librarians in Brooklyn and—because of my own great love and admiration for Huck—begged that he be allowed a place on the shelves of the children's rooms. It was no use. The good ladies assured me in effect that Huck was a deceitful boy; that he not only itched but scratched; and that he said *sweat* when he should have said *perspiration*. But my fervor amused them and they graciously gave me permission to plead his cause again at a later meeting if I wanted to. In desperation I wrote Mr. Clemens for help and promptly received the following reply:

Dear Sir:
I am greatly troubled by what you say. I wrote *Tom Sawyer* and *Huck Finn* for adults exclusively, and it always distresses me when I find that boys and girls have been allowed access to them. The mind that becomes soiled in youth can never again be washed clean; I know this by my own experience, and to this day I cherish an unappeasable bitterness against the unfaithful guardians of my young life, who not only permitted but compelled me to read an unexpurgated Bible through before I was 15 years old. None can do that and ever draw a clean sweet breath again this side of the grave. Ask that young lady—she will tell you so.

Most honestly do I wish I could say a softening word or two in defence of Huck's character, since you wish it, but really in my opinion it is no better than God's (in the Ahab chapter and 97 others) and those of Solomon, David, Satan, and the rest of the sacred brotherhood.

If there is an unexpurgated in the Children's Department, won't you please help that young woman remove Huck and Tom from that questionable companionship?

Sincerely yours,
(signed) S. L. Clemens.

I shall not show your letter to anyone—it is safe with me.

I was very young and very naïve in those days and this letter astonished and puzzled me not a little. I can see now that he wrote and mailed it on the spur of the moment when—as always—he was angry as well as hurt at the Nice-Nellieism of the lady librarians. They were easily shocked, it seemed. Well, then, he would say a few things that would shock them good and plenty. The Censor, alas, had been dead and gone for many a year and he was just a sensitive old man, lonely in the midst of a world's adulation.

The day for the second meeting came and, with many misgivings, I read Mark's letter. Needless to say, it fluttered the library dovecotes not a little, and all agreed that silence was golden. Mark Twain's name had a publicity value in those days only comparable to Roosevelt's in this. Public interest in his lightest word was unbounded and as uncontrollable as a prairie fire.

Let him tell what followed in his own words.

Four months drifted tranquilly by. Then there was music. [Some journalist had at last got wind of the letter.] There came a freshet of newspaper reporters and they besieged my secretary all day. Of course I was in bed. I am always in bed. She barred the stairs against them. They were bound to see me, if only for a moment, but none of them got by her guard. They said a report had sprung up that I had written a letter some months before to the Brooklyn Public Library; that according to that report the letter was pungent and valuable, and they wanted a copy of it. They said the head officials of the Brooklyn Library declared that they had never seen the letter and that they had never heard of it until the reporters came and asked for it. I judged by this that my man—who was not in the head library, but in a branch of it—was keeping his secret all right, and I believed he could be trusted to continue to keep that secret, for his own sake as well as mine. That letter would be a bombshell for me if it got out—but it would hoist him, too. So I felt pretty confident that for his own sake, if for no other, he would protect me.

My secretary had a hard day of it, but I had a most enjoyable one. She never allowed any reporter to get an idea of the nature of the letter; she smoothed all those young fellows down and sent them away empty.

They renewed the assault next day, but I told her to never mind—human nature would win the victory for us. There would be an earthquake somewhere, or a municipal upheaval *here*, or a threat of war in Europe—something would be sure to happen in the way of a big excitement that would call the boys away from No. 21 Fifth Avenue for twenty-four hours, and that would answer every purpose; they wouldn't think of that letter again, and we should have peace.

I knew the reporters would get on the right track very soon, so I wrote Mr. Dickinson and warned him to keep his mouth hermetically sealed.

Indeed Mark seemed even more badly scared than I was at all this excitement. He had kept no copy of his letter, probably, remembered only that "Liddy" certainly would not have liked it, and that he had been good and mad when he wrote it. From his own past performances he feared it might be even more outrageous than it actually was. So he put a special delivery stamp on his second letter to me. "Be wise as a serpent and wary as a dove!" he wrote. "The newspaper boys want that letter—don't you let them get hold of it. They say you refuse to let them see it without my consent. Keep on refusing, and I'll take care of this end of the line."

I sent him a re-assuring reply, explained that Tom and Huck had never been and would never be thrown out of the Brooklyn Public Library, that they were to be found on open shelves among adult fiction, that any child was free to seek them there if he chose, and that I was looking forward to seeing him at a public meeting the next evening. In his *Autobiography* he concludes his account of the incident as follows:

I saw him at the Waldorf the next night, where Choate and I made our public appeal in behalf of the blind, and found him to be a very pleasant and safe and satisfactory man. . . . I think the incident is closed. . . . When people let Huck alone he goes peacefully along, damaging a few children here and there and yonder, but there will be plenty of children in heaven without those, so it is no great matter. It is only when well-meaning people expose him that he gets his real chance to do harm. Temporarily, then, he spreads havoc all around in the nurseries and no doubt does prodigious harm while he has his chance. By and by, let us hope, people that really have the best interests of the rising generation at heart will become wise and not stir Huck up.

BOOKS IN GENERAL

V. S. PRITCHETT

After reading Hemingway and Faulkner and speculating upon the breach of American with English literature, the mind goes back to the two decisive, indigenous Americans who opened the new vein—Mark Twain and Edgar Allan Poe. Everything really American, really nonEnglish, comes out of that pair of spiritual derelicts, those two scarecrow figures with their half-lynched minds. We have never had the obverse of Puritanism in England, for the political power of Puritanism lasted only a decade. If an Englishman hated Puritanism, he could fall back on the rest of the elaborate English tradition; if an American hated that philosophy (which had become almost totalitarian in the United States), he found himself alone in a wilderness, with nothing but bottomless cynicism and bitterness for his consolation. There has never been in English literature a cynicism to compare with the American; at any rate we have never had the American kind, with its broken chopper edge and its ugly wound. We have also never had its by-product: the humorous practical philosophers, the Josh Billings, Artemus Wards, Will Rogers, the Pudd'nhead Wilsons with their close-fisted proverbs.

Training is everything. The peach was once a bitter almond: cauliflower is nothing but cabbage with a college education.

Or:

Consider well the proportions of things. It is better to be a young June bug than an old bird of Paradise.

Pudd'nhead Wilson was, of course, Twain's invention.

I say we have never had this kind of rumination, but there is one exception to prove the rule and to prove it very well, for he also is an uprooted and, so to speak, colonial writer. The Anglo-Indian Kipling with his "A woman is always a woman, but a good cigar is a smoke," is our first writer in the American school, with a cynicism, a brand of humour and a jungle book of beliefs which, I think, would be characteristic of our literature if we become seriously totalitarian in the future. For English totalitarianism would create the boredom and bitterness of the spiritual wilderness, as surely as Puritanism did in America.

When Mark Twain turned upon the religion of his childhood because it was intolerable, he was unaware that it would destroy him by turning him into a money-grubber of the most disastrously Puritan kind. Fortunately the resources of the imagination are endless even when a fanatical philosophy wrecks human life, genius and happiness. Out of the mess which Twain made of his life, amid the awful pile of tripe which he wrote, there does rise one book which has the serenity of a thing of genius. *Huckleberry Finn* takes the breath away. Knowing Mark Twain's life, knowing the hell of vulgarity from which the book has ascended, one dreads as one turns from page to page the seemingly inevitable flop. How can a low comedian, so tortured and so angry, refrain from blackguarding God, Man and Nature for the narrow boredom of his early life, and ruining the perfect comedy and horror of this story? But imaginative writers appear to get at least one lucky break in their careers; for a moment the conflicts are assimilated, the engine ceases to work against itself. *Huckleberry*

Finn does not flop. America gets its first truly indigenous masterpiece. The small boyhood of Huck Finn is the small boyhood of a new culture.

The curious thing about *Huckleberry Finn* is that, although it is one of the funniest books in all literature and really astonishing in the variety of its farce and character, we are even more moved that we are amused by it. Why are we moved? Do we feel the sentiment of sympathy only? Are we sighing with some envy and self-pity? "Alas, Huck Finn is just what I would have been in my boyhood if I had had half a chance?" Are we sorry for the vagrant, or are we moved by his rebellion? These minor feelings may play their part; but they are only sighs on the surface of the main stream of our emotion. Mark Twain has brought to his subject far more than this personal longing; he has become the channel of the generic emotion which floods all really American literature—the emotion of nostalgia. In that absurd, brilliant, hit-or-miss book, *Studies in Classical American Literature*, which is so often dead right, D. H. Lawrence called this feeling the longing of the rebel for a master. It may be simply the longing for a spiritual home, but it is as strong in Mark Twain as it is implicit in Hemingway. One finds this feeling in Anglo-Irish literature which is also colonial and, in a less lasting way, in the work of Kipling. The peculiar power of American nostalgia is that it is not only harking back to something lost in the past, but suggests also the tragedy of a lost future. As Huck Finn and old Jim drift down the Mississippi from one horrifying little town to the next and hear the voices of men quietly swearing at one another across the water; as they pass the time of day with the scroungers, rogues, murderers, the lonely women, the frothing revivalists, the maundering boatman and fantastic drunks of the river towns, we see the human wastage that is left in the wake of a great effort of the human will, the hopes frustrated, the idealism which has been whittled down to eccentricity and craft. These people are the price paid for building a new country. It is not, once you have faced it—which Dickens did not do in *Martin Chuzzlewit*, obsessed as he was with the negative pathos of the immigrant—it is not a disheartening spectacle; for the value of a native humour like Twain's is that it expresses a profound reality in human nature: the ability of man to adjust himself to circumstance and to live somehow.

Movement is one of the great consolers of human woe; movement, a sense of continual migration, is the history of America. This factor gives Twain's wonderful descriptions of the journey down the Mississippi their haunting overtone. His natural sensibility which is shown nowhere else in his writings and which is indeed vulgarly repressed in them is awakened:

. . . then we set down on the sandy bottom where the water was about knee-deep and watched the daylight come. Not a sound anywhere—perfectly still—just like the whole world was asleep, only sometimes the bullfrogs a-clattering maybe. The first thing to see, looking away over the water, was a kind of dull line—that was the woods on t'other side—you couldn't make nothing else out; then a pale place in the sky; then more paleness, spreading around; then the river softened up, away off, and wasn't black any more but grey; you could see little dark spots drifting along, ever so far away—trading scows and such things; and long black streaks—rafts; sometimes you could hear a sweep screaking; or jumbled-up voices, it was so still, and sounds come so far; and by-and-by you could see a streak on the water which you know by the look of the streak that there's a snag in the swift current which breaks on it and that makes that streak look that way; and you see the mist curl up off the water, and the east reddens up, and the river, and you make out a log cabin in the edge of the woods, away on the bank t'other side of the river, being a woodyard likely, and piled by them cheats so you can throw a dog through it anywheres. . . .

The subject of *Huckleberry Finn* is the comical but also brutal effect of an anarchic rebellion against civilization and especially its tradition:

> I reckon I got to light out for the Territory ahead of the rest, because Aunt Sally she's going to adopt me and sivilize me and I can't stand it. I been there before.

Huck isn't interested in "Moses and the Bulrushers" because Huck "don't take no stock of dead people." He garbles European history when he is discussing Kings with Jim, the negro. Whether Huck is the kind of boy who will grow up to build a new civilization is doubtful; Tom Sawyer obviously would do so because he is imaginative. Huck never imagines anything except fears. Huck is "low-down plain ornery," in trouble because of the way he was brought up with "Pap." He is a natural anarchist and bum. He can live without civilization, depending on simple affections and workaday loyalties. He is the first of those typical American portraits of the underdog, which have culminated in the "poor white" literature and Charlie Chaplin—an underdog who gets along on horse sense, so to speak. Romanticism, ideas, ideals, are repugnant to Huck.

Mark Twain obliges you to accept the boy as the humorous norm. Without him the violence of the book would be stark reporting of low life. For if this is a great comic book it is also a book of terror and brutality. Think of the scenes: Pap with d.t.'s chasing Huck round the cabin with a knife; Huck sitting up all night with a gun preparing to shoot the old man; Huck's early familiarity with corpses; the pig killing scene; the sight of the frame house (evidently some sort of brothel) floating down the Mississippi with a murdered man in it; the fantastic events at the Southerner's house where two families are shooting each other down in a vendetta; the drunken Boggs who comes into town to pick a quarrel and is eventually coolly shot dead before the eyes of his screaming young daughter by the man he has insulted. The "Duke" and "the King," those cynical rascals whose adventures liven up the second half of the story, are sharpers, twisters and crooks of the lowest kind. Yet a child is relating all this with a child's detachment and with a touch of morbidity. Marvellous as it all is as picaresque episode and as a description of the mess of frontier life, it is strong meat. Sometimes we wonder how Twain's public stomached such illusionless reporting. The sardonic humour and the important fact that in this one book Mark Twain never forced a point nor overwrote—in the Dickens way, for example—are of course the transfiguring and beguiling forces. The corpse and coffin humour is a dry wine which raises his animal spirits. Old Jim not only looked like a dead man after "the King" had painted him blue, but like one "who had been dead a considerable time." Judiciousness is carried to the comic limit.

Is *Huckleberry Finn* one of the great works of picaresque literature? It is, granting the limits of a boy's mind in the hero and the author, a comic masterpiece; but this limitation is important. It is not a book which grows spiritually, if we compare it to *Quixote, Dead Souls* or even *Pickwick*; and it is lacking in that civilized quality which you are bound to lose when you throw over civilization—the quality of pity. One is left with the cruelty of American humour, a cruelty which is softened by the shrewd moralisings of the humorous philosophers—the Josh Billings, the Artemus Wards, the Will Rogers. And once Mark Twain passed this exquisite moment of his maturity, he went to bits in that morass of sentimentality, cynicism, melodrama and vulgarity which have damned him for the adult reader. I advise those who haven't read *Huckleberry Finn* since their school days to read it again.

COME BACK TO THE RAFT AG'IN, HUCK HONEY!

LESLIE FIEDLER

It is perhaps to be expected that the Negro and the homosexual should become stock literary themes, compulsive, almost mythic in their insistence, in a period when the reassertion of responsibility and of the inward meaning of failure has become again a primary concern of our literature. Their locus is, of course, discrepancy—in a culture which has no resources (no tradition of courtesy, no honored mode of cynicism) for dealing with a contradiction between principle and practice. It used once to be fashionable to think of puritanism as a force in our life encouraging hypocrisy; quite the contrary, its rigid emphasis upon the singleness of belief and action, its turning of the most prosaic areas of common life into arenas where one's state of grace is symbolically tested, confuse the outer and the inner and make among us, perhaps more strikingly than ever elsewhere, hypocrisy *visible*, visibly detestable, a cardinal sin. It is not without significance that the shrug of the shoulders (the acceptance of circumstance as a sufficient excuse, the vulgar sign of self-pardon before the inevitable lapse) seems in America an unfamiliar, an alien gesture.

And yet before the underground existence of crude homosexual love (the ultimate American epithets of contempt notoriously exploit the mechanics of such affairs), before the blatant ghettos in which the cast-off Negro conspicuously creates the gaudiness and stench that offend him, the white American must over and over make a choice between coming to uneasy terms with an institutionalized discrepancy, or formulating radically new ideologies. There are, to be sure, stop-gap devices, evasions of that final choice; not the least interesting is the special night club: the fag café, the black-and-tan joint, in which fairy or Negro exhibit their fairyness, their Negro-ness as if they were mere divertissements, gags thought up for the laughs and having no reality once the lights go out and the chairs are piled on the tables for the cleaning-woman. In the earlier minstrel show, a negro performer was required to put on with grease paint and burnt cork the formalized mask of blackness.

The situations of the Negro and the homosexual in our society pose precisely opposite problems, or at least problems suggesting precisely opposite solutions: Our laws on homosexuality and the context of prejudice and feeling they objectify must apparently be changed to accord with a stubborn social fact, whereas it is the social fact, our overt behavior toward the Negro, that must be modified to accord with our laws and the, at least official, morality they objectify.

It is not, of course, quite so simple. There is another sense in which the fact of homosexual passion contradicts a national myth of masculine love, just as our real relationship with the Negro contradicts a myth of that relationship, and those two myths with their betrayals are, as we shall see, one.

The existence of overt homosexuality threatens to compromise an essential aspect of American sentimental life: the camaraderie of the locker-room and ball park, the good fellowship of the poker game and fishing trip, a kind of passionless passion, at once gross and delicate, homoerotic in the boy's sense, possessing an innocence above suspicion. To doubt for a moment this innocence, which can survive only as *assumed*, would destroy our stubborn belief in a relationship simple, utterly satisfying, yet immune to lust: physical as the handshake is physical, this side of copulation. The nineteenth-century myth of the immaculate Young Girl has failed to survive in any *felt* way into our time; rather in the dirty jokes shared among men in the smoking-car, the barracks, or the dormitory there is a common male revenge against women for having flagrantly betrayed that myth, and under the revenge, there is the rather smug assumption of the chastity of the group as a masculine society. From what other source could that unexpected air of good clean fun which overhangs such sessions arise? It is this self-congratulatory buddy-buddiness, its astonishing naiveté, that breeds at once endless opportunities for inversion and the terrible reluctance to admit its existence, to surrender the last believed-in stronghold of love without passion.

It is, after all, what we know from a hundred other sources that is here verified: the regressiveness, in a technical sense, of American life, its implacable nostalgia for the infantile, at once wrongheaded and somehow admirable. The mythic America is boyhood—and who would dare be startled to realize that two (and the two most popular, the two most *absorbed*, I think) of the handful of great books on our native heritage are customarily to be found, illustrated, on the shelves of the Children's Library. I am referring of course to *Moby Dick* and *Huckleberry Finn*, splendidly counterpoised in their oceanic complexity and fluminal simplicity, but alike children's books, or more precisely, *boys'* books.

Among the most distinguished novelists of the American past, only Henry James escapes completely classification as a writer of juvenile classics; even Hawthorne, who did write sometimes for children, must in his most adult novels endure, though not as Mark Twain and Melville submit to, the child's perusal; a child's version of *The Scarlet Letter* would seem a rather far-fetched joke if it were not a part of our common experience. On a lower level of excellence, there are the Leatherstocking Tales of Cooper and Dana's *Two Years Before the Mast*, books read still, though almost unaccountably in Cooper's case, by boys. What do all these novels have in common?

As boys' books we would expect them shyly, guilelessly as it were, to proffer a chaste male love as the ultimate emotional experience—and this is spectacularly the case. In Dana, it is the narrator's melancholy love for the *kanaka*, Hope; in Cooper, the lifelong affection of Natty Bumpo and Chingachgook; in Melville, Ishmael's love for Queequeg; in Twain, Huck's feeling for Nigger Jim. At the focus of emotion, where we are accustomed to find in the world's great novels some heterosexual passion, be it Platonic love or adultery, seduction, rape or long-drawn-out flirtation, we come instead upon the fugitive slave and the no-account boy lying side by side on the raft borne by the endless river towards an impossible escape, or the pariah sailor waking in the tatood arms of the brown harpooner on the verge of their impossible quest. "Aloha, aikane, aloha nui," Hope cries to the lover who prefers him above his fellow-whites; and Ishmael, in utter frankness tells us: "Thus, then, in our heart's honeymoon, lay I and Queequeg—a cosy, loving pair." Physical it all is, certainly, yet of an ultimate innocence; there is between the lovers no sword but a childlike ignorance, as if the possibility of a fall to the carnal had not yet been discovered. Even in the *Vita Nuova* of Dante there is no vision of love less offensively, more unremittingly chaste; that it is not adult seems sometimes beside the point.

The tenderness of Huck's repeated loss and refinding of Jim, Ishmael's sensations as he wakes under the pressure of Queequeg's arm, the role of almost Edenic helpmate played for Bumpo by the Indian—these shape us from childhood: we have no sense of first discovering them, of having been once without them.

Of the infantile, the homoerotic aspects of these stories we are, though vaguely, aware, but it is only with an effort that we can wake to a consciousness of how, among us who at the level of adulthood find a difference in color sufficient provocation for distrust and hatred, they celebrate, all of them, the mutual love of *a white man and a colored.*

So buried at a level of acceptance which does not touch reason, so desperately repressed from overt recognition, so contrary to what is usually thought of as our ultimate level of taboo—the sense of that love can survive only in the obliquity of a symbol, persistent, archetypical, in short, as a myth: the boy's homoerotic crush, the love of the black fused at this level into a single thing.

I hope I have been using here a hopelessly abused word with some precision; by myth I mean a coherent pattern of beliefs and feelings, so widely shared at a level beneath consciousness that there exists no abstract vocabulary for representing it, and (this is perhaps another aspect of the same thing) so "sacred" that unexamined, irrational restraints inhibit any explicit analysis. Such a complex achieves a formula or pattern story, which serves both to embody it, and, at first at least, to conceal its full implications. Later the secret may be revealed, the myth (I use a single word for the formula and what is formulized) "analyzed" or "allegorically interpreted" according to the language of the day.

I find the situation we have been explicating genuinely mythic; certainly it has the concealed character of the true myth, eluding the wary pounce of Howells or of Mrs. Twain who excised from *Huckleberry Finn* the cussin' as unfit for children, but left, unperceived, a conventionally abhorrent doctrine of ideal love. Even the writers in whom we find it, attained it, in a sense, dreaming. The felt difference between *Huckleberry Finn* and Twain's other books must lie surely in the release from conscious restraint inherent in the author's assumption of the character of Huck; the passage in and out of darkness and river mist, the constant confusion of identities (Huck's ten or twelve names—the questions of who is the real uncle, who the true Tom), the sudden intrusions into alien violences without past or future, give the whole work for all its carefully observed detail, the texture of a dream. For *Moby Dick*, such a point need scarcely be made. Even Cooper; despite his insufferable gentlemanliness, his civilized tedium, cannot conceal from the kids who continue to read him the secret behind the overconscious, stilted prose: the childish impossible dream. D. H. Lawrence saw in him clearly the kid's Utopia: the absolute wilderness in which the stuffiness of home yields to the wigwam and "My Wife" to Chingachgook.

I do not recall ever having seen in the commentaries of the social anthropologist or psychologist an awareness of the role of this profound child's dream of love in our relation to the Negro. (I say Negro, though the beloved in the books we have mentioned is variously Indian and Hawaiian, because the Negro has become more and more exclusively for us *the* colored man, the colored man par excellence.) Trapped in what has by now become a shackling cliché: the concept of the white man's sexual envy of the Negro male, they do not sufficiently note the complementary factor of physical attraction, the mythic love of white male and black. I am deliberately ignoring here an underlying Indo-European myth of great antiquity, the Manichaean notion of an absolute Black and White, hostile yet needing each other for completion, as I ignore more recent ideologies that have nourished the view that concerns us: the Shakespearian myth of good homosexual love opposed to an evil heterosexual attachment, the Rousseauistic concept of the Noble Savage; I have tried to stay within the limits of a single unified myth, re-enforced by disparate materials.

Ishmael and Queequeg, arm in arm, about to ship out, Huck and Jim swimming beside the raft in the peaceful flux of the Mississippi,—it is the motion of water which completes the syndrome, the American dream of isolation afloat. The Negro as homoerotic lover blends with the myth of running off to sea, of running the great river down to the sea. The immensity of water defines a loneliness that demands love, its strangeness symbolizes the disavowal of the conventional that makes possible all versions of love.

In *Two Years Before the Mast*, in *Moby Dick*, in *Huckleberry Finn* the water is there, is the very texture of the novel; the Leatherstocking Tales propose another symbol for the same meaning: the virgin forest. Notice the adjective—the virgin forest and the forever inviolable sea. It is well to remember, too, what surely must be more than a coincidence, that Cooper who could dream this myth invented the novel of the sea, wrote for the first time in history the sea-story proper. The rude pederasty of the forecastle and the Captain's cabin, celebrated in a thousand jokes, is the profanation of a dream. In a recent book of Gore Vidal's an incipient homosexual, not yet aware of his feelings, indulges in the apt reverie of running off to sea with his dearest friend. The buggery of sailors is taken for granted among us, yet it is thought of usually as an inversion forced on men by their isolation from women, though the opposite case may well be true, the isolation sought more or less consciously as an occasion for male encounters. There is a context in which the legend of the sea as escape and solace, the fixated sexuality of boys, the dark beloved are one.

In Melville and Twain at the center of our tradition, in the lesser writers at the periphery, the myth is at once formalized and perpetuated; Nigger Jim and Queequeg make concrete for us what was without them a vague pressure upon the threshold of our consciousness; the proper existence of the myth is in the realized character, who waits, as it were, only to be asked his secret. Think of Oedipus biding in silence from Sophocles to Freud.

Unwittingly we are possessed in childhood by the characters and their undiscriminated meaning, and it is difficult for us to dissociate them without a sense of disbelief. What! these household figures clues to our subtlest passions! The foreigner finds it easier to perceive the remoter significance; D. H. Lawrence saw in our classics a linked mythos of escape and immaculate male love; Lorca in *The Poet in New York* grasped instinctively the kinship of Harlem and Walt Whitman, the fairy as bard. Yet in every generation of our own writers the myth appears; in the gothic reverie of Capote's *Other Voices, Other Rooms*, both elements of the syndrome are presented, though disjunctively: the boy moving between the love of a Negro maidservant and his inverted cousin.

In the myth, one notes finally, it is always in the role of outcast, ragged woodsman, or despised sailor (Call me Ishmael!), or unregenerate boy (Huck before the prospect of being 'sivilized' cries, "I been here before!") that we turn to the love of a colored man. But how, we must surely ask, does the vision of the white American as pariah correspond with our long-held public status: the world's beloved, the success? It is perhaps only the artist's portrayal of *himself*, the notoriously alienated writer in America, at home with such images, child of the town drunk, the survivor. But no, Ishmael is all of us, our unconfessed universal fear objectified in the writer's status as in the sailor's: that compelling anxiety, which every foreigner notes, that we may not be loved, that we are loved for our possessions and not ourselves, that we are really—*alone*! It is that underlying terror which explains our almost furtive incredulity in the face of adulation or favor, what is called (once more the happy adjective) our "boyish modesty."

Our dark-skinned beloved will take us, we assure ourselves, when we have been cut off, or have cut ourselves off from all others, without rancor or the insult of forgiveness; he will fold us in his arms saying "Honey" or "Aikane!", he will comfort us, as if our offense against him were long ago remitted, were never truly *real*. And yet we cannot really forget our guilt ever; the stories that embody the myth dramatize almost compulsively the role of the colored man as victim: Dana's Hope is shown dying of the white man's syphilis; Queequeg is portrayed as racked by fever, a pointless episode except in the light of this necessity; Cooper's Indian smolders to a hopeless old age conscious of the imminent disappearance of his race; Jim is shown loaded down with chains, weakened by the hundred torments of Tom's notion of bullyness. The immense gulf of guilt must be underlined, just as is the disparity of color (Queequeg is not merely brown but monstrously tatooed, Chingachgook is horrid with paint, Jim is shown as the Sick A-rab dyed blue), so that the final reconciliation will seem more unbelievable, more tender. The myth makes no attempt to whitewash our outrage as a fact; it portrays it as meaningless in the face of love.

There would be something insufferable, I think, in that final vision of remission if it were not for the apparent presence of a motivating anxiety, the sense always of a last chance; behind the white American's nightmare that someday, no longer tourist, inheritor, or liberator, he will be rejected, refused—he dreams of his acceptance at the breast he has most utterly offended. It is a dream so sentimental, so outrageous, so desperate that it redeems our concept of boyhood from nostalgia to tragedy.

In each generation we *play* out the impossible mythos, and we live to see our children play it, the white boy and the black we can discover wrestling affectionately on any American street, along which they will walk in adulthood, eyes averted from each other, unwilling to touch. The dream recedes; the immaculate passion and the astonishing reconciliation become a memory, and less, a regret, at last the unrecognized motifs of a child's book. "It's too good to be true, Honey," Jim says to Huck. "It's too good to be true."

INTRODUCTION

T.S. ELIOT

The Adventures of Huckleberry Finn is the only one of Mark Twain's various books which can be called a masterpiece. I do not suggest that it is his only book of permanent interest; but it is the only one in which his genius is completely realized, and the only one which creates its own category. There are pages in *Tom Sawyer* and in *Life on the Mississippi* which are, within their limits, as good as anything with which one can compare them in *Huckleberry Finn*; and in other books there are drolleries just as good of their kind. But when we find one book by a prolific author which is very much superior to all the rest, we look for the peculiar accident or concourse of accidents which made that book possible. In the writing of *Huckleberry Finn* Mark Twain had two elements which, when treated with his sensibility and his experience, formed a great book: these two are the Boy and the River.

Huckleberry Finn is, no doubt, a book which boys enjoy. I cannot speak from memory: I suspect that a fear on the part of my parents lest I should acquire a premature taste for tobacco, and perhaps other habits of the hero of the story, kept the book out of my way. But *Huckleberry Finn* does not fall into the category of juvenile fiction. The opinion of my parents that it was a book unsuitable for boys left me, for most of my life, under the impression that it was a book suitable only for boys. Therefore it was only a few years ago that I read for the first time, and in that order, *Tom Sawyer* and *Huckleberry Finn*.

Tom Sawyer did not prepare me for what I was to find its sequel to be. *Tom Sawyer* seems to me to be a boys' book, and a very good one. The River and *the* Boy make their appearance in it; the narrative is good; and there is also a very good picture of society in a small mid-Western river town (for St. Petersburg is more Western than Southern) a hundred years ago. But the point of view of the narrator is that of an adult observing a boy. And Tom is the ordinary boy, though of quicker wits, and livelier imagination, than most. Tom is, I suppose, very much the boy that Mark Twain had been: he is remembered and described as he seemed to his elders, rather than created. Huck Finn, on the other hand, is the boy that Mark Twain still was, at the time of writing his adventures. We look at Tom as the smiling adult does: Huck we do not look at—we see the world through his eyes. The two boys are not merely different types; they were brought into existence by different processes. Hence in the second book their roles are altered. In the first book Huck is merely the humble friend—almost a variant of the traditional valet of comedy; and we see him as he is seen by the conventional respectable society to which Tom belongs, and of which, we feel sure, Tom will one day become an eminently respectable and conventional member. In the second book their nominal relationship remains the same; but here it is Tom who has the secondary role. The author was probably not conscious of this, when he wrote the first two chapters: *Huckleberry Finn* is not the kind of story in which the author knows, from the beginning, what is going to happen. Tom then disappears from our view; and when he returns, he has only two functions. The first is to provide a foil for Huck. Huck's persisting admiration for Tom only exhibits more clearly to our eyes the unique qualities of the former and the commonplaceness of the latter. Tom has the imagination of a lively boy who has read a good deal of romantic fiction: he might, of course, become a writer—he might become Mark Twain. Or rather, he might become the more commonplace aspect of Mark Twain. Huck has not imagination, in the sense in which Tom has it: he has, instead, vision. He sees the real world; and he does not judge it—he allows it to judge itself.

Tom Sawyer is an orphan. But he has his aunt; he has, as we learn later, other relatives; and he has the environment into which he fits. He is wholly a social being. When there is a secret band to be formed, it is Tom who organizes it and prescribes the rules. Huck Finn is alone: there is no more solitary character in fiction. The fact that he has a father only emphasizes his loneliness; and he views his father with a terrifying detachment. So we come to see Huck himself in the end as one of the permanent symbolic figures of fiction; not unworthy to take a place with Ulysses, Faust, Don Quixote, Don Juan, Hamlet and other great discoveries that man has made about himself.

It would seem that Mark Twain was a man who—perhaps like most of us—never became in all respects mature. We might even say that the adult side of him was boyish, and that only the boy in him, that was Huck Finn, was adult. As Tom Sawyer grown up, he wanted success and applause (Tom himself always needs an audience). He wanted prosperity, a happy domestic life of a conventional kind, universal approval, and fame. All of these things he obtained. As Huck Finn he was indifferent to all these things; and being composite of the two, Mark Twain both strove for them, and resented their violation of his integrity. Hence he became the humorist and even clown: with his gifts, a certain way to success, for everyone could enjoy his writings without the slightest feeling of discomfort, self-consciousness or self-criticism. And hence, on the other hand, his pessimism and misanthropy. To be a misanthrope is to be in some way divided; or it is a sign of an uneasy conscience. The pessimism which Mark Twain discharged into *The Man That Corrupted Hadleyburg* and *What is Man?* springs less from observation of society, than from his hatred of himself for allowing society to tempt and corrupt him and give him what he wanted. There is no wisdom in it. But all this personal problem has been diligently examined by Mr. Van Wyck Brooks; and it is not Mark Twain, but *Huckleberry Finn*, that is the subject of this introduction.

You cannot say that Huck himself is either a humorist or a misanthrope. He is the impassive observer: he does not interfere, and, as I have said, he does not judge. Many of the episodes that occur on the voyage down the river, after he is joined by the Duke and the King (whose fancies about themselves are akin to the kind of fancy that Tom Sawyer enjoys) are in themselves farcical; and if it were not for the presence of Huck as the reporter of them, they would be no more than farce. But, seen through the eyes of Huck, there is a deep human pathos in these scoundrels. On the other hand, the story of the feud between the Grangerfords and the Shepherdsons is a masterpiece in itself: yet Mark Twain could not have written it so, with that economy and restraint, with just the right details and no more, and leaving to the reader to make his own moral reflections, unless he had been writing in the person of Huck. And the *style* of the book, which is the style of Huck, is what makes it a far more convincing indictment of slavery than the sensationalist propaganda of *Uncle Tom's Cabin*. Huck is passive and impassive, apparently always the victim of events; and yet, in his acceptance of his world and of what it does to him and others, he is more powerful than his world, because he is more *aware* than any other person in it.

Repeated readings of the book only confirm and deepen one's admiration of the consistency and perfect adaptation of the writing. This is a style which at the period, whether in America or in England, was an innovation, a new discovery in the English language. Other authors had achieved natural speech in relation to particular characters—Scott with characters talking Lowland Scots, Dickens with cockneys: but no one else had kept it up through the whole of a book. Thackeray's Yellowplush, impressive as he is, is an obvious artifice in comparison. In *Huckleberry Finn* there is no exaggeration of grammar or spelling or speech, there is no sentence or phrase to destroy the illusion that these are Huck's own words. It is not only in the way in which he tells his story, but in the details he remembers, that Huck is true to himself. There is, for instance, the description of the Grangerford interior as Huck sees it on his arrival; there is the list of the objects which Huck and Jim salvaged from the derelict house:

> We got an old tin lantern, and a butcher-knife without any handle, and a bran-new Barlow knife worth two bits in any store, and a lot of tallow candles, and a tin candlestick, and a gourd, and a tin cup, and a ratty old bedquilt off the bed, and a reticule with needles and pins and beeswax and buttons and thread and all such truck in it, and a hatchet and some nails, and a fish-line as thick as my little finger, with some monstrous hooks on it, and a roll of buckskin, and a leather dog-collar, and a horseshoe, and some vials of medicine that didn't have no label on them; and just as we was leaving I found a tolerable good curry-comb, and Jim he found a ratty old fiddle-bow, and a wooden leg. The straps was broke off of it, but barring that, it was a good enough leg, though it was too long for me and not long enough for Jim, and we couldn't find the other one, though we hunted all round.
>
> And so, take it all round, we made a good haul.

This is the sort of list that a boy reader should pore over with delight; but the paragraph performs other functions of which the boy reader would be unaware. It provides the right counterpoise to the horror of the wrecked house and the corpse: it has a grim precision which tells the reader all he needs to know about the way of life of the human derelicts who had used the house; and (especially the wooden leg, and the fruitless search for its mate) reminds us at the right moment of the kinship of mind and the sympathy between the boy outcast from society and the negro fugitive from the injustice of society.

Huck in fact would be incomplete without Jim, who is almost as notable a creation as Huck himself. Huck is the passive observer of men and events, Jim the submissive sufferer from them; and they are equal in dignity. There is no passage in which their relationship is brought out more clearly than the conclusion of the chapter in which, after the two have become separated in the fog, Huck in the canoe and Jim on the raft, Huck, in his impulse of boyish mischief, persuades Jim for a time that the latter had dreamt the whole episode.

> '. . . my heart wuz mos' broke bekase you wuz los', en I didn' k'yer no mo' what become er me en de raf'. En when I wake up en fine you back agin', all safe en soun', de tears come en I could a got down on my knees en kiss' yo' foot, I's so thankful. En all you wuz thinkin' 'bout wuz how you could make a fool uv ole Jim wid a lie. Dat truck dah is *trash*; en trash is what people is dat puts dirt on de head er dey fren's en makes 'em ashamed.' . . .
>
> It was fifteen minutes before I could work myself up to go and humble myself to a nigger—but I done it, and I warn't ever sorry for it afterwards, neither.

This passage has been quoted before; and if I quote it again, it is because I wish to elicit from it one meaning that is, I think, usually overlooked. What is obvious in it is the pathos and dignity of Jim, and this is moving enough; but what I find still more disturbing, and still more unusual in literature, is the pathos and dignity of the boy, when reminded so humbly and humiliatingly, that his position in the world is not that of other boys, entitled from time to time to a practical joke; but that he must bear, and bear alone, the responsibility of a man.

It is Huck who gives the book style. The River gives the book its form. But for the River, the book might be only a sequence of adventures with a happy ending. A river, a very big and powerful river, is the only natural force that can wholly determine the course of human peregrination. At sea, the wanderer may sail or be carried by winds and currents in one direction or another; a change of wind or tide may determine fortune. In the prairie, the direction of movement is more or less at the choice of the caravan; among mountains there will often be an alternative, a guess at the most likely pass. But the river with its strong, swift current is the dictator to the raft or to the steamboat. It is a treacherous and capricious dictator. At one season, it may move sluggishly in a channel so narrow that, encountering it for the first time at that point, one can hardly believe that it has travelled already for hundreds of miles, and has yet many hundreds of miles to go; at another season, it may obliterate the low Illinois shore to a horizon of water, while in its bed it runs with a speed such that no man or beast can survive in it. At such times, it carries down human bodies, cattle and houses. At least twice, at St. Louis, the western and the eastern shores have been separated by the fall of bridges, until the designer of the great Eads Bridge devised a structure which could resist the floods. In my own childhood, it was not unusual for the spring freshet to interrupt railway travel; and then the traveller to the East had to take steamboat from the levee up to Alton, at a higher level on the Illinois shore, before he could begin his rail journey. The river is never wholly chartable; it changes its pace, it shifts its channel, unaccountably; it may suddenly efface a sandbar, and throw up another bar where before was navigable water.

It is the River that controls the voyage of Huck and Jim; that will not let them land at Cairo, where Jim could have reached freedom; it is the River that separates them and deposits Huck for a time in the Grangerford household; the River that re-unites them, and then compels upon them the unwelcome company of the King and the Duke. Recurrently we are reminded of its presence and its power.

When I woke up, I didn't know where I was for a minute. I set up and looked around, a little scared. Then I remembered. The river looked miles and miles across. The moon was so bright I could a counted the drift-logs that went a-slipping along, black and still, hundreds of yards out from shore. Everything was dead quiet, and it looked late, and *smelt* late. You know what I mean—I don't know the words to put it in.

It was kind of solemn, drifting down the big still river, laying on our backs looking up at the stars, and we didn't ever feel like talking loud, and it warn't often that we laughed, only a little kind of a low chuckle. We had mighty good weather as a general thing, and nothing ever happened to us at all, that night, nor the next, nor the next.

Every night we passed towns, some of them away up on black hillsides, nothing but just a shiny bed of lights, not a house could you see. The fifth night we passed St. Louis, and it was like the whole world lit up. In St. Petersburg they used to say there was twenty or thirty thousand people in St. Louis, but I never believed it till I see that wonderful spread of lights at two o'clock that still night. There warn't a sound there; everybody was asleep.

We come to understand the River by seeing it through the eyes of the Boy; but the Boy is also the spirit of the River. *Huckleberry Finn*, like other great works of imagination, can give to every reader whatever he is capable of taking from it. On the most superficial level of observation, Huck is convincing as a boy. On the same level, the picture of social life on the shores of the Mississippi a hundred years ago is, I feel sure, accurate. On any level, Mark Twain makes you see the River, as it is and was and always will be, more clearly than the author of any other description of a river known to me. But you do not merely see the River, you do not merely become acquainted with it through the senses: you experience the River. Mark Twain, in his later years of success and fame, referred to his early life as a steamboat pilot as the happiest he had known. With all allowance for the illusions of age, we can agree that those years were the years in which he was most fully alive. Certainly, but for his having practised that calling, earned his living by that profession, he would never have gained the understanding which his genius for expression communicates in this book. In the pilot's daily struggle with the River, in the satisfaction of activity, in the constant attention to the River's unpredictable vagaries, his consciousness was fully occupied, and he absorbed knowledge of which, as an artist, he later made use. There are, perhaps, only two ways in which a writer can acquire the understanding of environment which he can later turn to account: by having spent his childhood in that environment—that is, living in it at a period of life in which one experiences much more than one is aware of; and by having had to struggle for a livelihood in that environment—a livelihood bearing no direct relation to any intention of writing about it, of *using* it as literary material. Most of Joseph Conrad's understanding came to him in the latter way. Mark Twain knew the Mississippi in both ways: he had spent his childhood on its banks, and he had earned his living matching his wits against its currents.

Thus the River makes the book a great book. As with Conrad, we are continually reminded of the power and terror of Nature, and the isolation and feebleness of Man. Conrad remains always the European observer of the tropics, the white man's eye contemplating the Congo and its black gods. But Mark Twain is a native, and the River God is his God. It is as a native that he accepts the River God, and it is the subjection of Man that gives to Man his dignity. For without some kind of God, Man is not even very interesting.

Readers sometimes deplore the fact that the story descends to the level of *Tom Sawyer* from the moment that Tom himself re-appears. Such readers protest that the escapades invented by Tom, in the attempted "rescue" of Jim, are only a tedious development of themes with which we were already too familiar—even while admitting that the escapades themselves are very amusing, and some of the incidental observations memorable.[1] But it is right that the mood of the end of the book should bring us back to that of the beginning. Or, if this was not the right ending for the book, what ending would have been right?

In *Huckleberry Finn* Mark Twain wrote a much greater book than he could have known he was writing. Perhaps all great works of art mean much more than the author could have been aware of meaning: certainly, *Huckleberry Finn* is one book of Mark Twain's which, as a whole, has this unconsciousness. So what seems to be the rightness, of reverting at the end of the book to the mood of *Tom Sawyer*, was perhaps unconscious art. For Huckleberry Finn, neither a tragic nor a happy ending would be suitable. No worldly success or social satisfaction, no domestic consummation would be worthy of him; a tragic end also would reduce him to the level of those whom we pity. Huck Finn must come from nowhere and be bound for nowhere. His is not the independence of the typical or symbolic American Pioneer, but the independence of the vagabond. His existence questions the values of America as much as the values of Europe; he is as much an affront to the "pioneer spirit" as he is to "business enterprise"; he is in a state of nature as detached as the state of the saint. In a busy world, he represents the loafer; in an acquisitive and competitive world, he insists on living from hand to mouth. He could not be exhibited in any amorous encounters or engagements, in any of the juvenile affections which are appropriate to Tom Sawyer. He belongs neither to the Sunday School nor to the Reformatory. He has no beginning and no end. Hence, he can only disappear; and his disappearance can only be accomplished by bringing forward another performer to obscure the disappearance in a cloud of whimsicalities.

Like Huckleberry Finn, the River itself has no beginning or end. In its beginning, it is not yet the River; in its end, it is no longer the River. What we call its headwaters is only a selection from among the innumerable sources which flow together to compose it. At what point in its course does the Mississippi become what the Mississippi *means*? It is both one and many; it is the Mississippi of this book only after its union with the Big Muddy—the Missouri; it derives some of its character from the Ohio, the Tennessee and other confluents. And at the end it merely disappears among its deltas: it is no longer there, but it is still where it was, hundreds of miles to the North. The River cannot tolerate any design, to a story which is its story, that might interfere with its dominance. Things must merely happen, here and there, to the people who live along its shores or who commit themselves to its current. And it is as impossible for Huck as for the River to have a beginning or end—a *career*. So the book has the right, the only possible concluding sentence. I do not think that any book ever written ends more certainly with the right words:

But I reckon I got to light out for the Territory ahead of the rest, because Aunt Sally she's going to adopt me and civilize me, and I can't stand it. I been there before.

NOTES

1. e.g. "*Jim* don't know anybody in China."

MR. ELIOT, MR. TRILLING, AND *HUCKLEBERRY FINN*

LEO MARX

In the losing battle that the plot fights with the characters, it often takes a cowardly revenge. Nearly all novels are feeble at the end. This is because the plot requires to be wound up. Why is this necessary? Why is there not a convention which allows a novelist to stop as soon as he feels muddled or bored? Alas, he has to round things off, and usually the characters go dead while he is at work, and our final impression of them is through deadness.

—E.M. FORSTER

The Adventures of Huckleberry Finn has not always occupied its present high place in the canon of American literature. When it was first published in 1885, the book disturbed and offended many reviewers, particularly spokesmen for the genteel tradition.[1] In fact, a fairly accurate inventory of the narrow standards of such critics might be made simply by listing epithets they applied to Clemens' novel. They called it vulgar, rough, inelegant, irreverent, coarse, semi-obscene, trashy and vicious.[2] So much for them. Today (we like to think) we know the true worth of the book. Everyone agrees that *Huckleberry Finn* is a masterpiece: it is probably the one book in our literature about which highbrows and lowbrows can agree. Our most serious critics praise it. Nevertheless, a close look at what two of the best among them have recently written will likewise reveal, I believe, serious weaknesses in a current criticism. Today the problem of evaluating the book is as much obscured by unqualified praise as it once was by parochial hostility.

I have in mind essays by Lionel Trilling and T.S. Eliot.[3] Both praise the book, but in praising it both feel obligated to say something in justification of what so many readers have felt to be its great flaw: the disappointing "ending," the episode which begins when Huck arrives at the Phelps place and Tom Sawyer reappears. There are good reasons why Mr. Trilling and Mr. Eliot should feel the need to face this issue. From the point of view of scope alone, more is involved than the mere "ending"; the episode comprises almost one-fifth of the text. The problem, in any case, is unavoidable. I have discussed *Huckleberry Finn* in courses with hundreds of college students, and I have found only a handful who did not confess their dissatisfaction with the extravagant mock rescue of Nigger Jim and the denouement itself. The same question always comes up: "What went wrong with Twain's novel?" Even Bernard DeVoto, whose whole-hearted commitment to Clemens' genius is well known, has said of the ending that "in the whole reach of the English novel there is no more abrupt or more chilling descent."[4] Mr. Trilling and Mr. Eliot do not agree. They both attempt and on similar grounds, to explain and defend the conclusion.

Of the two, Mr. Trilling makes the more moderate claim for Clemens' novel. He does admit that there is a "falling off" at the end; nevertheless he supports the episode as having "a certain formal aptness." Mr. Eliot's approval is without serious qualification. He allows no objections, asserts that "it is right that the mood of the end of the book should bring us back to the beginning." I mean later to discuss their views in some detail, but here it is only necessary to note that both critics see the problem as one of form. And so it is. Like many questions of form in literature, however, this one is not finally separable from a question of "content," of value, or, if you will, of moral insight. To bring *Huckleberry Finn* to a satisfactory close, Clemens had to do more than find a neat device for ending a story. His problem, though it may never have occurred to him, was to invent an action capable of placing in focus the meaning of the journey down the Mississippi.

I believe that the ending of *Huckleberry Finn* makes so many readers uneasy because they rightly sense that it jeopardizes the significance of the entire novel. To take seriously what happens at the Phelps farm is to take lightly the entire downstream journey. What is the meaning of the journey? With this question all discussion of *Huckleberry Finn* must begin. It is true that the voyage down the river has many aspects of a boy's idyl. We owe much of its hold upon our imagination to the enchanting image of the raft's unhurried drift with the current. The leisure, the absence of constraint, the beauty of the river—all these things delight us. "It's lovely to live on a raft." And the multitudinous life of the great valley we see through Huck's eyes has a fascination of its own. Then, of course, there is humor—laughter so spontaneous, so free of the bitterness present almost everywhere in American humor that readers often forget how grim a spectacle of human existence Huck contemplates. Humor in this novel flows from a bright joy of life as remote from our world as living on a raft.

Yet along with the idyllic and the epical and the funny in *Huckleberry Finn*, there is a coil of meaning which does for the disparate elements of the novel what a spring does for a watch. The meaning is not in the least obscure. It is made explicit again and again. The very words with which Clemens launches Huck and Jim upon their voyage indicate that theirs is not a boy's lark but a quest for freedom. From the electrifying moment when Huck comes back to Jackson's Island and rouses Jim with the news that a search party is on the way, we are meant to believe that Huck is enlisted in the cause of freedom. "Git up and hump yourself, Jim!" he cries. "There ain't a minute to lose. They're after us!" What particularly counts here is the *us*. No one is after Huck; no one but Jim knows he is alive. In that small word Clemens compresses the exhilarating power of Huck's instinctive humanity. His unpremeditated identification with Jim's flight from slavery is an unforgettable moment in American experience, and it may be said at once that any culmination of the journey which detracts from the urgency and dignity with which it begins will necessarily be unsatisfactory. Huck realizes this himself, and says so when, much later, he comes back to the raft after discovering that the Duke and the King have sold Jim:

After all this long journey . . . here it was all come to nothing, everything all busted up and ruined, because they could have the heart to serve Jim such a trick as that, and make him a slave again all his life, and amongst strangers, too, for forty dirty dollars.

Huck knows that the journey will have been a failure unless it takes Jim to freedom. It is true that we do discover, in the end, that Jim is free, but we also find out that the journey was not the means by which he finally reached freedom.

The most obvious thing wrong with the ending, then, is the flimsy contrivance by which Clemens frees Jim. In the end we not only discover that Jim has been a free man for two months, but that his freedom has been granted by old Miss Watson. If this were only a mechanical device for terminating the action, it might not call for much comment. But it is more than that: it is a significant clue to the import of the last ten chapters. Remember who Miss Watson is. She is the Widow's sister whom Huck introduces in the first pages of the novel. It is she who keeps "pecking" at Huck, who tries to teach him to spell and to pray and to keep his feet off the furniture. She is an ardent proselytizer for piety and good manners, and her greed provides the occasion for the journey in the first place. She is Jim's owner, and he decides to flee only when he realizes that she is about to break her word (she can't resist a slave trader's offer of eight hundred dollars) and sell him down the river away from his family.

Miss Watson, in short, is the Enemy. If we expect a predilection for physical violence, she exhibits all the outstanding traits of the valley society. She pronounces the polite lies of civilization that suffocate Huck's spirit. The freedom which Jim seeks, and which Huck and Jim temporarily enjoy aboard the raft, is accordingly freedom *from* everything for which Miss Watson stands. Indeed, the very intensity of the novel derives from the discordance between the aspirations of the fugitives and the respectable code for which she is a spokesman. Therefore, her regeneration, of which the deathbed freeing of Jim is the unconvincing sign, hints a resolution of the novel's essential conflict. Perhaps because this device most transparently reveals that shift in point of view which he could not avoid, and which is less easily discerned elsewhere in the concluding chapters, Clemens plays it down. He makes little attempt to account for Miss Watson's change of heart, a change particularly surprising in view of Jim's brazen escape. Had Clemens given this episode dramatic emphasis appropriate to its function, Miss Watson's bestowal of freedom upon Jim would have proclaimed what the rest of the ending actually accomplishes—a vindication of persons and attitudes Huck and Jim had symbolically repudiated when they set forth downstream.

It may be said, and with some justice, that a reading of the ending as a virtual reversal of meanings implicit in the rest of the novel misses the point—that I have taken the final episode too seriously. I agree that Clemens certainly did not intend us to read it so solemnly. The ending, one might contend, is simply a burlesque upon Tom's taste for literary romance. Surely the tone of the episode is familiar to readers of Mark Twain. The preposterous monkey business attendant upon Jim's "rescue," the careless improvisation, the nonchalant disregard for common sense plausibility—all these things should not surprise readers of Twain or any low comedy in the tradition of "Western humor." However, the trouble is, first, that the ending hardly comes off as burlesque: it is *too* fanciful, *too* extravagant; and it is tedious. For example, to provide a "gaudy" atmosphere for the escape, Huck and Tom catch a couple of dozen snakes. Then the snakes escape.

No, there warn't no real scarcity of snakes about the house for a considerable spell. You'd see them dripping from the rafters and places every now and then; and they generly landed in your plate, or down the back of your neck. . . .

Even if this were good burlesque, which it is not, what is it doing here? It is out of keeping; the slapstick tone jars with the underlying seriousness of the voyage.

Huckleberry Finn is a masterpiece because it brings Western humor to perfection and yet transcends the narrow limits of its conventions. But the ending does not. During the final extravaganza we are forced to put aside many of the mature emotions evoked earlier by the vivid rendering of Jim's fear of capture, the tenderness of Huck's and Jim's regard for each other, and Huck's excruciating moments of wavering between honesty and respectability. None of these emotions are called forth by the anticlimactic final sequence. I do not mean to suggest that the inclusion of low comedy per se is a flaw in *Huckle-*

berry Finn. One does not object to the shenanigans of the rogues; there is ample precedent for the place of extravagant humor even in the works of high seriousness. But here the case differs from most which come to mind: the major characters themselves are forced to play low comedy roles. Moreover, the most serious motive in the novel, Jim's yearning for freedom, is made the object of nonsense. The conclusion, in short, is farce, but the rest of the novel is not.

That Clemens reverts in the end to the conventional manner of Western low comedy is most evident in what happens to the principals. Huck and Jim become comic characters; that is a much more serious ground for dissatisfaction than the unexplained regeneration of Miss Watson. Remember that Huck has grown in stature throughout the journey. By the time he arrives at the Phelps place, he is not the boy who had been playing robbers with Tom's gang in St. Petersburg the summer before. All he has seen and felt since he parted from Tom has deepened his knowledge of human nature and of himself. Clemens makes a point of Huck's development in two scenes which occur just before he meets Tom again. The first describes Huck's final capitulation to his own sense of right and wrong: "All right, then, I'll *go* to Hell." This is the climactic moment in the ripening of his self-knowledge. Shortly afterward, when he comes upon a mob riding the Duke and the King out of town on a rail, we are given his most memorable insight into the nature of man. Although these rogues had subjected Huck to every indignity, what he sees provokes this celebrated comment:

Well, it made me sick to see it; and I was sorry for them poor pitiful rascals, it seemed like I couldn't ever feel any hardness against them any more in the world. It was a dreadful thing to see. Human beings can be awful cruel to one another.

The sign of Huck's maturity here is neither the compassion nor the skepticism, for both had been marks of his personality from the first. Rather, the special quality of these reflections is the extraordinary combination of the two, a mature blending of his instinctive suspicion of human motives with his capacity for pity.

But at this point Tom reappears. Soon Huck has fallen almost completely under his sway once more, and we are asked to believe that the boy who felt pity for the rogues is now capable of making Jim's capture the occasion for a game. He becomes Tom's helpless accomplice, submissive and gullible. No wonder that Clemens has Huck remark, when Huck first realizes Aunt Sally has mistaken him for Tom, that "it was like being born again." Exactly. In the end, Huck regresses to the subordinate role in which he had first appeared in *The Adventures of Tom Sawyer.* Most of those traits which made him so appealing a hero now disappear. He had never, for example, found pain or misfortune amusing. At the circus, when a clown disguised as a drunk took a precarious ride on a prancing horse, the crowd loved the excitement and danger: "it warn't funny to me, though," said Huck. But now, in the end, he submits in awe to Tom's notion of what is amusing. To satisfy Tom's hunger for adventure he makes himself a party to sport which aggravates Jim's misery.

It should be added at once that Jim doesn't mind too much. The fact is that he has undergone a similar transformation. On the raft he was an individual, man enough to denounce Huck when Huck made him the victim of a practical joke. In the closing episode, however, we lose sight of Jim in the maze of farcical invention. He ceases to be a man. He allows Huck and "Mars Tom" to fill his hut with rats and snakes, "and every time a rat bit Jim he would get up and write a line in his journal whilst the ink was fresh." This creature who bleeds ink and feels no pain is something less than human. He has been made over in the image of a flat stereotype: the submissive stage-Negro. These antics divest Jim, as well as Huck, of much of his dignity and individuality.[5]

What I have been saying is that the flimsy devices of plot, the discordant farcical tone, and the disintegration of the major characters all betray the failure of the ending. These are not aspects merely of form in a technical sense, but of meaning. For that matter, I would maintain that this book has little or no formal unity independent of the joint purpose of Huck and Jim. What components of the novel, we may ask, provide the continuity which links one adventure with another? The most important is the unifying consciousness of Huck, the narrator, and the fact that we follow the same principals through the entire string of adventures. Events, moreover, occur in a temporal sequence. Then there is the river; after each adventure Huck and Jim return to the raft and the river. Both Mr. Trilling and Mr. Eliot speak eloquently of the river as a source of unity, and they refer to the river as a god. Mr. Trilling says that Huck is "the servant of the river-god." Mr. Eliot puts it this way: "The River gives the book its form. But for the River, the book might be only a sequence of adventures with a happy ending." This seems to me an extravagant view of the function of the neutral agency of the river. Clemens had a knowledgeable respect for the Mississippi, and, without sanctifying it, was able to provide excellent reasons for Huck's and Jim's intense relation with it. It is a source of food and beauty and terror and serenity of mind. But above all, it provides motion; it is the means by which Huck and Jim move away from a menacing civilization. They return to the river to continue their journey. The river cannot, does not, supply purpose. That purpose is a facet of their consciousness, and without the motive of escape from society, *Huckleberry Finn* would indeed "be only a sequence of adventures." Mr. Eliot's remark indicates how lightly he takes the quest for freedom. His somewhat fanciful exaggeration of the river's role is of a piece with his neglect of the theme at the novel's center.

That theme is heightened by the juxtaposition of sharp images of contrasting social orders: the microcosmic community Huck and Jim establish aboard the raft and the actual society which exists along the Mississippi's banks. The two are separated by the river, the road to freedom upon which Huck and Jim must travel. Huck tells us what the river means to them when, after the Wilks episode, he and Jim once again shove their raft into the current: "it *did* seem so good to be free again and all by ourselves on the big river, and nobody to bother us." The river is indifferent. But its sphere is relatively uncontaminated by the civilization they flee, and so the river allows Huck and Jim some measure of freedom at once, the moment they set foot on Jackson's Island or the raft. Only on the island and the raft do they have a chance to practice that idea of brotherhood to which they are devoted. "Other places do seem so cramped and smothery," Huck explains, "but a raft don't. You feel mighty free and easy and comfortable on a raft." The main thing is freedom.

On the raft the escaped slave and the white boy try to practice their code: "What you want, above all things, on a raft, is for everybody to be satisfied, and feel right and kind towards the others." This human credo constitutes the paramount affirmation of *The Adventures of Huckleberry Finn*, and it obliquely aims a devastating criticism at the existing social order. It is a creed which Huck and Jim bring to the river. It neither emanates from nature nor is it addressed to nature. Therefore I do not see that it means much to talk about the river as a god in this novel. The river's connection with this high aspiration for man is that it provides a means of escape, a place where the code can be tested. The truly profound meanings of the novel are generated by the impingement of the actual world of slavery, feuds, lynching, murder, and a spurious Christian morality upon the ideal of the raft. The result is a tension which somehow demands release in the novel's ending.

But Clemens was unable to effect this release and at the same time control the central theme. The unhappy truth about the ending of *Huckleberry Finn* is that the author, having revealed the tawdry nature of the culture of the great valley, yielded to its essential complacency. The general tenor of the closing scenes, to which the token regeneration of Miss Watson is merely one superficial clue, amounts to just that. In fact, this entire reading of *Huckleberry Finn* merely confirms the brilliant insight of George Santayana, who many years ago spoke of American humorists, of whom he considered Mark Twain an outstanding representative, as having only "half escaped" the genteel tradition. Santayana meant that men like Clemens were able to "point to what contradicts it in the facts; but not in order to abandon the genteel tradition, for they have nothing solid to put in its place." This seems to me the real key to the failure of *Huckleberry Finn*. Clemens had presented the contrast between the two social orders but could not, or would not, accept the tragic fact that the one he had rejected was an image of solid reality and the other an ecstatic dream. Instead he gives us the cozy reunion with Aunt Polly in a scene fairly bursting with approbation of the entire family, the Phelpses included.

Like Miss Watson, the Phelpses are almost perfect specimens of the dominant culture. They are kind to their friends and relatives; they have no taste for violence; they are people capable of devoting themselves to their spectacular dinners while they keep Jim locked in the little hut down by the ash hopper, with its lone window boarded up. (Of course Aunt Sally visits Jim to see if he is "comfortable," and Uncle Silas comes in "to pray with him.") These people, with their comfortable Sunday-dinner conviviality and the runaway slave padlocked nearby, are reminiscent of those solid German citizens we have heard about in our time who tried to maintain a similarly *gemütlich* way of life within virtual earshot of Buchenwald. I do not mean to imply that Clemens was unaware of the shabby morality of such people. After the abortive escape of Jim, when Tom asks about him, Aunt Sally replies: "Him? . . . the runaway nigger? . . . They've got him back, safe and sound, and he's in the cabin again, on bread and water, and loaded down with chains, till he's claimed or sold!" Clemens understood people like the Phelpses, but nevertheless he was forced to rely upon them to provide his happy ending. The satisfactory outcome of Jim's quest for freedom must be attributed to the benevolence of the very people whose inhumanity first made it necessary.

But to return to the contention of Mr. Trilling and Mr. Eliot that the ending is more or less satisfactory after all. As I have said, Mr. Trilling approves of the "formal aptness" of the conclusion. He says that "some device is needed to permit Huck to return to his anonymity, to give up the role of hero," and that therefore "nothing could serve better than the mind of Tom Sawyer with its literary furnishings, its conscious romantic desire for experience and the hero's part, and its ingenious schematization of life. . . ." Though more detailed, this is essentially akin to Mr. Eliot's blunt assertion that "it is right that the mood at the end of the book should bring us back to that of the beginning." I submit that it is wrong for the end of the book to bring us back to that mood. The mood of the beginning of *Huckleberry Finn* is the mood of Huck's attempt to accommodate himself to the ways of St. Petersburg. It is the mood of the end of *The Adventures of Tom Sawyer*, when the boys had been acclaimed heroes, and when Huck was accepted as a candidate for respectability. That is the state in which we find him at the beginning of *Huckleberry Finn*. But Huck cannot stand the new way of life, and his mood gradually shifts to the mood of rebellion which dominated the novel until he meets Tom again. At first, in the second chapter, we see him still eager to be accepted by the nice boys of the town. Tom leads the gang in re-enacting adventures he has culled from books, but gradually Huck's pragmatic turn of mind gets him in trouble. He has little tolerance for Tom's brand of make-believe. He irritates Tom. Tom calls him a "numbskull," and finally Huck throws up the whole business:

So then I judged that all that stuff was only just one of Tom Sawyer's lies. I reckoned he believed in the A-rabs and the elephants, but as for me I think different. It had all the marks of a Sunday school.

With this statement, which ends the third chapter, Huck parts company with Tom. The fact is that Huck has rejected Tom's romanticizing of experience; moreover, he has rejected it as part of the larger pattern of society's make-believe, typified by Sunday school. But if he cannot accept Tom's harmless fantasies about the A-rabs, how are we to believe that a year later Huck is capable of awe-struck submission to the far more extravagant fantasies with which Tom invests the mock rescue of Jim?

After Huck's escape from his "pap," the drift of the action, like that of the Mississippi's current, is *away* from St. Petersburg. Huck leaves Tom and the A-rabs behind, along with the Widow, Miss Watson, and all the pseudo-religious ritual in which nice boys must partake. The return, in the end, to the mood of the beginning therefore means defeat—Huck's defeat; to return to that mood *joyously* is to portray defeat in the guise of victory.

Mr. Eliot and Mr. Trilling deny this. The overriding consideration for them is form—form which seems largely to mean symmetry of structure. It is fitting, Mr. Eliot maintains, that the book should come full circle and bring Huck once more under Tom's sway. Why? Because it begins that way. But it seems to me that such structural unity is *imposed* upon the novel, and therefore is meretricious. It is a jerry-built structure, achieved only by sacrifice of characters and theme. Here the controlling principle of form apparently is unity, but unfortunately a unity much too superficially conceived. Structure, after all, is only one element—indeed, one of the more mechanical elements—of unity. A unified work must surely manifest coherence of meaning and clear development of theme, yet the ending of *Huckleberry Finn* blurs both. The eagerness of Mr. Eliot and Mr. Trilling to justify the ending is symptomatic of that absolutist impulse of our critics to find reasons, once a work has been admitted to the highest canon of literary reputability, for admiring every bit of it.

What is perhaps most striking about these judgments of Mr. Eliot's and Mr. Trilling's is that they are so patently out of harmony with the basic standards of both critics. For one thing, both men hold far more complex ideas of the nature of literary unity than their comments upon *Huckleberry Finn* would suggest. For another, both critics are essentially moralists, yet here we find them turning away from a moral issue in order to praise a dubious structural unity. Their efforts to explain away the flaw in Clemens' novel suffer from a certain narrowness surprising to anyone who knows their work. These facts suggest that we may be in the presence of a tendency in contemporary criticism which the critics themselves do not fully recognize.

Is there an explanation? How does it happen that two of our most respected critics should seem to treat so lightly the glaring lapse of moral imagination in *Huckleberry Finn*? Perhaps—and I stress the conjectural nature of what I am saying—perhaps the kind of moral issue raised by *Huckleberry Finn* is not the kind of moral issue to which today's criticism readily addresses itself. Today our critics, no less than our novelists and poets, are most sensitively attuned to moral problems which arise in the sphere of individual behavior. They are deeply aware of sin, of individual infractions of our culture's Christian ethic. But my impression is that they are, possibly because of the strength of the reaction against the mechanical sociological criticism of the thirties, less sensitive to questions of what might be called social or political morality.

By social or political morality I refer to the values implicit in a social system, values which may be quite distinct from the personal morality of any given individual within the society. Now *The Adventures of Huckleberry Finn*, like all novels, deals with the behavior of individuals. But one mark of Clemens' greatness is his deft presentation of the disparity between what people do when they behave as individuals and what they do when forced into roles imposed upon them by society. Take, for example, Aunt Sally and Uncle Silas Phelps, who consider themselves Christians, who are by impulse generous and humane, but who happen also to be staunch upholders of certain degrading and inhuman social institutions. When they are confronted with an escaped slave, the imperatives of social morality outweigh all pious professions.

The conflict between what people think they stand for and what social pressure forces them to do is central to the novel. It is present to the mind of Huck and, indeed, accounts for his most serious inner conflicts. He knows how he feels about Jim, but he also knows what he is expected to do about Jim. This division within his mind corresponds to the division of the novel's moral terrain into the areas represented by the raft on the one hand and society on the other. His victory over his "yaller dog" conscience therefore assumes heroic size: it is a victory over the prevailing morality. But the last fifth of the novel has the effect of diminishing the importance and uniqueness of Huck's victory. We are asked to assume that somehow freedom can be achieved in spite of the crippling power of what I have called the social morality. Consequently the less importance we attach to that force as it operates in the novel, the more acceptable the ending becomes.

Moreover, the idea of freedom, which Mr. Eliot and Mr. Trilling seem to slight, takes on its full significance only when we acknowledge the power which society exerts over the minds of men in the world of *Huckleberry Finn*. For freedom in this book specifically means freedom from society and its imperatives. This is not the traditional Christian conception of freedom. Huck and Jim seek freedom not from a burden of individual guilt and sin, but from social constraint. That is to say, evil in *Huckleberry Finn* is the product of civilization, and if this is indicative of Clemens' rather too simple view of human nature, nevertheless the fact is that Huck, when he can divest himself of the taint of social conditioning (as in the incantatory account of sunrise on the river), is entirely free of anxiety and guilt. The only guilt he actually knows arises from infractions of a social code. (The guilt he feels after playing the prank on Jim stems from his betrayal of the law of the raft.) Huck's and Jim's creed is secular. Its object is harmony among men, and so Huck is not much concerned with his own salvation. He repeatedly renounces prayer in favor of pragmatic solutions to his problems. In other words, the central insights of the novel belong to the tradition of the Enlightenment. The meaning of the quest itself is hardly reconcilable with that conception of human nature embodied in the myth of original sin. In view of the current fashion of reaffirming man's innate depravity, it is perhaps not surprising to find the virtues of *Huckleberry Finn* attributed not to its meaning but to its form.

But "if this was not the right ending for the book," Mr. Eliot asks, "what ending would have been right?" Although this question places the critic in an awkward position (he is not always equipped to rewrite what he criticizes), there are some things which may justifiably be said about the "right" ending of *Huckleberry Finn*. It may be legitimate, even if presumptuous, to indicate certain conditions which a hypothetical ending would have to satisfy if it were to be congruent with the rest of the novel. If the conclusion is not to be something merely tacked on to close the action, then its broad outline must be immanent in the body of the work.

It is surely reasonable to ask that the conclusion provide a plausible outcome to the quest. Yet freedom, in the ecstatic sense that Huck and Jim knew it aboard the raft, was hardly to be had in the Mississippi Valley in the 1840's, or, for that matter, in any other known human society. A satisfactory ending would inevitably cause the reader some frustration. That Clemens felt such disappointment to be inevitable is borne out by an examination of the novel's clear, if unconscious, symbolic pattern. Consider, for instance, the inferences to be drawn from the book's geography. The river, to whose current Huck and Jim entrust themselves, actually carries them to the heart of slave territory. Once the raft passes Cairo, the quest is virtually doomed. Until the steamboat smashes the raft, we are kept in a state of anxiety about Jim's escape. (It may be significant that at this point Clemens found himself unable to continue work on the manuscript, and put it aside for several years.) Beyond Cairo, Clemens allows the intensity of that anxiety to diminish, and it is probably no accident that the fainter it becomes, the more he falls back upon the devices of low comedy. Huck and Jim make no serious effort to turn north, and there are times (during the Wilks episode) when Clemens allows Huck to forget all about Jim. It is as if the author, anticipating the dilemma he had finally to face, instinctively dissipated the power of his major theme.

Consider, too, the circumscribed nature of the raft as a means of moving toward freedom. The raft lacks power and maneuverability. It can only move easily with the current—southward into slave country. Nor can it evade the mechanized power of the steamboat. These impotencies of the raft correspond to the innocent helplessness of its occupants. Unresisted, the rogues invade and take over the raft. Though it is the symbolic locus of the novel's central affirmations, the raft provides an uncertain and indeed precarious mode of traveling toward freedom. This seems another confirmation of Santayana's perception. To say that Clemens only half escaped the genteel tradition is not to say that he failed to note any of the creed's inadequacies, but rather that he had "nothing solid" to put in its place. The raft patently was not capable of carrying the burden of hope Clemens placed upon it.[6] (Whether this is to be attributed to the nature of his vision or to the actual state of American society in the nineteenth century is another interesting question.) In any case, the geography of the novel, the raft's powerlessness, the goodness and vulnerability of Huck and Jim, all prefigure a conclusion quite different in tone from that which Clemens gave us. These facts constitute what Hart Crane might have called the novel's "logic of metaphor," and this logic—probably inadvertent—actually takes us to the underlying meaning of *The Adventures of Huckleberry Finn*. Through the symbols we reach a truth which the ending obscures: the quest cannot succeed.

Fortunately, Clemens broke through to this truth in the novel's last sentences:

But I reckon I got to light out for the territory ahead of the rest, because Aunt Sally she's going to adopt me and civilize me, and I can't stand it. I been there before.

Mr. Eliot properly praises this as "the only possible concluding sentence." But one sentence can hardly be advanced, as Mr. Eliot advances this one, to support the rightness of ten chapters. Moreover, if this sentence is right, then the rest of the conclusion is wrong, for its meaning clashes with that of the final burlesque. Huck's decision to go west ahead of the inescapable advance of civilization is a confession of defeat. It means that the raft is to be abandoned. On the other hand, the jubilation of the family reunion and the proclaiming of Jim's freedom create a quite different mood. The tone, except for these last words, is one of unclouded success. I believe this is the source of the almost universal dissatisfaction with the conclusion. One can hardly forget that a bloody civil war did not resolve the issue.

Should Clemens have made Huck a tragic hero? Both Mr. Eliot and Mr. Trilling argue that that would have been a mistake, and they are very probably correct. But between the ending as we have it and tragedy in the fullest sense, there was vast room for invention. Clemens might have contrived an action which left Jim's fate as much in doubt as Huck's. Such an ending would have allowed us to assume that the principals were defeated but alive, and the quest unsuccessful but not abandoned. This, after all, would have been consonant with the symbols, the characters, and the theme as Clemens had created them—and with history.

Clemens did not acknowledge the truth his novel contained. He had taken hold of a situation in which a partial defeat was inevitable, but he was unable to—or unaware of the need to—give imaginative substance to that fact. If an illusion of success was indispensable, where was it to come from? Obviously, Huck and Jim could not succeed by their own efforts. At this point Clemens, having only half escaped the genteel tradition, one of whose pre-eminent characteristics was an optimism undaunted by disheartening truth, returned to it. *Why* he did so is another story, having to do with his parents and his boyhood, with his own personality and his wife's, and especially with the character of his audience. But whatever the explanation, the faint-hearted ending of *The Adventures of Huckleberry Finn* remains an important datum in the record of American thought and imagination. It has been noted before, both by critics and non-professional readers. It should not be forgotten now.

To minimize the seriousness of what must be accounted a major flaw in so great a work is, in a sense, to repeat Clemens' failure of nerve. This is a disservice to criticism. Today we particularly need a criticism alert to lapses of moral vision. A measured appraisal of the failures and successes of our writers, past and present, can show us a great deal about literature and about ourselves. That is the critic's function. But he cannot perform that function if he substitutes considerations of technique for considerations of truth. Not only will such methods lead to errors of literary judgment, but beyond that, they may well encourage comparable evasions in other areas. It seems not unlikely, for instance, that the current preoccupation with matters of form is bound up with a tendency, by no means confined to literary quarters, to shy away from painful answers to complex questions of political morality. The conclusion to *The Adventures of Huckleberry Finn* shielded both Clemens and his audience from such an answer. But we ought not to be as tender-minded. For Huck Finn's besetting problem, the disparity between his best impulses and the behavior the community attempted to impose upon him, is as surely ours as it was Twain's.

NOTES

1. I use the term "genteel tradition" as George Santayana characterized it in his famous address "The Genteel Tradition in American Philosophy," first delivered in 1911 and published the following year in his *Winds of Doctrine*. Santayana described the genteel tradition as an "old mentality" inherited from Europe. It consists of the various dilutions of Christian theology and morality, as in transcendentalism—a fastidious and stale philosophy of life no longer relevant to the thought and activities of the United States. "America," he said, "is a young country with an old mentality." (Later references to Santayana also refer to this essay.)

2. For an account of the first reviews, see A. L. Vogelback, "The Publication and Reception of *Huckleberry Finn* in America," *American Literature* 11 (November 1939), pp. 160-272.

3. Mr. Eliot's essay is the introduction to the edition of *Huckleberry Finn* published by Chanticleer Press, New York, 1950. Mr. Trilling's is in the introduction to an edition of the novel published by Rinehart, New York, 1948, and later reprinted in his *The Liberal Imagination*, Viking, New York, 1950.

4. *Mark Twain At Work* (Cambridge, 1942), p. 92.

5. For these observations on the transformation of Jim in the closing episodes, I am indebted to the excellent unpublished essay by Mr. Chadwick Hansen on the subject of Clemens and Western humor.

6. Gladys Bellamy (*Mark Twain As a Literary Artist*, Norman, Oklahoma, 1950, p. 221) has noted the insubstantial, dream-like quality of the image of the raft. Clemens thus discusses travel by a raft in *A Tramp Abroad*: "The motion of the raft is . . . gentle, and gliding, and smooth, and noiseless; it calms down all feverish activities, it soothes to sleep all nervous . . . impatience; under its restful influence all the troubles and vexations and sorrows that harass the mind vanish away, and existence becomes a dream . . . a deep and tranquil ecstasy."

CRITICISM 1960–1985

A SOUND HEART AND A DEFORMED CONSCIENCE

HENRY NASH SMITH

Mark Twain worked on *Adventures of Huckleberry Finn* at intervals over a period of seven years, from 1876 to 1883. During this time he wrote two considerable books (*A Tramp Abroad* and *The Prince and the Pauper*), expanded "Old Times on the Mississippi" into *Life on the Mississippi*, and gathered various shorter pieces into three other volumes. But this is all essentially minor work. The main line of his development lies in the long preoccupation with the Matter of Hannibal and the Matter of the River that is recorded in "Old Times" and *The Adventures of Tom Sawyer* and reaches a climax in his book about "Tom Sawyer's Comrade. Scene: The Mississippi Valley. Time: Forty or Fifty Years Ago."

In writing *Huckleberry Finn* Mark Twain found a way to organize into a larger structure the insights that earlier humorists had recorded in their brief anecdotes. This technical accomplishment was of course inseparable from the process of discovering new meanings in his material. His development as a writer was a dialectic interplay in which the reach of his imagination imposed a constant strain on his technical resources, and innovations of method in turn opened up new vistas before his imagination.

The dialectic process is particularly striking in the gestation of *Huckleberry Finn*. The use of Huck as a narrative persona, with the consequent elimination of the author as an intruding presence in the story, resolved the difficulties about point of view and style that had been so conspicuous in the earlier books. But turning the story over to Huck brought into view previously unsuspected literary potentialities in the vernacular perspective, particularly the possibility of using vernacular speech for serious purposes and of transforming the vernacular narrator form a mere persona into a character with human depth. Mark Twain's response to the challenge made *Huckleberry Finn* the greatest of his books and one of the two or three acknowledged masterpieces of American literature. Yet this triumph created a new technical problem to which there was no solution; for what had begun as a comic story developed incipiently tragic implications contradicting the premises of comedy.

Huckleberry Finn thus contains three main elements. The most conspicuous is the story of Huck's and Jim's adventures in their flight toward freedom. Jim is running away from actual slavery, Huck from the cruelty of his father, from the will-intentioned "sivilizing" efforts of Miss Watson and the Widow Douglas, from respectability and routine in general. The second element in the novel is social satire of the towns along the river. The satire is often transcendently funny, especially in episodes involving the rascally Duke and King, but it can also deal in appalling violence, as in the Grangerford-Shepherdson feud or Colonel Sherburn's murder of the helpless Boggs. The third major element in the book is the developing characterization of Huck.

All three elements must have been present to Mark Twain's mind in some sense from the beginning, for much of the book's greatness lies in its basic coherence, the complex interrelation of its parts. Nevertheless, the intensive study devoted to it in recent years, particularly Walter Blair's establishment of the chronology of its composition, has demonstrated that Mark Twain's search for a structure capable of doing justice to his conceptions of theme and character passed through several stages. He did not see clearly where he was going when he began to write, and we can observe him in the act of making discoveries both in meaning and in method as he goes along.

The narrative tends to increase in depth as it moves from the adventure story of the early chapters into the social satire of the long middle section, and thence to the ultimate psychological penetration of Huck's character in the moral crisis of Chapter 31. Since the crisis is brought on by the shock of the definitive failure of Huck's effort to help Jim, it marks the real end of the quest for freedom. The perplexing final sequence on the Phelps plantation is best regarded as a maneuver by which Mark Twain beats his way back from incipient tragedy to the comic resolution called for by the original conception of the story.

2

Huck's and Jim's flight from St. Petersburg obviously translates into action the theme of vernacular protest. The fact that they have no means of fighting back against the forces that threaten them but can only run away is accounted for in part by the conventions of backwoods humor, in which the inferior social status of the vernacular character placed him in an ostensibly weak position. But it also reflects Mark Twain's awareness of his own lack of firm ground to stand on in challenging the established system of values.

Huck's and Jim's defenselessness foreshadows the outcome of their efforts to escape. They cannot finally succeed. To be sure, in a superficial sense they do succeed; at the end of the book Jim is technically free and Huck still has the power to light out for the Territory. But Jim's freedom has been brought about by such an implausible device that we do not believe in it. Who can imagine the scene in which Miss Watson decides to liberate him? What were her motives? Mark Twain finesses the problem by placing this crucial event far offstage and telling us nothing about it beyond the bare fact he needs to resolve his plot. And the notion that a fourteen-year-old boy could make his escape beyond the frontier is equally unconvincing. The writer himself did not take it seriously. In an unpublished sequel to *Huckleberry Finn* called "Huck Finn and Tom Sawyer among the Indians," which he began soon after he finished the novel, Aunt Sally takes the boys and Jim back to Hannibal and then to western Missouri for a visit "with some of her relations on a hemp farm out there." Here Tom revives the plan mentioned near the end of *Huckleberry Finn*: he "was dead set on having us run off, some night, and cut for the Injun country and go for adventures." Huck says, however, that he and Jim "kind of hung fire. Plenty to eat and nothing to do. We was very well satisfied." Only after an extended debate can Tom persuade them to set out with him. Their expedition falls into the stereotyped pattern of Wild West stories of travel out the Oregon Trail, makes a few gibes at Cooper's romanticized Indians, and breaks off.

The difficulty of imagining a successful outcome for Huck's and Jim's quest had troubled Mark Twain almost from the beginning of his work on the book. After writing the first section in 1876 he laid aside his manuscript near the end of Chapter 16. The narrative plan with which he had impulsively begun had run into difficulties. When Huck and Jim shove off from Jackson's Island on their section of a lumber raft (at the end of Chapter 11) they do so in haste, to escape the immediate danger of the slave hunters Huck has learned about from Mrs. Loftus. No long-range plan is mentioned until the beginning of Chapter 15, when Huck says that at Cairo they intended to "sell the raft and get on a steamboat and go way up the Ohio amongst the free states, and then be out of trouble." But they drift past Cairo in the fog, and a substitute plan of making their way back up to the mouth of the Ohio in their canoe is frustrated when the canoe disappears while they are sleeping: "we talked about what we better do, and found there warn't no way but just to go along down with the raft till we got a chance to buy a canoe to go back in." Drifting downstream with the current, however, could not be reconciled with the plan to free Jim by transporting him up the Ohio; hence the temporary abandonment of the story.

3

When Mark Twain took up his manuscript again in 1879, after an interval of three years, he had decided upon a different plan for the narrative. Instead of concentrating on the story of Huck's and Jim's escape, he now launched into a satiric description of the society of the prewar South. Huck was essential to this purpose, for Mark Twain meant to view his subject ironically through Huck's eyes. But Jim was more or less superfluous. During Chapters 17 and 18, devoted to the Grangerford household and the feud, Jim has disappeared from the story. Mark Twain had apparently not yet found a way to combine social satire with the narrative scheme of Huck's and Jim's journey on the raft.

While he was writing his chapter about the feud, however, he thought of a plausible device to keep Huck and Jim floating southward while he continued his panoramic survey of the towns along the river. The device was the introduction of the Duke and the King. In Chapter 19 they come aboard the raft, take charge at once, and hold Huck and Jim in virtual captivity. In this fashion the narrative can preserve the overall form of a journey down the river while providing ample opportunity for satire when Huck accompanies the two rascals on their forays ashore. But only the outward form of the journey is retained. Its meaning has changed, for Huck's and Jim's quest for freedom has in effect come to an end. Jim is physically present but he assumes an entirely passive role, and is hidden with the raft for considerable periods. Huck is also essentially passive; his function now is that of an observer. Mark Twain postpones acknowledging that the quest for freedom has failed, but the issue will have to be faced eventually.

The satire of the towns along the banks insists again and again that the dominant culture is decadent and perverted. Traditional values have gone to seed. The inhabitants can hardly be said to live a conscious life of their own; their actions, their thoughts, even their emotions are controlled by an outworn and debased Calvinism, and by a residue of the eighteenth-century cult of sensibility. With few exceptions they are mere bundles of tropisms, at the mercy of scoundrels like the Duke and the King who know how to exploit their prejudices and delusions.

The falseness of the prevalent values finds expression in an almost universal tendency of the townspeople to make spurious claims to status through self-dramatization. Mark Twain has been concerned with this topic from the beginning of the book. Chapter 1 deals with Tom Sawyer's plan to start a band of robbers which Huck will be allowed to join only if he will "go back to the widow and be respectable"; and we also hear about Miss Watson's mercenary conception of prayer. In Chapter 2 Jim interprets Tom's prank of hanging his hat on the limb of a tree while he is asleep as evidence that he has been bewitched. He "was most ruined for a servant, because he got stuck up on account of having seen the devil and been rode by witches." Presently we witness the ritual by which Pap Finn is to be redeemed from drunkenness. When his benefactor gives him a lecture on temperance it will be recalled,

the old man cried, and said he'd been a fool, and fooled away his life; but now he was a-going to turn over a new leaf and be a man nobody wouldn't be ashamed of, and he hoped the judge would help him and not look down on him. The judge said he could hug him for them words; so *he* cried, and his wife she cried again; pap said he'd been a man that had always been misunderstood before, and the judge said he believed it. The old man said that what a man wanted that was down was sympathy, and the judge said it was so; so they cried again.

As comic relief for the feud that provides a way of life for the male Grangerfords Mark Twain dwells lovingly on Emmeline Grangerford's pretensions to culture—her paintings with the fetching titles and the ambitious "Ode to Stephen Dowling Bots, Dec'd.," its pathos hopelessly flawed by the crudities showing through like the chalk beneath the enameled surface of the artificial fruit in the parlor: "His spirit was gone for to sport aloft/In the realms of the good and great."

The Duke and the King personify the theme of fraudulent role-taking. These rogues are not even given names apart from the wildly improbable identities they assume in order to dominate Huck and Jim. The Duke's poses have a literary cast, perhaps because of the scraps of bombast he remembers from his experience as an actor. The illiterate King has "done considerable in the doctoring way," but when we see him at work it is mainly at preaching, "workin' camp-meetin's, and missionaryin' around." Pretended or misguided piety and other perversions of Christianity obviously head the list of counts in Mark Twain's indictment of the prewar South. And properly: for it is of course religion that stands at the center of the system of values in the society of this fictive world and by implication in all societies. His revulsion, expressed through Huck, reaches its highest pitch in the scene where the King delivers his masterpiece of "soul-butter and hogwash" for the benefit of the late Peter Wilks's fellow townsmen.

By and by the king he gets up and comes forward a little, and works himself up and slobbers out a speech, all full of tears and flapdoodle, about its being a sore trial for him and his poor brother to lose the diseased, and to miss seeing diseased alive after the long journey of four thousand mile, but it's a trial that's sweetened and sanctified to us by this dear sympathy and these holy tears, and so he thanks them out of his heart and out of his brother's heart, because out of their mouths they can't, words being too weak and cold, and all that kind of rot and slush, till it was just sickening; and then he blubbers out a pious goody-goody Amen, and turns himself loose and goes to crying fit to bust.

4

Huck is revolted by the King's hypocrisy: "I never see anything so disgusting." He has had a similar reaction to the brutality of the feud: "It made me so sick I most fell out of the tree." In describing such scenes he speaks as moral man viewing an immoral society, an observer who is himself free of the vices and even the weaknesses he describes. Mark Twain's satiric method requires that Huck be a mask for the writer, not a fully developed character. The method has great ironic force, and is in itself a technical landmark in the history of American fiction, but it prevents Mark Twain from doing full justice to Huck as a person in his own right, capable of mistakes in perception and judgment, troubled by doubts and conflicting impulses.

Even in the chapters written during the original burst of composition in 1876 the character of Huck is shown to have depths and complexities not relevant to the immediate context. Huck's and Jim's journey down the river begins simply as a flight from physical danger; and the first episodes of the voyage have little bearing on the novelistic possibilities in the strange comradeship between outcast boy and escaped slave. But in Chapter 15, when Huck plays a prank on Jim by persuading him that the separation in the fog was only a dream, Jim's dignified and moving rebuke suddenly opens up a new dimension in the relation. Huck's humble apology is striking evidence of growth in moral insight. It leads naturally to the next chapter in which Mark Twain causes Huck to face up for the first time to the fact that he is helping a slave to escape. It is as if the writer himself were discovering unsuspected meanings in what he had thought of as a story of picaresque adventure. The incipient contradiction between narrative plan and increasing depth in Huck's character must have been as disconcerting to Mark Twain as the difficulty of finding a way to account for Huck's and Jim's continuing southward past the mouth of the Ohio. It was doubtless the convergence of the two problems that led him to put aside the manuscript near the end of Chapter 16.

The introduction of the Duke and the King not only took care of the awkwardness in the plot but also allowed Mark Twain to postpone the exploration of Huck's moral dilemma. If Huck is not a free agent he is not responsible for what happens and is spared the agonies of choice. Throughout the long middle section, while he is primarily an observer, he is free of inner conflict because he is endowed by implication with Mark Twain's own unambiguous attitude toward the fraud and folly he witnesses.

In Chapter 31, however, Huck escapes from his captors and faces once again the responsibility for deciding on a course of action. His situation is much more desperate than it had been at the time of his first struggle with his conscience. The raft has borne Jim hundreds of miles downstream from the pathway of escape and the King has turned him over to Silas Phelps as a runaway slave. The quest for freedom has "all come to nothing, everything all busted up and ruined." Huck thinks of notifying Miss Watson where Jim is, since if he must be a slave he would be better off "at home where his family was." But then Huck realizes that Miss Watson would probably sell Jim down the river as a punishment for running away. Furthermore, Huck himself would be denounced by everyone for his part in the affair. In this fashion his mind comes back once again to the unparalleled wickedness of acting as accomplice in a slave's escape.

The account of Huck's mental struggle in the next two or three pages is the emotional climax of the story. It draws together the theme of flight from bondage and the social satire of the middle section, for Huck is trying to work himself clear of the perverted value system of St. Petersburg. Both adventure story and satire, however, are now subordinate to an exploration of Huck's psyche which is the ultimate achievement of the book. The issue is identical with that of the first moral crisis, but the later passage is much more intense and richer in implication. The differences appear clearly if the two crises are compared in detail.

In Chapter 16 Huck is startled into a realization of his predicament when he hears Jim, on the lookout for Cairo at the mouth of the Ohio, declare that "he'd be a free man the minute he seen it, but if he missed it he'd be in a slave country again and no more show for freedom." Huck says: "I begun to get it through my head that he *was* most free—and who was to blame for it? Why, *me*. I couldn't get that out of my conscience, no how nor no way." He dramatizes his inner debate by quoting the words in which his conscience denounces him: "What had poor Miss Watson done to you that you could see her nigger go off right under your eyes and never say one single word? What did that poor old woman do to you that you could treat her so mean? Why, she tried to learn you your book, she tried to learn you your manners, she tried to be good to you every way she knowed how. *That's* what she done." The counterargument is provided by Jim, who seems to guess what is passing through Huck's mind and does what he can to invoke the force of friendship and gratitude: "Pooty soon I'll be a-shout'n' for joy, en I'll say, it's all on accounts of Huck; I's a free man, en I couldn't ever ben free ef it hadn' ben for Huck; Huck done it. Jim won't ever forgit you, Huck; you's de bes' fren' Jim's ever had; en you's de *only* fren' ole Jim's got now." Huck nevertheless sets out for the shore in the canoe "all in a sweat to tell on" Jim, but when he is intercepted by the two slave hunters in a skiff he suddenly contrives a cunning device to ward them off. We are given no details about how his inner conflict was resolved.

In the later crisis Huck provides a much more circumstantial account of what passes through his mind. He is now quite alone; the outcome of the debate is not affected by any stimulus from the outside. It is the memory of Jim's kindness and goodness rather than Jim's actual voice that impels Huck to defy his conscience: "I see Jim before me all the time: in the day and in the night-time, sometimes moonlight, sometimes storms, and we a-floating along, talking and singing and laughing." The most striking feature of this later crisis is the fact that Huck's conscience, which formerly had employed only secular arguments, now deals heavily in religious cant:

At last, when it hit me all of a sudden that here was the plain hand of Providence slapping me in the face and letting me know my wickedness was being watched all the time from up there in heaven, whilst I was stealing a poor old woman's nigger that hadn't ever done me no harm, and now was showing me there's One that's always on the lookout, and ain't a-going to allow no such miserable doings to go only just so fur and no further, I most dropped in my tracks I was so scared.

In the earlier debate the voice of Huck's conscience is quoted directly, but the bulk of the later exhortation is reported in indirect discourse. This apparently simple change in method has remarkable consequences. According to the conventions of first-person narrative, the narrator functions as a neutral medium in reporting dialogue. He remembers the speeches of other characters but they pass through his mind without affecting him. When Huck's conscience speaks within quotation marks it is in effect a character in the story, and he is not responsible for what it says. But when he paraphrases the admonitions of his conscience they are incorporated into his own discourse. Thus although Huck is obviously remembering the bits of theological jargon from sermons justifying slavery, they have become a part of his vocabulary.

The device of having Huck paraphrase rather than quote the voice of conscience may have been suggested to Mark Twain by a discovery he made in revising Huck's report of the King's address to the mourners in the Wilks parlor (Chapter 25). The manuscript version of the passage shows that the King's remarks were composed as a direct quotation, but in the published text they have been put, with a minimum of verbal change, into direct discourse. The removal of the barrier of quotation marks brings Huck into much more intimate contact with the King's "rot and slush" despite the fact that the paraphrase quivers with disapproval. The voice of conscience speaks in the precise accents of the King but Huck is now completely uncritical. He does not question its moral authority; it is morality personified. The greater subtlety of the later passage illustrates the difference between the necessarily shallow characterization of Huck while he was being used merely as a narrative persona, and the profound insight which Mark Twain eventually brought to bear on his protagonist.

The recognition of complexity in Huck's character enabled Mark Twain to do full justice to the conflict between vernacular values and the dominant culture. By situating in a single consciousness both the perverted moral code of a society built on slavery and the vernacular commitment to freedom and spontaneity, he was able to represent the opposed perspectives as alternative modes of experience for the same character. In this way he gets rid of the confusions surrounding the pronoun "I" in the earlier books, where it sometimes designates the author speaking in his own person, sometimes an entirely distinct fictional character. Furthermore, the insight that enabled him to recognize the conflict between accepted values and vernacular protest as a struggle within a single mind does justice to its moral depth, whereas the device he had used earlier—in *The Innocents Abroad*, for example—of identifying the two perspectives with separate characters had flattened the issue out into melodrama. The satire of a decadent slaveholding society gains immensely in force when Mark Twain demonstrates that even the outcast Huck has been in part perverted by it. Huck's conscience is simply the attitudes he has taken over from his environment. What is still sound in him is an impulse from the deepest level of his personality that struggles against the overlay of prejudice and false valuation imposed on all members of the society in the name of religion, morality, law, and refinement.

Finally, it should be pointed out that the conflict in Huck between generous impulse and false belief is depicted by means of a contrast between colloquial and exalted styles. In moments of crisis his conscience addresses him in the language of the dominant culture, a tawdry and faded effort at a high style that is the rhetorical equivalent of the ornaments in the Grangerford parlor. Yet

speaking in dialect does not in itself imply moral authority. By every external
criterion the King is as much a vernacular character as Huck. The conflict in
which Huck is involved is not that of a lower against an upper class or of an
alienated fringe of outcasts against a cultivated elite. It is not the issue of
frontier West versus genteel East, or of backwoods versus metropolis, but of
fidelity to the uncoerced self versus the blurring of attitudes caused by social
conformity, by the effort to achieve status or power through exhibiting the
approved forms of sensibility.

The exploration of Huck's personality carried Mark Twain beyond satire
and even beyond his statement of a vernacular protest against the dominant
culture into essentially novelistic modes of writing. Some of the passages he
composed when he got out beyond his polemic framework challenge comparison with the greatest achievements in the world's fiction.

The most obvious of Mark Twain's discoveries on the deeper levels of
Huck's psyche is the boy's capacity for love. The quality of the emotion is
defined in action by his decision to sacrifice himself for Jim, just as Jim attains
an impressive dignity when he refuses to escape at the cost of deserting the
wounded Tom. Projected into the natural setting, the love of the protagonists
for each other becomes the unforgettable beauty of the river when they are
allowed to be alone together. It is always summer, and the forces of nature
cherish them. From the refuge of the cave on Jackson's Island the thunder-
storm is an exhilarating spectacle; Huck's description of it is only less poetic
than his description of the dawn which he and Jim witness as they sit
half-submerged on the sandy bottom.

Yet if Mark Twain had allowed these passages to stand without qualification as a symbolic account of Huck's emotions he would have undercut the
complexity of characterization implied in his recognition of Huck's inner
conflict of loyalties. Instead, he uses the natural setting to render a wide range
of feelings and motives. The fog that separates the boy from Jim for a time is
an externalization of his impulse to deceive Jim by a Tom Sawyerish practical
joke. Similarly Jim's snake bite, the only injury suffered by either of the
companions from a natural source, is the result of another prank played by
Huck before he has learned what friends owe one another.

Still darker aspects of Huck's inner life are projected into the natural setting
in the form of ghosts, omens, portents of disaster—the body of superstition that
is so conspicuous in Huck's and Jim's world. At the end of Chapter 1 Huck is
sitting alone at night by his open window in the Widow Douglas' house:

I felt so lonesome I most wished I was dead. The stars was shining, and the leaves rustled in
the woods ever so mournful; and I heard an owl, away off, who-whooing about somebody that was
dead, and a whippowill and a dog crying about somebody that was going to die; and the wind was
trying to whisper something to me, and I couldn't make out what it was, and so it made the cold
shivers run over me. Then away out in the woods I heard that kind of a sound that a ghost makes
when it wants to tell about something that's on its mind and can't make itself understood, and so
can't rest easy in its grave, and has to go about that way every night grieving. I got so downhearted
and scared I did wish I had some company.

The whimpering ghost with something incommunicable on its mind and
Huck's cold shivers suggest a burden of guilt and anxiety that is perhaps the
punishment he inflicts on himself for defying the mores of St. Petersburg.
Whatever the source of these sinister images, they develop the characterization
of Huck beyond the needs of the plot. The narrator whose stream of consciousness is recorded here is much more than the innocent protagonist of the

pastoral idyl of the raft, more than an ignorant boy who resists being civilized. The vernacular persona is an essentially comic figure; the character we glimpse in Huck's meditation is potentially tragic. Mark Twain's discoveries in the buried strata of Huck's mind point in the same direction as does his intuitive recognition that Huck's and Jim's quest for freedom must end in failure.

A melancholy if not exactly tragic strain in Huck is revealed also by the fictitious autobiographies with which he so often gets himself out of tight places. Like the protocols of a thematic apperception test, they are improvisations on the basis of minimal clues. Huck's inventions are necessary to account for his anomalous situation as a fourteen-year-old boy alone on the river with a Negro man, but they are often carried beyond the demands of utility for sheer fable-making. Their luxuriant detail, and the fact that Huck's hearers are usually (although not always) taken in, lend a comic coloring to these inventions, which are authentically in the tradition of the tall tale. But their total effect is somber. When Huck plans his escape from Pap in Chapter 7, he does so by imagining his own death and planting clues which convince everyone in St. Petersburg, including Tom Sawyer, that he has been murdered. In the crisis of Chapter 16 his heightened emotion leads him to produce for the benefit of the slave hunters a harrowing tale to the effect that his father and mother and sister are suffering smallpox on a raft adrift in mid-river, and he is unable to tow the raft ashore. The slave hunters are so touched by the story that they give him forty dollars and careful instructions about how to seek help—farther downstream. Huck tells the Grangerfords "how pap and me and all the family was living on a little farm down at the bottom of Arkansaw, and my sister Mary Ann run off and got married and never was heard of no more, and Bill went to hunt them and he warn't heard of no more, and Tom and Mort died, and then there warn't nobody but just me and pap left, and he was just trimmed down to nothing, on account of his troubles; so when he died I took what there was left, because the farm didn't belong to us, and started up the river, deck passage, and fell overboard."

5

A number of characters besides Huck are presented in greater depth than is necessary either for purposes of satire or for telling the story of his and Jim's quest for freedom. Perhaps the most striking of these is Pap Finn. Like most of the book, Pap comes straight out of Mark Twain's boyhood memories. We have had a glimpse of him as the drunkard sleeping in the shade of a pile of skids on the levee in the opening scene of "Old Times on the Mississippi." His function in the plot, although definite, is limited. He helps to characterize Huck by making vivid the conditions of Huck's childhood. He has transmitted to his son a casual attitude toward chickens and watermelons, a fund of superstitions, a picaresque ability to look out for himself, and even the gift of language. Pap takes Huck away from the comfort and elegance of the Widow's house to the squalor of the deserted cabin across the river, and then by his sadistic beatings forces the boy to escape to Jackson's Island, where the main action of the flight with Jim begins. After the three chapters which Pap dominates (5-7) we do not see him again except as a corpse in the house floating down the river, but Huck refers to him several times later, invoking Pap's testimony to authenticate the aristocratic status of the Widow Douglas, and to support the family philosophy of "borrowing."

In the sociological scheme of the novel Pap provides a matchless specimen of the lowest stratum of whites who are fiercely jealous of their superiority to all Negroes. His monologue on the "govment" in Chapter 6, provoked by the spectacle of the well-dressed free Negro professor from Ohio, seizes in a few lines the essence of Southern race prejudice. Huck shrewdly calls attention to his father's economic code. When the flooded river brings down part of a log raft, he says: "Anybody but pap would 'a' waited and seen the day through, so as to catch more stuff; but that warn't pap's style. Nine logs was enough for one time; he must shove right over to town and sell," mainly in order to buy whiskey.

But these documentary data supply only a minor part of the image of Pap in *Huckleberry Finn*. He provides some of the most mordant comedy in the book. The fashion in which he gives himself away in the monologue on "govment" is worthy of Jonson or Molière:

> It was 'lection day, and I was just about to go and vote myself if I warn't too drunk to get there; but when they told me there was a state in this country where they'd let that nigger vote, I drawed out. I says I'll never vote ag'in. Them's the very words I said; they all heard me; and the country may rot for all me—I'll never vote ag'in as long as I live. And to see the cool way of that nigger—why, he wouldn't 'a' give me the road if I hadn't shoved him out o' the way.

Even when the comedy verges on slapstick it retains its function as characterization. Pap is so completely absorbed in his diatribe that he barks his shins on the pork barrel:

> He hopped around the cabin considerable, first on one leg and then on the other, holding first one shin and then the other one, and at last he let out with his left foot all of a sudden and fetched the tub a rattling kick. But it warn't good judgment, because that was the boot that had a couple of his toes leaking out of the front end of it; so now he raised a howl that fairly made a body's hair raise, and down he went in the dirt, and rolled there, and held his toes; and the cussing he done then laid over anything he had ever done previous. He said so his own self afterwards. He had heard old Sowberry Hagan in his best days, and he said it laid over him, too; but I reckon that was sort of piling it on, maybe.

Pap's detached evaluation of his own accomplishment in swearing gives to his character an almost medieval flavor. In all his degradation he conceives of himself as enacting a role which is less a personal destiny than part of an integral natural-social reality—a reality so stable that he can contemplate it as if it were external to him. On election day he was drunk as a matter of course; it was an objective question, like an effort to predict the weather, whether he might be too drunk to get to the polls. When he settles down for a domestic evening in the cabin, he "took the jug, and said he had enough whiskey there for two drunks and one delirium tremens."

But when the delirium comes, it belies the coolness of his offhand calculation. Huck's description of the drunkard's agony is a nightmare of neurotic suffering that blots out the last vestige of comedy in Pap's image and relates itself in Huck's mind to the ominous sounds he had heard from his window in the Widow's house:

> [Pap] rolled over and over wonderful fast, kicking things every which way, and striking and grabbing at the air with his hands, and screaming and saying there was devils a-hold of him . . . Then he laid stiller, and didn't make a sound. I could hear the owls and the wolves away off in the woods, and it seemed terrible still . . . By and by he raised up part way and listened, with his head to one side. He says, very low:

"Tramp—tramp—tramp; that's the dead; tramp—tramp—tramp; they're coming after me; but I won't go. Oh, they're here! don't touch me—don't! hands off—they're cold; let go. Oh, let a poor devil alone!"

Then he went down on all fours and crawled off, begging them to let him alone, and he rolled himself up in his blanket and wallowed in under the old pine table, still a-begging; and then he went to crying. I could hear him through the blanket.

Pap's hallucinations externalize inner suffering in images of ghosts and portents. Presently he sees in Huck the Angel of Death and chases him around the cabin with a knife "saying he would kill me, and then I couldn't come for him no more." In fact, the mystery of Pap's anguished psyche has had a supernatural aura all along. He is in a sense a ghost the first time we see him, for his faceless corpse has been found floating in the river; and immediately before his dramatic appearance in Huck's room Jim's hair-ball oracle has announced, "Dey's two angels hoverin' roun' 'bout him. One uv 'em is white en shiny, en t'other one is black. De white one gits him to go right a little while, den de black one sail in en bust it all up. A body can't tell yit which one gwyne to fetch him at de las'." Coming early in the story, at a time when Mark Twain had apparently not yet worked out the details of the plot, this sounds as if he had in mind the possibility of involving Pap more elaborately in the course of events. But aside from the relatively minor incidents that have been mentioned, what the angels might have led Pap to do is never revealed.

He does, however, have an important thematic function. He serves as a forceful reminder that to be a vernacular outcast does not necessarily bring one into contact with the benign forces of nature. Physical withdrawal from society may be plain loafing, without moral significance. Huck's life with Pap in the cabin foreshadows his life with Jim on the raft, but lacks the suggestion of harmony with the natural setting:

It was kind of lazy and jolly, laying off comfortable all day, smoking and fishing, and no books nor study. Two months or more run along, and my clothes got to be all rags and dirt, and I didn't see how I'd ever got to like it so well at the widow's, where you had to wash, and eat on a plate, and comb up, and go to bed and get up regular, and be forever bothering over a book, and have old Miss Watson pecking at you all the time. I didn't want to go back no more . . . It was pretty good times up in the woods there, take it all around.

More explicitly, Pap's denunciation of Huck for the civilized habits the Widow and Miss Watson have imposed on him is a grotesque version of vernacular hostility toward the conventions of refined society:

Starchy clothes—very. You think you're a good deal of a big-bug, *don't* you? . . . You're educated, too, they say—can read and write. You think you're better'n your father, now, don't you, because he can't? . . . you drop that school, you hear? I'll learn people to bring up a boy to put on airs over his own father and let on to be better'n what *he* is . . . First you know you'll get religion, too. I never see such a son.

This adds another nuance to the book by suggesting that civilized values have something to be said for them after all.

The extent to which Mark Twain's imagination was released in *Huckleberry Finn* to explore multiple perspectives upon the Matter of Hannibal and the Matter of the River can be realized if one compares Pap with the sociologically similar backwoodsmen observed from the steamboat in "Old Times." These "jeans-clad, chills-racked, yellow-faced miserables" are merely comic animals. Pap is even more degraded than they are, lazier, more miserable, but he is not an object of scorn. The fullness with which his degradation and his misery are presented confers on him not so much a human dignity—although it is also that—as the impersonal dignity of art.

In relation to the whole of *Huckleberry Finn*, Pap serves to solidify the image of Huck's and Jim's vernacular paradise by demonstrating that Mark Twain is aware of the darker possibilities confronting them when they escape from the shore to the river. The mass of superstitions with which Pap is so vividly connected (we recall the cross of nails in his boot heel to ward off the devil), standing in contrast to the intimations of blissful harmony with nature in the passages devoted to Huck and Jim alone on the raft, keeps that lyrical vision from seeming mere pathetic fallacy. And the appalling glimpse of Pap's inner life beneath the stereotype of the town drunkard makes him into what might be called a note of tragic relief in a predominantly comic story.

6

It has become a commonplace of criticism that the drastic shift in tone in the last section of *Huckleberry Finn*, from Chapter 31 to the end, poses a problem of interpretation. The drifting raft has reached Arkansas, and the King and the Duke have delivered Jim back into captivity. They make their exit early in the sequence, tarred and feathered as punishment for one more effort to work the "Royal Nonesuch" trick. Tom Sawyer reappears by an implausible coincidence and takes charge of the action, which thereafter centers about his schemes to liberate Jim from confinement in a cabin on the plantation of Tom's Uncle Silas Phelps.

These events have for their prelude a vivid description of Huck's first approach to the Phelps place:

> When I got there it was all still and Sunday-like, and hot and sunshiny; the hands was gone to the fields; and there was them kind of faint dronings of bugs and flies in the air that makes it seem so lonesome and like everybody's dead and gone; and if a breeze fans along and quivers the leaves it makes you feel mournful, because you feel like it's spirits whispering—spirits that's been dead ever so many years—and you always think they're talking about *you*. As a general thing it makes a body wish *he* was dead, too, and done with it all.

And a few lines later:

> I went around and clumb over the back stile by the ash-hopper, and started for the kitchen. When I got a little ways I heard the dim hum of a spinning-wheel wailing along up and sinking along down again; and then I knowed for certain I wished I was dead—for that *is* the lonesomest sound in the whole world.

This passage has much in common with Huck's meditation before his open window in Chapter 1. They are the two most vivid expressions of his belief in ghosts, and in both cases the ghosts are associated in his mind with a deep depression not fully accounted for by the context of the story.

It would be reasonable to suppose that the cause of Huck's depression is the failure of his long effort to help Jim toward freedom. The reader knows that even if Huck could manage to rescue Jim from the Phelpses, they face insuperable difficulties in trying to make their way back up the Mississippi to free territory. Yet oddly enough, Huck does not share this estimate of the situation. He is confident he can find a way out of the impasse: "I went right along, not fixing up any particular plan, but just trusting to Providence to put the right words in my mouth when the time come; for I'd noticed that Providence always did put the right words in my mouth if I left it alone." Somewhat later, Huck points out to Tom that they can easily get Jim out of the log cabin by stealing the key, and "shove off down the river on the raft with Jim, hiding daytimes and running nights, the way me and Jim used to do before. Wouldn't that plan work?" Tom agrees: "Why, cert'nly it would work, like rats a-fighting. But it's too blame' simple; there ain't nothing *to* it. What's the good of a plan that ain't no more trouble than that?"

The tone as much as the substance of the references to the problem of rescuing Jim makes it plain that Huck's view of his predicament cannot account for his depression as he approaches the Phelps plantation. The emotion is the author's rather than Huck's, and it is derived from sources outside the story. In order to determine what these were we must consult Mark Twain's autobiographical reminiscences. The Phelps place as he describes it in the novel has powerful associations for him because it is patterned on the farm of his Uncle John A. Quarles where he spent summers as a boy. "I can see the farm yet, with perfect clearness," he wrote in his *Autobiography.*

> I can see all its belongings, all its details; the family room of the house, with a "trundle" bed in one corner and a spinning-wheel in another—a wheel whose rising and falling wail, heard from a distance, was the mournfulest of all sounds to me, and made me homesick and low spirited, and filled my atmosphere with the wandering spirits of the dead.

Additional associations with the Quarles farm are recorded in Mark Twain's "The Private History of a Campaign That Failed," written a few months after the publication of *Huckleberry Finn.* This bit of fictionalized autobiography describes his experiences as second lieutenant of the Marion Rangers, a rather informal volunteer militia unit organized in Hannibal in the early months of the Civil War. The Quarles farm is here assigned to a man named Mason:

> We stayed several days at Mason's; and after all these years the memory of the dullness, and stillness, and lifelessness of that slumberous farm-house still oppresses my spirit as with a sense of the presence of death and mourning. There was nothing to do, nothing to think about; there was no interest in life. The male part of the household were away in the fields all day, the women were busy and out of our sight; there was no sound but the plaintive wailing of a spinning-wheel, forever moaning out from some distant room—the most lonesome sound in nature, a sound steeped and sodden with homesickness and the emptiness of life.

The emotional overtones of the memories recorded in "The Private History" are made more explicit in a letter Mark Twain wrote in 1890:

> I was a *soldier* two weeks once in the beginning of the war, and was hunted like a rat the whole time . . . My splendid Kipling himself hasn't a more burnt-in, hard-baked and unforgettable familiarity with that death-on-the-pale-horse-with-hell-following-after which is a raw soldier's first fortnight in the field—and which, without any doubt, is the most tremendous fortnight and the vividest he is ever going to see.

But while there are references to fear of the enemy in "The Private History," they are mainly comic, and the dullness and lifelessness that afflict the neophyte soldiers at the Mason farm do not suggest the feeling of being hunted like a rat. More significant, perhaps, is an incident Mark Twain places a few pages later in "The Private History." Albert B. Paine says it was invented; and it does have the air of fiction. But it reveals the emotional coloring of the author's recollections. He relates that he fired in the dark at a man approaching on horseback, who was killed. Although five other shots were fired at the same moment, and he did not at bottom believe his shot had struck its mark, still his "diseased imagination" convinced him he was guilty. "The thought shot through me that I was a murderer; that I had killed a man—a man who had never done me any harm. That was the coldest sensation that ever went through my marrow."

Huck also experiences a strong and not easily explicable feeling of guilt a few pages after his arrival at the Phelpses'. When he sees the Duke and the King ridden out of the nearby town on a rail, surrounded by a howling mob, he says:

> It was a dreadful thing to see. Human beings *can* be awful cruel to one another . . . So we poked along back home, and I warn't feeling so brash as I was before, but kind of ornery, and humble, and to blame, somehow—though *I* hadn't done nothing. But that's always the way; it don't make no difference whether you do right or wrong, a person's conscience ain't got no sense, and just goes for him *anyway*. If I had a yaller dog that didn't know no more than a person's conscience does I would pison him.

The close linkage of the Phelps and Mason farms with Mark Twain's memory of the Quarles place strongly suggests that Huck's depression is caused by a sense of guilt whose sources were buried in the writer's childhood. It is well known that Mark Twain was tormented all his life by such feelings. A fable written in 1876, "The Facts Concerning the Recent Carnival of Crime in Connecticut," makes comedy of his sufferings; but they were serious and chronic. In his twenties, because of an imaginary error in administering an opiate, he had insisted he was to blame for the death of his brother from injuries received in the explosion of a steamboat. Later he accused himself of murdering his son Langdon when he neglected to keep him covered during a carriage ride in cold weather, and the child died of diphtheria.

But why was Mark Twain's latent feeling of guilt drawn up into consciousness at a specific moment in the writing of *Huckleberry Finn*? The most probable explanation is that at this point he was obliged to admit finally to himself that Huck's and Jim's journey down the river could not be imagined as leading to freedom for either of them. Because of the symbolic meaning the journey had taken on for him, the recognition was more than a perception of difficulty in contriving a plausible ending for the book. He had found a solution to the technical problem that satisfied him, if one is to judge from his evident zest in the complicated pranks of Tom Sawyer that occupy the last ten chapters. But in order to write these chapters he had to abandon the compelling image of the happiness of Huck and Jim on the raft and thus to acknowledge that the vernacular values embodied in his story were mere figments of the imagination, not capable of being reconciled with social reality. To be sure, he had been half-aware from the beginning that the quest of his protagonists was doomed. Huck had repeatedly appeared in the role of a Tiresias powerless to prevent the deceptions and brutalities he was compelled to witness. Yet Providence had always put the right words in his mouth when the time came, and by innocent guile he had extricated himself and Jim from danger after danger. Now the drifting had come to an end.

At an earlier impasse in the plot Mark Twain had shattered the raft under the paddle wheel of a steamboat. He now destroys it again, symbolically, by revealing that Huck's and Jim's journey, with all its anxieties, has been pointless. Tom Sawyer is bearer of the news that Jim has been freed in Miss Watson's will. Tom withholds the information, however, in order to trick Huck and Jim into the meaningless game of an Evasion that makes the word (borrowed from Dumas) into a devastating pun. Tom takes control and Huck becomes once again a subordinate carrying out orders. As if to signal the change of perspective and the shift in his own identification, Mark Twain gives Huck Tom's name through an improbable mistake on the part of Aunt Sally Phelps. We can hardly fail to perceive the weight of the author's feeling in Huck's statement on this occasion: "it was like being born again, I was so glad to find out who I was." Mark Twain has found out who he must be in order to end his book: he must be Tom.

In more abstract terms, he must withdraw from his imaginative participation in Huck's and Jim's quest for freedom. If the story was to be stripped of its tragic implications, Tom's perspective was the logical one to adopt because his intensely conventional sense of values made him impervious to the moral significance of the journey on the raft. Huck can hardly believe that Tom would collaborate in the crime of helping a runaway slave, and Huck is right. Tom merely devises charades involving a man who is already in a technical sense free. The consequences of the shift in point of view are strikingly evident in the treatment of Jim, who is subjected to farcical indignities. This is disturbing to the reader who has seen Jim take on moral and emotional stature, but it is necessary if everything is to be forced back into the framework of comedy. Mark Twain's portrayal of Huck and Jim as complex characters has carried him beyond the limits of his original plan: we must not forget that the literary ancestry of the book is to be found in backwoods humor. As Huck approaches the Phelps plantation the writer has on his hands a hybrid—a comic story in which the protagonists have acquired something like tragic depth.

In deciding to end the book with the description of Tom's unnecessary contrivances for rescuing Jim, Mark Twain was certain to produce an anti-climax. But he was a great comic writer, able to score local triumphs in the most unlikely circumstances. The last chapters have a number of brilliant touches—the slave who carries the witch pie to Jim, Aunt Sally's trouble in counting her spoons, Uncle Silas and the ratholes, the unforgettable Sister Hotchkiss. Even Tom's horseplay would be amusing if it were not spun out to such length and if we were not asked to accept it as the conclusion of *Huckleberry Finn*. Although Jim is reduced to the level of farce, Tom is a comic figure in the classical sense of being a victim of delusion. He is not aware of being cruel to Jim because he does not perceive him as a human being. For Tom, Jim is the hero of a historical romance, a peer of the Man in the Iron Mask or the Count of Monte Cristo. Mark Twain is consciously imitating *Don Quixote*, and there are moments not unworthy of the model, as when Tom admits that "we got to dig him out with the picks, and *let on* it's case-knives."

But Tom has no tragic dimension whatever. There is not even any force of common sense in him to struggle against his perverted imagination as Huck's innate loyalty and generosity struggle against his deformed conscience. Although Mark Twain is indulgent toward Tom, he adds him to the list of characters who employ the soul-butter style of false pathos. The inscriptions Tom composes for Jim to "scrabble onto the wall" of the cabin might have been composed by the Duke:

1. Here a captive heart busted.
2. Here a poor prisoner, forsook by the world and friends, fretted his sorrowful life.
3. Here a lonely heart broke, and a worn spirit went to its rest, after thirty-seven years of solitary captivity.
4. Here, homeless and friendless, after thirty-seven years of bitter captivity, perished a noble stranger, natural son of Louis XIV.

While he was reading these noble sentiments aloud, "Tom's voice trembled . . . and he most broke down."

7

Mark Twain's partial shift of identification from Huck to Tom in the final sequence was one response to his recognition that Huck's and Jim's quest for freedom was only a dream: he attempted to cover with a veil of parody and farce the harsh facts that condemned it to failure. The brief episode involving Colonel Sherburn embodies yet another response to his disillusionment. The extraordinary vividness of the scenes in which Sherburn figures—only a half-dozen pages all told—is emphasized by their air of being an intrusion into the story. Of course, in the episodic structure of *Huckleberry Finn* many characters appear for a moment and disappear. Even so, the Sherburn episode seems unusually isolated. None of the principal characters is involved in or affected by it: Jim, the Duke, and the King are offstage, and Huck is a spectator whom even the author hardly notices. We are told nothing about his reaction except that he did not want to stay around. He goes abruptly off to the circus and does not refer to Sherburn again.

Like Huck's depression as he nears the Phelps plantation, the Sherburn episode is linked with Mark Twain's own experience. The shooting of Boggs follows closely the murder of "Uncle Sam" Smarr by a merchant named Owsley in Hannibal in 1845, when Sam Clemens was nine years old. Although it is not clear that he actually witnessed it, he mentioned the incident at least four times at intervals during his later life, including one retelling as late as 1898, when he said he had often dreamed about it. Mark Twain prepares for the shooting in *Huckleberry Finn* by careful attention to the brutality of the loafers in front of the stores in Bricksville. "There couldn't anything wake them up all over, and make them happy all over, like a dog-fight—unless it might be putting turpentine on a stray dog and setting fire to him, or tying a tin pan to his tail and see him run himself to death." The prurient curiosity of the townspeople who shove and pull to catch a glimpse of Boggs as he lies dying in the drugstore with a heavy Bible on his chest, and their pleasure in the re-enactment of the shooting by the man in the big white fur stovepipe hat, also help to make Bricksville an appropriate setting for Sherburn's crime.

The shooting is in Chapter 21, and the scene in which Sherburn scatters the mob by his contemptuous speech is in the following chapter. There is evidence that Mark Twain put aside the manuscript for a time near the end of Chapter 21. If there was such an interruption in his work on the novel, it might account for a marked change in tone. In Chapter 21 Sherburn is an unsympathetic character. His killing of Boggs is motivated solely by arrogance, and the introduction of Boggs's daughter is an invitation to the reader to consider Sherburn an inhuman monster. In Chapter 22, on the other hand, the Colonel appears in an oddly favorable light. The townspeople have now become a mob; there are several touches that suggest Mark Twain was recalling the descriptions of mobs in Carlyle's *French Revolution* and other works of history and fiction. He considered mobs to be subhuman aggregates generating psychological pressures that destroyed individual freedom of choice. In a passage written for *Life on the Mississippi* but omitted from the book Mark Twain makes scathing generalizations about the cowardice of mobs, especially in the South but also in other regions, that closely parallel Sherburn's speech.

In other words, however hostile may be the depiction of Sherburn in Chapter 21, in Chapter 22 we have yet another instance of Mark Twain's identifying himself, at least partially, with a character in the novel other than Huck. The image of Sherburn standing on the roof of the porch in front of his house with the shotgun that is the only weapon in sight has an emblematic quality. He is a solitary figure, not identified with the townspeople, and because they are violently hostile to him, an outcast. But he is not weaker than they, he is stronger. He stands above the mob, looking down on it. He is "a heap the best dressed man in that town," and he is more intelligent than his neighbors. The scornful courage with which he defies the mob redeems him from the taint of cowardice implied in his shooting of an unarmed man who was trying to escape. Many members of the mob he faces are presumably armed; the shotgun he holds is not the source of his power but merely a symbol of the personal force with which he dominates the community.

The Colonel's repeated references to one Buck Harkness, the leader of the mob, whom he acknowledges to be "half-a-man," suggest that the scene represents a contest between two potential leaders in Bricksville. Harkness is the strongest man with whom the townspeople can identify themselves. In his pride Sherburn chooses isolation, but he demonstrates that he is stronger than Harkness, for the mob, including Harkness, obeys his command to "*leave*—and take your half-a-man with you."

Sherburn belongs to the series of characters in Mark Twain's later work that have been called "transcendent figures." Other examples are Hank Morgan in *A Connecticut Yankee*; Pudd'nhead Wilson; and Satan in *The Mysterious Stranger*. They exhibit certain common traits, more fully developed with the passage of time. They are isolated by their intellectual superiority to the community; they are contemptuous of mankind in general; and they have more than ordinary power. Satan, the culmination of the series, is omnipotent. Significantly, he is without a moral sense—that is, a conscience, a sense of guilt. He is not torn by the kind of inner struggle that Huck experiences. But he is also without Huck's sound heart. The price of power is the surrender of all human warmth.

Colonel Sherburn's cold-blooded murder of Boggs, his failure to experience remorse after the act, and his withering scorn of the townspeople are disquieting portents for the future. Mark Twain, like Huck, was sickened by the brutality he had witnessed in the society along the river. But he had an adult aggressiveness foreign to Huck's character. At a certain point he could no longer endure the anguish of being a passive observer. His imagination sought refuge in the image of an alternative persona who was protected against suffering by being devoid of pity or guilt, yet could denounce the human race for its cowardice and cruelty, and perhaps even take action against it. The appearance of Sherburn in *Huckleberry Finn* is ominous because a writer who shares his attitude toward human beings is in danger of abandoning imaginative insight for moralistic invective. The slogan of "the damned human race" that later became Mark Twain's proverb spelled the sacrifice of art to ideology. Colonel Sherburn would prove to be Mark Twain's dark angel. His part in the novel, and that of Tom Sawyer, are flaws in a work that otherwise approaches perfection as an embodiment of American experience in a radically new and appropriate literary mode.

THE RAFT EPISODE IN *HUCKLEBERRY FINN*

PETER G. BEIDLER[*]

Included in the original manuscript of *Huckleberry Finn* was the "raft episode," a fifteen-page passage recording Huck's visit to a large raft to discover how far he and Jim were from Cairo. Twain had previously lifted the passage from the unfinished novel and printed it in *Life on the Mississippi*, for it was interesting in itself as an account of river life and the bragging and tall tales that river men are fond of. Before he sent the manuscript of his completed novel to Charles Webster, his nephew and publisher, he restored the passage to its original position after the second paragraph of Chapter XVI. Webster, however, persuaded Twain to leave the passage out of the final published version of the novel, and most subsequent editors have printed *Huckleberry Finn* as he did. The purpose of the present paper is to question Twain's decision to allow the deletion of the raft episode and then to consider briefly the editorial problem that has resulted.

Since Twain was determined not to let Webster publish *Huckleberry Finn* until at least 40,000 copies had been ordered, he impressed upon his nephew the need for forceful canvassing and a well-selected "canvassing book." Apparently afraid that prospective buyers would recognize the passage from *Life on the Mississippi*, Twain, in a letter written on April 14, 1884, specifically cautioned Webster to "Be particular & don't get any of that *old* matter into your canvassing book—(the *raft* episode.)." A week later, on April 21, Webster wrote to Twain suggesting that the episode be left out of the novel altogether: "The book is so *much* larger than Tom Sawyer would it not be better to omit that old Mississippi matter? I think it would improve it." Since the letter was postmarked in New York at 6 P.M., we may assume that Twain did not receive it in Hartford until the next day. He answered promptly that same day, April 22: "Yes, I think the raft chapter can be left wholly out, by heaving in a paragraph to say Huck visited the raft to find out how far it might be to Cairo, but got no satisfaction. Even *this* is not necessary unless that raft-visit is referred to later in the book. I think it is, but am not certain."[1]

These letters make clear two important facts. First, it was Webster who suggested dropping the raft episode from the published novel, apparently only because he wanted the new novel to be short enough to look like a companion to *Tom Sawyer*. Second, Twain's decision to approve Webster's suggestion was made rapidly and apparently without his having checked a manuscript of the novel; he was not even sure whether a possible later reference to the visit to the raft would necessitate a new paragraph. Twain's failure to remember very clearly the details of his narrative is not surprising when we recall that much of the novel had been written eight years earlier in 1876.[2] Under these circumstances we need not consider the author's rapid editorial decision as necessarily artistically justified. We have the time and the materials, which Twain apparently did not have, to examine the function of the passage in its original context, and we are not being pressed, as Twain was, by a publisher who is more interested in counting words than in reading them.

That Twain so readily permitted the deletion of the raft episode testifies apparently to his awareness of the basically episodic nature of *Huckleberry*

[*] *Modern Fiction Studies*, copyright 1968, by Purdue Research Foundation, West Lafayette, Indiana 47907. Reprinted with permission.

Finn: eliminate a passage here and there and no real harm is done. This attitude toward the episodes, however, is inconsistent with the second of his "nineteen rules governing literary art": "the episodes of a tale shall be necessary parts of the tale and shall help to develop it."[3] I believe that the raft episode *is* a necessary part of the novel and *does* help to develop it, and I believe that it should not have been removed.

In the first place, the deletion of the raft episode leaves a curious narrative gap in the novel, for Twain never did "heave in" a paragraph about Huck's unsuccessful visit to the large raft to find out about Cairo. In the second paragraph of Chapter XVI Huck and Jim discuss how they might recognize Cairo when they do come to it. Huck fears they may drift right on past it if they go by at night, and so he determines to paddle ashore the first time they see a light and ask how far ahead Cairo is. In the published version this paragraph is immediately followed by a paragraph beginning, "There warn't nothing to do now but to look out sharp for the town and not pass it without seeing it" (p. 307). Such a statement is puzzling indeed when it follows immediately Huck's resolution *not* to count on recognizing the town when they come to it but to make an attempt to discover before they get there how far ahead it is. In the original manuscript, of course, the lengthy raft episode came between the second and third paragraphs, and, because Huck's attempt to discover the location of Cairo by swimming to the raft had not only failed but had nearly gotten him into serious trouble, it fully explained his statement that now there was nothing to do but wait and hope they would recognize the town when they came to it. Huck was not anxious to make a second dangerous inquiry that night.

The raft episode serves other functions than that of a bridge between two otherwise awkwardly juxtaposed paragraphs. It gives us, for example, just as it gives Huck himself, technical information about the place where the two rivers come together. In the second paragraph of the chapter, as I have said, Huck and Jim discuss how they will know when they reach Cairo: "Jim said if the two big rivers joined together there, that would show. But I said maybe we might think we was passing the foot of an island and coming into the same old river again. That disturbed Jim—and me too" (p. 291). Huck is apparently unaware that the two rivers will be distinguishable or that any difference between them will show up after they have joined at Cairo. After all, he has never been down the river before; how could he know? A few pages later in the originally published volume, however, Huck somehow *does* know enough about the condition of the two rivers to recognize that he has passed Cairo. He and Jim have tied up for the day on a towhead near the left (east) shore of the river. When daylight comes, Huck sees that "here was the clear Ohio water inshore, sure enough, and outside was the old regular Muddy! So it was all up with Cairo" (p. 314). That Huck can now recognize the difference between the two rivers and interpret the difference correctly shows that since the second paragraph he must have learned about the merging of the rivers below Cairo. In the published version, however, we are not told how he learned this.

The mystery is, of course, cleared up if we reinsert the raft episode. While hidden on the raft, Huck overhears Ed say that "the muddy Mississippi water was wholesomer to drink than the clear water of the Ohio" (p. 297), so he would now know that the rivers were not of identical consistency. And Huck would also have learned that the difference between the two rivers would be apparent for some distance below Cairo, for the raftsmen talk about "how Ohio water didn't like to mix with Mississippi water. Ed said if you take the Mississippi on a rise [and the Mississippi now *is* on a rise] when the Ohio is low, you'll find a wide band of clear water all the way down the east side of the Mississippi for a hundred mile or more, and the minute you get out a quarter of a mile from shore and pass the line, it is all thick and yaller the rest of the way across" (p. 298). Twain clearly used the raft episode as a device to give Huck and the equally naive reader the technical background to interpret properly the condition of the river below Cairo. Twain apparently forgot that, in permitting the excision of the episode, he was leaving unexplained Huck's sudden ability to understand the phenomenon and was leaving unanswered for many readers the question of why the inshore water on the left bank was clearer than the water further out, and what that difference had to do with the location of Cairo.

The raft episode also provides the careful reader with a different kind of information about the location of Cairo, information which this time Huck himself does not get. Twain subtly tells us that Huck and Jim have already drifted past the destination they seek. I suspect that the very fact that the raftsmen are discussing the mixing of the two rivers in the first place is a hint that they have passed the point where the two rivers come together. The real clue comes, however, when Huck is being questioned by the raftsmen about why he has come to their raft. Huck quickly makes up a lie about how his pap, who had "traded up and down here all his life," had told him to swim to the raft to ask one of them "to speak to a Mr. Jonas Turner, in Cairo, and tell him—" (p. 306). Here, after he mentions Cairo, Huck is interrupted by the raftsmen and accused of lying. I suggest that they are already past Cairo and so could not deliver a message to anyone there. They therefore know Huck is lying when he mentions Cairo because no one who knows as much about the region as Huck says his pap knows could possibly *not* know that they were below Cairo. Huck himself never understands how they know he is lying, but we readers can see that this is the only possible inconsistency in his lie.

Dramatic irony, then, is made possible by the raft episode. When Jim thinks every light he sees is Cairo, we know he will be disappointed; when Huck asks the fisherman if that town up ahead is Cairo, we know why the man thinks Huck "must be a blame' fool" (p. 313); and when Huck wrestles with his "conscience" because he thinks he has helped bring Jim to the town where Jim will be free, we know that they are already well south into slave territory and are beyond the place where Jim could have found his freedom. In letting us know ahead of time what Jim and Huck have yet to find out, Twain makes sure that our chief interest is not in the location of Cairo but in the states of mind of Jim and, especially, Huck as they anticipate an event which we know will not happen. If we read the novel without the raft episode, this dramatic irony is lost. We learn the location of Cairo no sooner than Huck and Jim do, and our interest is more likely to be in the suspense of the action than in the psychology of the characters.

It is, of course, Huck's psychological nature that is our chief interest in the novel, and no attempt to justify the raft episode can be finally convincing unless it can show that the episode is important for its development of, or its contribution to our understanding of, Huck's character. Huck plays only a small part in the action of the raft episode. During most of it he is hidden and listening to the others talking. What he hears, however, makes a deep impression on him, and his reaction to what he hears is significant. The account of Ed's story of Dick Allbright and the haunted barrel, like the immediately preceding account of the "fight" between the two raftsmen, is valuable for its addition to Twain's fictional version of life on the Mississippi; it is also important for its effect on Huck. Before we can refer in detail to Ed's story and its effect on Huck, however, it is necessary to examine Huck's generally morbid outlook on life, his repeated identification with dead and suffering human beings.

Huck's many lies on his downward journey are, I feel, central to an understanding of his character. I cannot agree with Wyatt Blassingame that Twain used the lie, "simply a variation of the old vaudeville gag," merely as an excuse to "release his full flamboyant genius" by setting up "a situation which he wished to described [sic] in detail." In other words, Blassingame feels that Huck's lies are not an organic part of the novel, are usually not necessary, and represent merely Twain's indulging his desire to write scenes which "he could get his teeth into."[4] If we examine Huck's lies carefully, however, we find a pattern emerging from them which reveals something of Huck's psychological nature: in many of them Huck casts himself in the role of a boy who is alone in the world and whose family is dead, sick, or in grave danger.

Let us look at some of those lies. Huck tells Mrs. Loftus that "my mother's down sick and out of money and everything" (p. 256). A moment later he tells her that "my father and mother was dead and the law had bound me out to a mean old farmer . . . and he treated me so bad I couldn't stand it no longer" (p. 261). He tells the ferryboat captain about the "awful peck of trouble" his family is in up on the wrecked *Walter Scott* (p. 276). He lets the two men in the skiff believe that his father and mother and sister all have the smallpox and that "I've told everybody before, and they just went away and left us" (p. 311). He tells the Grangerfords that his sister "run off and got married and never was heard of no more, and Bill went to hunt them and he warn't heard of no more, and Tom and Mort died, and then there warn't nobody but just me and pap left, and he was just trimmed down to nothing, on account of his troubles; so when he died I took what there was left, because the farm didn't belong to us, and started up the river, deck passage, and fell overboard" (p. 320). He tells the King and the Duke that his folks "all died off but me and pa and my brother Ike." When their raft collided with the steamboat, "pa was drunk, and Ike was only four years old, so they never come up no more" (p. 351).

It might be argued that these lies show us nothing about Huck except that he was extremely adept at making up convincing stories to explain his being where he was without any family. Huck's lies certainly do show his ability to explain his way out of difficult situations, but it seems to me that Huck's lies are identifiably *Huck's*, and that Tom Sawyer, for example, under similar conditions, would have dreamed up equally effective but very different lies. The particular lies Huck tells are prescribed not only by circumstances but also by Huck's own character and background. If Huck were not, in effect, an orphan, and if he had known no loneliness and brutality, I doubt that he would have come up with such mournful imaginary accounts of his past.

As evidence for my contention I refer to an instance where Huck's lying is quite unnecessary and even cumbersome when only the demands of the situation are considered. When the King accuses Huck of trying to give him and the Duke the slip at Peter Wilks's grave, Huck might simply have told the truth:

the man who held him let go his arm in the excitement of the discovery of the gold. This explanation would surely have sufficed, for that is exactly the way the King and the Duke themselves escaped. Instead, Huck fabricates a lie that the man who held him prisoner took a liking to him because Huck reminded him of his own "boy about as big as me that died last year" (p. 441). Since the lie cannot be explained by the circumstances under which Huck told it, it can be explained only by Huck's character. In saying that the man identified him with his dead son, Huck is identifying *himself* with the imaginary dead son, since it is Huck who quite unnecessarily makes up the lie. Huck's lies, then, make real to others, and perhaps temporarily to himself, the fantasy world of his imagination. It can hardly be accidental that in his stories Huck takes on the role of the suffering child, separated through sickness, accident, or death from his family.

It is important to note before we go on that when Huck is cast in a different role, he convinces no one with his lies. In trying to be the English "valley," for example, Huck almost immediately has "the hare-lip" suspecting that he has been telling her "a lot of lies" (p. 405). When Huck gives his account of himself in the tavern, the lawyer Levi Bell does not even let him finish: "I reckon you ain't used to lying, it don't seem to come handy; what you want is practice. You do it pretty awkward" (p. 434). Huck is usually anything but an awkward liar, and he has certainly had plenty of practice. Perhaps one of the reasons why his lies are usually not questioned is that if his fictitious role is psychologically congenial to him, he *lives* the role as he plays it, and so he is being true, if not to actual fact, then to his own nature.

Huck's lie about his escape from the graveyard, revealing his identification with a dead boy, leads us directly into another important matter: Huck's almost obsessive concern with death. It is necessary that we be aware of this concern if we are to understand why the raft episode belongs in *Huckleberry Finn*. Throughout the novel we find evidence of the darkness of Huck's imagination and his intuitive awareness of death. In the first chapter, for example, when Huck hears an owl in the woods, he imagines that it is "who-whooing about somebody that was dead." When he hears a dog and a "whippowill," he imagines that they are "crying about somebody that was going to die." He hears another sound in the woods, the "kind of a sound that a ghost makes when it wants to tell about something that's on its mind and can't make itself understood, and so can't rest easy in its grave" (p. 196). The house in which he sits is "as still as death" (p. 197). Often Huck's intense concern with death is more obviously related to himself. After his experience with the *Walter Scott*, for example, he tells us that he and Jim "slept like dead people" (p. 278). When he loses his way in the fog he finds that he has no more idea which way he is going "than a dead man" (p. 284), and feels that he is "laying dead still on the water" (p. 286).

One aspect of Huck's obsessive concern with death is his desire for it. I suspect that Huck's elaborate efforts to have his pap and the townspeople think he has been murdered are more an expression of his own desire for death than of any real fear that they might attempt to follow him. He must know that if he just runs away the townspeople will not care enough to stage much of a search, even if they have any idea where to look, and he knows his pap well enough to know that he will not wander far from the six thousand dollars. If this is so, then the "murder" is at least in part an outward manifestation of Huck's desire for death.

The plausibility of such an interpretation is supported by Huck's many explicit statements of his desire for death and his envy of those who are dead. In the first chapter of the novel, for example, Huck's reaction to Miss Watson's description of "the bad place" is "I wished I was there" (p. 195). Later, as Huck sits in his room, he tells us that "I felt so lonesome I most wished I was dead" (p. 196). When he describes the plight of those who are stranded on the wrecked *Walter Scott*, he adds as part of his lie the information—quite unnecessary to his story, it must be remembered—that Bill Whipple had been killed when the scow had "saddle-baggsed" on the wreck. What we are chiefly interested in here is Huck's comment about the imaginary Bill Whipple's death: "I most wisht it had been me, I do" (p. 277). When Huck's conscience begins to bother him about his part in helping Jim to escape, Huck "got to feeling so mean and so miserable I most wished I was dead. . . . I reckoned I would die of miserableness" (p. 308). Later he thinks that Emmeline Grangerford had had such a death-centered disposition that she was better off dead than alive: "I reckoned . . . she was having a better time in the graveyard" (p. 324). And I wonder if it is just a coincidence that the poem he chooses to quote as an example of her "very good poetry" is the "Ode to Stephen Dowling Bots, Dec'd," a poem about a boy "that fell down a well and was drownded" (p. 324). At any rate, when he makes his escape from the Grangerfords after the fighting, Huck seems pleased that "they'll think I've been killed, and floated down the river" (p. 340). During Peter Wilks's funeral Huck reflects that the dead man "was the only one that had a good thing, according to my notion" (p. 413). When he approaches the Phelps place to find out about Jim, Huck finds that the droning of insects and the gentle breezes make "a body wish *he* was dead . . . and done with it all." As he gets closer to the house he hears the mournful hum of a spinning wheel, "and then I knowed for certain I wished I was dead—for that *is* the lonesomest sound in the whole world" (p. 456). In view of such explicit and repeated expressions there can be little question that Huck, whether fully aware of it or not, is attracted to death as a release from the cruelty and suffering that is life—at least "sivilized" life.

With this much background, then, on the nature of Huck's lying and his yearning for death, we can get to the matter at hand: how these motifs figure in the raft episode. In the part of the passage with which we are concerned, Ed tells the story of his experience with Dick Allbright and the haunted barrel. It seems that Dick Allbright had had a son named Charles William Allbright. One night the child had cried, and in a rage the father had choked him to death and buried him in a barrel and run away to take up rafting. For three years the floating barrel had haunted Dick Allbright along a certain stretch of the river as he went by on a raft, bringing bad luck in the form of sprained ankles and death to other men of the raft with him. On one trip the captain of the raft, wondering what was in the barrel and why it seemed to bring bad luck, brought the barrel aboard, opened it, and found the baby. Dick Allbright confessed that the baby was his and told how he had choked it, "not intending to kill it" (p. 303). Then, before the crew could lynch him, Dick Allbright grabbed the baby, jumped into the river with it, and was never seen again.

It is not important whether the story is true or false, or whether the other raftsmen believe Ed. What is important is that Huck, from his dark hiding place on the raft, hears the story and is apparently much affected by it. A moment after the story is completed, Huck is discovered, brought out into the light, and questioned. When asked what his name is Huck "didn't know what to say, so I just says 'Charles William Allbright'" (p. 306)—the name of the dead baby.[5]

Can there be any doubt, in view of what we have seen about the psychological revelations of Huck's other lies and about his desire for death, that in blurting out the name of the mistreated child whose sufferings have been ended by death, Huck is unconsciously identifying with the child? Both boys have been mistreated by their fathers. Both are alone and naked in the dark when they are discovered and brought into the light by raftsmen. And it can be no coincidence when Huck later lies to them and tells them that he lives in a scow "up at the head of the bend" (p. 306); Charles William had lived "up at the head of this bend" (p. 303) when he was killed. The raftsmen are amused at Huck's lies, and so, perhaps, are we, but surely there is a psychologically significant meaning in them. They tell us, I am sure, much more than Huck thinks they do.

The raft episode, then, very much belongs in its original context in Chapter XVI. It supplies narrative connections which are otherwise rather conspicuously missing. It affects our reading of the rest of the chapter by giving information about Cairo which Huck and Jim do not yet have. And most important, it helps us to understand Huck by bringing into sharp focus his identification with suffering children and his desire for refuge in death. To read the novel without all this is to miss a great deal.

The problem is finally an editorial one. Ought we to respect Twain's "final intention" and print the novel as he finally permitted it to be printed—without the raft episode? Hamlin Hill thinks so: "To add the raftsmen passage to the body of Mark Twain's text is a literary tampering as serious as removing the *Walter Scott* passage would be; the former belongs out (good or bad) because Mark Twain left it out and the latter belongs in (good or bad) because Twain put it in."[6] There is some merit in this argument, but I wonder if the question is quite so simple as Hill makes it sound. Twain did not, we must remember, leave the episode out of the manuscript he sent to his publisher. It was Webster who suggested the deletion, and then only because he wanted to make the book smaller in size. Twain's decision to permit the deletion was made rapidly and apparently without his having consulted the manuscript. I have tried to show that that was an ill-advised and unfortunate decision, and I wonder if we are right, under the circumstances, to hold Twain to it. In printing the novel without the raft episode, an editor is insisting that the reader read what Charles Webster published, not what Mark Twain wrote.

NOTES

1. Excerpts from the two letters by Twain are quoted from *Mark Twain, Business Man*, ed. Samuel Charles Webster (Boston, 1946), pp. 249-250. For his assistance in locating the letter by Webster, I am indebted to Frederick Anderson, Editor of the Mark Twain Papers in the General Library of the University of California in Berkeley. I have decided to refer to what is usually called the "raftsmen passage" as the "raft episode" because that is what Twain himself called it, not only in the first letter quoted above, but also in a letter written to Howells on July 20, 1883. Twain mentioned that he was at work on "a kind of companion to Tom Sawyer. There's a raft episode from it in second or third chapter of *Life on the Mississippi*" (see *Mark Twain-Howells Letters*, ed. Henry Nash Smith *et al.* [Cambridge, Mass., 1960], I, 435).

2. For a full discussion of the writing of the novel, see Walter Blair, *Mark Twain & Huck Finn* (Berkeley and Los Angeles, 1960).

3. From "Fenimore Cooper's Literary Offenses" in *The Portable Mark Twain*, ed. Bernard DeVoto (New York, 1946), pp. 541-542. Subsequent page references to quotations from *Huckleberry Finn* will be included in parentheses in the text and are from this viking portable edition, one of the very few which print the raft episode in its original position in Chapter XVI of the novel.

4. Wyatt Blassingame, "The Use of the Lie in *Huckleberry Finn* as a Technical Device," *Mark Twain Quarterly*, IX (Winter 1953), 11-12.

5. Kenneth S. Lynn thinks Huck replies "jokingly," but I find no evidence that the frightened Huck intended "the release of laughter triggered by this superbly timed response." Lynn is the only critic I have read who has seriously attempted to explain the function of the raft episode. He finds it "an episode of extraordinary richness, of great beauty and humor, which takes us to the heart of the novel." Lynn connects the episode with the "parenthood problem" (Charles William Allbright and Huck both search for fathers on the river), with the theme of death and rebirth ("having died, both boys have come alive again in the flowing waters of the great Mississippi"), and with "the novel's grand theme. . . , the Mosaic drama of liberation." My quotations are from pages 212-213 of Lynn's *Mark Twain and Southwestern Humor* (Boston, 1959); see also his earlier article "Huck and Jim" in *Yale Review*, XLVII (Spring 1958), 421-431.

6. See Hill's "Introduction" to the Facsimile of the First Edition of the novel (San Francisco, 1962), p. xii.

THE FORM OF FREEDOM IN *ADVENTURES OF HUCKLEBERRY FINN*

ALAN TRACHTENBERG

Certain literary works accumulate an aura which possesses the reader before he ventures into reading itself; it gives him a readiness to respond, and a set of expectations to guide his response. Who has come to *Adventures of Huckleberry Finn* free of associations, even of some intimacy with characters and episodes? An aura can be considered a mediation which situates the book and guides the reader toward an available interpretation. This is to say that books like *Huckleberry Finn* can be powerfully predetermined experiences; we encounter them, especially at certain stages of their career, from deep within the culture shared by reader, author, and work. How any book achieves an aura is a problem for the historian of culture: a book's career implicates the history of its readers. *Huckleberry Finn* became a cultural object of special intensity during a period after World War II when many Americans seized upon literary experiences as alternatives to an increasingly confining present. Mark Twain's idyll seemed to project an answerable image—an image of wise innocence in conflict with corruption, of natural man achieving independence of a depraved society. It seemed to project an image, in short, of freedom. But not freedom in the abstract; the values of the book were seen by readers as the precise negation of all the forces felt as oppressive in the 1950's. Common to the several major interpretations of the book was one absolute theme, that the book's most prominent meanings were, as Henry Nash Smith wrote, "against stupid conformity and for the autonomy of the individual." Autonomy vs. conformity: the terms condense a memorable passage of recent American history. The conception of freedom and individualism which pervades the criticism reveals as much of the subliminal concerns of the critics as it does the themes of the book, and should be understood in light of the political and social anxieties of the postwar period.

But does *Huckleberry Finn* deserve its celebration as a testimony to freedom? What exact place, in fact, does freedom have among the book's themes? To say that a theme does not exist apart from its verbal matrix may seem commonplace. But criticism has often addressed itself to extractable elements in this novel such as imagery, symbol, and episode rather than to the total and continuous verbal performance. Granted, the book's susceptibility to a variety of readings—its ability to come apart into separate scenes and passages which affect us independent of the continuous narrative—is a mark of strength. But a firm grip upon the complete and total text is necessary to understand the form freedom takes in the book.

We want first to locate the problem implied by "autonomy" and "conformity," the problem of freedom, within the text, and if possible, to identify the thematic problem with a formal problem. In the broadest sense, the theme of freedom begins to engage us at the outset: Huck feels cramped and confined in his new condition as ward of Widow Douglas and closet neophyte of Miss Watson. The early episodes with Tom Sawyer add a complicating paradox: to enjoy the freedom of being "bad"—joining Tom's gang—Huck must submit himself to his adopted household and appear "respectable." With Pap's arrival the paradox is reversed; now he can enjoy his former freedom to lounge and choose his time, but the expense is a confinement even more threatening, a virtual imprisonment. The only release is escape, flight, and effacement of the identity through which both town and Pap oppress him; he can resume autonomy only by assuming "death" for his name.

In brief and general terms, such is the inner logic of the theme of freedom as we arrive at the Jackson Island episode. With Jim's appearance as a runaway slave a new and decisive development begins. We now have two runaways, and their conjunction generates the rest of the narrative, deepens the theme, and forces nuances to the surface. Jim's situation is both simpler and more urgent than Huck's. His freedom is no more or less than escape from bondage, escape to free territory. He expects there to assume what is denied him in slave society, his identity as an adult man, husband, and father. The fact that the reader is made to share this expectation with Jim, that the novel does not allow us to anticipate a reversal of hope if Jim reaches free territory, is important; as readers we are freed of normal historical ambiguities in order to accept as a powerful given the possibility of fulfilled freedom for Jim. Thus by confining the action to the area of slave society, Mark Twain compels us (at the expense of historical accuracy, perhaps) to imagine the boundary between "slave" and "free" as real and unequivocal, and to accept that boundary as the definition of Jim's plight: on the one side, enslaved; on the other, free.

Jim presents himself, then, unencumbered by the paradoxes of Huck's problem: to be free, to possess himself, to reveal a firm identity—these will be equal consequences of the single act of crossing the border. The effect of such a simplifying and unambiguous presence in the book is, first, to bring into relief the more subtle forms of denial of freedom, forms which cannot be overcome by simple geographical relocation, and second, to force Huck, once the boy commits himself to the slave, into a personal contradiction. Jim can say, as soon as he escapes from Miss Watson, "I owns myself," while Huck is still "owned" by the official values supervised by his "conscience." Once Jim's freedom becomes Huck's problem, the boy finds himself at odds with what Mark Twain called his "deformed conscience." Huck's "sound heart" may respond to Jim's desire to recover his humanity at the border, but his conscience wants to repress that response.

In light of this conflict, implicit in Huck's words at the end of Chapter 11, "They're after us!" what would constitute freedom for Huck? Clearly, getting Jim to the free states would not be enough. He would need to free himself of moral deformity before he too can say "I owns myself." Just as clearly neither issue is resolved in the novel. And the book's indecision is reflected in the criticism. The controversies regarding the "Evasion" at the Phelps farm need not be reviewed here, but it is useful to point out that the question of the ending eventually becomes a question of *form*, of judgment about the book's unity of tone and intention. Those who wish for Jim's release through a heroic act by Huck tend to feel the ending flawed, and those who wish for Huck's escape from all consciences, including a "good" abolitionist conscience, tend to accept the ending. In either case the burden of both meaning and form has fallen on the question of unity, of the wholeness of the narrative as a patterned action.

The question of unity is, however, only one of the formal problems of the book. If form is understood as the shape given to the reader's consciousness, as the unique engagement the text makes available, criticism might profit by an account of that engagement, of the reader's participation in the book's flow of words. And from this point of view the first fact we encounter is that the book is the speech of a single voice. At the outset we learn that Huck is the teller as well as actor, that we are listeners as well as witnesses of action.

Reading begins by acceding to the demands of the voice. "You don't know about me," Huck begins, and his accents identify him immediately as a recognizable type, a western or frontier speaker whose vernacular diction and syntax stand for a typology which includes dress and posture along with characteristic verbal strategies. Huck asks to be heard, as if he faced a live audience from a stage. The first edition Frontispiece has him posing with a smile for the reader, in rags and tatters, the familiar long-barrelled rifle in hand; the bow and flourish in the concluding illustration confirms the quasi-theatrical stance. Huck appears before us, at least in part, within the conventions of an oral tradition. But if Huck is by convention a storyteller, Mark Twain is at the same time a novelist, a maker of a book which asks to be read as "literature" even if its mode is in some ways preliterary.

The book is born for us, in short, under the aegis of a dual tradition, a dual vision of art. The dualities are not always in accord with each other, and some tensions between an oral and a written, especially a "high" or sophisticated tradition, account for technical problems, problems which, I mean to show, bear on the theme of freedom. The book is marked by an uneasy accommodation between seriously differing modes of literary art. Before detailing some of these, it is worth commenting that the pressure to fuse a vernacular verbal style and its methods of narrative with an accepted form of "literature"—a book-length fiction—characterized all of Mark Twain's mature work. As Justin Kaplan has made clear, Clemens' career contained many unresolved tensions and ambivalences, and none had more consequence for his work than his simultaneous though uneven commitment to two kinds of audience. On the one hand he saw himself as popular spokesman for a vast, nonliterary readership. "My audience is dumb," he wrote: "it has no voice in print." He claimed "the Belly and the Members" as his people, not the "thin top crust of humanity," and insisted, not without defensiveness, that it was unfair to judge his work by "the cultivated-class standard." At the same time that standard appealed to him, and even if his paranoia before it represented social as well as literary anxieties, he did bow toward the established conception of "literature" held by readers of the *Atlantic Monthly*. "*It* is the only audience that I sit down before in complete serenity," he confessed. Writing books which resemble novels is one capitulation to that audience, while marketing his books through the subscription system kept him in touch with his large "dumb" audience.

Even as an "author," however, Mark Twain clung to his root notion of literary art as a performance by a speaking character, usually a nonliterary figure with a calculatedly vernacular voice. Such a figure—Simon Wheeler in "Jumping Frog" is a good instance—characteristically deflates expectations and values associated with the "cultivated-class standard." But he does so on behalf of a standard of "common sense," of common and humble humanity. Rather than pose one class standard against another, the vernacular tradition in American humor offers a universal standard, open to all, skeptical of hierarchies, self-evident in its truths. Through a fusion of vernacular values with "literature," Mark Twain strived to achieve exactly such a universal, classless appeal. "I can't stand George Eliot, & Hawthorne & those people," he wrote to Howells in 1885; their "labored & tedious analyses of feeling & motives" were suspiciously aristocratic. Instead he preferred Howells's own *Indian Summer*: "It is a beautiful story, & makes a body laugh all the time, & cry inside." This describes just the kind of response he wished from his own readers: direct and uncomplicated and moving.

What better means did he have toward this end than to create vernacular characters, unencumbered by analysis or excessive introspection, whose universality was obvious to every reader? Matching his manner of creation to his self-conception as a popular writer, Clemens seemed always more comfortable inventing such characters than filling out complete books or imagining narrative actions. He might even be better considered a maker of figures, like Huck and Tom and Jim, and "Mark Twain," who populate a general fictional realm unconfined by specific verbal contexts than a maker of particular books. The tendency of his characters to live in the mind apart from their texts is a revealing feature of Clemens' talent.

But our aim is to hold the characters fast within their verbal settings. Transforming an oral art to a written one presented Mark Twain with difficulties apparent in almost all his long narratives. Consider the matter of filling out a book that wants to be the "adventures" of a vernacular voice. One difficulty is simply how to bring such a book to a close. The ending of *Huckleberry Finn* does, to be sure, bring the action to a point of general resolution: Jim is freed, masks are stripped away, misunderstandings cleared up, some sort of order restored. But the loose plot which calls for resolution has been kept out of sight during much of the narrative, and we cannot avoid feeling that the plain duration of the book has depended more upon the arbitrary postponement of any event (such as the recapture of Jim) which might end things too soon than upon an inner logic of plot. The only conclusive ending is the drop of the curtain, the final words, "The End. Yours Truly, Huck Finn," and silence. The performance of Huck's voice does not so much complete itself as exhaust itself.

To begin with, then, the problem of the ending is a technical problem of *an* ending. The source of the problem is the attempt to accommodate the opening convention of a vernacular storyteller, whose story simply unwinds, to the imperatives of a book-length written narrative. But the ending is a relatively minor matter. Of more consequence are the pressures upon the narrative voice through the entire course of its performance. An enormous burden is placed upon Huck, who must not only tell the story but enact it as the leading player. My discussion will focus on this double role, will attempt to assess Huck's role as the verbalizer of the narrative in order to assess his role as a character within the narrative. What freedom means in the book, and what form freedom takes, cannot be understood at all without such assessments.

What part of Huck's life in the book derives from the inner necessities of his "character," and what part derives from the outer necessities of his role as speaking voice? Huck has precisely the split identity this question implies. The consequent tensions within the narrative have been obscured in criticism by the great attention given to "identity" as a theme. The pervasive deployment of disguises, verbal and sartorial, through which Huck extricates himself from tight spots alerts the reader to the significance of hidden and revealed identities. When Huck is taken for Tom Sawyer in Chapter 32, he accepts the name with relief (it saves him the trouble of having to invent yet another name), "for it was like being born again, I was so glad to find out who I was." The line follows one of Huck's meditations on death, and some critics have been moved to discover a pattern of death and rebirth throughout, a pattern in which Huck's true name finds protection in the "death" of assumed identities. The motif is familiar in oral literature (see the excised "Raftsmen" passage), and the fact that Huck is legally dead through most of the book adds suggestive weight. At least as long as Pap lives, and as long as Huck is associated with Jim's escape, it seems impossible for the boy to own up to his true identity. The motif of disguise thus seems to harbor a dilemma directly related to the question of freedom: is it possible for Huck to both show and be his true self? To show himself as a runaway who has faked his own death and is aiding an escaped slave would invite disaster. This is a given of the narrative: to be himself Huck must hide himself.

What are the sources of this commanding paradox? Social reality, for one: Miss Watson, Pap, slavery, general avariciousness, all constitute an environment of treachery. Some critics argue too that the need to hide derives from deep psychic needs, from the extreme vulnerability expressed in Huck's character, especially his recurrent feelings of guilt. In this view colored by psychoanalytic rhetoric, Huck's disguises represent a shrewd reality principle which acts to protect the very shaky equilibrium of his inner life, the life of a "lost" boy who prefers the pleasure of a precivilized and precharacterological state of nature. This is a compelling and widely held view of Huck. "You feel mighty free and easy and comfortable on a raft." Pleasurable drift and unruffled harmony seem the conditions Huck demands for "free and easy" selfhood.

The issue is subtle and difficult. Do Huck's traits derive in fact from an inner life at odds with a social necessity, or from, I want to add, imperatives of his role as narrator? Obviously we need not make an either/or choice. But the second alternative has been so little present in criticism it is worth considering at some length. The crux of the matter is whether Huck presents a consistent character, whether a sentient inner life is always present. Some critics have suggested not. Richard Poirier finds that after his reversal of attitude toward Jim in Chapter 15 (the "trash" episode) and the defeat of his "white" conscience in Chapter 16, Huck gradually disappears as an active agent in the narrative. Unable to continue the developing consciousness implicit in these scenes, Poirier argues, Mark Twain became absorbed in sheer "social panorama," to which Huck is a more or less passive witness. Henry Nash Smith makes a similar point. After losing Cairo in the fog, and losing the raft in Chapter 16, Mark Twain set aside the manuscript, and when he resumed several years later, he "now launched into a satiric description of the society of the prewar South." Huck becomes Mark Twain's satiric mask, which prevents him, Smith argues, from developing in his own right.

These are promising hints regarding Huck's status as a fictional character. Of course any criticism which charges Mark Twain with failing to continue a developing consciousness assumes such a development is a hallmark of fictional character. It might be countered that such a standard is inappropriate to this book, as Clemens himself may have suggested in his attack on the "cultivated-class standard," or that Huck's so-called disappearance in the middle section is actually another disguise, profoundly enforced by an increasingly hostile setting. His retreat, then, after the Grangerford episode, might be consistent with what had already developed as his character.

Even to begin to discuss this issue we need to understand what we mean by a "fictional character." Our expectations derive, in brief, from the novelistic tradition, in which character and action have a coextensive identity. Henry James insisted in "The Art of Fiction" (consider the differences implied by the title of Mark Twain's comparable essay, "How to Tell a Story") upon the inseparability of character and action by describing the novel as "a living thing, all one and continuous, like any other organism." "What is character," he wrote, "but the determination of incident? What is incident but the illustration of character?" The reciprocity of character and action implies, moreover, a process, a twofold development in which character fulfills itself just as it reveals itself to the reader. By development we expect a filling out, a discovery of possibilities and limitations. We also expect a certain degree of self-reflectiveness in character to register what is happening internally.

We need not remind ourselves that *Huckleberry Finn* is not a Jamesian novel. But it is important to know what sort of novel it is, to know what to expect of Huck as a character. What happens to Huck in the course of the narrative? Is he a changed being at the end from what he was at the beginning? In the opening scene Huck chafes at the "dismal regular and decent" routine of Widow Douglas, says he can't stand it "no longer," and "lights out" to his old rags and hogshead and "was free and satisfied." He returns only to qualify for Tom's gang. At the end of the book he again "lights out," this time for "howling adventures amongst the Injuns, over in the Territory." Has anything changed? The final words rejecting civilization, this time Aunt Sally's, do seem to register a difference: "I been there before." These are precious words for the reader; they confirm what he has discovered about civilization. But do they mean the same thing to Huck?

The difference we want to feel between the two rejections of civilization which frame the book parallels the indisputable difference between the two instances when Huck decides to go to hell rather than obey moral conscience. In Chapter 1, Miss Watson tries to frighten the child into sitting up straight by preaching about the bad place and what is in store for boys who don't behave. Huck retorts that he wishes he were there; if Miss Watson is heading for heaven, he would rather not try for it. In Chapter 31, in Huck's famous struggle with his conscience, this comedy of inverted values recurs, but with much expanded significance. In the first instance the preference for hell is expressed in a raffish, offhanded manner, it is a joke, not a serious commitment. In Chapter 31, in a much analyzed passage, we witness a genuine choice, preceded by an inward struggle. The language, first of self-condemnation ("here was the plain hand of Providence slapping me in the face"), then of self-reproach ("and he was so grateful, and said I was the best friend old Jim ever had in the world, and the *only* one he's got now"), externalizes the opposite perspectives of sound heart and deformed conscience. The feat of language itself convinces us that Huck has now earned a meaningful damnation on behalf of his friendship with Jim. This episode has a structure of modulated feeling entirely missing in the first case. Moreover the much deeper implications for Huck's freedom in the second instance are affected by the location of the moment in the narrative, after the exposure of greed, corruption, hypocrisy, and violence in the river society. If the Grangerfords and all the others name heaven as their goal, then hell is by far a better aspiration. Huck's decisive words, "All right, then, I'll *go* to hell," are a release for the reader, for he too has been in "a close place." The line affirms Huck's fundamental rightness.

In short, the deepened implications of "I'll go to hell" and "I been there before," implications which have led critics to impute to Huck a self-generated liberation from moral deformity, arise from the context of narrative action. But does Huck actually catch the same implications? Does he know and understand exactly what he is saying? Of course we might argue that the implications are finally comic precisely because Huck does not understand them. But if this is the case, can we also say that he is a conscious character?

If we cannot believe that Huck shows himself just at the moment when we most approve of his words, then we necessarily claim we are superior to him. We fix him in an ironic relation to his own words: he says more than he knows. But then again, does he not by nature *feel* rather than think? If we say so, if we excuse him from an intellectual act we perform, then are we not exploiting our sense of superiority and condescending toward him? Of course Huck is clearly mindful of the seriousness of his impasse, that he is deciding "forever, betwixt two things." Even earlier in the narrative, however, Huck had settled moral dilemmas by choosing what to him is the easiest, most comfortable course; we approve his choices, and smile at his handy rationalizations (some of which he learns from Pap). A similar pattern finally emerges in Chapter 31; after his "awful thoughts, and awful words" about hell, he "shoved the whole thing out of my head; and said I would take up wickedness again, which was in my line, being brung up to it." A beautiful line; but beautiful because of its perfect ironic tone. Is Huck aware of the irony? Has he learned what we have learned as witnesses, overhearers of his conflict? Can we be sure, here or at the end of the book, that we are not extrapolating from our own lessons in expecting Huck to share our recognitions?

In at least one episode Huck does achieve an unequivocal self-awareness, and the scene is the measure of Huck's behavior elsewhere in the book. I refer to the colloquy with Jim that concludes Chapter 15, after Huck had played his joke on Jim during the fog. The scene is unusual in the book, in part because of its realized tension between Huck and Jim, in part because of the completely unfettered, "free" and honest speech by Jim ("What do dey stan' for? I's gwyne to tell you. . . . Dat truck dah is *trash*; en trash is what people is dat puts dirt on de head er dey fren's en makes 'em ashamed"). Huck is forced by the speech to reckon with Jim as a person who has developed specific human expectations regarding Huck. By reckoning with such expectations Huck must reckon with, must confront himself, as a social being whose acts make a difference. He experiences himself through the sense compelled by Jim's speech of how another person experiences him. Huck once more wins our approval, but more important, he wins a self-conception which issues into an action—his apology "to a nigger."

The implications of a deepening human relation between Huck and Jim fail to materialize in the book; they have no other dramatic conflicts of this sort. But perhaps one confrontation is sufficient; perhaps the implications are buried in order to return in Huck's comparably "free" speech in Chapter 31, which recalls the circumstances of his friendship with Jim on the raft. It is curious, however, in light of the growing consciousness of these moments of mutual perception and self-perception, that the book, filled as it is with so many characters, is so barren of human relationships. The superficial quality of how people deal with each other (and themselves) is, of course, a deliberate element in Mark Twain's portrait of river society. It is also true that in Huck's experience people usually represent problems rather than possibilities, objects rather than subjects. His disguises are manipulative; he usually plays the role of the victimized orphan boy in order to exact enough sympathy to permit an escape. His many encounters leave him relatively untouched by memory (with a few notable exceptions); threads of meaning do not appear between episodes. Pap, Miss Watson, Tom, cannot be said to exist for Huck as subjectivities in their own right: if Tom were here he would do this or that, Miss Watson is a nuisance, Pap is a threat.

The scarcity of complicating relations, of *dramatic* encounters, does in fact qualify the reader's relation to Huck. To repeat what I propose is the critical issue at stake, we want to learn if these features of the narrative follow from Huck's "character," the demanding needs of his inner being, or if they in some way reflect the double role he plays, as a narrator who tells a story and a character who has a story. We need to look more closely at Huck's technical and dramatic roles.

The absence of serious complications helps account for the book's universal appeal. Compared to the "analytic" works Mark Twain condemned, *Huckleberry Finn* seems "easy" reading. Mark Twain could rely upon a readership already trained to recognize and "read" a comic vernacular speaker, to place him within its verbal universe; Huck appears within the guise of local color conventions (dialect, regional dress, essential "goodness" of heart). As a storyteller he intervenes very little between the events and the reader; he rarely projects a mind that calls attention to itself apart from the immediate experiences it records. Verbally, Huck displays a prepositional exactness in defining himself in space, but more or less imprecision in regard to time; his language is keyed more to geography than to the clock—as befits a mind with little active memory. The intervals between episodes, which themselves have fairly concrete temporal structures, are filled usually with drift: "So we would put in the day, lazying around, listening to the stillness." The mythic force of many separate passages in the book arises from the absence of an obtruding sense of historical time. In the drift, one thing follows another without more relation than sequence: "Two or three days and nights went by"; "Soon as it was night"; "One morning."

But if sequential time matters little in the narrative structure, "timing," the arch device of the real storyteller, does. In "How to Tell a Story" Mark Twain speaks of the importance of a studied nonchalance, and appearance of rambling purposelessness, and of the strategic pause. The storyteller holds his listener in a relation which has a strict temporal order of its own. Within that order, generated by the verbal posture of casualness, the placement or the withholding of details is of first importance. Thus the comic story tends to appear within longer narratives as a set piece, such as Huck's account of the Grangerford household, or his colloquy with Jim about "Sollermun." Within these pieces, Huck's role follows what Clemens called "the first virtue of a comedian"—to "do humorous things with grave decorum and without seeming to know they are funny." Grave decorum and seeming humorlessness well describe Huck's appearance. But is he so guileful as to dissemble his appearance for the reader? Who is the controlling comedian of the book, Huck or Mark Twain? Is humorlessness, the dead pan, Huck's trick on us, or Mark Twain's? Is grave decorum a feature of Huck's own character, or of Mark Twain's deployed mask?

We need to consider dead pan, not only as a mode operative in specific passages, but as the dominant mode of the entire narrative, even when it does not lead to a punch line or reversal. The mode is based on a form of trickery, of saying less than one means. As such it can be taken as a form of insincerity, benign though it may be. "I never seen anybody but lied, one time or another," says Huck in the fifth sentence of the book. The comment disarms in several ways. It evokes a village world where the highest premium is placed upon "telling the truth." To admit that the official value of truth telling is often violated by everyone, including Miss Watson and Widow Douglas, requires either the courage of an iconoclast, which Huck is not, or a personal station outside the official values. As a vernacular character, Huck is free to speak this way; his manner is not aggressive or muckraking, but grave, decorous, and deadpan. (Contrast, for example, the tone of Colonel Sherburn's speech). At the same time, the offhanded, flat manner of the admission hides the fact that the statement is of more than passing importance in the book. Lying, indeed, is a major and complex theme. The reader will eventually recognize instance after instance of lies passing as truths, deceptions sanctioned by the social order. Moreover, liars often believe their own lies, are unable to distinguish truth from appearance. On a level of considerable abstraction, the book offers as a basic deception the notion that Jim is "worth" $800, or that money can be traded for human value. Tom seems to think so when he pays Jim forty dollars "for being prisoner for us so patient"; Jim's being "pleased most to death" is one of the jarring notes in the Phelps conclusion. Another variation of the theme belongs to the Duke and the King, perhaps the supreme liars of the book. Cynicism liberates them to purvey appearance as truth without qualms. For this reason they are among the abstractly "free" characters; without thoughts of heaven, without conscience, they menace not only the social order but the fragile harmony of the raft. They represent an ultimate freedom in which the "other" is entirely an object, a freedom Huck ostensibly has overcome in himself after his elaborate lie to Jim after the fog in Chapter 15.

Dead pan exists in a complex relation to lies. It too is a falsehood, a manipulated appearance. But it is a lie in the service of truth or "reality," an honest lie whose effect as humor is based on our ultimate recognition of its falseness. As James Cox writes of the tall tale—a variant of dead pan—it "is true in that it is the only lie in a world of lies which reveals itself to be a lie." Commonly the procedure is to dramatize in the comic voice an apparently unrecognized discrepancy between what is perceived (the awful gimcrackery of the Grangerford sitting room) and what is felt (Huck's sentimental approval). The reader is allowed to accept the feelings as provisionally his own, only to be thwarted by the details which normally arouse a contrary response; he is released from the false feelings by recognizing their cause to be ludicrously inadequate. The reader is initially taken in by Huck's manner so that he may, so to speak, be saved from Huck's foolish approval.

But does Huck really approve? If so, he is indeed a fool, and we laugh at him as well as the complacent Grangerfords. In the convention of dead pan the teller is only apparently a fool. We permit him to practice deception on us because in the end some absurdity will be exposed to the light of universal common sense; we will gain an advantage over the world. The teller's manner is a mask which steadily, deliberately, misleads us, until at the critical moment the mask falls. Behind the mask we might expect to find the real Huck, sharing our laughter, perhaps laughing at us for being momentarily taken in. The revealed comedian becomes at least our equal. But is this model at work here? Again we face Huck's paradoxical situation, as teller and as character. If we say that Huck's manner is a deliberate guise on his part, what happens to his gravity, his solemnity, his innocence, which we have normally taken as traits of character? Apart from depriving, or freeing, him of these elements of personality, such a reading would seriously upset the balance established between reader and narrative voice established at the outset. The voice presents itself as genuinely literal-minded; it presents itself as inferior in its own mind to the civilization of Widow Douglas and Tom Sawyer. We quickly make the judgment Huck seems unable to make for himself, that literal-mindedness is notably superior to the respectable lies of the town. The obvious superiority of Huck's frankness frees the reader from the deceptions of a world where respectability is the qualification for membership in a gang of robbers. To assign duplicity to Huck (by claiming he knows more than he is saying) would disturb this effect. To serve as our liberator Huck must remain ignorant and solemn. He must remain so in order to serve as Mark Twain's comic mask. In short, Mark Twain may have removed himself from the frame of the book, as the guileful, controlling voice, but the control remains in force, internalized and sublimated. The outside speaker who in earlier versions of vernacular presentation appeared, as in the Sut Lovingood stories, as a colloquist, now hides in the mask, a secret character in the book.

Dead pan predominates, and with it, Mark Twain's use of Huck's surface manner to reach the reader on a level of common values. But Huck's speech periodically escapes studied solemnity to become either lyrical, as in the sunrise passage which opens Chapter 19, or dramatic, as when he faces up to himself after Jim's "trash" speech. Such moments usually occur after actions which begin within the comic mode. Dead pan in part neutralizes the world, holds it at bay, seems to remove the threat of harm. But genuine harm frequently springs up to threaten the comic mode itself. One of many instances occurs in Chapter 18; the deadpan technique exposes Buck's explanation of the feud as absurd (the scene parallels the exposure of Tom's absurdities in trying to enforce an oath upon his fellow robbers in chapter 2). Before long the slaughter begins and we hear "Kill them, kill them!" The sunrise passage and the idyllic account of the raft follow in Chapter 19. Huck's lyric-dramatic voice seems to require a violation of his surface deadpan manner for release. The book alternates between a voice given over to deadpan trickery and narrative, and undisguised, direct feeling. The second voice generates needs for dramatic realization the author does not accommodate. Mark Twain's own needs, perhaps for some revenge against Southern river society, seemed to require a Huck Finn who is ignorant, half-deformed, and permanently humorless. To put the case strongly, we might say that Huck's character is stunted by his creator's need for him to serve as a technical device. The same devices of irony which liberate the reader by instructing him about civilization and human nature also repress Huck by using him; they prevent his coming into his own.

Huck's freedom, I want finally to argue, requires that he achieve a conscious moral identity. Huck cannot be free in this sense unless Mark Twain permits him a credible and articulate inner being, with dramatic opportunities to realize his self. Of course this is to make perhaps impossible and therefore inappropriate demands upon this novel. But I think Mark Twain came close enough to such a realization for us to judge the book by its on best moments. Consider, for example, the raft, often taken as the symbol of freedom. The ethic of the raft is stated eloquently: "You feel mighty free and easy and comfortable on a raft." Yes; but this mood is possible because Huck had earlier humbled himself before Jim and decided to give up the pleasure of playing tricks. The raft has a tacit code, what we might call its own conscience. When the Duke and King arrive, that code bends to accommodate the rascals, for, as Huck tells himself as justification for not letting on to Jim that the men are frauds, "what you want, above all things, on a raft, is for everybody to be satisfied, and feel right and kind towards the others . . . . it's the best way; then you don't have no quarrels, and don't get into no trouble." "Free and easy" of the first passage has become "satisfied" and "no quarrels . . . no trouble." The difference is subtle but crucial. The raft is no longer free. Dissembling has returned. Huck decides in the name of "peace in the family" not to share with Jim his insights into the intruders: "it warn't no use to tell Jim." No one but the wary reader recognizes that trickery and deception have returned for the sake of the comedy Mark Twain can wring from Jim's ignorant wisdom about kings. True, Jim plays a pastoral role in his discussions about royalty with Huck, but his stature is reduced. Long before the Phelps episode he is required to submit to being tied up and left alone in the wigwam, or to donning "King Lear's outfit" to play a "Sick Arab." No one protests, and "Jim was satisfied."

The raft cannot defend itself against imposture. In the end imposture itself seems the only resort for Huck and Jim. From this point of view the elaborate theatricals at the Phelps farm seem an appropriate conclusion: how else might the two fugitives be returned to a possible world without real harm, without damaging the comic expectations of the novel? But what then can we say about freedom? Are we to judge the vulnerability of the raft, the necessity of a concluding "Evasion" (necessary to have any conclusion at all), to mean that by *its nature* the difficult freedom of owning oneself is impossible? Are we too hard with this book to blame it for failing to sustain the self-consciousness and process of self-discovery implicit in several scenes? Or more to the point, is that failure part of Mark Twain's design, or a result of technical limitations? Does the book project a fully realized vision, or is the vision blocked by the author's inability to sustain a novelistic development? These questions characterize the critic's dilemma in assessing the book.

Of course a vision and the verbal means of its realization and execution are virtually inseparable. Mark Twain saw the world the best he was able to, given his special verbal resources. My argument has meant to say that the formal problems which proceed from the initial conception of a book-length narrative in a mainly deadpan vernacular voice themselves enforce a certain vision. Mark Twain's work as a whole suggests that he seriously doubted the possibilities of personal freedom within a social setting. He seems to have taken freedom as true only when absolute and abstract, outside time. The imagery of drift in this novel is invested with such longing perhaps because it represents a condition already lost and insubstantial the moment it is imagined. The other side of the image reveals the fully invulnerable trickster, whose cynicism releases him from the control of any conscience. The dream voyages and mysterious strangers which obsessed Mark Twain's later years are anticipated in *Huckleberry Finn*.

The book is finally more persuasive as a document of enslavement, of the variety of imprisonments within verbal styles and fictions than as a testimony to freedom. Of course its negativity implies an ideal. I would like to identify that ideal with the "free" speech of Huck and Jim at the moments of engagement. I have tried to explain why such speech breaks out so rarely, why moral identity was so difficult to attain given the technical resources of the book. But we should recognize that the limits placed upon Huck's character are also forceful imperatives from the society within which Mark Twain portrays him. Moral character requires that social roles be credible to young people about to assume them. The society rendered in *Huckleberry Finn* deprives all roles of credibility when viewed from a literal-minded vernacular perspective. Rationalization and improvisation have convincing survival value, and virtuosity of disguise earns our admiration. Pap, after all, did bequeath a fatherly heritage by teaching Huck how to cheat and get away with no more than a bruised conscience. Perhaps the book's Americanness is most profoundly revealed in this heritage of eluding fixed definitions, in the corrosive decreation of established roles. Jim's presence reminds us, however, of the cost history has exacted from a society which drives its children to negativity. The cost is charged most heavily against Huck; he pays with his chance to grow up.

THE PARADOX OF LIBERATION IN *HUCKLEBERRY FINN*

NEIL SCHMITZ

The perennial dispute over the ending of the *Adventures of Huckleberry Finn*, whether Mark Twain's ingenious resolution possesses a "formal aptness," as Lionel Trilling reads it, or is a "failure of nerve," as Leo Marx would have it, regularly invokes that crucial term *freedom*. It is, as Marx so capably argued, what the book is about, but his own judgment that freedom in *Huckleberry Finn* "specifically means freedom from society and its imperatives,"[1] is far from satisfactory, if not simplistic, and the problem remains. Twain was rarely, if ever, a successful philosopher in his fiction. The aphorism was his mode of analysis and Pudd'nhead Wilson, an embittered crank, his notion of a radical theoretician. In *Huckleberry Finn*, where Twain restricts his tortured vision of the world to the consciousness of an urchin, this limitation is something of a dangerous virtue. Those large, potent abstractions—*freedom, civilization, morality*—are not dealt with conceptually, but rather issue their significance through the wrenching of Huck's psyche, through muted cries of pain. There is no Grand Inquisitor passage in the novel. Colonel Sherburn is the closest Twain comes to a *raissoneur*. We are instead made to feel the achievement and loss of freedom in the sensuous context of tight collars and loose rags, floating rafts and cramped sheds. Yet the forces engendering the calamities which pass before Huck's ingenuous gaze drag with them perplexing problems, the darkness of Twain's thought. That is the bewitching thing about *Huckleberry Finn*: it arouses such large and difficult ideas, and then gives us only feelings about those ideas. What Marx demanded some fifteen years ago was an ending to the novel that would elucidate those contorted lines of thought, a conclusion. Unfortunately we do not have it, but we do have, amid all the confusion and dead-ends, strokes of the imagination that cut, however clumsily, very near the bone of our experience.

"Our philosophical tradition," Hannah Arendt writes in *Between Past and Future*, "is almost unanimous in holding that freedom begins where men have left the realm of political life inhabited by the many, and that it is not experienced in association with others but in intercourse with one's self."[2] She then proceeds to argue the contrary: that the only meaningful freedom men can possess must be won in the sociopolitical realm. The notion that men can constitute an impregnable inner freedom within the self simply by taking themselves out of the social world, she argues, is essentially illusory, an escape from the responsibilities of action. Mrs. Arendt's critique of those who would separate freedom from politics, placing it either in the withdrawn self or in a mythicized state of nature, is useful to keep in mind when discussing the nature of freedom in *Huckleberry Finn*, if only because it makes us re-examine the idyllic life established on the river, that "free zone" cutting through the murderous world of politics. What student of the novel does not know that the Shore signifies constraint and the River freedom, or that the "free and easy" life on the raft affirms the sacred practice of brotherhood, specifically Huck's celebrated leap over the color bar? The word keeps bubbling up, often simply serving as a convenient heading for all those apolitical things that Huck and Jim desire. Yet Twain's understanding of what constitutes freedom in his book is largely intuitive, not systematic, and consequently does not fit into the libertarian categories that have been painstakingly constructed to hold it. Indeed, there is a kind of pathos in that criticism which neatly irons out all the contradictions in *Huckleberry Finn*, turning that sprawling, ambivalent narrative into a finely contrived Austenian novel. This approach constrains the most sensitive of Twain's critics. Huck "knows how he feels about Jim, but he also knows what he is expected to do about Jim. This division within his mind corresponds to the division of the novel's moral terrain into the areas represented by the raft on the one hand and society on the other."[3] In short, there is a shared concept of freedom that Huck and Jim struggle to obtain, "their code," and a common understanding of the constrictive rules that society inflicts on its members. The novel's "moral terrain" is accordingly partitioned into precise districts. Only those who do not know the river with its hidden snags and treacherous undercurrents, Twain wrote in *Life on the Mississippi*, can see poetic harmonies in its devious flow.

Clearly Huck and Jim have different ideas of where they want to go and what their flight means, points of view that come increasingly into conflict in the first part of the novel. Faced with a symbolic *point d' appui* as Cairo loomed in his imagination, Twain had to deal with that paradox and found himself staring into the abyss of the Reconstruction. The question is not Jim's freedom per se, but whether he will seize it or be given it, and then, most horrifying of all—what is to be done with him in either case, this emancipated, alien black man? In these proceedings Huck's intentions are finally, though grudgingly, good, but Jim as citizen and dutiful breadwinner is not the Jim who primarily interests him. It is Jim as *magus*, uncomplicated and sensuous, immediate in his feelings, the dark tutor who helps unlock the "sound heart" imprisoned in Huck's breast, who is the cherished soulmate. At the very outset, once Jackson's Island is left behind, the slave and the child are journeying in different directions—Huck within to reassert his instinctual self, Jim outward into the world, toward Cairo and purposeful social activity. It was Twain's recognition of this impending crises, I feel, that led him to abandon the novel in 1876, leaving Huck and Jim safely neutralized at the bottom of the Mississippi.

The freedom Huck strives to attain is his right to be a child, not an impertinent manikin like Tom Sawyer, but the unregenerate poetic child alive in his body and sensitive to the mystery of being in the world. Miss Watson correctly perceives the subversive nature of this desire, and she moves to suppress it with the conventional weaponry of dutiful elders: grisly textbooks, uncomfortable chairs, "smothery" clothes, and incomprehensible lessons pounded home from a dogmatic religiosity. Twain knew in what small measures and with what anxious solicitude the spirit of a child is curbed. The seductive powers of clean sheets and regular hours keep Tom Sawyer's prankish rebellion in bounds, and for a time in *Huckleberry Finn* almost snare Huck: "So the longer I went to school the easier it got to be. I was getting sort of used to the widow's ways, too, and they warn't so raspy on me" (p. 17).[4] But the "old thing" remains, those rasping arbitrary forms into which the child squeezes his experience. Early in the novel, having been buttoned, buckled, and combed, Huck is driven to the table at the designated time. The dinner plate with its cut and segregated food appalls him. He prefers stew, the meal where "things get mixed up, and the juice kind of swaps around, and the things go better" (p. 7). It is consciousness soaked in the flesh, the self as a fluent whole, that Huck seeks to sustain, and the stakes in that struggle, as Twain represents them, are indeed high. Huck's refusal to become "respectable," to bend his body and then his mind, enables him to keep operative the lucid stare that plumbs hypocrisies and pierces shams. It preserves him from the fate of young Buck Grangerford, who has lost that battle. "Do you like to comb up, Sundays," Huck is asked, "and all that kind of foolishness? You bet I don't, but ma she makes me. Confound these ole britches, I reckon I'd better put 'em on, but I'd ruther not, it's so warm" (p. 81). Buck's acquiescence to that "foolishness" characterizes all the young Grangerfords. Each morning they consecrate themselves to "sir, and Madam," lifting cocktails to their father's rigid, maniacal face and pledging their filial "duty." The continuance of the feud, which ultimately consumes Buck, depends on this ritualistic obeisance, this tacit acceptance of parental madness. "I don't like that shooting from behind a bush," the Colonel reprimands Buck. "Why didn't you step into the road, my boy?" (p. 88). The enemy is sharply focused here. It is the cannibalistic parent or the surrogate Miss Watson "pecking at you all the time" (p. 24). The murderous look Pap Finn casts on Huck is at least undisguised.

Against his powerful elders the child seems to have as his only defense the instinct to be "lazy and jolly," which in *Huckleberry Finn* always figures as a kind of sanctifying grace. Tom Sawyer's antisocial fantasies, acted out in savage games, are "lies," what Huck scornfully calls "just pretending," and have finally all the "marks of a Sunday school" (p. 17). Huck's resistance to oppressive authority always begins at his skin. He chooses "rags and dirt," his tobacco, the good feel of artful "cussing," knowing that they mean an overt repudiation of Miss Watson's meticulous world. There is no posturing or bookish declamation in Huck's rebellion, no desire for the power of revenge. The substance of his challenge is his unwashed face and tattered shirt, that placid concern he manifests for the comfort of his body. Feeling "free and easy" is what he wants, and it is only on the river, cut off from the world of combs and clocks, hard chairs and tight clothes, that he can perfect this liberation. Only there does life become good to possess. When he returns to the raft after the Grangerford catastrophe, Buck's murdered face burning in his memory, his reclamation begins with a feast: "I hadn't had a bite to eat since yesterday; so Jim he got out some corn dodgers and buttermilk, and pork and cabbage, and greens—there ain't nothing in the world so good, when it's cooked right—and whilst I eat my supper we talked and had a good time" (p. 95). The fellowship that follows the feast is also "cooked" in natural juices: the raft is abandoned to the current, Huck and Jim are "always naked, day and night" (p. 97). Huck's description of this idyllic interlude is purely sensuous, redolent with smells and sounds, with the rapture of "listening to the stillness" (p. 96). The mythic imagination flourishes once more: "We used to watch the stars that fell, too, and see them streak down. Jim allowed they'd got spoiled and was hove out of the nest" (p. 97).

What lies coiled in the child is the aboriginal self, an effortless beauty that mocks the repressed, fiercely civilized adult. "This is the grace for which every society longs, irrespective of its beliefs, its political regime, its level of civilization," Claude Lévi-Strauss writes at the end of *Tristes Tropiques*. "It stands, in every case, for leisure, and recreation, and freedom, and peace of body and mind. On this opportunity, this chance of for once detaching oneself from the implacable process, life itself depends."[5] Surely this is the vision Twain glimpsed in Huck's experience, Twain who responded to that "implacable process" with furious anguish all his life. Children were the only savages he knew. Twain rendered Huck "exactly" from his recollection of Tom Blankenship, the only "really independent person" in Hannibal. Ignorant and unwashed, free of parental supervision, Blankenship was "continuously happy" in this wild, unruly state of existence. Both in his fiction and on tour as a performer, Twain constantly impersonated the figure of Blankenship-Huck, the bad boy who fascinates the beseiged children around him. There he was in all his colorful extravagance, speaking to staid frock-coated, tightly corseted audiences about the virtue of his vices, those cherished "bad habits" of drinking whisky, smoking cigars, and sleeping late. Then, as now, Twain's audience responded warmly to this pose, remembering their own childish insight into the fraudulence of the great world—in sum, the whole dimly understood drama of their preadolescence. It was the bad boy metamorphosed into the cantankerous uncle drawling blasphemies who reminded them of what they had lost and who brought to life again the villains of childhood, the nay-saying parent and authoritarian teacher. But in *Huckleberry Finn* this was only part of the drama.

What the Brazilian Indian is for Lévi-Strauss, the preceptor of "what our species has been and still is, beyond thought and beneath society,"[6] Jim in his blackness is for Twain, the dark guide who welcomes Huck back to the raft, whose presence relieves him of an aimless loneliness. On Jackson's Island Jim assumes almost immediately the role of interpreter. He understands the natural world, ciphers a certain flight of "little birds," takes Huck literally out of the rain, gives him a short course in reading signs, and in general sharpens Huck's sense of being in the woods, which, given the baneful moons and ominous snakeskins, is not all holiday loveliness. Daniel G. Hoffman has explored this aspect of Jim at great length in *Form and Fable in American Fiction*, suggesting that these powers enhance Jim's stature in the novel and endow him with "moral energy." Indeed this is the Jim who gains Huck's loving admiration: "Jim knowed all kinds of signs. He said he knowed most everything" (p. 41). It is a relationship that would seem to fit easily into a familiar pattern. Yet Jim is unlike Queequeg and Chingachgook, or any of that legion of dusky mates in nineteenth-century American fiction, not in what he has to give to his white companion, but in what he wants. For Huck the raft is the symbolic center of his flight, the attained end of his quest, but for Jim it is at first a precarious transport and then a prison. He is an escaped slave struggling for his life under nearly impossible conditions, a reality that haunted Twain.

In the *Autobiography* Twain's remembrance of the wild free life, the "unrestricted liberty" of Tom Blankenship, who served as a model for Huck, is clouded by his memory of the slaves. Were they happy, he wonders between lyrical passages on "the taste of maple sap" and "the look of green apples and peaches and pears on the trees," or were they mistreated?[7] He tries to remember whether there was a slave market in the area of Hannibal and recollects seeing Negroes in chains. Similarly Huck senses in Jim that obstinate dark presence, that lurking omnipresent fact. Jim may well serve him as *shaman*, as a brotherly father figure, but there is also that hidden side, the "nigger you can't learn to argue" (p. 67), the imponderable consciousness of the black man. "We were comrades," Twain wrote of his boyhood black friends, "and yet not comrades; color and condition interposed a subtle line which both parties were conscious of and which rendered complete fusion impossible."[8] Twain understood Huck's relish of the simple sensations and saw clearly enough how the freedom to feel comprehended the freedom to think and act, but he had, like any white man, only a glancing sense of Jim's psyche. Negroes *did* choose not to endure. Every Southerner knew that genial Uncle Dan'ls, marvelous story tellers, were capable of running away to die miserably in the swamps. What happened when the slave stood up, as Jim does on Jackson's Island, and declared, "I owns myself, en I's wuth eight hund'd dollars" (p. 42)? That determination to run, to break from the fixed point of being Miss Watson's "big nigger," imposes a psychical baptism on Jim, the taking of his life and his value into his own hands. It also imposes on Twain, the artist, difficult but unavoidable obligations—Jim's waking to consciousness, his emergence from racial type and ultimate assumption of selfhood, a problem complicated by the fact that this complex process could reveal itself only through Huck's limited vision.

One thing is clear. As long as Jim is headed toward Cairo, life on the raft is not particularly "free and easy." If anything, Twain demonstrates repeatedly the barriers between white and black consciousness—Jim's agony, his "level head," and Huck's inane adventurism. Only by painful degree does Huck come to appreciate Jim's dangerous position, and then it takes a figurative slap on the cheek to rouse him to an awareness of Jim's person. The nature of this perplexed relationship is treated in a number of scenes early in the book, each of which deals variously with their estrangement, all leading up to the climactic scene in which Huck decides to betray Jim. That Jim exists somewhere beyond the pale of Huck's perception is clearly insinuated in those passages. "They're after us," Huck declares at the end of Chapter 11, but his understanding of their mutual peril is almost immediately shown to be flawed by his decision to board the *Walter Scott*, a capricious stunt that nearly loses them the raft, Jim's only means of successfully achieving his escape. His rebuke, "he said he didn't want no more adventures," carefully states his dangerous situation:

He said that when I went in the texas and he crawled back to get on the raft and found her gone, he nearly died; because he judged it was all up with *him* anyway it could be fixed; for if he didn't get saved he would get drownded; and if he did get saved, whoever saved him would send him back home so as to get the reward, and then Miss Watson would sell him South, sure. Well, he was right; he was most always right; he had an uncommon level head, for a nigger. (p. 64)

The "uncommon level head" belongs to a man intent on surviving, as Huck ruefully recognizes. In the much maligned "Sollermun" episode, where Jim is ostensibly reduced to caricature by the comic device of a minstrel show routine, the "level head," I would argue, remains intact. Huck does assume the role of interlocutor, but Jim is neither the drawling bumpkin nor the capering rascal. The Bible story cloaks social and political realities, realities which Huck fails to discern, and it is an assertive Jim who rears up, suddenly touched and wanting to tell. The books found on the *Walter Scott* are examined, and Huck begins an admiring account of "kings and dukes" that draws steadily closer to an unwitting description of the white man's imperium in the South. Jim asks, "how much do a king git?" Huck replies that "they can have just as much as they want; everything belongs to them" (p. 64). Their life is leisurely, interrupted only by wars and politics, and they have their harems, their "million wives." The conversation then focuses on Solomon, the omnipotent ruler who enigmatically decides the fate of his subjects. Jim spiritedly attacks Solomon's proposal to split the child and when Huck intervenes by asserting that he "don't get the point." Jim passionately sweeps the objection aside:

"Blame de pint! I reck'n I knows what I knows. En mine you, de *real* pint is down furder—it's down deeper. It lays in de way Sollermun was raised. You take a man dat's got on'y one er two chillen; is dat man gwyne to be waseful o' chillen? No, he ain't; he can't 'ford it. *He* know how to value 'em. But you take a man dat's got 'bout five million chillen runnin' round de house, en

it's diffunt. *He* as soon chop a chile in two as a cat. Dey's plenty mo'. A chile er two, mo' er less,
warn't no consekens to Sollermun, dad fetch him!" (p. 65)

The real point *is* "down deeper." Jim has instinctively recognized in Solomon
the figure of the slaveholder, the white Southerner who regards the Negro as
chattel. He speaks from the depths of his own experience about the "chile er
two" that "warn't no consekens to Sollermun," his own children—all the black
families dismembered on the block. Significantly Jim refuses to accept Huck's
patronizing explanation. Indeed he rebukes the boy for what is essentially an
impertinence. "Go 'long. Doan' talk to *me* 'bout yo' pints. I reck'n I knows
sense when I sees it; en dey ain' no sense in sich doin's as dat" (p. 65). With
crushing authority, he adds, "doan' talk to me 'bout Sollermun, Huck, I knows
him by de back." Dumbfounded not so much by Jim's ignorance as by his
refusal to give up the "notion" in his head about Solomon, Huck changes the
topic. The subsequent discussion of language twists humorously around Jim's
refusal to accept the concept of foreign tongues as "natural." Huck is once
more superficially academic, concerned with simply ascertaining the fact, and
Jim again is somewhere else rooted in his experience of the world and not to
be argued from it. Frenchmen, Huck says by way of introducing the topic,
"gets on the police, and some of them learns people how to talk French." They
go from there. Language becomes an assertion of estrangement; French, the
discourse of authority. Isn't it "natural and right for a *Frenchman* to talk
different from us?" Huck asks. "Dad blame it," Jim responds, "Why doan he
talk like a man?" (pp. 66-67).

But if Jim proves intractable in Chapter 14, revealing an immovable
confidence in what he knows "down deeper," he clearly establishes himself in
the succeeding chapter. His celebrated reproach—"En all you wuz thinkin 'bout
wuz how you could make a fool uv ole Jim wid a lie. Dat truck dah is *trash* en
trash is what people is dat puts dirt on de head or dey fren's en makes 'em
ashamed" (p.71)—places Huck in a genus, white trash, the class that Pap Finn
in all his viciousness typifies, and strikes unerringly at a vulnerable spot. The
hurt is exchanged. Huck is compelled to recognize not only Jim's outraged self,
but also to separate himself from the onerous label Jim has affixed to his
behavior. It takes fifteen minutes for Huck to ponder the subtle gravity of the
charge. His immediate reaction is simply to prostrate himself, to kiss Jim's
foot, but upon reflection he formalizes his apology so that it comes not just
from Huck, but from the white boy, and goes not just to Jim, but to the black
man, the whole race. Huck has emerged from the "solid white fog" to discover
Jim, but the implications of his apology, the fright of suddenly seeing the
strangeness of his black friend, are not immediately clear to him.

As Cairo nears, Jim discloses for the first time the full extent of his plan, a
scheme that involves not just his own freedom but the deliverance of his family.
It is couched in such a way as to disregard the legal right of the slaveholder to
his property, and it reveals in one stroke Jim's notion of freedom. This
information comes late, it is important to note, only after Huck's abase-
ment. Huck's resentful aside that Jim "wouldn't ever dared" to speak in this
fashion before is remarkably apt. "Just see," he continues, "what a difference
it made in him the minute he judged he was about free" (p. 73). Jim has broken
the confining mask of the loyal slave and this new alien personality, as Huck
notes with alarm, "was fidgeting up and down past me" (p. 73). Their quick
movement about the raft is skillfully choreographed. Jim dances ecstatically and
Huck writhes with anxiety. Jim sings out joyously while Huck's conscience

whispers feverishly to him. When Huck finally leaves the raft, Jim incants their names, repeating them in such a way as to knit Huck-Jim tightly together, a chant that poignantly frames Huck's decision as a loyal white to betray Jim, the disloyal black man. "Pooty soon I'll be a-shout'n for joy, en I'll say it's all on accounts o' Huck; I's a free man, en couldn't ever ben free ef it hadn' ben for Huck; Huck done it. Jim won't ever forgit you, Huck; you's de bes' fren' Jim's ever had; en you's de *only* fren' ole Jim's got now" (p. 74). His final exhortation, called out at a distance of fifty yards—"Dah you goes, de ole true Huck; de on'y white genlman dat ever kep' his promise to ole Jim" (p. 74)—not only suggests Jim's despair, his lingering suspicion of Huck, but also involves a cunning piece of seductive praise. Pap Finn's delinquent, ragtag child is now declared a "white genlman."

What has burst in on Huck is the recognition that the flight down river has meant all along a return to civilization. In effect, Jim is going to leave him. Huck has wanted only to play, to ride the raft, sleep late, eat the fish he has caught, and poke around. The distance between the boy and the man, between the black man desperate for a secure and honorable place in society and the white youth in desperate flight from that same society, is here sharply defined. There is no mention of Huck in the plan which Jim excitedly relates. The Jim that Huck has "helped to run away" is the indulgent primitive black man, a storyteller and companion, certainly not an emancipated Jim free in Illinois and working for wages, involved with conspiratorial Abolitionists: "It was according to the old saying, 'give a nigger an inch and he'll take an ell.' Thinks I, this is what comes of my not thinking." The specter of that black man drives Huck back very close to Pap Finn's dread. In this crisis Huck's instincts serve him well, the swinish voice of his father is repudiated, but the victory is, after all, narrowly accomplished. Even as Huck seems to be delivering Jim, the river is nudging them past Cairo and the practical consequences of that decision. What needs to be stressed is that Huck is harassed from all sides, within and without. He not only defies his social conscience in shielding Jim from capture, but also, to a large extent, his own inner needs. There has been, as I have suggested, no formulation in his flight, no determined place to go. Until Chapter 16 Huck seems not to have understood the significance of Cairo. In a very real sense, Jim's freedom means the termination of his own, the abandonment of the raft and the river for concrete realities in Illinois.

It was at this impasse that Twain halted and shelved his manuscript. In a groping, often strangled fashion, he had uncovered a complex philosophical problem concerning the nature of freedom. Huck desires to be liberated from the trammels of society, to win for himself the freedom to feel and move about at will, but this is possible only in solitude. Here the right to do as one pleases is absolutely guaranteed. By feigning his death and ceasing to exist socially, Huck momentarily enters that condition of being on Jackson's Island: "And so for three days and nights. No difference—just the same thing" (p. 36). Huck, who has wrenched himself out of clocktime, discovers the enormity of inner space and immediately begins to struggle with his loneliness. His main task, as he so curiously phrases it, is to "put in time." It is Jim who nudges the bare fact of Huck's liberation toward the more complex matter of freedom in a sociopolitical context, whose presence as a hunted fugitive drives home the brutal truth that no one is free unless all are free. Huck finally perceives this truth, but he doesn't understand, as Twain did, that Jim is headed toward a catastrophe, the equally brutal truth that such a politically organized world (where all men are free) is not yet found, least of all in pre-Civil War Illinois. So it is that the white youth and the black man pass each other in flight, Huck searching for some primitive community and Jim looking for a place in modern society, a phenomenon that Eldridge Cleaver has brilliantly analyzed in *Soul on Ice*. The Supermasculine Menial (the black man) wishes to reclaim his Mind and the Omnipotent Administrator (the white man) seeks to regain his Body, but both are frustrated in their quest for the fused self (man politically and sensuously free) by a class society whose function depends on the fragmentation of the self. Cleaver's prescription in *Soul on Ice* is revolution, a level of discourse that is assuredly remote in *Huckleberry Finn*. The sweeping current of the Mississippi rushes Huck and Jim, who have no theories, southward. Before they can confront one another on the alien ground of Cairo, the steamboat, bearing its passengers and cargo, churns obliviously over the raft and the problems it represents.

Where the first part of the book narrows to an intense concentration of the "subtle line" dividing Huck and Jim, the second part, opening with the Grangerford episode, simply begins a comprehensive revelation of the ugliness of society, and in this new set of adventures Jim is a supernumerary. "Goodness sakes," Huck exclaims to the confidence men who commandeer the raft, "would a runaway nigger run south?" (p. 102). In fact, Jim has ceased to be a renegade black. The "chilling descent" that most critics find in the ending of the novel begins really at this point, with the deformation of Jim's psyche. The black man who had determined not only to seize his freedom, but who, with an audacity that stunned Huck, planned to return and "steal" his family, now becomes the gowned, besmirched "Sick Arab" amiably howling on the moored raft, the comic shambling burrhead who imperils the future of his own children for the sake of his principal tormentor, Tom Sawyer, an arrogant little white boy. The travesty in the final chapter originates in the travesty embedded in that much-praised idyllic sequence where Jim and Huck, far below Cairo, float down the Mississippi in a golden prelapsarian daze. We are asked there to accept a revised, implausible Jim drifting "free and easy" down river, calmly contemplating the heavens as he moves steadily toward the ninth circle of the black man's hell, the Deep South—the terror of which initially compelled him to make his perilous break. Where is the murder in Jim's heart?

In brief, Twain had turned restively from the difficulties Jim posed, but he could no longer evoke the rhapsodic dream of Huck's emancipation without the vexing clutter of Jim's presence. "What is Jim's function in this novel?" Chadwick Hansen asks. "I think it is, quite simply, to be the white man's burden."[9] By forcing Huck to that crises of conscience at the Phelps farm, Hansen argues, Jim fulfills his purpose: "Jim's chief function in the novel is over at that point . . . and so is the moral conflict. All that remains is to get the characters off stage as gracefully and plausibly as possible."[10] If that is Jim's significance in *Huckleberry Finn*, then Hansen's phrasing is too felicitous. The problem is how to throw the black man away after he has served as a "moral burden." But in fact Jim has struggled for his own life in the novel, and there is no "graceful" way to get him off the stage. Twain's method is to freeze that struggle and abort the development of Jim's self. What he retrieves in this maneuver is the black man as Uncle Dan'l, the old slave he eulogizes in the *Autobiography*, a "patient" friend who gave him his "strong liking" for the black race, his "appreciation of its fine qualities."[11] Having been shackled like an animal on the river, duped and betrayed at the Phelps farm, Jim suffers a final indignity—the affirmation of his "fine qualities." The alternative to that resolutely humane black man, it would seem, is Melville's Babo, duplicitous and deadly, the shadow who becomes flesh in *Benito Cereno*.

NOTES

1. Leo Marx, "Mr. Eliot, Mr. Trilling, and *Huckleberry Finn*," *The American Scholar*, 22 (Autumn, 1953), p. 439.

2. *Between Past and Future* (New York, 1968), p. 157.

3. Marx, p. 439.

4. All references are to the Norton Critical Edition of the *Adventures of Huckleberry Finn*, ed. Sculley Bradley, Richmond Croom Beatty, and E. Hudson Long (New York, 1961).

5. Claude Lévi-Strauss, *Tristes Tropiques* (New York, 1963), p. 398.

6. Ibid.

7. *The Autobiography of Mark Twain*, ed. Charles Neider (New York, 1959), p. 14.

8. Ibid., p. 6.

9. Chadwick Hansen, "The Character of Jim and the Ending of *Huckleberry Finn*," *Massachusetts Review*, 5 (Autumn, 1963), p. 58.

10. Ibid.

11. *Autobiography*, p. 6.

WAS *HUCKLEBERRY FINN* WRITTEN?

WALTER BLAIR

Reviewing *Adventures of Huckleberry Finn* a month or so before the American first printing came out, Brander Matthews commended Mark Twain for having readers "see everything through [Huck's] eyes" rather than "a pair of Mark Twain's spectacles," thereby letting "Huck set down, without any comment at all, scenes which would have afforded the ordinary writer matter for endless moral and political and social disquisition." For this and other reasons, scores of later critics also have praised the use of Huck as a fictional voice. Yet a meticulous critic bent on raising questions about Twain's use of his first-person narrator can come up with several. A review of some of these will, I believe, throw light on the book's artistry.

A reading of the very first paragraph will serve as a starter:

> You don't know about me, without you have read a book by the name of "The Adventures of Tom Sawyer". . . That book was made by Mr. Mark Twain, and he told the truth, mainly. There was things which he stretched, but mainly he told the truth. . . Tom's Aunt Polly . . . and Mary, and the Widow Douglas, is all told about in that book. . .

The last page of *Huckleberry Finn* has Huck say that he finished unfolding the story soon after his adventures ended. The title page of the novel tells us: "Time: Forty to Fifty Years Ago." Since the first American edition came out in 1885, that had to be some time between 1835 and 1845. But "Mr. Mark Twain" never signed his name to any piece of writing until 1863, and *The Adventures of Tom Sawyer*, which Huck is able to summarize, wasn't published until 1876.

There are other puzzlements, for instance: At the start of Chapters IV and VI, the facts about Huck's education are given. During the "three or four months" until "it was well into the winter," Huck went to school "most all the time," or if some of his statements are correct, he "didn't go to school much," perhaps because "whenever I got uncommon tired I played hookey." The result: he "could spell, and read, and write just a little, and could say the multiplication table up to six times seven is thirty-five, and I don't reckon I could go any further than that if I was to live forever." At this point, Pap began to interfere with Huck's attendance whenever he could. And in April or May, he ended his son's schooling by kidnapping him. Well, how did a boy of "thirteen or fourteen or along there" learn during less than a year of sporadic schooling to write this long novel spelling thousands of words in it correctly except when momentary ignorance or vernacular pronunciation dictated otherwise?

A couple of inconsistencies call attention to other problems. All the words in a 31-word note that Huck writes to Miss Watson (Chapter XXXI) are spelled correctly, and in Chapter XVII when Huck quotes himself as telling the Grangerfords his assumed name he spells it "George Jackson." But a few pages later, when his young friend Buck spells it "G-o-r-g-e J-a-x-o-n," Huck says, "you done it, but I didn't think you could"—and it is obvious that he isn't joking. When Huck quotes Tom Sawyer's writings, Tom, better educated than Huck, is inconsistent at greater length. In Chapter XXXVIII, when Tom composes graffiti for Jim to copy on his prison walls, he spells 60 words without an error. But at the end of the next chapter, when he writes a 200-word letter to the Phelpses, he misspells 3½% of the words.

A pair of Tom's spellings, it may be, represent dialect pronunciations (*northard* for *northward* and *stead* for *instead*); even so, Huck, after less schooling, is more restrained: he holds "dialect spelling," Robert J. Lowenherz calculates, to 1% of his total narrative. However, when the boy quotes himself in conversations, he uses twice as many such spellings as he uses in his narrative passages.

"Explanatory," just before the table of contents, leads to another inquiry. The book, it says, uses seven different dialects—that of Missouri blacks; "the extremest form of the backwoods South-Western dialect; the ordinary 'Pike-County' dialect; and four modified varieties of this last." What is more, it uses "shadings" of these, not haphazardly "or by guess-work, but painstakingly." How in the world could an unsophisticated teen-age kid manage to notice and to record such distinctions?

One answer that has been given to this question by some commentators is: He didn't. Some claim that "Notice" was just one of Mark Twain's jokes which it is silly to consider at all seriously. Edgar Lee Masters, who spent his youth in Fulton County, Illinois, about 50 miles from Hannibal, among folk whose "lingo" was "just the same" as Huck's, considered it seriously anyhow, and found the dialect "preposterous." The author, he says, "went wrong many times . . . in choosing words for Huck and other characters." Masters gives examples:

It doesn't sound true for Huck to say, "it don't make any difference." He must have said, "it don't make no difference." . . .

Would Huck, in speaking of his feelings, say "very well satisfied?" Would he not rather say, "and feelin' all right"? Would he use the word "reticule" instead of saying "one of them things they keep needles in, ratacoul or something"? Would he not say "et" instead of "eat"? Would he not say "the lightning showed her very plain," instead of "the lightning showed her very distinct"? Would he say "very gray whiskers" and not "whiskers all white," and "terbacker" instead of "tobacco"? At that Huck sometimes says "tobacker" as well as "tobacco." Would he speak of "astonishing things"? Would he say "gaudiest" and "pat" and "pleasure and astonishment," and "heptarchies" and "Domesday Book," "butt of maumsey" and "histrionic" with the slang word "doxologer" right by its side? Would he say "inscriptions" and "journals" and "responsibility" and "just so" when "that-a-way" was the colloquialism of Missouri and middle Illinois? . . . Huck would say "the other feller," and not "the other fellow." He would likely speak of sheet lightning as "winking and spreading," not as "squirting."

"There are passages, too, in the book," Masters claims, "where Twain is unmistakably talking and not Huck. They are too well expressed and compact for the unlettered brain of Huck to give utterance to." Masters doesn't say what these are; but William Van O'Connor cites examples:

Huck's parody (Chapter XVII) of the activities of Emmeline Grangerford, poetess, is extremely amusing, but the "voice" is more nearly Twain's than Huck's. Many other things are put into the mouth of the twelve or thirteen year old Huck that, sometimes only weakly humorous themselves, are Twain himself speaking. [An instance is Huck's scrambled history in Chapter XXIII, which O'Connor thinks inappropriate "from a boy with almost no schooling."] There are other witticisms about kings, a theme appropriate enough . . . , but Twain might have found some other way of introducing them. In "An Arkansas Difficulty" [Chapter XXI] . . . Twain . . . makes Huck relate an observation on "chawing tobacker" that one would expect to find as "filler" in a nineteenth-century newspaper or magazine. Most incongruous of all, perhaps, is Huck's rendition of Hamlet's soliloquy [Chapter XXI].

The juggled lines of Shakespeare's soliloquies really illustrate, not words "put into the mouth" of Huck but Huck's quotations of the words of other characters. They therefore illustrate what hostile critics might call another anomaly—Huck's remarkable ability to give us the speeches and writings of some people without injecting grammatical errors of dialect spellings. Some other instances include: the dialogue and the writings of the Grangerfords (except Buck) in Chapters XVII and XVIII, the preacher's exhortation in Chapter XXII, the playbills composed and displayed by the king in Chapter XXI, and Col. Sherburn's speeches—the short one to Boggs in Chapter XXI and the lengthy one to the mob in Chapter XXII.

These questionings are of particular passages. Hostile critics may raise a more sweeping one about the composition of the whole novel. For months—up to the very minute his account ends—Huck has been unceasingly busy having adventures—at the Widow Douglas's, in pap's cabin, or Jackson's Island, on the river, in riverside towns, in the homes of the Grangerfords, the Wilkses and the Phelpses. Whenever and how did he find time to put together this 366-page book?

A literal-minded critic, then, using "common-sense" yardsticks, can make numerous objections to Huck's performance as a narrator. Nevertheless, though commentators have lavished attention on Twain's technical ineptitudes, practically none has complained about any of the anomalies cited above. Instead, the overwhelming majority agree with Lewis Leary that "the honest observations of an attractive boy . . . and his view of the world" are what "secure for this book its high place in American writings." It seems worth while to ask why.

We may start with the most sweeping objections—that Huck couldn't possibly have told this lengthy story because he hadn't had enough education and he couldn't ever have found the time. Here a convention centuries old helped acceptance. Beginning in the sixteenth century, in hundreds of picaresque novels and their offspring, rascals, servants, social parasites, shady ladies and teen-age dropouts, many as illiterate and as busy with adventures as Huck, somehow got prose autobiographies assembled and published—the adult Lazo, Gil Blas, Jacke Wilton, Moll Flanders and Ferdinand, in the past, and in more modern times Holden Caulfield, Jaimie McPheeters and Addie Pray. Even more improbable autobiographers were accepted without too much trouble by some readers—dogs, cats, and a horse named Black Beauty.

Disparities between the language in the main narrative and in quoted speeches also had long been accepted without hesitation. Henry Nash Smith rightly has said: "As long as Mark Twain uses Huck simply to report dialogue, whether his own or others', he is following a convention which was familiar to Mrs. Stowe, or Cooper, or Scott, or for that matter Richardson. . . ."

Just as most amanuenses ignored awkward questions about such differing styles in dialogue, they usually didn't bother to explain the ways long first person stories came into being. Mark Twain by contrast took some pains to keep Huck from out-and-out claiming that he wrote his story. In his final paragraph, Huck speaks of himself doing what he reported, in his first paragraph, Mr. Twain had done—"making" a book: ". . . there ain't nothing more to write about, and I am rotten glad of it, because if I'd a knowed what a trouble it was to make a book I wouldn't a tackled it. . ."

To suggest how the story was told "in the vernacular, through the eyes and sensibility of a river rat," Huck, William M. Gibson imaginatively alleged that something comparable to a modern machine did the job:

[Huck] addresses the reader orally—for it is a *speaking* letter, dictated or tape-recorded as it were—and ingratiatingly in the first paragraph; and he confides his plans to the reader in the last paragraph and signs his communication "Yours truly/Huck Finn" to conclude the work. But the absurdity of the form is glimpsed only momentarily as the reader enters into and emerges from the imaginary world of the story, and it vanishes entirely while he is inside that world. The skill, that is, with which Clemens speaks through the double mask of "Mark Twain" and that of the vernacular-voiced adolescent is all but flawless.

Illuminating though it is, Professor Gibson's analogy between the style of the book and that of a tape recording, like most analogies, isn't quite impeccable. As Mark Twain fully realized, the style wasn't exactly that of talk. It was a talk like style, one modified to give the impression of talk—literary dialect. Twain, as he himself said, knew that "the best and most telling speech [in print] is not the actual impromptu one, but the counterfeit of it, [speech that] will seem impromptu." "Written things," he saw, "have to be limbered up, broken up, colloquialized, and turned into the common form of unpremeditated talk" thanks to "a touch of indifferent grammar flung in here and there, apparently at random." He knew what H. Allen Smith has called "the secret of dialect writing"—"always to stop some distance short of perfection." "Rigid consistency," Smith continues, "is a sin committed by many who try to write in dialect. It's the spacing of the dialect words that is important."

Huck doesn't do what some nineteenth-century humorists, local colorists and poor spellers did—set up so many dialect roadblocks that would-be readers today are unwilling or unable to track down his meanings. His selective version of vernacular speech is economical and suggestive rather than exhaustive and exhausting. In terms of what it is, Huck's lingo therefore can't legitimately be criticized the way Masters criticizes it. Even granting, for the sake of argument, that every work and phrase which Masters cites isn't one that a Missouri hobbledehoy would know or utter, we can dismiss his gripes as irrelevant, incompetent and immaterial.

As they justify their all but unanimous liking for the "voice" that tells Huck's story, critics often say why they aren't much bothered by any of the novel's "illogicalities." In addition to Professor Gibson, whom I have quoted, three critics, in fact, offer reasons in passages about the boy's anachronism-filled first paragraph: Carl Van Doren writes that the author, "with the very first sentence. . . fell into an idiom and rhythm flawlessly adapted to the naive, nasal, drawling little vagabond . . . mouthpiece for himself so completely that the whole of his tough, ignorant, generous, loyal, mendacious nature lies revealed." In Huck's brief first sentence, says Pascal Covici, Jr., he "persuades us to take his existence for granted. . . . The illusion that Huck is real is so intense that we never ask ourselves when in the world of time Huck is actually writing his story. He is immediately present as an actor." And Robert J. Lowenherz says of the paragraph: "In 108 words, Mark Twain firmly establishes the vernacular speech of his narrator Huck, characterizes him, enunciates one of the major themes of the story, provides a frame of reference for the action, and even works in some free advertisement for . . . *Tom Sawyer.*"

As these commentators argue, two interrelated elements erase most readers' possible worries—the brilliant fleshing out of Huck's rounded character and the highly appropriate style that makes him completely acceptable as a narrator. Frank Baldanza puts it very well:

Because Huck tells his story himself, the stylistic richness is immeasurably deepened by the rhythms, intonations, and choice of words of this magnificent child. . . . Huck's own vulgar but richly beautiful lingo. . . carries the narration along as smoothly and majestically as the river itself. . . . The highest accolades . . . must be reserved for the complexity of moral awareness on the part of this growing boy.

Bothersome or not (and luckily not) and anachronistic or not, Huck's early mention of "Mr. Mark Twain," preceded as it is in the first edition of the book by Twain's name on the cover, the title page, and (as a signature) under a photograph of a bust of him, stresses an important disparity—between the actual and the fictitious narrators. Unsophisticated, innocent, completely without humor, and sure that his most virtuous acts are wicked enough to damn him to hell, Huck constantly differs from his creator, and time after time the resulting incongruity is essential to the humor of America's funniest classic.

THE DIALECTS IN *HUCKLEBERRY FINN*

DAVID CARKEET

Mark Twain's "Explanatory" preface to *Adventures of Huckleberry Finn* is straightforward enough:

> In this book a number of dialects are used, to wit: the Missouri negro dialect; the extremest form of the backwoods South-Western dialect; the ordinary "Pike-County" dialect; and four modified varieties of this last. The shadings have not been done in a hap-hazard fashion, or by guesswork; but pains-takingly, and with the trustworthy guidance and support of personal familiarity with these several forms of speech.
> I make this explanation for the reason that without it many readers would suppose that all these characters were trying to talk alike and not succeeding.[1]

Yet an apparent lack of fit between this announcement and the linguistic facts of the novel has long confounded investigators trying to decide just who speaks what dialect. Some have given up the fight and concluded that the preface is a joke. Others have taken the preface seriously but have still failed to decode it.[2] The question of what Clemens meant with the preface is a complex one divisible into several parts: (1) Does a close linguistic analysis of the speech of the characters in the novel show the seven-way dialectal differentiation of which Clemens speaks? (2) What did the preface mean to Clemens? That is, in his lexicon what was the meaning of "dialect," "extremest," "backwoods South-Western," and "ordinary 'Pike-County'"? (3) When Clemens wrote the preface, what could he have *thought* he had done in the way of differentiating dialects? This question is distinct from (1) above, for Clemens's sense of the language of the novel may have been different from the linguistic facts of the novel. (4) Finally, what is the relation between the dialects in the novel and linguistic reality of the Mississippi Valley in the mid-nineteenth century? The first three of these questions will be taken up below. The last question, because it has been dealt with elsewhere and because answering it sheds little light on the meaning of the preface, will not be treated.[3]

It is a characteristic flaw of published research in dialectology to dwell ponderously on methodological preliminaries. Eschewing this practice—which exists, I think, to disguise leanness in the body of many studies of dialects—I will not discuss here the notion of "literary dialect."[4] I will say only that dialects—in literature and out in the field—can differ from each other in their pronunciation (Huck says *get*, Pap says *git*), grammar (Huck says *you want*, Jim says *you wants*), and vocabulary or lexicon (Huck says *smouch* for 'steal,' the King says *hook*).

As to the first question raised above, a detailed examination of *Huckleberry Finn* shows that there are differences in the way people speak that are too systematic to be accidental. For purposes of discussion, Huck's dialect can be taken as the norm from which other dialects, to varying degrees, depart. This approach, besides being convenient, makes sense precisely because our goal is to understand the author's intention. Since Clemens wrote the novel in Huck's dialect, that dialect must have been uppermost in his mind. In a sense it is the "standard" dialect of the novel. Systematic departures from that dialect must, then, reflect conscious choices by the author. Given this approach, it is not necessary to list the hundreds of features distinguishing Huck's dialect from Standard English.[5] Instead, I will focus on the departures from Huck's dialect in the speech of the other characters.

First, there is an obvious difference between the speech of Jim (and the four other black speakers in the novel, whose dialects are identical with Jim's) and that of Huck. Phonologically, Jim shows widespread loss of *r* (*do'* 'door,' *heah* 'here,' *thoo* 'through'), palatalization (i.e., the insertion of a palatal glide—the initial sound of *yes*—in certain environments: *k'yer* 'care,' *dish-yer* 'this here'), (*a*) *gwyne* as the present participle of *go*, and substitution of voiceless *th* with *f* (*mouf* 'mouth'), of voiced *th* with *d* (*dese* 'these'), and of the negative prefix *un*— with *on*— (*oneasy*). Huck has none of these features. Also, where Huck and Jim share a rule producing nonstandard forms, Jim's use of the rule is much higher in frequency. This holds for final consonant cluster reduction (*ole* 'old'), deletion of initial unstressed syllables (*'crease* 'increase'), and epithetic *t* (*wunst* 'once'). Jim also shows much more eye dialect (nonstandard spellings for standard pronunciations, like *uv* 'of' and *wuz* 'was') than Huck. Grammatically, Huck's and Jim's dialects are very similar. However, Jim's dialect additionally shows the *done*-perfect construction (*she done broke loose*), deletion of the copula, and an *-s* suffix on second-person present-tense verbs. Lexically, Jim's dialect differs from Huck's only in a few exclamations: Jim says *dadblamedest, dad fetch him,* and *ding-busted,* and Huck does not.

The differences between Huck's dialect and the dialects of the other white characters in the novel are less striking but still significant. As in the treatment of Jim's dialect, these differences will be presented in terms of nonstandard features exhibited in the speech of others (Pap, the King, etc.) that are *not* exhibited in Huck's dialect. This approach rather than the reverse is taken because Huck's corpus is much larger than the corpora of the other characters, and nonoccurrence of a form in a large body of data is more significant than nonoccurrence in a small body of data. That is, it cannot be maintained that the features below fail to appear in Huck's dialect because there is insufficient occasion for them to appear. Rather, they fail to appear because Clemens more than likely chose not to make them a characteristic of Huck's dialect.

The lists below are arranged as follows. Characters are given in order of appearance in the novel. Under each character's name are given the features of phonology, grammar, and lexicon that distinguish that dialect from Huck's, i.e., features of which there is no evidence in Huck's corpus.[6] The three categories are separated by lines of ellipses; if no grammatical or lexical features distinguish the dialect from Huck's, a dash is entered. In the phonology section of each dialect I have listed the features in descending order of importance (by frequency and salience, the latter being a subjective impression). Items subject to the same phonological rule (e.g., the King's palatalization) are listed across the same line. Items subject to a rule evidenced in Huck's dialect are not given, even though the particular word in question may not appear in the data from Huck; for example, Pap says *'lection* 'election,' showing a rule deleting initial unstressed syllables, and although Huck never says *'lection,* it is clear from spellings like *'low* 'allow' and *'deed* 'indeed' that he has the same rule. Consequently, *'lection* is not given as a distinguishing feature of Pap's dialect.[7] An asterisk means that the form fails to appear in any other white dialect in the novel, that is, that the form is unique to the dialect under whose name it is entered. The number in parentheses indicates the number of instances of a form. The few examples of eye dialect and idioms in these dialects are not given.

Some of the identifying names below need an explanation. Judith Loftus is the Illinois woman whom Huck tries to fool with his girl's disguise; "*Sir Walter Scott*" refers to the dialect spoken by the three thieves on the wreck of that name; "Raftsmen" refers to the dialect of the six speakers in the "Raft

Passage," which was first published in *Life on the Mississippi* (chapter 3) and was part of *Huckleberry Finn* (in Chapter 16) when Clemens sent the manuscript to his publisher;[8] the Bricksville loafers are the tobacco-chewing sluggards (nine or ten different speakers) in the town where Colonel Sherburn shoots Boggs; and the Arkansas Gossips are Sister Hotchkiss et al. (five identifiable speakers), who discuss Jim's strange housekeeping on the Phelps plantation.[9]

Pap

*p'fessor (1)
*suthin' (something, 1)
agin (2), git (3)
o' (of, 5)
fitten (fitting, 1)
wust (worst, 1)

. . . .

—

. . . .
*big-bug (big shot, 1)
*hifalutin' (1)
*palaver (talk, 1)
*pungle (pay, 1)

Judith Loftus

*sence (since, 3)
*cheer (chair, 1)
ben (been, 1)

. . . .

—

. . . .

—

Sir Walter Scott[10]

*orter (ought to, 1)
forgit (1), git (2), yit (2)
jest (1), jist (4)
befo' (1), yo' (1)
shore (sure, 1)
't (that: *conj.*, 1)
wrack (wreck, 1)

. . . .

—

. . . .
*pickins (transportables, 1)
*unfavorable to (opposed to, 1)

Raftsmen

*furder (further, 1)
*Sent Louis (1)
*yander (yonder, 1)
bar'l (barrel, 4), thar (there, 2),
    whar (where, 1)
oncomfortable (1), oneasy (1)
tech (1)

. . . .

ye (1)

. . . .
*jigger (jerk, 1)
*squench (suppress, 1)
*whoo-oop (*exclamation*, 7)

King

*h-yer (here, 2), k'yer (care, 2),
    these-'yer (these here, 2),
    thish-yer (this here, 1)
*considable (1), misable (1)
*he'p (2)
*aluz (always, 1)
*drot (drat, 1)
*partickler (1)
agin (2), forgit (1), git (4),
    yisterday (1), yit (1)
jest (4), jist (2), sech (3), sich
    (1), shet (1)
oncomfortable (1), oncommon
    (1), oneasy (1)
thar (1), whar (2)
'at (that: *conj.*, 1; *rel. pro.*, 2)
ben (been, 2)
fitten (fitting, 2)
o' (of, 2)
out'n (out of, 2)
pore (poor, 2)
wisht (wish, 2)
hunderd (1)

. . . .

ye (1)

. . . .
*holt (specialty, 1)
*hook (steal, 1)

Bricksville Loafers

*(a) gwyne (going, 5)
*borry (borrow, 2)
*awready (1)
*cain't (1)
*wunst (once, 1)
thar (2), whar (1)
ben (been, 1)
f'm (from, 1)
jedge (1)
off'n (off of, 1)
waw-path (warpath, 1)
wisht (wish, 1)
. . . .
—
. . . .
—

Aunt Sally and Uncle Silas Phelps

*owdacious (audacious, 2)
*clo'es (clothes, 1)
*Newrleans (1)
*reely (1)
't (that: *conj.*, 3)
childern (1), hunderd (1)
Babtist (1)
shet (1)
shore (sure, 1)
. . . .
ye (3)
. . . .
*bang (surpass, 1)
*beat (that which surpasses, 3)
*Old Harry (devil, 1)
*pass (point, juncture, 1)
Sister, Brother (*forms of address*, 2)

Arkansas Gossips

*s'I (says I, 26), sh-she (says she, 4), s'e (says he, 3)
*that-air (that there, 6)
*Brer (brother, 4)

*amost (almost, 1)
*kiver (cover, 1)
*natcherl (natural, 1)
*sasser (saucer, 1)
jist (2), sich (2)
ben (been, 2)
out'n (out of, 2)
't (that: *conj.*, 1; *rel. pro.*, 1)
fust (first, 1)
git (1)
thar (1)
they (there: *expletive*, 1)
. . . .
hearn (heard: *preterite*, 1)
ye (1)
. . . .
Sister, Brother (*forms of address*, 14)

This list shows real dialectal differences. It is surely no accident that in the entire novel only one group of white speakers (the Bricksville Loafers) uses the typically black *(a) gwyne* participle, or that the King shows palatalization seven times, or that Sister Hotchkiss utters a reduced form of *says* thirty-three times in her brief appearance. In the light of facts like these, Rulon's claim in his dissertation (p. 50) and again in "Geographical Delimitation" (p. 12) that there are only two dialects in the novel, one spoken by blacks and the other by whites, is quite remarkable.

When we add Huck's dialect to the above list, we have nine distinct dialects spoken by white characters, whereas Clemens names only six in the preface. How can we identify the six dialects Clemens had in mind? The degree of divergence from Huck's dialect will certainly play some role, however elusive the principles involved in assessing this may be. One such principle is that asterisked (i.e., unique) forms must weigh heavily in marking a dialect as divergent. A second principle is that phonological features must weigh more heavily than lexical features, because a lexical omission in Huck's dialect is more likely to be accidental than the absence of a phonological feature, and because lexical choices often reflect a personality more than a dialect—Pap says "hifalutin'" not only because of where he was born but also because of who he is. Third, phonological rules affecting a class weigh more heavily than phonological rules affecting just one word. The sheer number of differences or of words exhibiting a difference is a fourth consideration. Finally, some of these characters speak more than others and thus have greater occasion to exhibit dialectal features different from Huck's; the more a character speaks, the more features distinct from Huck's he must show in order for us to consider his dialect markedly different from Huck's. A precise formula expressing "density" of features could easily be worked out, but such rigor would be foolish in the light of the subjective nature of our other considerations.

On the basis of these criteria, then, I would rank the eight dialects roughly in the following order, the dialect of the Arkansas Gossips being least like Huck's, and Judith Loftus's dialect being most like Huck's: Arkansas Gossips, King, Bricksville Loafers, Aunt Sally and Uncle Silas, Raftsmen, *Sir Walter Scott*, Pap, and Judith Loftus. What we have here is the beginning of a conclusion. But our notion "degree of divergence from Huck's dialect" is not sufficiently exact to allow us simply to subtract the last three dialects (or to say they are subspecies of Huck's dialect) and to declare the problem solved. Straight linguistic analysis of the novel takes us only so far. We now must turn our attention to the other questions raised in the opening paragraph.

What could Clemens have meant by "the extremest form of the backwoods South-Western Dialect"? The Old Southwest is of course a geographical region into which Huck and Jim move more deeply as the novel progresses. In this respect, characters appearing far down the river are more likely to be speakers of this dialect than, say, Pap or Judith Loftus, residents of St. Petersburg. "Southwestern" also has a literary meaning which is equally important to our question. Clemens was closely familiar with the antebellum literature of Southwestern humorists like George Washington Harris, Johnson J. Hooper, and William Tappan Thompson, both from his general reading and from his editing of *Mark Twain's Library of Humor*, which he worked on for several years before its publication in 1888.[11] Clemens drew from this tradition in his portrayal of the King, a typical Southwestern confidence man whose "conversion" at the camp meeting in chapter 20 recalls that of Hooper's roguish Simon

Suggs in "The Captain Attends a Camp-Meeting." The "Raft Passage" shows a similar indebtedness, with its boasting and brawling raftsmen, among them one "from the wilds of Arkansaw," and its spinners of tall tales—characters reminiscent of A. B. Longstreet and Thomas Bangs Thorpe. On these grounds, then, one might be tempted to identify the King or the Raftsmen as speakers of the Southwestern dialect. But the Southwestern humorists also provide us with orthographic criteria with which to make this judgment, for many of them wrote in heavy dialect whose features no doubt impressed Clemens. These criteria point clearly to Sister Hotchkiss and the other Arkansas Gossips as the Southwestern dialect speakers. Sister Hotchkiss's and Mrs. Damrell's unique *that-air* 'that there' appears, spelled *that air, that ere,* or *that ar,* in the sketches of Harris, Hooper, and Thorpe, the last also giving his characters the plural counterpart, *them ar* 'them there.' Brother Marples's *kiver* 'cover' is also used by Simon Suggs, and Sister Hotchkiss's *natcherl,* whatever pronunciation it is meant to indicate, brings to mind the reduced form in Sut Lovingood's recurring epithet, "a nat'ral born durn'd fool." The Arkansas Gossips also show lowering and backing of /ɛr/ to /ar/ (*thar*), neutralization of /I/ and /ɛ/ (*git*), and selective loss of /r/ with schwa (*fust* 'first'); all of these features are easily found in Southwestern tales.

Finally, when Sister Hotchkiss says *s'I* 'says I,' *s'e* 'says he,' and *sh-she* 'says she,' she uses a form that has some precedent, particularly in its rhythmic repetition, in stories by some of the writers mentioned above (compare her "s'I, he's crazy, s'I" with "says I, 'Bill,' says I, 'you're an ass,'" from Thorpe's "The Big Bear of Arkansas"). A more direct inspiration, however, appears to be Joel Chandler Harris's "At Teague Poteet's: A Sketch of the Hog Mountain Range," where we find dozens of occurrences of *s'I* 'says I' and *se' she* 'says she,' along with *Sister* as a form of address and *that air* 'that there.'[12] Modern literary historians view the Southwestern school as an antebellum phenomenon, but there is no reason to believe that Clemens did. Linguistically and artistically many of Harris's characters can be seen as "Southwestern." In borrowing these linguistic forms for this scene, as well as the *Brer* of the earlier Uncle Remus stories, Clemens shows his respect for Harris, whom he rightly considered a master of dialect writing. Clemens apparently drew more than dialect from Harris's story. A working note written by him in the summer of 1883 says, "He [Huck] must hear some Arkansas women, over their pipes & knitting (spitting from between teeth), swap reminiscences of Sister this & Brother that . . ." At the end of this note, added later without comment, is "s'I, sh-she, s'ze." A group of gossips very similar to that described here appears in "At Teague Poteet's," and they appear to be the inspiration for Clemens's Arkansas Gossips.[13]

No other speaker or group of speakers in *Huckleberry Finn* shows so many features that also appear in the works of the Southwestern humorists. The Arkansas Gossips reside at the southern extremity of the novel, so they meet the geographical test as well. Their speech is more dense in dialect than that of the other white speakers in the novel, and it is probably for this reason that Clemens calls it the "extremest" form of the Southwestern dialect. In this scene as in no other, Clemens has Huck step aside and for eight paragraphs of speech shows us rich local linguistic color.

If this much is correct we are left with eight white dialects in the novel: Huck, Pap, Judith Loftus, *Sir Walter Scott,* Raftsmen, King, Bricksville Loafers, and Aunt Sally and Uncle Silas. However, "the ordinary 'Pike-

County' dialect" and "four modified varieties" of it means that three of these
dialects must be disregarded or subsumed under another dialect. Which three?

We must first determine what "Pike County" meant to Clemens. In his
fiction it is the Missouri county in which St. Petersburg is located, named after
a Missouri county to the south of Hannibal. It is also an Illinois county immediately across the river, the home of Judith Loftus in *Huckleberry Finn* and
the locale of John Hay's *Pike County Ballads*. If we look hard enough we can
find five speakers in the novel, all clearly from Pike County, Missouri, or Pike
County, Illinois, and all speaking somewhat differently from each other: Huck,
Pap, Judith Loftus, Judge Thatcher, and—stretching it—Aunt Polly or Tom
Sawyer. But there are several things wrong with this approach. First, Judge
Thatcher speaks a standard variety of English, and Clemens, not being a
twentieth-century linguist, probably understood and used the word "dialect" to
refer to nonstandard systems only. Second, Aunt Polly and Tom Sawyer both
speak dialects identical with Huck's except for a very few features (Aunt Polly
says *y'r* once and Tom says *git* once and *per'aps* once; Huck says none of
these). Third and more important, if Clemens meant by "Pike County" this
small geographic area, then in the preface he perversely called our attention
to almost imperceptible dialectal differences (in the case of Aunt Polly or Tom)
while ignoring major differences in the speech of characters like the King and
the Bricksville Loafers. Such a reading in fact must ignore the speech occurring
in three-fourths of the novel.

There is still another reason to look beyond the geographical Pike Counties
for the speakers of "Pike County" dialect. Like "Southwestern," "Pike County"
is the name of a literary tradition well established by the time Clemens began
work on *Huckleberry Finn*. During the 1850's in California there emerged a
stock immigrant character known as "the Pike." He figured in early ballads
like "Joe Bowers," "California Bank Robbers," and "Sweet Betsey from Pike,"
and also in plays and sketches of the period. As to his roots, the Pike "was
named for Pike County, Missouri, but he came from Illinois, Arkansas, or
North Texas quite as frequently."[14] He spoke a dialect variously represented by
different writers, part literary artifact and part reflective of actual linguistic
features of the Pike County area in Missouri and Illinois. Well before Clemens
wrote *Huckleberry Finn*, "Pike County" had come to refer to a literary
representation of the speech of Missouri and points south. Clemens, fully aware
of this, punctuated the term with quotation marks in his preface.[15] Huck
participates actively in this tradition when he tells the King that he is from Pike
County, Missouri, and that his family "all died off but me and pa and my
brother Ike" (chapter 20); "Ike" is the name of a forever undeveloped character
in Pike County balladry, his sole claim to fame being his ability to rhyme with
"Pike." Clemens further highlights the geographical indefiniteness of "Pike" by
giving the towns along the river names that can be seen as variants: the camp
meeting is in Pokeville, the Phelps farm is in Pikesville, and "Bricksville"
translates the Greco-Germanic "(St.) Petersburg," the town in the heart of Pike
County.

Thus we are free to range down the river in our search for "Pike County"
speakers in *Huckleberry Finn*. But what could Clemens have meant by "ordinary" and "modified"? A reasonable guess is that Huck is the speaker of the
ordinary Pike County dialect, on the basis of the sheer bulk of his words—that
which dominates numerically is "ordinary"—and also considering his geographical roots: Pike County, Missouri. We find some corroboration of this guess if

we follow the procedure used above to identify the Southwestern dialect speakers in the novel, that is if we examine the Pike County literature antedating *Huckleberry Finn* for recurring dialect features. In an early version of "Joe Bowers" we find much that anticipates Huck's dialect—intrusive *r* pronunciations (*orful* 'awful'), deletion of initial unstressed syllables (*'most* 'almost'), preterite *cotched* 'caught,' and infinitival *for to*.[16] We find most of these same features, along with many others shared by Huck, in John Hay's *Pike County Ballads* and Bret Harte's *East and West Poems*, both published in 1871. Huck-like features appear sporadically in some of Clemens's early California newspaper sketches, such as "Those Blasted Children" (1864), but it is in "The Celebrated Jumping Frog of Calaveras County" (1865) that the dialect appears in full bloom. Simon Wheeler and Huck Finn would have little trouble understanding each other. They share nonstandard pronunciations like *jest* 'just,' *terbacker* 'tobacco,' *jint* 'joint,' *fur* 'for,' *'low* 'allow,' and *ca'mly* 'calmly'; they share grammatical forms like preterite *warn't* 'wasn't,' *come* 'came,' *ketched* 'caught,' *see* 'saw,' and *throwed* 'threw,' possessive *his'n*, unmarked plurals (*five pound*), and unmarked adverbs (*monstrous proud*); they even share lexical items like *bully-rag* 'abuse' and *snake* 'take.'

Insofar as the "Pike County" dialect in literature can be defined, Huck appears to be a speaker of it. But so do the speakers of the seven other white dialects in *Huckleberry Finn*. In fact some of them show pronunciations (like *thar, git,* and *this-yer*) that Huck does not show and that can occasionally be found in early Pike County works. This procedure, then, cannot tell us which three dialects to disregard. Let us assume that our earlier guess that Huck speaks the "ordinary" Pike County dialect is correct. We are left with seven dialects competing for four positions. At this point we must take up the third question raised in the opening paragraph: when Clemens wrote the "Explanatory" what could he have *thought* he had done in the way of differentiating the dialects of *Huckleberry Finn*? A glance at the history of the composition of the novel will help us answer this question and also tell us which three of the seven dialects in contention can be eliminated.

According to Walter Blair, *Huckleberry Finn* was written as described below.[17] Dates separated by one dash indicate known limits of a period of concentrated work on the novel; dates separated by three dashes mark limits of a period during which Clemens probably worked on *Huckleberry Finn* in addition to other projects:

July-August, 1876: chap. 1-middle chap. 12; chaps. 15 and 16
                                (beginning-raft struck by steamboat; includes
                                "Raft Passage")

October, 1879 - - - June, 1880: chaps. 17 and 18 (Grangerfords)

June, 1880 - - - - June, 1883: chaps. 19-21 (King and Duke
                                appear; Boggs shot in Bricksville)

June-August, 1883: middle of chap. 12-chap.14 (*Sir Walter Scott*;
                                King Solomon discussion); chaps. 22-43
                                (Colonel Sherburn's speech in Bricksville-end)

When Clemens returned to *Huckleberry Finn* after an interruption he frequently made notes to himself.[18] Some of these are concerned with what he had already written, while others contain suggestions for future scenes. Some are concerned with characters and events: one says "Widow Douglas—then who is 'Miss Watson?' Ah, she's W D's *sister*" (DeVoto, p. 71). A line crosses out the first sentence, apparently drawn by Clemens when he found (or remembered) the answer. Other notes are concerned with dialect. One apparently written in the summer of 1883 says, "Huck says Nuther," and it also contains notes on Jim's dialect—isolated entries like "hund'd," "kin," "Nuffn," "W'y," and so on (DeVoto, p. 74). These notes on dialect are apparently reminders of the features in Huck's and Jim's speech. Huck does indeed say "nuther," both early and late in the novel, and Jim shows the pronunciations attributed to him.

But Clemens's recall was imperfect; his attempt at consistency, at least in Huck's dialect, falls short. In the parts of the novel written in the summer of 1883 (the latter half of the novel and the chapters 12-14 interpolation), Huck shows several nonstandard features which do not appear in the parts of the novel written earlier. These features are listed below, again with members of a class listed across the same line and the number of instances of each given in parentheses:

phonology: fur 'for' (9)
            bile 'boil' (5), pison 'poison' (3), pint 'point' (1)
            kinder 'kind of' (9)

grammar: possessive ourn (5), his'n (4), hern (1), yourn (1),
               their'n (1)
            theirselves (2)
            redundant comparative marking (e.g., *more easier*; 4)

Some of these features are quite striking. Except for the summer, 1883, passages, Huck has the standard diphthong, spelled *oi*, in words like *boil*, *poison*, and *point*, in contrast to Pap's *jint* 'joint' and Jim's *pint* 'point.' Then, writing in 1883, Clemens gives Huck Pap's and Jim's nonstandard /aI/ pronunciation nine times. To take another example, prior to the summer of 1883 Huck has exclusively standard absolute possessives: *ours, yours,* etc. In 1883, however, Huck utters twelve of these with the nonstandard -*n* suffix. Standard versions of all of the forms listed above (*for, kind of, themselves,* etc.) can be found in those parts of the novel written before June, 1883.[19]

This inconsistency in Huck's dialect—along with the working notes on dialect—is strong evidence that in the summer of 1883, when Clemens wrote three-fifths of the novel, he had imperfect recollection of all the details of the dialects he had written in the other two-fifths. In addition, during the months he spent revising the novel before sending it to his publisher (August, 1883-April, 1884), he did not observe and correct these inconsistencies. This is not particularly surprising. After all, in order to make the two parts of *Huckleberry Finn* harmonious—the part written before the summer of 1883 and the part written during that summer—Clemens would have had to make the nonstandard spellings in the second part standard (changed *fur* to *for*, say), or he would have had to make the standard spellings in the first part nonstandard (changed *for* to *fur*); the nonstandard spellings, having just issued from his pen in the preceding months, would not be at all suspect, and the standard spellings in the first part would be very easy to overlook: when one reads dialect, one notices what is nonstandard more than what is standard.

There is no evidence as to when Clemens wrote the "Explanatory." He is most likely to have written it shortly before or after completing the novel, since it is improbable that he would write a preface which lists seven distinct dialects before he had actually written the scenes containing those dialects. Now considering what Clemens failed to recall (or notice) in 1883 about Huck's dialect early in the novel, it is reasonable to suspect that he failed to recall other linguistic features long ago written into the novel—features such as Pap's *suthin'* 'something,' Judith Loftus's three pronunciations of *sence* 'since,' or Raftsman Ed's *furder* 'further.' Clemens may once have carefully chosen these features and deliberately used them to distinguish these characters' dialects from Huck's; but he is likely to have forgotten in 1883 a choice made in 1876, and the features are sufficiently subtle to have gone undetected in revision.

When we left the question of the four modified Pike County dialects we were faced with seven dialects from which to choose. Three of these were written in 1876: Pap's, Judith Loftus's, and the Raftsmen's. Three of the four others were constructed in the summer of 1883 (*Sir Walter Scott's*, the King's—some of whose speech was also written earlier—and the Phelpses'), and the fourth (the Bricksville Loafers') was written no earlier than June 1880. It is reasonable to assume that in reporting on the differences among the dialects in the novel Clemens remembered the distinctions he had drawn most recently at the expense of those he had drawn earlier. Also, the dialects written in 1876 are not greatly different from Huck's—note that they cluster toward the end of our scale ranking the dialects in decreasing order of divergence from Huck's dialect. In addition, Pap and Judith Loftus are both from Pike County, and, with Huck, Tom Sawyer, Aunt Polly, and Ben Rogers, can be seen as speakers of the "ordinary" or Ur-Pike County dialect. Finally, the Raft Passage is suspect not only because it was written in 1876 and shows relatively few distinguishing features but for another reason as well. If Clemens had intended this passage to represent uniquely one of the seven dialects referred to in the preface, then in the letter to his publisher authorizing its deletion he probably would have indicated that the preface needed revising accordingly; but nowhere in this or any other correspondence with his publisher is there a reference to the preface.[20]

Our conclusion, then, is that while it is not the case that there are seven and only seven distinct dialects in *Huckleberry Finn*, it *is* the case that there are seven distinct dialects which Clemens had in mind when he wrote the "Explanatory." These are as follows:

Missouri Negro: Jim (and four other minor characters)
Southwestern: Arkansas Gossips (Sister Hotchkiss et al.)
Ordinary "Pike County": Huck, Tom, Aunt Polly, Ben Rogers, Pap,
                        Judith Loftus
Modified "Pike County": Thieves on the *Sir Walter Scott*
Modified "Pike County": King
Modified "Pike County": Bricksville Loafers
Modified "Pike County": Aunt Sally and Uncle Silas Phelps

The fact that intelligent sense can be made out of the preface falsifies the view that Clemens was joking when he wrote it. This view never had much merit anyway. While the last sentence of the "Explanatory" might raise a smile, there is nothing rib-splitting about a list of dialects. The existence of a separate comical preface (called "Notice" and published on a separate page in the first English and American editions) is irrelevant; it is certainly possible for an author to write two prefaces to a work, one comical and one serious.[21] Clemens's abiding interest in folk speech, his impatience with Harte's use of dialect, and his working notes on the dialects of *Huckleberry Finn* all point to earnestness in the representation of dialects in this novel—as does the evidence of extensive revision of dialect spellings. There are hundreds of corrections of dialect in the manuscript (or discrepancies between a dialect form in the manuscript and the final form in the first edition). A *just* might be corrected to *jest* in the manuscript, for example, and then end up as *jist* in the first edition. Such labored revision makes no sense if the "Explanatory" is frivolous.

Thus Clemens was serious when he wrote the "Explanatory." But he was also partly mistaken about the work he was describing. This makes for a blend of system with chaos which has either confused investigators or discouraged them at the outset. Also, while there is greater differentiation than stated in the "Explanatory" in terms of the number of distinguishable dialects, there is a somewhat smaller degree of differentiation of the dialects than one would expect from such a bold announcement. This is especially true of the varieties of "Pike County" dialect, where the differentiation is so fine that one must wonder what the author hoped the novel could gain from it. In this regard it is worth noting that the speakers of three of the four modified varieties of the "Pike County" dialect—the thieves on the *Sir Walter Scott*, the King, and the Bricksville Loafers—are morally reprehensible, and, in addition, that their speech differs from Huck's by virtue of features normally found in the speech of the blacks in the novel. The Bricksville Loafers' *gwyne*, for example, occurs elsewhere in the novel only in the speech of slaves. The same can be said for the King's palatalization, which in the manuscript is also given to the thieves on the *Sir Walter Scott* (see note 10). This last group also loses *r* in phonetic environments similar to those where *r* is lost in Jim's speech (*befo'*, *yo'*), whereas Huck very rarely loses *r* and never loses it word-finally (e.g., *stabboard, whippowill*). One's first thought is that it is surprising that Clemens, in a novel concerned with exposing weaknesses in the conventional values of society, calls upon those values in the way he taints these characters' dialects—to "lower" them he draws them with features of black speech. But in doing this Clemens was merely reflecting linguistic reality in his time and, indeed, in the present century: the speech of lower-class rural whites in the South shares a great deal with the speech of blacks.[22] In *Huckleberry Finn*, *gwyne*, palatalization, and *r*-lessness are—for both blacks and whites—physical signals of low social status, and—for whites only—physical signals of "substandard" morals. These white characters may share something of Jim's dialect, but they do not share in his goodness.

Finally, it is important to recognize the showmanship in this ambitious, seven-way dialectal differentiation and in the attention the author calls to it. Clemens composed *Huckleberry Finn* in the heyday of literary dialect in American literature, and no doubt he wanted to show what he too was capable of doing, especially with the "Pike County" dialect that he helped to create.

NOTES

1. Mark Twain, *Adventures of Huckleberry Finn*, ed. Henry Nash Smith (Boston, 1958), p. 2. All subsequent references are to this edition. I am grateful to the National Endowment for the Humanities for a summer Stipend enabling me to investigate Clemens's literary use of dialect.

2. In the first group are William Clark Brekenridge, "Missouri," in *Books Containing American Local Dialects*, ed. Arthur E. Bostwick (St. Louis, 1914), p. 9; Vance Randolph and George P. Wilson, *Down in the Holler: A Gallery of Ozark Folk Speech* (Norman, Okla., 1953), p. 7; and Curt Rulon, "Geographical Delimitation of the Dialect Areas in *The Adventures of Huckleberry Finn*," *Mark Twain Journal*, XIV (Winter, 1967), 9-12. In the second group are Katherine Buxbaum, "Mark Twain and American Dialect," *American Speech*, II (Feb., 1927), 233-236, whose sensible (though somewhat casual) analysis suffers because it antedated Walter Blair's determination of the dates of the composition of *Huckleberry Finn* (see note 17)—a determination which, as will be shown below, is essential in to an understanding of the preface—and, more recently, Sally Boland, "The Seven Dialects in *Huckleberry Finn*," *North Dakota Quarterly*, XXXVI (Summer, 1968), 30-40, a study flawed by errors of observation.

3. For treatments of this question see James Nathan Tidwell, "Mark Twain's Representation of Negro Speech," *American Speech*, XVII (Oct., 1942), 174-176; Curt Rulon, "The Dialects in *Huckleberry Finn*," (Ph.D. diss., University of Iowa, 1967); and Lee A. Pederson, "Negro Speech in *The Adventures of Huckleberry Finn*," *Mark Twain Journal*, XIII (Winter, 1965), 1-4. Pederson, in "Mark Twain's Missouri Dialects: Marion County Phonemics," *American Speech*, XLII (Dec., 1967), 261-278, reports on a 1964 dialect survey of northeastern Missouri. Four of his twelve informants were seventy-nine years old or older, and they in turn reported on remembered archaisms; thus there is some raw material here for a comparison of the dialects in *Huckleberry Finn* with actual nineteenth-century speech. Finally, Walt Wolfram and Donna Christian's *Appalachian Speech* (Arlington, Va., 1976) is a linguistic description of two West Virginian counties which lie in the larger South Midland area, whence came the bulk of the antebellum settlement of Missouri; despite the years separating the two, *Appalachian Speech* comes remarkably close to being a grammar of *Huckleberry Finn*.

4. See Sumner Ives's classic article on the subject, "A Theory of Literary Dialect," *Tulane Studies in English*, II (1950), 137-182.

5. This has already been done. For a partial list see Buxbaum, and for a nearly complete list see Rulon, "The Dialects in *Huckleberry Finn*," 59-95. It should be noted here that the nonstandard features characterizing Huck's dialect appear in both his speech and narration, although as Robert J. Lowenherz, "The Beginning of *Huckleberry Finn*," *American Speech*, XXXVIII (Oct., 1963), 196-201, points out, dialect spellings are somewhat more dense in Huck's speech than in his narration. Below, "Huck's dialect" refers to the language of both.

6. The lexical items are minimally glossed. For fuller treatment see Robert L. Ramsay and Frances Guthrie Emberson, *A Mark Twain Lexicon* (1938; rpt. New York, 1963).

7. I depart from this procedure in two instances. First, I give spellings showing neutralization of the contrast between the vowels of standard English *pit* (/I/) and *pet* (/ɛ/); such neutralization is indicated either with a nonstandard use of the *i* graph for /ɛ/ (*git* 'get') or a nonstandard use of *e* for /I/ (*sence* 'since'). Huck has just one example of this—*resk* 'risk'—and so in some sense has the rule of neutralization, but it is a striking feature of several other dialects and worthy of attention. Second, I give spellings showing /ɛ/ or /I/ for /ʌ/ in *just, such, touch*, etc. Again Huck has just one example (*jest*), whereas other characters have many more.

8. It is highly debatable that Clemens could have been referring to this passage in the preface, and my final conclusion below is that he was not. However, it is listed here for the sake of thoroughness.

9. Excluded from the list are minor characters of various types: speakers of dialects differing very slightly from Huck's (the watchman whom Huck sends to the *Sir Walter Scott*, Buck Grangerford, and the Duke), speakers whose dialects are virtually identical with Huck's (Tom Sawyer, Ben Rogers, Aunt Polly, and The Wilks daughters), and speakers who can be grouped in one of the categories below, e.g., Tim Collins (the "young country jake" from whom the King learns about the Wilkses), who can be grouped with the King by virtue of his two pronunciations of *g'yirls* 'girls,' and the Pikesville boy who tells Huck about Jim's capture, who with his *hunderd* and *Newrleans* belongs with Aunt Sally and Uncle Silas Phelps.

10. Two important dialect spellings in the speech of these characters appear in the partial holograph manuscript but do not appear in the first edition: *weepon* 'weapon' (p. 81-9 in the manuscript) and *thish-yer* 'this here' (p. 81-15). The first, which is unique to the thieves, fails to appear in the published version of the novel only because the passage containing it was deleted in revision. Clemens revised the second to *this*, perhaps because the characters are too far north to show palatalization, a feature he associated with the South (see *Life on the Mississippi*, chap. 44). Thus Clemens originally intended to distinguish the speech of these characters from Huck's speech even more than is evident in the published version. I am grateful to the Buffalo and Erie County Public Library for permission to examine the manuscript.

11. See Kenneth S. Lynn, *Mark Twain and Southwestern Humor* (1959; rpt. Westport, Conn., 1972), and Walter Blair, *Mark Twain and Huck Finn* (Berkeley, Calif., 1960), 243-244.

12. *The Century Magazine* XXVI (May, 1883), 137-150 and XXVI (June, 1883), 185-194. The story also appears in Harris's *Mingo and Other Sketches in Black and White* (Boston, 1884). Clemens wrote the Arkansas Gossips scene in the summer of 1883.

13. Clemens's note appears in Bernard DeVoto, *Mark Twain at Work* (Cambridge, Mass., 1942), p. 76.

14. *Literary History of the United States*, 4th ed., ed. Robert E. Spiller et al. (New York, 1974), I, 864. "The Pike" is fully described in Fred Lewis Pattee, *A History of American Literature Since 1870* (New York, 1915), 83-98, and in G. R. MacMinn, "'The Gentleman from Pike' in Early California," *American Literature*, VIII (May, 1936), 160-169.

15. The only other reference by Clemens to Pike County dialect that I know of is to be found among his marginalia to Bret Harte's *The Luck of Roaring Camp*, where he also uses quotation marks. Criticizing Harte's dialect, as he often did, Clemens writes of one passage, "This is much more suggestive of Dickens & an English atmosphere than 'Pike County'" (Bradford A. Booth, "Mark Twain's Comments on Bret Harte's Stories," *American Literature*, XXV [Jan., 1954], p. 494).

16. *Johnson's Original Comic Songs* (San Francisco, 1860).

17. "When Was *Huckleberry Finn* Written?," *American Literature*, XXX (March, 1958), 1-25.

18. The notes are given in DeVoto, 63-78, and are discussed there and in Blair, "When Was *Huckleberry Finn* Written?"

19. Tom Sawyer, another character who speaks early and late in the novel, is subject to the same winds of change. In chapter 2 he says *join*, while in chapter 42 he says *spile* 'spoil.'

20. Clemens's letter agreeing to the deletion of the passage, dated April 22, 1884, is in *Mark Twain, Business Man*, ed. Samuel C. Webster (Boston, 1946), 249-250.

21. The "Notice" reads, "Persons attempting to find a motive in this narrative will be prosecuted; persons attempting to find a moral in it will be banished; persons attempting to find a plot in it will be shot. BY ORDER OF THE AUTHOR PER G. G., CHIEF OF ORDNANCE."

22. Walt Wolfram, "The Relationship of White Southern Speech to Vernacular Black English," *Language*, L (Sept., 1974), 498-527.

MARK TWAIN, HUCK FINN, AND JACOB BLIVENS: GILT-EDGED, TREE-CALF MORALITY IN *THE ADVENTURES OF HUCKLEBERRY FINN*

HAROLD H. KOLB, JR.

Anchored in the middle of James Cox's *Mark Twain: The Fate of Humor* (1966) is a statement which, if true, reduces virtually all of the criticism on *Huckleberry Finn* to rubble:

[The] moment, when Huck says "All right, then, I'll *go* to hell," is characteristically the moment we fatally approve, and approve *morally*. But it is with equal fatality the moment at which Huck's identity is most precariously threatened. In the very act of choosing to go to hell he has surrendered to the notion of a *principle* of right and wrong. He has forsaken the world of pleasure to make a moral choice. Precisely here is where Huck is about to negate himself—where, with an act of positive virtue, he actually commits himself to play the role of Tom Sawyer which he *has* to assume in the closing section of the book. To commit oneself to the idea, the *morality* of freeing Jim, is to become Tom Sawyer.

This provocative (which of course means perverse) reading must be answered, not because it is eccentric, but because it unhinges the moral structure which has been assumed by the book's defenders and detractors alike. Having spent their ammunition on the border war of the ending, most 20th-century critics take for granted the proposition that the "*go* to hell" passage in Chapter 31 is the moral center of the book, and that Huck makes the right choice. Much of the large library of *Huckleberry Finn* criticism is a series of footnotes to the view first expressed by Joel Chandler Harris: "there is not in our fictive literature a more wholesome book than 'Huckleberry Finn'. . . . We are taught [by it] the lesson of honesty, justice, and mercy." The critics who have testified to Huck's moral victory need not be listed—their name is legion. Henry Nash Smith, whose *Mark Twain: The Development of a Writer* (1962) is the best of the many books on Mark Twain, can be taken as representative: "The account of Huck's mental struggle in [Chapter 31] is the emotional climax of the story. . . . The most obvious of Mark Twain's discoveries on the deeper levels of Huck's psyche is the boy's capacity for love. The quality of the emotion is defined in action by his decision to sacrifice himself for Jim." Because this view is often assumed rather than developed, and not always developed in the light of the evidence of the text, the best way to respond to Professor Cox's disturbing pronouncement is first to make a persuasive a case as possible for the moral integrity of *Adventures of Huckleberry Finn*, and then to suggest its inadequacy.

The novel exhibits three patterns of evidence concerning Huck's moral enlightenment. The first, and most celebrated, is developmental. In a series of episodes Huck gradually comes to recognize that Jim is a human being whose blackness dissolves, whose chains fall away, under the transforming power of friendship. Huck doesn't learn easily. Soon after he meets him on Jackson's Island, Huck plays a trick on Jim by coiling a dead rattlesnake on his blanket, "thinking there'd be some fun when Jim found him there." When Jim is bitten, Huck's reaction centers on himself rather than on Jim: "That all comes of my being such a fool as to not remember that wherever you leave a dead snake its mate always comes there and curls around it. . . . Then I slid out quiet and throwed the snakes clear away amongst the bushes; for I warn't going to let Jim find out it was all my fault, not if I could help it." And while Jim is suffering,

Huck is unconcerned enough to debate the relative potency of rattlesnake bites and Pap's whiskey.

His next trick comes after they have been separated in the fog. Huck, for a time, persuades a sleepy Jim that the episode was a dream. When Jim finally sees the debris on the raft and untangles its meaning, he lectures the white boy for the first and last time:

> En when I wake up en fine you back agin', all safe en soun', de tears come en I could a got down on my knees en kiss' yo' foot I's so thankful. En all you wuz thinkin 'bout wuz how you could make a fool uv ole Jim wid a lie. Dat truck dah is *trash*; en trash is what people is dat puts dirt on de head er dey fren's en makes 'em ashamed.

Huck accepts this lesson, humbles himself to Jim, and resolves to give up playing tricks on his friend. His resolve is tested immediately, and it holds. When two armed men in a skiff, searching for runaway blacks, challenge him on the river—"Is your man white or black?"—Huck responds with "He's white" and uncorks one of his Homeric lies to prevent the men from checking.

Jim is out of sight in the Grangerford chapters; and he is subdued, roped, and painted blue during the siege of the raft by the king and the duke. But Huck's newly won insight holds firm. He recognizes Jim's humanity and tells us that "he cared just as much for his people as white folks does for their'n. It don't seem natural, but I reckon it's so." This compassion arms Huck for his most difficult battle. When Jim is sold by the king to Silas Phelps, Huck is forced to review the companionship established during their rafting journey and choose between his love for Jim and his duty to report a runaway slave. "It was a close place," thinks Huck, in his steamboat vernacular, but he churns through with the courage and resolution of Horace Bixby running a dangerous channel at night. Huck rejects duty, religion, society, and his conscience, and chooses Jim by destroying the letter to Miss Watson and deciding to steal Jim out of slavery once more: "All right, then, I'll *go* to hell." After this moral crisis the novel, engineered by Tom Sawyer, takes its notorious downhill slide. Although he is powerless to stem Tom's evasion, Huck remains true to his friendship and to his opinion of Jim. When Jim refuses to go further until Tom's wound is treated, even though it will result in recapture, Huck summarizes the essential lesson of his adventures: "I knowed he was white inside."

The development of Huck's awareness of Jim's humanity provides satisfying narrative and moral continuity, but it apparently fails to harmonize with a second pattern of evidence. Many passages throughout the novel, and especially after Huck has presumably learned his lesson in chapter 31, give us pause. Huck tells us that Jim's ignorance proves "you can't learn a nigger to argue." He is appalled by Jim's freedom fever as they near the clear waters of the Ohio, and by his talk of stealing his children out of slavery, if necessary.

> It most froze me to hear such talk. He wouldn't ever dared to talk such talk in his life before. Just see what a difference it made in him the minute he judged he was about free. It was according to the old saying, "give a nigger an inch and he'll take an ell." Thinks I, this is what comes of my not thinking. Here was this nigger which I had as good as helped to run away, coming right out flat-footed and saying he would steal his children—children that belonged to a man I didn't even know; a man that hadn't ever done me no harm.

"Well," Huck says, when the king and the duke stage their lost-brother routine, "if ever I struck anything like it, I'm a nigger." Mistaken for Tom Sawyer late in the novel, Huck invents a steamboat disaster to explain his delayed appearance to Aunt Sally:

"We blowed out a cylinder-head."
"Good gracious! anybody hurt?"
"No'm. Killed a nigger."
"Well, it's lucky; because sometimes people do get hurt."

And at the end of the book Huck is relieved to discover that Jim had been free during the escapades on Silas Phelps' farm, so no blame can be attached to Tom as an abolitionist: "I couldn't ever understand, before, until that minute and that talk, how he *could* help a body set a nigger free, with his bringing-up." All this suggests that Huck somehow hasn't totally learned his lesson, that his knowledge about Jim is incomplete, that the smooth flow of moral development contains more rough water than first appeared.

These two contradictory patterns are further complicated by a third. A number of passages suggest that Huck has no need of moral development, that he has an instinctive compassion for Jim from the beginning. In Chapter 2, Tom Sawyer suggests that they "tie Jim [who is asleep] to the tree for fun." Huck's reply is instantaneous: "But I said no; he might wake and make a disturbance, and then they'd find out I warn't in." Huck's reply may be straightforward and thus show more concern for himself than Jim, but it may also be a lie to protect Jim and to dodge Tom's ridicule. Twice in the chapter Tom wants to trick Jim, and both times Huck refuses. When they meet on Jackson's Island, Huck quickly recovers from the "fan-tods" of finding his refuge inhabited: "I bet I was glad to see him. . . . I was ever so glad to see Jim." And Jim easily (and permanently, it turns out) extracts a promise from Huck not to tell on him: "I said I wouldn't and I'll stick to it. Honest *injun* I will. People would call me a low down Ablitionist and despise me for keeping mum—but that don't make no difference. I ain't agoing to tell." Huck's gift of friendship, offered instinctively and immediately and never withdrawn, generates a striking shift in pronouns in his cry of warning when Huck discovers that Mr. Loftus is hunting Jim for the reward money: "'Git up and hump yourself, Jim! There ain't a minute to lose. They're after us!'"

These three patterns—moral development, moral backsliding, moral stasis—complicate but do not contradict the lesson of honesty, justice, and mercy first recognized by Joel Chandler Harris. They fit together in a plausible whole as Mark Twain suggested in his 1895 notebook entry about "a book of mine where a sound heart & a deformed conscience come into a collision & conscience suffers defeat." Huck Finn does have a sound heart which beats steadily throughout the novel. In the first chapters and the last (although he fails to divert Tom Sawyer's tricks on Jim which bracket the novel) and in the rafting adventures between, Huck consistently, inevitably it seems, chooses the path of compassion. But there is development. As he comes to know Jim better, his sympathy, respect, and comradeship all deepen. "Miss Watson's big nigger, named Jim" (Chapter 2) becomes simply "Jim" as Huck discovers that this particular nigger is a man like any other man, a friend unlike any other friend. But Huck is unable to generalize from his experience. He has no insights into the Negro question. He never renounces slavery. The disquieting negatives that appear throughout—the clichés about learning a nigger to argue or giving him an inch; the cylinder-head manslaughter—are the products of Huck's diseased conscience, caught from a corrupt society, but they do not intrude in his relationship with Jim. Huck's age of innocence is below the age of abstraction, and the reader is left to draw the conclusion. Huck has made a friend; the reader castigates the society which defines such a friendship as illegal and immoral. Huck never defeats his deformed conscience—it is we who do that—he simply ignores it in relation to Jim.

So go the moral adventures of Huckleberry Finn. They are so satisfying, so wholesome, so perfect, that they invite suspicion. Nevertheless, the book's morality is not a "sell," as James Cox suggests. It is not a subtle trap, a confidence game, designed for naïve readers. The moral theme of *Huckleberry Finn* was created by Mark Twain at a time—1876 to 1883—when he was in full command of his talent; and it indicates precisely the way he understood his book ten years later. But we can make a distinction between Mark Twain's Huck Finn and ours, between the author's achievement in 1885 and the revisionist view that his later writings offer. Why didn't Mark Twain write another *Huckleberry Finn*? This question is not answered merely by assigning the book to the incomparable Everest reserved for *Oedipus Rex, Hamlet*, and *Paradise Lost*. The reason Mark Twain never wrote another *Huckleberry Finn* is that it became impossible for him to believe in his hero.

II

Mark Twain's writings contain an unceasing procession of moral idiots. One of the earliest is "Mamie Grant, the Child-Missionary," the heroine of a story composed during the summer of 1868 as the author relaxed on a three-week steamship journey from San Francisco to New York. Mamie is a nine-year-old devotee of Sunday school literature, an enthusiast of the "comfort & joy of true religion," whose relentless piety extends even to the breakfast table of her unregenerated aunt:

"Batter-cakes?"
"No auntie, I cannot, I dare not eat batter-cakes while your precious soul is in peril."

Mamie spends a visit with her aunt and uncle answering their doorbell and astonishing all callers with a barrage of holy advice and wholesome tracts ("Fire & Brimstone, or the Sinner's Last Gasp"; "The Doomed Drunkard or the Wages of Sin"; "The Blasphemous Sailor Awfully Rebuked"). Having driven the census-taker, the newspaper boy, her uncle's debtor, and the mortgage collector from the house, Mamie contemplates her "noble work today. I may yet see my poor little name in a beautiful Sunday School book, & maybe T. S. Arthur may write it." Her uncle has a different view of the efficacy of Mamie's missionary work:

"Alas, we are ruined. My newspaper is stopped, & I am posted on its bulletin board as a delinquent. The tax-collecting census-taker has set his black mark opposite my name. Martin, who should have returned the thousand dollars he borrowed has not come, & Phillips, in consequence, has foreclosed the mortgage, & we are homeless!"

Mamie Grant's good works are carried on in the manuscript fragments by Bolivar ("Autobiography of a Damned Fool"), and they have their counterparts throughout the published works. Mark Twain amuses himself constantly and his readers occasionally by stuffing moral platitudes in the mouths of the passengers on board the *Columbia (Mark Twain's Travels with Mr. Brown)* and the *Quaker City* (*The Innocents Abroad*). Pious fools abound in his books. Some of the morality-mouthing characters are hypocrites, like Sid Sawyer and Miss Watson. Others are merely stupid, like Mr. Walters, the Sunday school superintendent in *Tom Sawyer*. Sometimes the narrator is the straight man; sometimes he delivers the punchline. The game always is deflation, but it is Sunday school style rather than Sunday school morality that is the target. Mark Twain's early "Story of the Good Little Boy" perfectly defines the genre. Young Jacob Blivens, like the blonde heroine of the *Occidental's* composite novel in *Roughing It,* is "virtuous to the verge of eccentricity":

He always obeyed his parents, no matter how absurd and unreasonable their demands were; and he always learned his book, and never was late at Sabbath-school. He would not play hookey . . . he wouldn't lie . . . and he was so honest that he was simply ridiculous. The curious ways that Jacob had, surpassed everything. He wouldn't play marbles on Sunday, he wouldn't rob birds' nests, he wouldn't give hot pennies to organ-grinders' monkeys.

Instead, Jacob reads Sunday school books and resolves to emulate their heroes. The strategy of the tale is conveyed by Mark Twain's original title—"The Story of the Good Little Boy Who Did Not Prosper." Jacob's adventures invariably come to grief. He admonishes a boy not to steal apples and is rewarded with a broken arm. He befriends a lame dog and is bitten. He attempts to warn some youngsters about the dangers of Sunday sailing and nearly drowns. And his career of misfired benevolence abruptly ends when he interferes with a group of boys "in the old iron foundry fixing up a little joke on fourteen or fifteen dogs, which they had tied together in long procession, and were going to ornament with empty nitroglycerine cans made fast to their tails." Jacob explodes "through the roof and soar[s] away toward the sun, with the fragments of those fifteen dogs stringing after him like the tail of a kite. . . . Although the bulk of him came down all right in a tree-top in an adjoining country, the rest of him was apportioned around among four townships. . . . You never saw a boy scattered so."

The fun of "The Good Little Boy" lies in its satire of the lesson of morality rewarded in the Sabbatical literature that made the Front Room of the 1870's, as George Ade put it, a ponderous Mausoleum. But morality itself is not under attack, as a companion story demonstrates. Mark Twain arrives at the same satire from the other side of the street in the "Story of the Bad Little Boy." Jim, the bad boy, steals, lies, gets the widow's son in trouble, abuses animals, strikes his little sister, gets drunk and thrown into jail. "And he grew up and married, and raised a large family, and brained them all with an axe one night, and got wealthy by all manner of cheating and rascality; and now he is the infernalest wickedest scoundrel in his native village, and is universally respected, and belongs to the legislature." The two stories attack not the moral but the providential universe—at least the 19th-century version which demanded proof in this world. Virtue, Mark Twain insists, is not always rewarded; evil is not always punished.

Huck Finn superficially resembles bad Jim, but he is firmly in the camp of Jacob Blivens, a cousin to what Anne T. Trensky has called "The Saintly Child in Nineteenth-Century American Fiction" (in *Prospects*, 1975). Ms. Trensky doesn't consider Huck, but her formulation is suggestive:

We see the basic pattern for hundreds of stories that were the favorite reading of nineteenth-century America—the confrontation between an innocent child and a corrupt society. . . . [The saintly children often] are bereft of one or both parents. . . . The sign of inner grace is a supernatural beauty, marked either by pale skin and golden curls or by a spiritual glow that transforms otherwise plain features. The children frequently suffer hardship and pain, but are ultimately rescued by protective adults, the conversion of their persecutors, or early death.

Huck's curls are grimed by Mississippi mud, and he is translated to the Indian Territory rather than heaven, but the glow of his inner virtue makes him a bedfellow—however incongruously gritty and uncombed—with Ilbrahim, little Eva, Baby Rue, and Elsie Dinsmore. Ms. Trensky's two categories—the child born pure and the child initially imperfect—remind us of Leslie Fiedler's Good Good Boy and Good Bad Boy, which he uses to differentiate Sid Sawyer and Tom in *Love and Death in the American Novel*. Huck's badness is more vivid than Tom's, and his goodness is organized by an entirely different code, but Huck, too, is a good bad boy.

Huck steals and lies and abuses grammar, but his thefts are inevitably excusable and his lies are always benevolent. If Tom Sawyer were to suggest the hot penny trick, Huck would probably argue for keeping the penny themselves, for there warn't no use in giving it to a monkey who didn't know how to spend it. If there were sisters to be slapped or dogs to be tortured, Huck would undoubtedly slide out and try to turn the focus in a harmless direction. It is his naïve but compassionate eye which reports to us the shock of the slapping of Elizabeth, the deaf-mute, and the squalid brutality of the loafers in Bricksville: "There couldn't anything wake them up all over, and make them happy all over, like a dog-fight—unless it might be putting turpentine on a stray dog and setting fire to him, or tying a tin pan to his tail and see him run himself to death."

Huck Finn and Jacob Blivens differ mainly in the matter of baths and verb tenses, and of course in ability. But it is Jacob's incompetence that we laugh at, not his intention. Both characters are curious in ways that surpass everything, virtuous to the point of eccentricity. Jacob's pattern of disinterested benevolence to boys and dogs is mirrored by Huck's seemingly motiveless benignity, not just to Jim, but to everyone he encounters: the widow Douglas (she "looked so sorry that I thought I would behave a while if I could"); the murderers on board the *Walter Scott* ("I begun to think how dreadful it was, even for murderers, to be in such a fix"); the Grangerfords ("I liked all that family, dead ones and all, and warn't going to let anything come between us"); Mary Jane Wilks ("It made my eyes water a little, to remember her crying there all by herself in the night"); the king and the duke ("I was sorry for them poor pitiful rascals, it seemed like I couldn't ever feel any hardness against them any more"); Aunt Sally ("I wished I could do something for her, but I couldn't, only to swear that I wouldn't never do nothing to grieve her any more"); and the community in general ("We made up our minds they [the king and the duke] was going to break into somebody's house or store, or was going into the counterfeit-money business, or something. So then we . . . made up an agreement that we wouldn't have nothing in the world to do with such actions"). Huck provides the reader with an entertaining description of the Widow Douglas' religion ("'spiritual gifts' . . . was too many for me") and her sister's exhortation to prayer ("I tried it. Once I got a fish-line, but no hooks"), but in spite of his protests, his much proclaimed rebellion, Huck's code is precisely that of the Widow: "She told me what she meant—I must help other people, and do everything I could for other people, and look out for them all the time, and never think about myself."

The difference between Huck Finn and Jacob Blivens, just as that between Scotty Briggs and the minister in *Roughing It*, is one of style rather than substance. Like the Sunday school literature Mark Twain satirized all his life, *Adventures of Huckleberry Finn* presents a hero whose moral triumph soars on gratuitous wings. The story succeeds because we, like Mark Twain, wish to believe in the ethical ideal Huck represents, and because the saccharine piety associated with that ideal in third-rate literature is so effectively diluted by Huck's scruffy exterior, his venial sins, his Concord Library-defying vernacular, his ability to transmit a vision—both comic and tragic—which explodes stupidity and cruelty and hypocrisy. But Mark Twain's book has at its center an angel in homespun. The most realistic of our realists has created a hero who is a gilt-edged, tree-calf, hand-tooled, seven-dollar Friendship's Offering moral idealist.

III

Adventures of Huckleberry Finn, like all great books, is about the complexities of human experience. These complexities arise from Huck's confrontation with Mississippi Valley civilization, but they are located largely outside Huck's character. This is the price Mark Twain pays for Huck's innocence, for his worldly unworldliness. The difficulty with Huck is not that he carries a heavy moral burden, but that he carries it so lightly. His goodness is innate, instinctive, natural. He is a Rousseauan noble savage born free of the chains of civilization, a Lockean natural man nursed in principles of justice and charity that derive from the state of nature, a Wordsworthian blessed child trailing clouds of glory from God (or, in Lionel Trilling's version, waves of goodness from the river-god). Huck, like Uncle Tom in Augustine St. Clare's shrewd phrase, is a "moral miracle." He reminds us of Bret Harte's good-natured drunken cowboys, self-denying gamblers, and heart-of-gold prostitutes. The comparison would gravel Mark Twain, who, after their friendship had dissolved, denounced Harte as dishonest: "[His] pathetics, imitated from Dickens, used to be a godsend to the farmers of two hemispheres on account of the freshets of tears they compelled. He said to me once with a cynical chuckle that he thought he had mastered the art of pumping up the tear of sensibility." The two authors are separated by the gulf of genius as well as that of rancor, but Mark Twain's later writing suggests that Huck Finn is as impossible, or at least as unlikely, as pumped up, as Sandy, John Oakhurst, Mother Shipton, and the other great-hearted riders of the Slumgullion Stage, magnanimous denizens of Poker Flat, Red Gulch, and Roaring Camp.

Mark Twain lived for a quarter of a century after the publication of *Adventures of Huckleberry Finn*. He spent much of this period wrestling with three related issues that he never managed to pin down—the responsibility of the individual to the community, the origin of ethics, free will and determinism. The more he pondered these issues the more it appeared that human beings were accidents of necessity locked in a trap of response that served only the self. In his forays into W. E. H. Lecky's *History of European Morals from Augustus to Charlemagne* he discovered two theories of morality:

One of them is generally described as the stoical, the intuitive, the independent or the sentimental; the other as the epicurean, the inductive, the utilitarian, or the selfish. The moralists of the former school, to state their opinions in the broadest form, believe that we have a natural power of perceiving that some qualities, such as benevolence, chastity, or veracity, are better than

others. . . . The moralist of the opposite school denies that we have any such natural perception. He maintains that we have by nature absolutely no knowledge of merit and demerit . . . [that]
a desire to obtain happiness and to avoid pain is the only possible motive to action. The reason, and
the only reason, why we should perform virtuous actions, or in other words, seek the good of
others, is that on the whole such a course will bring us the greatest amount of happiness.

In spite of Lecky's bias toward the intuitive, Mark Twain chose, with
increasing vehemence, the utilitarian. Huck represents both points of view. In
small matters he is our archpragmatist: "Tom Sawyer called the hogs 'ingots,'
and he called the turnips and stuff 'julery' and we would go to the cave and
pow-wow over what we had done and how many people we had killed and
marked. But I couldn't see no profit in it." But in large affairs of conduct he
is an exemplar of the stoical, the intuitive, the independent, the sentimental. Thus Huck Finn is essentially out of harmony with the drift of his author's
convictions. Mark Twain wrote in the margin of Lecky's *History* that "all moral
perceptions are acquired by the influences around us," but that doctrine applied
to *Adventures of Huckleberry Finn* contradicts the notion of a sound heart,
uncorrupted by society, on which Huck's character is built. Huck has been to
two schools—Pap, and the Mississippi Valley society at large. He could not
have learned his morality from his father ("Every time he got money he got
drunk; and very time he got drunk he raised Cain around town; and every time
he raised Cain he got jailed. He was just suited—this kind of thing was right in
his line") or from a society in which every institution endorses slavery ("they
fetched the niggers in and had prayers"); a society whose worst elements enjoy
"putting turpentine on a stray dog and setting fire to him"; a society whose best
members "run along the [river] bank shooting at [the boys] and singing out,
'kill them, kill them!'" Huck's opposition to these influences governs the book.
How he could have reached beyond his environment and come to his unprece-
dented ethical purity is more than even Mark Twain finally could understand.

IV

Increasingly unable to account for his hero, the author could not support an
intuitive theory of morality in his writings after 1885. The difficulties of
interpretation in *A Connecticut Yankee in King Arthur's Court* (1889) rest
precisely on the moral ambiguity of Hank Morgan. His conduct careens wildly
from melodramatic sympathy ("down came the lash and flicked a flake of skin
from her naked shoulder. It stung me as if I had been hit instead") to comic
sadism ("during the next fifteen minutes we stood under a steady drizzle of
microscopic fragments of knights and hardware and horse-flesh"), making the
entire book, like a telephone in Camelot, "a fantastic conjunction of opposites
and irreconcilables." The bleakness of *Pudd'nhead Wilson* (1894) stems from
the lack of the steady moral beacon that illuminates *Adventures of Huckleberry
Finn*. Even Wilson and Roxy—intelligent, decent, sympathetic—are trained by
the society of Dawson's Landing to accept inhumanity as the normal condition
of human affairs. All the characters, black and white, good and evil, must
finally dance to the book's refrain (repeated 22 times): sold down the river in
slavery. The man that corrupted Hadleyburg has an easy task: Hadleyburg
corrupts itself. The harmless old couple, Mary and Edward Richards, are
relentlessly destroyed by the forces of greed and hypocrisy. There is no moral
center, no countercurrent, no voice of protest. Mark Twain's double vision in
the early works has hardened to a single vision in the late, and with the loss

of duality we suffer a loss of humor. Huck is resurrected to tell more tales in *Tom Sawyer Abroad* (1894) and *Tom Sawyer, Detective* (1896), but these ghostly imitations are appalling failures. No sequels to a great work were ever flatter, more insipid, more disappointing. The conventional explanation is that Mark Twain was grinding out uninspired potboilers in the midst of personal and financial chaos in a frenzied attempt to pay his creditors. Yet the books fail even as potboilers, and they are inferior to other works written at the same time. The biographical explanations are valid enough, but it is also true that Huck's lifelessness in these late stories results from the fact that he had died in his author's hands. Huck in his own book was free, free as his Hannibal prototype Tom Blankenship, who "was the only really independent person—boy or man—in the community," free to choose the path of virtue. By the late 1890's Mark Twain was uncertain about both free will and virtue.

He never gave up entirely on the possibility of human goodness—Theodore Fisher opposes a sound heart to Satan's artillery in *The Mysterious Stranger*—but he never found a satisfactory theoretical source. Mark Twain described his reading of Jonathan Edwards' *Freedom of the Will* as a "three day's tear with a drunken lunatic." In addition, he seemed to find the practice of virtue and the evidence of providence diminishing on every hand. Personal disasters obviously influenced his writing, but to these overtrumpeted events we need to add the political, economic, and social disasters that for Mark Twain made up *fin de siècle* history. The author's personal and public writings in his later years poignantly detail the deaths of Susy and Jean and the crash of his business affairs, but they also strike out at imperialism in the Philippines, colonialism in China, mass murder in the Belgian Congo, the Boer war, lynching, religious hypocrisy, corporate profiteering, tariff manipulation, the "constitutional monarchy" of Theodore Roosevelt, and the "teaching of Jay Gould" ("people had desired money before his day, but he taught them to fall down and worship it"). The list is endless, taxing even Mark Twain's voracious appetite for satire and entangling him in a dilemma that he had earlier described to Howells: "Of course a man can't write successful satire except he be in a calm judicial good-humor. . . . In truth I don't ever seem to be in a good enough humor with ANYthing to *satirize* it; no, I want to stand up before it & *curse* it, & foam at the mouth—or take a club & pound it to rags & pulp." *Adventures of Huckleberry Finn* was conceived in an adolescent America whose problems, substantial as they seemed at the time, were dwarfed in the 1890's by the agonies of maturity: industrialism apparently run amuck and generating class warfare; international power achieved so quickly and so effortlessly that it led to buccaneering adventures in imperialism and exploitation; booming cities crowded with foreigners; American life rerouted by a lust for technology and the worship of a new trinity of size, speed, success. By the end of the century, Mark Twain found the philosophical questioning that made Huck's morality an anachronism buttressed by every newspaper:

I have been reading the morning paper. I do it every morning—well knowing that I shall find in it the usual depravities and basenesses & hypocrisies & cruelties that make up Civilization, & cause me to put in the rest of the day pleading for the damnation of the human race.

The [London] correspondent mentions a few of our American events of the past twelvemonth, such as the limitless rottenness of our great insurance companies, where theft has been carried on by our most distinguished commercial men as a profession; the exposures of conscienceless graft, colossal graft, in great municipalities like Philadelphia, St. Louis, and other large cities; the recent exposure of millionfold graft in the great Pennsylvania Railway system—with minor uncoverings of commercial swindles from one end of the United States to the other; and finally today's lurid exposure, by Upton Sinclair, of the most titanic and death-dealing swindle of them all, the Beef Trust. . . . Europe is beginning to wonder if there is really an honest male human creature left in the United States.

Unsettled in philosophy, stunned by history, Mark Twain demonstrates in his later career a decreasing faith in Huck Finn—his Jacob Blivens in wolf's clothing. But even in 1885 there were premonitions, implicit in the closing chapters of the novel. With the possible exception of the wafer-sun in *The Red Badge of Courage*, the ending of *Adventures of Huckleberry Finn* is the best roasted chestnut in American literature. The ending is everything that has been said about it: Jim is debased and Huck is suppressed, the meaning of the rafting journey is lost, social criticism is reduced to a parody of romanticism, and it is too long. On the other hand the book has to end, the shore has to win, Tom is the rightful hero of Mississippi Valley society; Jim's debasement and Huck's suppression are precisely what the whole novel is about. The debate, like the Mississippi, flows on forever, but the debaters agree on one point—the last ten chapters do lower the vision of humanity, of moral possibility, attempted in the earlier sections. Perhaps these last chapters, with their lack of resolution and their reduction of Huck to the ineffective fool that he is in *Tom Sawyer Abroad*, represent as early as 1885 a half-buried uneasiness on Mark Twain's part about Huck's effortlessly achieved virtue and about the power of morality itself. The novel fails to achieve the rounded closure of *Bleak House* or *The Rise of Silas Lapham*, because even though Mark Twain created a spotless moral hero he was reluctant to let his hero triumph. His reluctance created a less neat but more complex novel, for our doubts about Huck Finn are doubts about ourselves, and they will continue to haunt us as they did Mark Twain.

THE MAKING OF A HUMORIST: THE NARRATIVE STRATEGY OF *HUCKLEBERRY FINN*

BARRY A. MARKS

The thing about *Adventures of Huckleberry Finn* is that it needs to be read backwards. And one of the rewards of doing so is that it becomes easier to see the book as the work of a humorist. Not the sloppy craftsmanship of a man who was really more comfortable with shorter fictional forms or with oral presentations. Not the serious social criticism of a man whose public reputation as a funny man masked his real talent and disposition. But a book which, while not itself entirely humorous, was written by a humorist and is profoundly *about* humor.

Most literature needs to be read both forwards and backwards. Such reading is essential to hearing clearly the resonance of repetition, partial repetition, repetition by antithesis, etc. And, finally, as E. M. Forster suggests in *Aspects of the Novel*, at the end of one's reading, full comprehension depends on reaching all the way back to the beginning and apprehending the entire work in a single flash of recognition.

First person narration like Mark Twain's masterpiece makes a special kind of demand on this style of reading. A story told by a narrator about past events in which he was himself a participant entails necessarily a double tiered structure. As it unfolds, the author must tell the story of his narrator's speaking—what I have elsewhere called "the narrative present."[1] And at the same time he must also of course relate the events which the narrator is speaking about, or the "narrative past." One of the principal aims in adopting this strategy is that some authors have found they can make of the narrative present a mimetic version of the narrative past and thus communicate with greater immediacy than they could with other narrative strategies. In the double tiered structure of *Huckleberry Finn*, in any event, the unfolding of the narrative present unfolds also the narrative past.

But the reader, particularly as he recaptures the kind of total apprehension to which Forster referred, experiences *Huckleberry Finn* in a different way as well. In his mind's eye he can place the narrative past and the narrative present end to end. From this purely chronological point of view, a sequence of events occurred in the narrative past, and then after a period of time the narrator begins to talk about those past events at the beginning of the narrative present. This perspective on the novel permits us, as it does generally with the first person narrative, to think clearly about Huck's motivation for beginning his tale. The point is particularly important because the text makes clear that Huck begins his story within a matter of hours after the climactic events which mark the end of the narrative past.

The climactic events are the twin revelations that each of his two closest friends has told Huck a critically important lie, the kind of lie which Mark Twain once denoted "the lie of withheld truth." Tom acknowledges the previously withheld information that Jim had been freed by the terms of Miss Watson's will. Jim acknowledges the previously withheld information that Huck's father is dead. Obviously, the events at the Phelps farm would have been avoided if Tom had told Huck about Jim's liberation. If Jim had told Huck about his father's death when he first discovered it, the entire escape down the Mississippi could have been avoided—for Huck, at least. It was, after all, his father he was running away from. Whatever their motives may have been, Huck discovers that his two closest friends could have saved him a world of trouble if they had been fully honest with him, and it is precisely at this point that Huck begins to tell the story of his adventures. Small wonder that the opening paragraph should sound the theme, to be played on in hundreds of different ways, of lying and telling the truth.

You don't know about me without you have read a book by the name of *The Adventures of Tom Sawyer*; but that ain't no matter. That book was made by Mr. Mark Twain, and he told the truth, mainly. There was things which he stretched, but mainly he told the truth. That is nothing. I never seen anybody but lied one time or another, without it was Aunt Polly, or the widow, or maybe Mary.

The Huck Finn of the narrative past is a materialist and a pragmatist. He believes in sincerity. He believes in telling the truth. He believes in first-hand evidence. He is of course an endlessly inventive liar, but other people's lies—the Widow's prayers, Tom Sawyer's book logic, the Duke and the King's con games—call forth reactions ranging from skepticism to contempt. Mark Twain used to refer to Huck as a "goodhearted but ignorant village boy." One of the marks of his ignorance and youth is that in the narrative past he is either unaware of or unconcerned about the discrepancy between his values and his behavior. The revelations at the end of the narrative past are, however, profoundly shocking. He is himself the victim of deceit. His trust in his friends and in his own judgment has been violated. The act of telling his story is appropriately seen as an effort to reevaluate the fundamental nature of truth and the possibility of open and sincere human relationships. Huck himself would not of course have put the matter this way. Huck is no philosopher. The casual colloquialism of Huck's language reflects his age and education. It also reflects, I think, his initial inability—one might even say, his unwillingness—to confront directly the intellectual and emotional problem which nevertheless motivates his storytelling. He will improvise his story and hopefully discover the answer to his questions as he goes.

Huckleberry Finn's search for the truth in the narrative present moves along smoothly enough until Chapter 9 in which he tells about his and Jim's discovery of a dead man in a frame house floating down the Mississippi. Although he did not of course know it at the time, as he is telling the story he does know that the dead man was his own father. As storyteller-truthseeker Huck is confronted with a dilemma. To tell the truth, the whole truth, and nothing but the truth, is simply not a live option. He cannot be true both to himself as he was and to himself as he is. One would dictate that he wait to reveal his father's death until he arrives, in his chronicling of the events of the past, at the moment when he himself had *learned* of his father's death; the other, of course, would dictate that he reveal now that the dead man was his father because that is what he *knows* now. To put the problem in aesthetic rather than moral terms, he cannot speak the full truth that he knows at this point in his narration and yet expect the later narration of his moment of discovery to communicate the impact and immediacy which were themselves critical parts of that discovery.

What does Huck decide? He decides at this point in his narration to withhold from his reader the same information which in the narrative past Jim had withheld from him. And his narration continues. But with an implicit difference: from this point on, the boy who set out on a narrative voyage to discover and tell the truth about truths and falsehoods has become a liar. He is committed to "the lie of withheld truth."

The past which Huck Finn is narrating contains an almost endless number of similar dilemmas. One might speculate that Huck is peculiarly perceptive in his descriptions of such dilemmas precisely because of his having had to face such an important one in his role as a narrator. But whether such speculation is fruitful or not, it is certainly the case that the dilemmas of Huck's past take on additional resonance when they are heard through the dilemmas of Huck's present task as a storyteller.

No narrative problem in the book is so excruciatingly difficult as the one Huck faces in Chapter 31, "You Can't Pray a Lie." Here Huck describes in great detail the moral agony he underwent trying to decide how best to free Jim when, as he narrates the incident, he knows that Jim was in fact already a free man. The incident differs from the "house of death." No person had lied to him. It bears more resemblance to Chapter 15, "Fooling Poor Old Jim," in which fog had deceived Huck and Jim and caused them to miss their destination—Cairo and the mouth of the Ohio River. The problem in Chapter 31 is unrelated even to a natural phenomenon however. Life itself produced the monstrous absurdity of his having agonized over freeing an already free man.

How does Huck handle this problem? Once again, he lies. In the narrative present he withholds his knowledge that even as he made that momentous past decision Jim was already free.

By contrast to the emotional crisis implicit in the narrative present of "You Can't Pray a Lie," the problem two chapters later in "The Pitiful Ending of Royalty" is easy. Huck tells about meeting Tom Sawyer and about Tom's obviously having considered the possibility of telling Huck the truth about Jim and having decided not to.

I says:
"All right; but wait a minute. There's one more thing—a thing that nobody don't know but me. And that is, there's a nigger here that I'm a-trying to steal out of slavery, and his name is *Jim*—old Miss Watson's Jim."
He says:
"What! Why, Jim is—"
"I know what you'll say. You'll say it's dirty, low-down business; but what if it is? I'm low down; and I'm a-going to steal him, and I want you to keep mum and not let on. Will you?"
His eye lit up, and he says:
"I'll *help* you steal him!"

Huck of course has had to face a narrative dilemma once again. This one is easy, however, in the sense that it is *so* absurd that not even humorless Huck can take it seriously. As he told about his decision to "go to hell," he was forced for the first time to see himself as a fool of life. One can appreciate the impact of such a recognition. Yet, beyond his having experienced intense anguish in the narrative past and, presumably, in the narrative present, he was aware that his past decision, arrived at—God knows!—in all sincerity, yet also in all ignorance, had had no significant, practical consequences. Now, however, he was faced with narrating an incident in which his friend Tom had deliberately lied to him, and Huck, in the narrative present, must have been keenly aware of the considerable consequences which had followed from that decision—Tom shot, Jim a victim of pain and humiliation, and the Phelps family and the surrounding community massively upset.

How does Huck handle this narrative problem? Once again, he lies. He handles the situation in the same way he had handled Jim's lie in Chapter 9. In the narrative present he lies to the reader in the same way that Tom had lied to him in the narrative past. He continues to withhold the information that Jim is already free.

This lie marks a major turning point, however, in the narrative present. From this point on, almost to the end of the book, Huck's narrative style undergoes a marked change. Huck cannot now escape the reality of his situation. The boy-narrator who set out to discover the meaning of a sequence of events which could easily have been obviated by simple truths uttered at the right moments now finds himself inescapably trapped in his own lies.

The decision he has now made is not unlike the one made in the narrative past by the audience at the first performance of The Royal Nonesuch.

> Everybody sings out, "Sold!" and rose up mad, and was a-going for that stage and them tragedians. But a big, fine-looking man jumps on a bench and shouts:
> "Hold on! Just a word, gentlemen." They stopped to listen.
> "We are sold—mighty badly sold. But we don't want to be the laughing-stock of this whole town, I reckon, and never hear the last of this thing as long as we live. No. What we want is to go out of here quiet, and talk this show up, and sell the *rest* of the town! Then we'll all be in the same boat."

It is not, I think, necessary to see Huck as mean-spirited at this point. Nevertheless, he had been "badly sold" by Tom; he is now committed to selling us. And, in light of what follows, it might be well to recall the way Huck had concluded a previous great decision. After saying, "All right, then I'll go to hell," he had concluded,

> I shoved the whole thing out of my head, and said I would take up wickedness again, which was in my line, being brung up to it, and the other warn't. And for a starter I would go to work and steal Jim out of slavery again; and if I could think up anything worse, I would do that, too; because as long as I was in, and in for good, I might as well go the whole hog.

Huck's style in his narration of the Phelps farm sequence is a going of "the whole hog."

Or to borrow a different metaphor from the text itself: having decided to adopt a Tom Sawyerish role vis à vis the reader, Huck, throughout most of the remainder of his narration, will adopt what he has always taken as Tom's most distinctive feature—his sense of "style." He will "throw in the fancy touches" as Tom would if Tom were to tell Huck's story.

The result is well known. Huck frequently loses his grasp of the plausible in his narration of the incident. Tom and Jim, not to mention himself, become unrecognizable as characters. Tom suddenly develops a total insensitivity and Jim, an absolute subservience which are utterly out of keeping with Huck's treatment of them earlier in the narrative present. Just as he did in the snakeskin and the fog incidents of the narrative past, Huck as a storyteller in the narrative present frequently miscalculates his efforts.

Mark Twain once referred to a tall tale he had told as "a string of roaring absurdities, albeit they were told with an unfair pretense of truth that even imposed upon me to some extent, and I was in some danger of believing in my own fraud." Huck Finn may have been similarly proud of his handiwork, but I think Mark Twain knew better. Mark Twain, it seems to me, knew perfectly well that, while Huck had told a "string of roaring absurdities," he had failed to make them plausible enough to compel the reader's belief. But then Mark Twain would probably not have expected more from a boy of Huck's age and education, particularly not on his first time out.

On the other hand, Mark Twain might have considered that Huck had matured as a teller of tall tales in the process of telling one, and he almost certainly admired the way Huck handled his ending. In his famous essay, "How to Tell a Story," Mark Twain noted that the narrator of the American tall tale tells his story gravely, doing "his best to conceal the fact there is anything funny about it." The pose of gravity is particularly important at the moment when the narrator drops the nub, point, or snapper of the story. The narrator, he said, is likely "to divert attention from that nub by dropping it in a carefully casual and indifferent way, with the pretense that he does not know it is a nub."

There are two nubs to Huck's story, and they are of course that the father from whom Huck had been running was dead before he and Jim had started downstream and that Jim was a free man before Tom had even begun designing the "evasion." And, of course, the famous last line of the story, "But I reckon I got to light out for the territory ahead of the rest, because Aunt Sally she's going to adopt me and civilize me, and I can't stand it. I been there before," is an important part of Huck's "carefully casual and indifferent way" of dropping his nubs with the pretense he does not know them for what they are.

If the story of the narrative present is, then, as I have said it is, the story of Huck Finn's setting out to tell the truth, finding that he is not permitted that luxury, sensing that life itself had played him for a fool at a moment when he had thought he had been most conscientious, and becoming finally a teller of the tall tale, it is important to remember also that Mark Twain had his own tall tale to tell. He warned us in his published notice:

Persons attempting to find a motive in this narrative will be prosecuted; persons attempting to find a moral in it will be banished; persons attempting to find a plot in it will be shot.

He warned us again in his opening sentence, "You don't know about me without you have read a book by the name of *The Adventures of Tom Sawyer*." In a "carefully casual and indifferent way" he dropped *his* nub in the book's last paragraph when he has Huck say, "There ain't nothing more to write about, and I am rotten glad of it, because if I'd 'a' knowed what trouble it was to make a book I wouldn't 'a' tackled it, and ain't a-going to no more."

Using the ingenuous voice of Huckleberry Finn, Mark Twain told us we had been "sold" into believing seriously in a "goodhearted but ignorant village boy" whose only reality was as a character in another book but who had presumed to step forth to write a book about himself.[2]

NOTES

1. "Retrospective Narrative in Nineteenth Century American Literature," *College English* (February 1970), pp. 366-375.
2. See also my discussion of Mark Twain's understanding and use of the tall tale in "The Huck Finn Swindle," *Western American Literature* (Summer 1979), especially pp. 115-121. With the exception that the present article takes a more favorable view of Huck's intelligence than the earlier one, the two articles complement one another.

HUCKLEBERRY FINN IS A MORAL STORY

ROBERT NADEAU

When the principal of Mark Twain Intermediate School in Fairfax County followed the advice of the school's racially mixed human relations committee and recommended that *The Adventures of Huckleberry Finn* be removed from the school's curriculum he was not acting without precedent. Misguided guardians of the moral integrity of schoolchildren have often attempted, particularly in Twain's own lifetime, to prevent young minds from being exposed to the profoundly moral views of the 13-year-old, pipe-smoking marvelously imaginative liar whose love for the runaway slave, Jim, grows to such proportions that he would risk eternal damnation to protect him.

A letter written by Twain to a Brooklyn librarian who was seeking to ban both *Tom Sawyer* and *Huckleberry Finn* from the children's room of the library has not, I suspect, been read by most faculty members teaching at a school named in honor of one of our greatest American artists. Let me share a portion of it with them:

> I wrote *Tom Sawyer* and *Huckleberry Finn* for adults exclusively, and it always distresses me when I find that boys and girls have been allowed access to them. The mind that becomes soiled in youth can never again be washed clean. I know this by my own experience, and to this day I cherish an unappeasable bitterness against the unfaithful guardians of my young life, who not only permitted but compelled me to read an unexpurgated Bible before I was 15 years old. . . . More honestly do I wish that I could say a softening word or two in defense of Huck's character since you wish it, but really, in my opinion, it is no better than those of Solomon, David, and the rest of the sacred brotherhood.

That Twain firmly believed that the behavior and character of his first-person narrator was designed to be morally instructive to young people is obvious. Countless individuals in this culture, including myself, know from the experience of reading the book at an early age that he was absolutely correct.

Apparently the faculty members as well as the parents and the administrators who concurred with the recommendation to bar teachers from assigning the novel—or even reading it aloud in class—feel otherwise. They object, we are told, to "the flagrant use of the word *nigger* and the demeaning way in which black people are portrayed in the book." *Nigger* is, of course, a terribly offensive word in our own time and should definitely not be used by anyone who respects the rights and integrities of others. But it might help to explain to those students who might continue to study the book at the intermediate school that in slave states the word was merely the ordinary colloquial term for a slave, and not necessarily abusive.

More important, however, as the historical record also shows, Twain was a violent opponent of the institution of slavery, and *Huckleberry Finn* can and should be read as one of the most forceful indictments ever made against the subjugation of any class of human beings by another.

Anyone, including adolescents, who has carefully read the book should have little difficulty recognizing the many instances in which this theme is abundantly obvious. Since there is not sufficient space here to detail all of them, I will only touch briefly on that climactic moment when Huck, in defiance of what he has been taught to be the will of God in his own morally bankrupt society, elects to imperil his mortal soul.

Subjected, as many children in this country continue to be, to a religious education in which the interpreters of spiritual verities seek to sanction the view of black people as innately inferior. Huck reflects late in the narrative upon his many efforts to help Jim to escape and concludes:

And at last when it hit me all of a sudden that here was the plain hand of Providence slapping me in the face and letting me know my wickedness was being watched all the time from up there in Heaven, whilst I was stealing a poor old woman's nigger that hadn't ever done me no harm, and now was showing me there's One that's always on the lookout, and ain't a going to allow such miserable doings to go only just so fur and no further, I almost dropped in my tracks I was so scared.

Feeling oppressed with guilt, realizing that "people that acts as I'd been acting about that nigger goes to everlasting fire," Huck writes a letter to Mrs. Watson indicating where Jim can be found. But then immediately thereafter he recalls—in a passage that is one of the best illustrations in literature of the power of agape love—the many acts of kindness displayed by Jim toward himself, looks once again at the letter, and says to himself, "'All right, then, I'll *go* to hell'—and tore it up."

The message here, which is pervasive in this marvelous novel, is that truly moral acts are, often enough, undertaken in defiance of a so-called moral majority. And it is that which this particular member of the sacred brotherhood has chosen to do. If studying *Huckleberry Finn* is in anyway to hurt students at Mark Twain Intermediate School, it can only be because those who teach the book have failed to understand it.

But there is, of course, a larger issue here. When we prevent our children from being exposed in the classroom to the best that has been known and said in our literary tradition, we not only narrow the range of their educational experience, but we also—unintentionally to be sure—help them to grow into individuals, like the members of the Shepherdson and Grangerford families in the novel, who might commit senseless acts of destruction out of a lack of understanding of the complexities of moral life. If *Huckleberry Finn* is, as an administrative aide at the school put it, "poison," then I suspect my own 11-year-old daughter must have a remarkably immune system. She even appears to thrive on it.

HUCKLEBERRY FINN IS OFFENSIVE

JOHN H. WALLACE

Ever since it was written Mark Twain's *The Adventures of Huckleberry Finn* has provoked great controversy—and it runs on unabated even now in Fairfax County. After reading the book at least six times, I think it's perfectly all right for college class use, especially at the graduate level, where students can gain insight into the use and writing of satire and an uncensored flavor of the times. The caustic and abusive language is less likely to offend students of that age level because they tend to be mature enough to understand the ridicule.

Huckleberry Finn uses the pejorative term *nigger* profusely. It speaks of black Americans with implications that they are not honest, they are not as intelligent as whites and they are not human. All of this, of course, is meant to be satirical. It is. But at the same time, it ridicules blacks. This kind of ridicule is extremely difficult for black youngsters to handle. I maintain that it constitutes mental cruelty, harassment and outright racial intimidation to force black students to sit in a classroom to read this kind of literature about themselves.

I read *Huck Finn* when I was in high school—and I can remember feeling betrayed by the teacher. I felt humiliated and embarrassed. Ten years ago, my oldest son went through the same experience in high school, until I went to talk to the teachers about it; and he lost all interest in English classes. Before reading this book, this bright, energetic youngster was inquisitive and liked school; but afterward—after he had been asked to participate in the reading with an all white class—I could see a definite negative change in his attitude toward teachers and school. (I'm happy to say he has recovered now.)

For years, black families have trekked to schools in just about every district in America to say that "this book is bad for our children," only to be turned away by insensitive and often unwittingly racist teachers and administrators responding that "this is a classic." Classic or not, it should not be allowed to continue to make our children feel bad about themselves.

I am convinced that the assignment and reading aloud of *Huck Finn* in our classrooms causes black children to have a low esteem of themselves and of their race. It also causes white students to have little or no respect for blacks. The resulting attitudes can lead to tension, discontent and fights. If the book is removed from the curriculums of our schools, there will be much better student-to-student, student-to-teacher and teacher-to-teacher relationships; and black students will definitely enjoy school a little bit more.

Every black child is the victim of the history of his race in this country. As John Fisher, former president of Columbia Teachers College has noted, "On the day he enters kindergarten, he carries a burden no white child can ever know, no matter what handicaps or disabilities he may suffer." Add to this the reading of a book like *Huckleberry Finn*, and the experience can be devastatingly traumatic.

Many of my friends have cited First Amendment rights. But I am convinced that the continued use of pejorative materials about one particular racial group is a violation of the equal protection clause of the 14th Amendment. It also may violate the right to liberty as applied to reputation in that the book maligns all black people.

I have no problem with *Huckleberry Finn* being on the library shelf for any youngster or his parents to check out and read to their hearts' content, in school or at home. But as a professional educator with 28 years of teaching at all levels, I cannot see the slightest need to use disparaging language to identify any racial, ethnic or religious group. If the lesson cannot be taught in positive terms, maybe it should not be taught.

We must be sensitive, creative teachers, encouraged to understand the special factors in the backgrounds of all the children—with curriculums that reflect these varied needs. And no sensitive, loving teacher would use *Huckleberry Finn* in class.

I am exceedingly shocked that *The Post* has taken an editorial position that seventh-graders ought to be able to read the book in class. Many seventh- and eight-graders have come to me and said they did not understand the language of the book, nor what it was about. Here *The Post* misses a most salient point: that black students do not see the same thing in this book that a white teacher sees. We school administrators have to be selective and help our teachers use good judgment about their students and their teaching materials. That is a mandate from the state of Virginia that we must carry out.

Huckleberry Finn did not stand up to the scrutiny of two committees of experts: the human relations committee, made up of teachers and administrators, and a book review committee of teachers, administrators and parents. *Post* editors should take a closer look at the book and talk to black educators and students about its effect before blindly endorsing the use of this book by youngsters.

"SIVILIZING" HUCK FINN

ROGER SUTTON

Despite Mark Twain's notice that "Persons attempting to find a moral in this narrative will be banished," the woods surrounding his *Adventures of Huckleberry Finn* are thick with thieves; the only thing being banished is this book. While in a gentler time Louisa May Alcott could remark, "If Mr. Clemens cannot think of something better to tell our pure-minded lads and lasses, he had best stop writing for them," the issue today is not coarseness, but racism.

My interest here is in *The Adventures of Huckleberry Finn Adapted*, published by John H. Wallace, (John H. Wallace & Sons Co., 1983). A letter accompanying the review copy states, "Very little has been changed. The term 'nigger' has been exorcised, as have the stereotypical assumptions that blacks steal, are not intelligent, and are not human." Wallace, who is black, had attempted to ban Twain's book from the Mark Twain Intermediate School in Fairfax, Virginia. "I don't care about the First Amendment, I care about children," he was quoted in the *Chicago Sun-Times* (April 11, 1982).

Now, we care about the First Amendment, precisely because we care about children. But Wallace believes that children—particularly black children—are hurt and humiliated by this book. Since his unsuccessful attempt to ban it, he wrote a "sivilized" version.

But given Wallace's premise that the book is racist, can we say that his "edited" version has rendered it less so? I don't think it has. In fact, I believe he has taken *Hucklebery Finn*, a book containing some strong anti-racist sentiment, and turned it into a very different book, one that is racist "by omission" (to borrow a phrase from the Council on Interracial Books for Children). Wallace's changes are of several kinds. Most prominent is the complete expurgation (Wallace calls it "exorcism") of the word "nigger," replacing it most often with "slave," and occasionally "servant" or "fellow." Sometimes he omits phrases or sentences containing the offending word.

Wallace says, "Very little has been changed"—"nigger" is a word occurring countless times in Twain's book. It is (and was in Twain's time) an ugly word. "Slave," on the other hand, is only descriptive, carrying no value judgment or emotional freight. For the most part, changing "nigger" to "slave" doesn't distort the literal, narrative sense of Twain's book. For example, Wallace changes "By and by they fetched the niggers in and had prayers," to "By and by they fetched the slaves in and had prayers." Despite the change, readers still know, nominally, to whom Twain is referring.

Twain, however, used "nigger," not "slave," and he used it on purpose. Remember, Huck tells the story, and "nigger" is the word he would use. The point of the story is that Huck is an ignorant, uneducated racist who, when faced with a choice between his racism and helping a slave escape, says, "All right, then, I'll *go* to hell," choosing to aid his friend Jim, a "nigger."

By changing "nigger" to "slave," Wallace rewrites not only Twain but history, fashioning Huck's society to appear less racist than it really was. Whites of that time did believe "Give a nigger an inch and he'll take an ell," but not in Wallace's book—he deleted that sentence. With Wallace's removal of the "nigger," and his softening of white bigotry in Twain's book, readers can conclude that life wasn't so bad for blacks in the South. Indeed, they can conclude that blacks scarcely existed. By simply referring to them as "slaves," readers can forget why they were enslaved to begin with.

Wallace also changes Huck's relationship with Jim. Huck, by Wallace, doesn't believe "He was a mighty good nigger, Jim was." Instead, "He was a mighty good man, Jim was." In Twain's book, Huck, expressing approval of Jim, says, "I knowed he was white inside." In Wallace's, this becomes "I knowed he was good." Why is Wallace so eager to let Huck Finn off the hook? What was, in Twain, a telling exposure of how racism infects even the most sympathetic of characters becomes, in Wallace, just a coupla guys sitting around on a raft, talkin'. Huck is no Simon Legree. He does love Jim, but cannot escape his own racism entirely. That's the point. The world would be a lot simpler if we had bad guys and good guys, but what we do have is a whole lot of mixed-up, uneasy people positively bustling with ignorance. And that's Huck—us—the good guys.

Look at how Wallace sweetens up Aunt Sally. When Huck tells her a fabricated story of a steamboat accident, the old dear replies, "Good gracious! Anybody hurt?" And when Huck replies "No'm," she's relieved. "Well, it's lucky because sometimes people do get hurt." Let's see this same exchange in Twain:

"It warn't the grounding—that didn't keep us back but a little. We blowed out a cylinder-head."
"Good gracious! Anybody hurt?"
"No'm. Killed a nigger."
"Well, it's lucky; because sometimes people do get hurt."

Different, isn't it? Aunt Sally, sweet Aunt Sally, doesn't care if it "killed a nigger" so long as "people" didn't "get hurt." It is as if she didn't hear Huck's response; like Wallace, she ignores the "nigger's" existence. Wallace reduces Twain's neat irony to a pointless exchange, like Aunt Sally, complacently ignorant.

I can say what I do about these two *Huckleberry Finns* only because (unlike the intended audience of Wallace's book) I have both books in front of me. I can see that in Twain's book the angels "hoverin' round" Huck's father are black and white, the ones in Wallace's are white and "yaller." (The white angel is still the good 'un.) I can see that Jim calls Huck "Honey" in Twain, but not in Wallace (and that change begs more questions than it answers). What I can't see is what Wallace expects students to get out of his book. Twain's stern moral vision, his irony—the reasons this book is taught—are gone. What is left?

What's left is ignorance. Wallace, who has called Twain's book "the most grotesque example of racist trash ever written" (*Chicago Sun-Times*, May 25, 1984), has revealed his own; and through his "sivilizing" of Huck, seeks to pass it on.

"I reckon I got to light out for the Territory ahead of the rest, because Aunt Sally she's going to adopt me and sivilize me, and I can't stand it." Me neither, Huck. Have a safe trip.

HUCKLEBERRY FINN : LITERATURE OR RACIST TRASH?

In New York

TED KOPPEL   Anchor

Guests
In Chicago

MESHACH TAYLOR   Actor
JOHN WALLACE, Ph.D.   Educator

In New York

NAT HENTOFF   Syndicated Columnist

Report from ABC Correspondent
JEFF GREENFIELD, in New York

RICHARD N. KAPLAN   Executive Producer

TED KOPPEL: Good evening. I'm Ted Koppel and this is Nightline.

[clip from the film "Huckleberry Finn"]

[voice over]: An American classic since it was first published one hundred years ago. But is *Huckleberry Finn* one of our greatest works of literature or, as some now charge, racist trash?

ANNOUNCER: This is ABC News Nightline. Reporting from New York, Ted Koppel.
KOPPEL: It was Ernest Hemingway, who stands as one of the giants of 20th century American literature, who said of the work we discuss tonight that all modern American literature comes from one book by Mark Twain called *Huckleberry Finn*. But the question perhaps ought not to be whether *Huckleberry Finn* is a classic. There comes a time when by virtue of survival alone a work takes on classical proportions. The question ought to be whether the pain it causes to some children and to their families provides sufficient reason to remove it from our schools and perhaps even from our libraries. Tonight in Chicago, as Nightline correspondent Jeff Greenfield reports, Huck Finn reemerged once again, and once again he has stirred controversy.

    ACTOR, playing Huckleberry Finn: I've never seen such a nigger. He got a notion in his head once, there was no getting it out again.
    JEFF GREENFIELD *[voice over]*: A play opened tonight in Chicago, a stage version of Mark Twain's hundred-year-old novel *Huckleberry Finn*, a book many literary critics say is the closest thing we have to the great American novel. At the end of the book Huck says, "If I'd a knowed what a trouble it was to make a book, I wouldn't a tackled it." A century later, Huck Finn is still kicking up trouble.
    JOHN WALLACE, Ph.D., educator: It is the most grotesque example of racist trash ever written.
    GREENFIELD *[voice-over]*: Dr. John Wallace, a Chicago educator, has traveled across America attacking the book. He says the frequent references to Nigger Jim, Huck Finn's companion on his adventures, and the use of rural black dialect, portrays blacks in demeaning, insulting terms.

Dr. WALLACE: One hundred percent of the black young people whom I spoke to are humiliated and embarrassed when they've had to sit in the classroom and read this kind of filth.

GREENFIELD *[voice-over]*: The controversy in Chicago grew hot enough for the Goodman Theater, where the play is being staged, to hold a roundtable discussion on the meaning of *Huck Finn*. Chicago drama critic Lenny Kleinfeld says bigotry was in fact Mark Twain's target.

LENNY KLEINFELD, drama critic: The book is set up to embarrass white people into seeing how poisoned their minds are and their attitudes towards black people are. The assertions about black people's inadequacies are being made in this book by a bunch of white murderers and white thieves and white con men and white homicidal maniacs who are the Southern aristocracy, and in fact if you can't see that irony there is nothing that can be done about it.

GREENFIELD *[voice-over]*: Robert Evans, an alderman in the Chicago suburb of Waukegan, says the book doesn't belong in public school libraries.

ROBERT EVANS, alderman: Black children don't need to read Mark Twain's *Huckleberry Finn* in order to understand how white folks treat black folks.

GREENFIELD: This controversy reminds us again that literature becomes great when it stirs the emotions, when it moves us to anger, joy, pity, terror. But because a piece of writing has been declared a classic does not necessarily mean that the emotions it triggers are all positive. Look at some other works that have become the target of attacks.

[voice-over] Shakespeare's *Merchant of Venice*, a frequent target because of alleged anti-Semitism in the character of Shylock, the Jewish merchant. John Steinbeck's *Grapes of Wrath*. The book, which became a celebrated movie, was banned in an Iowa high school for obscene language and for blasphemy. *The Wizard of Oz*, banned from the Detroit public library system in the 1950's for negativism, *Fahrenheit 451*, Ray Bradbury's bleak look at a futuristic book-burning society. That book, later adapted into a motion picture, was removed from a Texas high school for being too negative. And *Mary Poppins*, removed from a San Francisco library in 1981 because of stereotypical black dialect.

American literature Professor Jack Saltzman says the problem erupts because readers fail to understand why a writer would use a term like "Nigger Jim" to expose racism.

Prof. JACK SALTZMAN: It is a rhetoric that we use. We speak about people as being spics and wops and kikes, and it is a common kind of parlance that we use, and in large part it identifies who we are. And if we don't always articulate those terms, we most frequently think those terms. And if we try to obliterate that and forget that then we forget who we are.

GREENFIELD *[voice-over]*: But John Wallace says a book like *Huckleberry Finn* will be taken literally by black children. That's why he's rewritten the book to eliminate all objectionable phrases.

Dr. WALLACE: It's got to be changed so that we don't hurt any children, make them feel bad about themselves, you see.

GREENFIELD: Mark Twain wrote in his preface to *Huck Finn* that "Persons attempting to find a motive in this narrative will be prosecuted. People attempting to find a moral in it will be banished. People attempting to find a plot in it will be shot." Well, Twain's warning, it seems, has been replaced by a twist on an old childhood nursery rhyme: sticks and stones may break my bones, but words will *really* hurt me. This is Jeff Greenfield for Nightline in New York.

KOPPEL: When we come back, we'll talk live with Dr. John Wallace, an educator, who has described *Huckleberry Finn* as the most grotesque example of racist trash ever written, and with Meshach Taylor, the actor playing the part of the runaway slave, Jim, in the production of *Huckleberry Finn* that opened tonight in Chicago.

[commercial break]

KOPPEL: Joining us live now in our Chicago bureau, Dr. John Wallace, researcher for the Chicago School Board, who's been fighting to ban *Huckleberry Finn* from schools since 1972. And also in Chicago, actor Meshach Taylor, who plays the role of the slave, Jim, in the dramatic version of *Huckleberry Finn* that opened tonight at the Goodman Theater in Chicago, and who has just come from that opening night performance. You must have gone through a little bit of soul-searching, I suspect, Mr. Taylor, given all this controversy, about whether indeed you should even be in the production. Did you, and if so, why did you decide to do it?

MESHACH TAYLOR, actor: Initially I did, Ted. Ten years ago was the first time that we did the particular adaptation that we've done, with the Organic Theater. And when I was asked to do it initially, all the experience that I have had with *Huckleberry Finn* was from seeing it in old movies; I'd never read the book. I read the book because the director asked me to do so. I read it, and when I read it I felt that it was one of the best indictments against racism in the United States that I had ever read. And the character of Jim appealed to me because I felt that an individual who speaks with a dialect is not necessarily an ignorant individual. It's an individual who maybe is uneducated but not stupid. And I thought I could bring something to this character because I have some facility with the dialect.

KOPPEL: And you do not feel that it enhances bigotry when words like "nigger" are used on the stage, that this somehow gives the bigots out there perhaps a feeling that it's all right?

Mr. TAYLOR: No. First of all, let me say that I feel that the word "nigger" is an offensive word. I do feel that slavery was offensive as well. I think that if we're going to be true to the time, however, that we must speak the way the people spoke during that time. And I think it's important for people to understand exactly what the history of racism in this country is.

KOPPEL: All right. Mr. Wallace, let me turn then to you, because it seems to me that what Mr. Taylor has just enunciated is probably a fairly prevalent view in this country. The book is a classic, the book reflects the dialect of an era, the book is fundamentally an antislavery rather than a proslavery book. But let me hear your side.

JOHN WALLACE, Ph.D.: Well, I certainly disagree with what we have just heard. And I think the book is certainly the most racist book, among many, that is printed in the United States of America.

KOPPEL: Well, we've heard you say that already two or three times on this broadcast on videotape; now explain to me why.

Dr. WALLACE: Well, because it says that black people steal, we lie, we're not as intelligent as white people and that we are not human. And plus—

KOPPEL: Well, the book also—

Dr. WALLACE: Plus it says—uses the word "nigger" roughly 200 times.

KOPPEL: Forgive me for interrupting. The point I'm making, that, you know, what *Huck Finn* says is also, if you want to use particular examples, that white people are liars, drunkards, thieves, murderers.

Dr. WALLACE: But now, in that book he does not call white people honkies, nor does he call them kikes. He refers to them as white—they are white people, right?

KOPPEL: Only, I suspect, because the term—

Dr. WALLACE: I am offended—

KOPPEL: Because the term "honky" was not commonly in use a hundred years ago.

Dr. WALLACE: I am offended by the use of the word "nigger." There is no place for the word "nigger" in our classrooms today. And by the way, I am more interested in what is going on in the classrooms of the United States of America. And what we are doing with these pieces of trash like *Huck Finn* is that we are teaching racism in the schools, and we have to get it out.

KOPPEL: Why is it necessary to condemn the entire book? And I can understand, I mean, if I had a child in a school and I was black and the child was required to read from that book and repeat the word "nigger" several times, I can see how that would be painful, how it would be offensive. But why do you insist on dismissing the whole book?

Dr. WALLACE: Well, let me say this. It was painful to me, it was painful to my son. The research that I have done, I've questioned over 200 young people—it has been very detrimental to them, it has embarrassed and humiliated them in the classroom. And they have gone along with it; some of them have recovered, some of them have not. So this book and books like it are doing a great deal of damage to black children, and I want the world to know about that.

Mr. TAYLOR: Mr. Koppel? Even though—I have—I don't know anyone personally who has been ruined by *Huck Finn*, but I can agree with Mr. Wallace to an extent. I don't think that *Huck Finn* is a children's book. I think it's been wrongly promoted as a children's book, but I don't think it's a children's book. I think that an individual has to have a certain amount of sophistication to understand what satire is. I think an individual has to have a certain amount of sophistication to understand what irony is. So perhaps it should be taught in college or the latter years of high school. I have no problem with not teaching it to junior high school kids, because I don't think it's a book that was written for children.

KOPPEL: But that's not really what you want, is it, Mr. Wallace?

Dr. WALLACE: Well, no, no, Mr. Taylor and I agree there. I mean, I—you know, it's adult entertainment. In fact, it was written for adults, as Twain said, it was written for adults. And if adults want to pick it up and read that piece of racist trash, fine. But I don't want racism taught in the schools of the United States of America.

KOPPEL: Well, gentlemen, you've got to excuse me. I mean, you say you agree; I don't think you agree at all.

Mr. TAYLOR: No, I don't agree.

KOPPEL: I don't hear Mr. Taylor dismissing it as a piece of racist trash.

Mr. TAYLOR: No, I definitely cannot dismiss *Huckleberry Finn* as a piece of racist trash.

Dr. WALLACE: I'm not saying he's going to go that far either, but as far as it being an adult piece of literature, that's what I'm agreeing to. It is an adult piece of literature; it's not for children.

KOPPEL: Yeah, but I mean, you're saying that the same way you would say that—I don't know—some piece of pornography is an adult piece of literature.

Dr. WALLACE: Well, that's true too.

KOPPEL: Well, but you see, there's where I think we're having a little bit of trouble coming to some kind of a meeting of the minds here. Mr. Taylor, you are not suggesting that this is a piece of trash; you're just suggesting—

Mr. TAYLOR: I'm not suggesting that it's trash at all, no.

KOPPEL:—that it's a little more subtle than perhaps some children's—you know, than a classic comic book.

Mr. TAYLOR: As I said before, I think it takes a certain level of sophistication to understand exactly what *Huckleberry Finn* is trying to do. And I think that—

Dr. WALLACE: But you know, if *Huckleberry Finn* says that black people are not as intelligent as white people—

Mr. TAYLOR: It's just—

Dr. WALLACE: Wait a minute. And that's what it says, and that is what is believed throughout the country, then it is not irony. That's what I'm trying to get you to see; it is not irony, because—

Mr. TAYLOR: It is irony. *[crosstalk]* I'm not certain who believes that, Dr. Wallace.

Dr. WALLACE:—trying to prove that through empirical data.

Mr. TAYLOR: I don't know whether you believe it or who believes it. I certainly don't believe black people are inferior.

Dr. WALLACE: But I would wager that most of the people in the United States of America actually believe that.

KOPPEL: All right, gentlemen, let's take a break on that point. When we come back, we'll be joined by author and syndicated columnist Nat Hentoff, who's written a novel about a controversy in a high school where students and parents demand that *Huckleberry Finn* be banned from the school library.

ACTOR, playing Jim *[from the film "Huckleberry Finn"]*: You know, I'm going there one of these days, Huck. I'm saving up enough money to buy myself, and when I gets enough money to buy me with, I'm gonna head straight for that old free state. And I'm gonna see my wife and little Joey, and I'm going to sling around and be free.

[commercial break]

KOPPEL: Joining us now live in our New York studio, author, columnist Nat Hentoff, whose novel *The Day They Came to Arrest the Book* is about a high school controversy sparked by efforts to ban *Huckleberry Finn*. And with that background alone, let me ask you something. Let's take for granted, let's accept that arguendo, as the lawyers would say, that *Huckleberry Finn* is indeed a classic. But let us also accept that it must cause pain to black youngsters who have to read it in junior high school or in high school, especially when you have to read it out loud.

NAT HENTOFF, syndicated columnist: Sure, and that's part of the learning process. I've talked to kids, and I've watched classes, particularly in a junior high school in Brooklyn over the years. And the kids will say, "Yeah, when I started this, this book, and I see 'nigger' page after page, it was pretty awful." Then they begin to read the book and see what's happening. And what happens to them then is what is called education. What Dr. Wallace does, unwittingly, unintentionally, is to underestimate the intelligence of black kids. I mean, what is learning? To begin with, it's to know language, to control language, to not be afraid of language. If you protect kids by saying, no, no, they can't hear these words like "nigger," they go out in the world and it is still mystification. You demystify language.

KOPPEL: All right. Without categorizing now, let us assume that there is another book that really is a piece of racist trash, that does use all this language but doesn't have the redeeming value of *Huck Finn*. What then are your reasons for keeping that out of a school? It can also be educational, right?

Mr. HENTOFF: Well, yeah, but first of all, you can't buy every book. Second of all, there are so many first-class books that never get read, I have no problem saying this thing isn't even worth reading.

KOPPEL: All right, but if there are so many first-class books that haven't been read, why does one have to read a book like *Huck Finn* which uses words which may be painful?

Mr. HENTOFF: Because, I mean, Hemingway aside, if you read the novel again and again—and every time you read it, and I'm now getting along, and it means different things all the time and it means a special thing to kids. It's the first novel in America written by an adolescent, that is, in the guise of an adolescent—something that kids can identify with. It's an extraordinary relationship between a boy and an older man. You know, Jim is Huck's father, because Huck's real father is a terrible person who gets killed, thank God, in the course of the book. And what it also is, is that it's a rite of passage. Here is Huck Finn, a kid reared in, steeped in the racism of his period and his region, and through knowing this man on that raft he becomes aware of this man as a person. And he has that—that climax of the book. He's been taught that if he commits a crime by not returning a runaway slave, he will go to hell—he will literally go to hell. And he thinks about it and he thinks about it, and he says, "I got to do it, I got to do it." Then he says, "I won't do it. I won't do it. All right, I'll go to hell." That's a hell of an experience for kids to see in front of them.

KOPPEL: Mr. Wallace, Dr. Wallace, we really have not heard about that side of *Huck Finn* from you, and I wonder why not.

Dr. WALLACE: Yes, well, I think that Nat does not really understand black schoolchildren. I think he certainly ought to go back to school and take a course in educational psychology, and one, a course that I've taught, called institutional racism, and then go back and read that book. Now, children are going to tell you, you know, what you want to hear, especially Nat Hentoff.

Mr. HENTOFF: No, they don't know who I am, believe me, and the classrooms that I'm in are run by teachers that enable the kids to inquire and to argue. They don't talk to me; I listen to them argue with each other. You really, you really undervalue—and that's where I disagree with Mr. Taylor too—this is not a book for college only; this is a book for junior high school. This is *the* book for junior high school kids of all kinds.

Mr. TAYLOR: I submit to you, though, Mr. Hentoff, that in order for it to be taught properly—the situation that we had here in Chicago was pretty unique. We have a school system in Waukegan that's 50% black students, 3% black teachers. And the parents were concerned that the book, if it was taught, it would not be taught sympathetically, that it wouldn't be taught with historical perspective.

Mr. HENTOFF: Well, I agree with that entirely.

Mr. TAYLOR: Okay, this is why I say that.

Mr. HENTOFF: Yeah. We have a teacher in Texas, for example, in the spring where there was a real protest against the book. The teacher starts off the class saying "We're going to read *Huckleberry Finn*," and she starts writing on the blackboard, "Okay, what is a nigger?" The other kids turn around and look at the black kids. Now, that teacher should have been fired on the spot? You're absolutely right.

Dr. WALLACE: But yet you want to trust every teacher with this book. That's what you're saying.

Mr. HENTOFF: If you're running a decent school—

Dr. WALLACE: You want to trust every English teacher with this book.

Mr. HENTOFF: Oh no, oh no. I—

Dr. WALLACE: That maligns blacks.

Mr. HENTOFF: I am insisting that parents get involved not only in the teaching of *Huck Finn* but in everything else, so they see what's going on in the classrooms. Not every teacher can teach anything, for that matter.

Dr. WALLACE: Okay. Now, if you know anything about psychology, the minute the word "nigger" is brought into the classroom, the black kid has a tendency to set up a block. And he internalizes his frustrations, which makes him hate his blackness.

Mr. HENTOFF: Then you talk about it, and you say—

Dr. WALLACE: No, I don't think any measure of talking—

Mr. HENTOFF: And you say, "Why is Mark Twain showing these—"

Dr. WALLACE: Nat Hentoff, I think I know black psychology better than you.

Mr. TAYLOR: But I'm not certain that you know it better than I.

Mr. HENTOFF: I'm not so sure you know psychology. *[crosstalk]*

KOPPEL: Dr. Wallace, let me interrupt for just a moment. Let's take it away just for a moment from *Huck Finn*. What if we're talking here about *The Merchant of Venice*. Should every Jewish kid who feels offended by the Anti-Semitic representation of Shylock then—

Dr. WALLACE: Of course not, of course not, because he—

KOPPEL:—insist that—

Dr. WALLACE: Shylock is not called a kike; he's referred to as a Jew.

KOPPEL: Yeah, but he's—

Dr. WALLACE: Now, if you want to call me a black or if you want to call me a Negro, you know, you can ridicule me.

Mr. TAYLOR: You can say whatever you want to as long as—to you, not to me.

KOPPEL: Yeah, but just hold on—

Mr. TAYLOR: I don't feel that same way.

KOPPEL: Just hold on one second, Dr. Wallace, because what we're talking about now is whatever was common in Elizabethan times for Shakespeare. And when we're talking about Twain we're talking about 19th century America, not 20th century America. And those terms, the fact that that term was used in 19th century America is a fact of life. It is an unfortunate fact of life.

Dr. WALLACE: Well, Ted, it is a fact of life that it is used today. So what are you speaking about, what are you saying?

Mr. HENTOFF: Look, let me give you one example from the novel. Toward the end of the novel, Huck is saying to Aunt Sally, he's describing to her an incident, a blowing up of a steamboat coming up the river from New Orleans. And Aunt Sally says—Aunt Sally's a good Christian, good white Christian. She says, "Huck, did anybody get killed?" And Huck says, "No, ma'am, no, ma'am, just a nigger." And Aunt Sally says, "Good, good, because sometimes folks do get killed." Now, what does that show the kid? Obviously Mark Twain and Huck know what's going on here.

Dr. WALLACE: Well, it says that black people are not human. That's what it says.

Mr. HENTOFF: To Aunt Sally, who is the kind of person that Mark Twain is criticizing and making fools of. Don't you understand that?

Mr. TAYLOR: That's right. He does not understand irony at all.

Mr. WALLACE: I can understand what you're saying, but how do the children understand it?

Mr. HENTOFF: Of course they understand it.

Dr. WALLACE: Wait a minute. You've got to be able to empathize with the black student. You've got to be able to put yourself in his place.

Mr. TAYLOR: I can do that, I can do that more recently than you can.

Dr. WALLACE: And you're not doing that, Nat.

Mr. TAYLOR: I'm doing that.

Mr. HENTOFF: I listen to them, which is something you might do.

Mr. TAYLOR: Could I say this? I'm doing this show now. I've done this show in Europe; I've done it all over the United States. And we have done it for schoolchildren, high school children a great many times. And the thing that I get from them is that they do understand exactly what is happening in *Huckleberry Finn*, and even if black children are embarrassed initially by it, the fact that they are exposed to it and it's explained to them with historical perspective—

Mr. HENTOFF: Let me tell you. In a class just like that—I've got to say this or I'll blow up. In a class, in that class, in the eighth grade class—

KOPPEL: You've got 20 seconds, Nat.

Mr. HENTOFF: Okay. I go to the class, outside there are four black kids, and they're hopping up and down, and they want to talk. You know what they want to say? They say, "You know, we're furious because there are people out there who think that we, we kids, are so dumb we don't know the difference between a racist book and a good book like *Huck Finn*." They understood; they were in the eighth grade.

KOPPEL: Gentlemen, I thank you all very much. Nat Hentoff, Dr. John Wallace; Meshach Taylor—hope your production goes well. Thank you very much. I'll be back in a moment.

[commercial break]

KOPPEL: Another reminder. Tomorrow on a special Tuesday 20/20, the childhood vaccine that experts say can sometimes itself be a killer, DPT. That's our report for tonight. I'm Ted Koppel in New York. For all of us here at ABC News, good night.

REAGAN AND HUCK FINN: THE TWAIN MEET
The President Defends the Values of an American Classic

LAWRENCE FEINBERG

"We catched fish and talked, and we took a swim now and then to keep off sleepiness," President Reagan said. "It was kind of solemn, drifting down the big, still river. . . ."

In the ballroom of the Washington Hilton Hotel, the president was reading yesterday from *The Adventures of Huckleberry Finn*.

Mark Twain's novel has been controversial for most of its 100 years, both hailed as an American classic scornful of bigotry and periodically criticized as "racist." Occasionally the book has been removed from schools.

Yesterday Reagan said he read it in school himself. He said the book, about the mischievous Huck and his friend Jim, a runaway slave, floating down the Mississippi River on a raft, epitomized values American schools should be teaching.

"Huck works hard to keep Jim free, and in the end he succeeds," Reagan said. "I believe the book says much about the moral aims of education—about the qualities of heart that we seek to impart to our children."

The president spoke to about 1,500 persons at the annual meeting of the National Association of Independent Schools, a group of private-school educators. He said students at their schools, as well as public ones, "should not only learn basic subjects, but basic values." The values to be taught, Reagan said, should include "the importance of justice, equality, religion, liberty and standards of right and wrong."

In 1982 *Huckleberry Finn* was at the center of sharp controversy in Fairfax County when a junior high school named after Mark Twain sought to remove the book from its curriculum. The school's human relations committee said the book was "racist" because of its "demeaning" portrayal of blacks and liberal use of the word "nigger."

Senior Fairfax administrators overruled the decision. But last summer it was removed from school reading lists in Waukegan, Ill., for similar reasons.

Just before a stage adaptation of *Huckleberry Finn* opened in Chicago last month, the book was criticized at a forum as "racist trash." The criticism was led by John H. Wallace, who had spearheaded the drive against it in Fairfax.

Yesterday, however, Reagan said the book, far from being antiblack, teaches a "hatred of bigotry."

"In the decades to come, may our schools give to our children the skills to navigate through life as gracefully as Huck navigated the Mississippi," Reagan declared. "May they teach our students the same hatred of bigotry and love of their fellow men that Huck shows on every page, and especially in his love for his big friend, Jim. And may they equip them to be as thankful for the gift of life in America in the 21st century as was one Huckleberry Finn in the 19th."

Mark Twain, Reagan said, "presents the humor, openness and purity of heart so characteristic of the American spirit."

Yesterday several literary scholars agreed with Reagan's view that the book tells a tale against racial prejudice, but they were skeptical that *Huckleberry Finn* is as positive about the values the president wishes to promote as Reagan takes it to be.

"Huck has the conventional [prejudiced] views of his time," said Sterling Brown, a retired Howard University English professor. "But he overthrows them, and convinces Huck he is wrong. . . . There's a great deal of irony there. But it's irony in the right direction."

"Much of what Reagan says is true," said Doris Grumbach, a professor at American University and former literary editor of *The New Republic*. "But why would Huck run away if he was appreciative of life in America? He wants to be wild and free, to smoke when he pleases and not go to school."

Grumbach agreed that Huck "does have a purity of heart, but the point is that this boy knows more about human good and evil than any schoolboy would. . . . Mark Twain had a deeply held belief that education doesn't matter a bit."

CENTENNIAL CELEBRATION

HUCK FINN: 100 YEARS OF DURN FOOL PROBLEMS

LOU WILLETT STANEK

Huck Finn is a hundred years old this month. Troubles? For poor old Huck, it has just been one durn fool thing after another. Celebrating his birthday in the pages of *School Library Journal* would not make him very comfortable. He has had his problems with librarians from the start when, in 1885, those "moral icebergs," the Library Committee of Concord—symbolic seat of freedom—pronounced the book rough, coarse, inelegant, and expelled it from the library shelves. "Trash and suitable only for the slums," they said.

Now Huck probably wouldn't have given a hoot, but he was a sensitive boy who thought his author told the truth, "mostly." And although Mark Twain managed to present a public image of confidence and good humor, saying he was not disturbed by their "moral gymnastics," he was disturbed.

Louisa May Alcott, a member of the Library Committee, expressed the view of its members, saying that if Mr. Clemens could not think of something better to tell pure-minded lads and lasses, he had better stop writing for them. Emerson's son was also on that committee, and their labeling Clemens as "crude" summoned the ghost of the infamous Whittier dinner. Like Huck, Twain's manners had been criticized, too.

As Twain was not to forget until the day he died, he had been asked to give a speech at a dinner given by the *Atlantic Monthly* to celebrate John Greenleaf Whittier's seventieth birthday. The guest list was a roster of honored American men of letters—Whittier, Longfellow, Emerson—a group of extraordinary dignity from whom the poor boy from Hannibal, Missouri, who felt he had married above his class and only pretended to be a Connecticut Yankee, longed to gain acceptance.

The keynote of the evening was reverence. Twain the humorist (whom even Mrs. Clemens could not always persuade to behave) chose to tell an irreverent story he invented about Mr. Emerson, Mr. Longfellow, and Mr. Holmes. Twain was always to remember how the expressions on the faces of the guests turned to a "sort of black frost." William Dean Howells, who along with Livy often expurgated his friend's bawdy humor, described the fiasco:

There fell a silence, weighing many tons to the square inch, which deepened from moment to moment and was broken only by the hysterical and blood-curdling laughter of a single guest. . . . Nobody knew whether to look at the speaker or down at his plate. . . . I chose my plate.[1]

Newspaper accounts of the story called it in bad taste, entirely out of place, and said the instincts of a gentleman would have prevented its presentation. Speaking from the town of Thoreau and Emerson, the brightest intellectual center in America, the Concord Library Committee's decision to expel *Huckleberry Finn* rubbed salt in that old wound.

Publicly, however, Twain, the first of many writers to realize that being banned in Boston had its material rewards, said Huck's success was made. The Concord Committee had given them a "rattling tip-top puff" that would sell 25,000 more books. But in his notebook he would protest too much saying "those idiots in Concord are not a court of last resort." Later he would regain his humor and make the often-quoted response to Asa Don Dickinson, a Brooklyn librarian, concerning the removal of both Huck and Tom from the shelves of the children's rooms of the Brooklyn Public Library:

I wrote *Tom Sawyer* and *Huck Finn* for adults exclusively, and it always distresses me when I find that boys and girls have been allowed access to them. The mind that becomes soiled in youth can never again be washed clean. I know this by my own experience, and to this day I cherish an unappeasable bitterness against the unfaithful guardians of my young life, who not only permitted but compelled me to read an unexpurgated Bible through before I was 15 years old. . . . More honestly do I wish that I could say a softening word or two in defense of Huck's character since you wish it, but really in my opinion, it is no better than . . . those of Solomon, David, Satan and the rest of the sacred brotherhood.[2]

If librarians ever doubt their power and influence, tracing the *Huck Finn* story should remove their concerns and increase their sense of responsibility. For the past hundred years, scholars have been speculating on the rather surprising neglect of reviewers to comment on the book at the time of publication. Currently, approximately twenty contemporary reviews have been located, while *The Innocents Abroad* and *The Gilded Age*, certainly lesser novels, both received over fifty. Bad publicity from the Library Committee is one of the reasons most often cited. Although additional reviews have been uncovered since Arthur Vogelback's study in 1939, no one quibbles with his finding that the famous Concord banning had the effect of drawing out newspaper and magazine comments from editors who were otherwise silent, but who wished to express their agreement with the book ban.

For the most part . . . the critical reaction to the book followed the course set by the Concord Library. . . . That the critical denunciation was widespread and powerful, is shown by the reluctance of anyone to venture a defense . . . it seems clear that most critics received the book unfavorably, and for reasons unconnected with its artistic aspects. Few seemed aware of the great character painting in the book, its magnificent passages of description, its vigor of style, and the appropriateness of the picaresque structure to the material.[3]

Huck & Censors

Although a conservative estimate says *Huck Finn* has sold 20 million copies in 100 editions in 30 languages, for the last century someone has always managed to find something wrong with Huck's character. He has been banned from more libraries and schools than any other book in history. Nat Hentoff has even written a young adult novel about his problems, called *The Day They Came to*

Arrest the Book (Delacorte, 1982). Either Huck represents something the world does not want to know or there have been many cooperative censors in the schools and libraries who find it easier to go along or who have not read the story and therefore cannot defend it. It was Twain himself who, perhaps prophetically, said a classic is something everybody wants to have read and nobody wants to read.

To the Victorian Americans, Huck was crude. Some blacks say he is a racist. Feminists find him sexist. Critic Leslie Fiedler thinks he might be gay.

In 1907, librarian E. L. Pearson, in "The Children's Librarians versus *Huckleberry Finn*," caricatured the attitudes of a censorious children's librarian (no surprise to find her female) as follows:

"No, no," she says, "Tom Sawyer, and you, you horrid Huckleberry Finn, you musn't come here. All the boys and girls in here are good and pious; they have clean faces, they go to Sunday school, and they love it, too. . . . But you—you naughty, bad boys, your faces aren't washed, and your clothes are all covered with dirt. I don't believe either of you brushed your hair this morning. . . . As for you, Huckleberry, you haven't any shoes or stockings at all, and everyone knows what your father is."[4]

Huck Banned

Although in 1881, before the book was even finished, William Livingston Alden, editorial writer, *New York Times* columnist, and founder of The Lotus Club, said it was the best book ever written, in 1957, New York City's board of Education excised Huck from its approved reading lists. When this happened Eva Taylor, assistant director of the Steele Library in Elmira, N.Y., commented:

There is much kindliness and friendship between races in *Huckleberry Finn* and the real villains of the piece are white men. Miss Watson thought so highly of Jim, her slave, that she freed him in her will.

Mark Twain gave a realistic portrayal of frontier character and experience in the days of slavery. Words that are longer in good standing are used, but it is a book true to its time.

As Negro boys and girls grow up they must, it seems to me, learn the history of their own race in America. That history should shame the white man rather than the Negro. I cannot see anything wrong in learning something of that history from a man as basically humane as Mark Twain.

One of the more widely publicized censorship cases occurred in 1982 when a black Virginia school administrator [John Wallace] tried to have Huck removed from America's school curriculums. "Poison," he said, "anti-American, works against the melting-pot theory." Twain the humorist would have had to appreciate the irony—this administrator worked at the Mark Twain Intermediate School and spoke as a member of its Human Relations Committee. In a letter of protest, a group of students describing themselves as white, black, Catholics, Jews, and agnostics, called the censorship a pointless withdrawal from reality.

Michael Patrick Hearn, author of *The Annotated Huckleberry Finn*, also wondered if anybody out there was reading the book. His response to the school administrator (in *The Nation*) was:

Wow! is it possible that the *Huckleberry Finn* taught in Fairfax County is the same *Huckleberry Finn* that describes how a poor white boy befriends a runaway slave in his flight down the Mississippi? . . . Anyone who labels *Huckleberry Finn* 'racist trash' doesn't recognize that the principal purpose of the novel was to describe an ignorant 14-year-old boy's awakening to the injustices of slavery. . . . In his flight with Jim, Huck denies everything—his people, his country,

his God . . . this boy believes that there are laws greater than men's laws. Like Martin Luther
King, Jr., Huck concludes that if a law be unjust, one has the right to break it. If Huck Finn is a
racist, then God help the country.[5]

The Russians used to ban Mark Twain as a petit-bourgeois writer. Then one
of them read *Huck Finn* carefully and discovered he was a critic of American
capitalism, imperialism, and racism, and Huck was put back on the shelves.

The case in Virginia was settled when Fairfax County ruled that *Huckleberry
Finn* may be taught, but only with "appropriate planning." A sure bet is that
there will be more such incidents. As Huck said, "Human beings can be awful
cruel to one another."

According to Stavely and Gerson, one month after Ronald Reagan's first
election to the presidency in 1980, Judith Krug, director of the American
Library Association's Office for Intellectual Freedom, reported that the number
of demands for removal of materials from public libraries received by her office
had increased on average from three to five a week to three to five per day.[6]
More recently, Arthur Sulzberger, publisher of *The New York Times*, said, "If
Mr. Reagan has his way, I fear for how a new and truly conservative Supreme
Court will interpret the first Amendment."[7] And Judy Blume is still being
banned in Hanover, Pennsylvania.[8]

Huck's Centennial

In 1985, however, people all over the country will celebrate Huck's centennial—on Broadway, on public television, and on the banks of the Mississippi.
The presses are also rolling. Teachers or librarians who think only they have
read *Huckleberry Finn* will have a multitude of editions to draw from. As a
reporter with the *Philadelphia Ledger* said in 1896, "We are suspicious of the
middle-aged person who hasn't read *Huckleberry Finn*; we envy the young
person who has it still in store."[9]

In 1885, William Glick, an enterprising librarian who was building the book
collection for the Buffalo and Erie County Library, was able to talk Mark
Twain out of the partial *Huck Finn* manuscript. All the other Twain papers and
his working papers for *Huck* are housed in the Mark Twain Library at the
University of California, Berkeley (with the exception of *Joan of Arc* which is
at Yale). The University of California Press is in the process of publishing new
editions of all of Twain's work. They contain the original illustrations and have
been carefully edited by leading Twain scholars to provide schools and libraries
with copies that have not been tampered with as was the original edition of his
manuscript for *The Mysterious Stranger*. It was no mystery and no stranger,
but Twain's official biographer and publisher who patched together four manuscripts, deleted a character, added another, and posthumously published a book
they claimed had been written by Mark Twain. The University of California
Press, under the auspice of The Mark Twain Library, published the only
authentic version of *No. 44, The Mysterious Stranger* in 1982.

The year 1985 has been reserved for Huck. To celebrate his birthday, the
University of California Press will publish three editions for schools and
colleges—an edition with apparatus for scholars, a trade hardback, and an
inexpensive, durable softcover for the schools, with an introduction by Walter
Blair and Victor Fis[c]her. A fine edition, using the U. of C. Press text and
illustrated by Barry Moser (who is known to educators for his *Alice in
Wonderland* illustrations), will be published by Pennyroyal Press. Sensing that

Huck has often been abandoned to the censors by teachers and librarians, The Twain Library is also publishing a teacher's guide to address the issues which have caused periodic uproar.

T.S. Eliot, Ernest Hemingway, and William Faulkner—three American winners of the Nobel Prize—as well as scores of other writers, have paid homage to Twain as the father of American Literature. After discovering Huck, James Joyce played not only with the name Finn, but also with the theme of a river journey in *Finnegan's Wake*. Hemingway said in *Green Hills of Africa*, "All modern literature comes from one book by Mark Twain called *Huckleberry Finn*." Critics have suggested that Holden Caulfield's journey in *Catcher in the Rye* is a continuation of Huck's odyssey, which is our national myth.

Like millions of students who were to follow him, Huck would skip school when he could get away with it. It's up to teachers and librarians to see that we keep that boy on the premises.

NOTES

1. For this and other details about the banquet, see Henry Nash Smith, "That Hideous Mistake of Poor Clemens's," *Harvard Library Bull.*, IX (Spring 1955), pp. 145-180.

2. Asa Don Dickinson, "*Huckleberry Finn* is Fifty Years Old—Yes; But is He Respectable?" *Wilson Bulletin for Librarians* (Nov. 1935), pp. 180-185.

3. Arthur L. Vogelback, "The Publication and Reception of *Huckleberry Finn* in America," *American Literature*, 11 (Nov. 1939), pp. 263.

4. E. L. Pearson, "The Children's Librarian versus *Huckleberry Finn*," *Library Journal*, XXXII (July 1907), p. 313.

5. Michael Patrick Hearn, "Expelling Huck Finn," *The Nation* (August 7-14, 1982), p. 117.

6. Keith Stavely, and Lani Gerson, "We Didn't Wait for the Censor: Intellectual Freedom at the Watertown Public Library," *Library Journal* (Sept. 1, 1983), p. 1654.

7. William Greer, "Publisher of *Times* Cites Concern for Press in Second Reagan Term," *The New York Times*, 11 Nov. 1984, p. 23.

8. "Peoria, Ill., Bans 3 Books from School Libraries," *The New York Times*, 11 Nov. 1984, p. 34.

9. Advertiser, *Harper's Monthly*, 93 (Sept. 1896).

HUCK AT 100

LEO MARX

Ever since it was published, exactly one hundred years ago, Mark Twain's
Adventures of Huckleberry Finn has been a target of moral disapproval. Many
of the novel's first reviewers found it disturbing and offensive. They called it,
among other things, vulgar, inelegant, ungrammatical, coarse, irreverent,
semi-obscene, trashy and vicious. The library in Concord, Massachusetts,
promptly banned it, but the book soon won the affection of a large audience,
and during the next fifty years critics, scholars and writers succeeded in
rescuing it from the mincingly refined standards of what George Santayana
aptly named "the genteel tradition." In the 1930s Ernest Hemingway praised
Huckleberry Finn as the work from which all modern American writing stems,
and T. S. Eliot later described Mark Twain's vernacular style as nothing less
than "a new discovery in the English language." By the 1950s the initial
objections to the novel had been dispelled, and it was quietly installed, along
with *The Scarlet Letter* and some other "classic" American books, in the more
or less standard high-school English curriculum.

But then, having survived the disdain of the genteel critics, the book became
the object of another, angrier and more damaging kind of moral condemnation.
In 1957 the National Association for the Advancement of Colored People called
Huckleberry Finn racially offensive, and since then we have seen a mounting
protest against this novel whose first-person narrator, the 14-year-old son of the
town drunk, routinely refers to blacks as "niggers." Huck's repeated use of that
demeaning epithet is enough to convince many black Americans that schoolchildren should not be required to read the book. (Another, somewhat less
obvious reason for their disquiet is a certain resemblance between the novel's
leading black character, the escaped slave, Jim, and the stereotypical minstrel-
show darkie.) In the last few years the protest has been gaining adherents. In
a number of cities across the country, indignant parents, educators and
school-board members have demanded that the book be removed from the
curriculum and even, in some instances, that it be banned from school or public
libraries. This past year a group of black parents succeeded in having the novel
taken off the list of required reading in Waukegan, Illinois, and John
H. Wallace, an educator with the school board in Chicago, is now conducting
a nationwide campaign against Mark Twain's greatest work, which he calls "the
most grotesque example of racist trash ever written."

One result of this protest is that the centenary of *Huckleberry Finn* has been
marked by a curious conjunction of celebration and denunciation. In March,
when Shelley Fisher Fishkin, a literary scholar at Yale University, came to
Mark Twain's defense, she attracted national attention to the dispute about his
racial views. In an announcement treated as front-page news by *The New York
Times*, she reported the authentication of an 1885 letter in which Twain offered
to provide financial support for a black student at Yale Law School. There he
wrote that "we have ground the manhood out of . . . [black men] & the shame
is ours, not theirs; and we should pay for it." (He subsequently did provide the
money.) Because the letter reveals "the personal anguish that Twain felt
regarding the destructive legacy of slavery," Fishkin evidently thought that it
might help to overcome the objections of black people to *Huckleberry Finn*. The
implication was that a man of such enlightened views could not possibly have
written a racially offensive novel and that once those views were established,
the controversy would be resolved.

But as it turned out, the Yale letter merely provoked the contending parties to recast their arguments in less compromising, more strident language. Thus Sterling Stuckey, a historian at Northwestern University who is black, was moved to reaffirm the received scholarly-critical estimate of Mark Twain's masterwork. Of the letter he said that it "couldn't be a clearer, more categorical indictment of racism in American life," and he went on to praise *Huckleberry Finn* as "one of the most devastating attacks on racism ever written." But Wallace, perhaps the novel's most outspoken critic, was unmoved by Fishkin's announcement. When asked to comment on the new evidence of Mark Twain's sympathy for blacks, he said that it "still does not mitigate the problems that children have with *Huck Finn*. . . . The book teaches blatant racism. . . . We ought to get it off the school reading list."

What shall we make of this unusual controversy? Unlike most issues of public policy involving opposed literary judgments, the current argument about the place of *Huckleberry Finn* in the public school curriculum does not involve censorship or First Amendment rights. Whether or not high-school students are required to read a particular novel has nothing to do with anyone's freedom of speech. (I am putting aside the very different and, to my mind, intolerable proposal to remove the book from school or public libraries.) Another striking feature of the dispute is the extremity of the antagonists' views. Most public quarrels about the merit of literary works turn on relatively subtle questions of interpretation, but in this case an enormous gulf separates those who consider *Huckleberry Finn* to be "one of the most devastating attacks on racism ever written" from those who denounce it as "racist trash"—who claim that it actually "teaches" blatant racism. At first sight, indeed, the two parties seem to be so far apart as to make the controversy irresolvable, and perhaps it is. But it may be useful, as a step toward a resolution, to consider why this novel lends itself to such antithetical readings. How is it possible for *Huckleberry Finn* to convey such diametrically opposed attitudes toward American racism?

The explanation should begin, I think, with a decisive though perhaps insufficiently appreciated fact: the racial attitudes to which this novel lends overt expression are not Mark Twain's, they are those of an ignorant adolescent boy. This fact also explains, incidentally, why evidence from other sources about what the writer, Samuel L. Clemens, may have thought or said on the subject of race (as in the Yale letter) proves to be largely beside the point. That a considerable disparity often exists between what writers believe and what their work conveys is an axiom of modern criticism. In the case of a first-person narrative like *Huckleberry Finn*, of course, Clemens's viewpoint is manifestly disguised, and can only make itself felt obliquely, in the voice of—from behind the mask of—the boy narrator, Huck.

In accounting for the ability of readers to arrive at radically opposed conclusions about the racial attitudes embodied in this novel, the importance of the first-person narrative method cannot be exaggerated. Every word, every thought, every perception, emanates from Huck or, in passages where other characters speak, is reported by him—filtered through his mind. *Adventures of Huckleberry Finn* is a tour de force of sustained impersonation. It is a tale told by a boy who is a vagrant and a virtual outcast, who has no mother (she is never mentioned), whose father is an illiterate drunk, bigot and bully, and who is inclined to accept society's view of people like himself as being, in his own words, irremediably "wicked and low-down and ornery."

Of course Huck calls black people "niggers"; for him to refer to them any other way would be inconceivable. But to say this can be misleading if it is taken to imply that the difficulty comes down to a mere question of usage, as if Mark Twain might have absolved his narrator (and himself) of the charge of racism merely by cleaning up Huck's vocabulary. The truth is that *Huckleberry Finn* is written from the viewpoint of a racist, or, to be more precise, a semiracist—a racist with a difference. The difference stems in part from Huck's exceptionally empathic nature (or, as Mark Twain puts it, his "sound heart") and in part from his disreputable upbringing on the fringe of antebellum Southern society. Unlike Tom Sawyer and his other friends whose parents belong to "the quality," Huck has been spared much of the formative influence of family, church and school. His racial prejudice is not supported by a sense of family or social superiority. On the contrary, he is a distinct outsider, a boy who is only half "civilized" or, in social science idiom, he has been incompletely acculturated. Although he has picked up the received version of white racism along with other bits and pieces of the dominant belief system, that viewpoint has been less deeply implanted in him than in respectable children like Tom Sawyer.

In moments of crisis, accordingly, Huck comes up against the discrepancy between the standard conception of black people as "niggers"—a conception he shares—and what he has learned as a result of his direct experience with Jim. During such crises his inner struggle characteristically begins with an unquestioning endorsement of the culture's stock prejudices, but then, when he tries to enact them, he balks and, in consequence, he inadvertently reveals their inhumanity. When, for example, it suddenly occurs to him that his journey with an escaped slave will determine what people back home think about him, his first reaction is wholly conventional: "It would get all around that Huck Finn helped a nigger to get his freedom; and if I was ever to see anybody from that town again, I'd be ready to get down and lick his boots for shame." He knows what he is supposed to do if he wants the respect of law-abiding citizens, but the thought of turning Jim in calls up vivid memories of Jim's loyalty and friendship, and he finally decides that he can't do it; he would rather go to hell. The conflict between Huck's stock racist ideas and his compassionate nature exemplifies the way the controlling irony works: when he thinks he is behaving ignobly, we are invited to recognize his innate nobility. What makes the outcome so powerful is that the novel's readers are compelled to effect the ironic reversal. That Huck can acknowledge Jim's humanity only by violating the moral code of a racist society is an implication that the boy is unable to grasp or put into words. It is a thought that Mark Twain's readers must formulate for themselves.

But of course the centrality of that irony also explains why some readers consider *Huckleberry Finn* a racist book. For whatever reason, and one can imagine several, they mistake the hero's flagrant if erratic racism for the novel's—the author's—viewpoint. It may be difficult, admittedly, for admirers of this wonderful book to believe that an average, reasonably competent reader could fail to recognize that its satirical thrust is directed against slavery and racial bigotry, but it does happen. Leaving aside the incontrovertible evidence that some adult readers do miss the point, it must be emphasized that Wallace and those who share his views are not chiefly concerned about the novel's effect on mature, competent readers. They are concerned about its effect on schoolchildren, all schoolchildren, but especially black American children, whose special experience might very well hinder their responsiveness to the ironic treatment of racial oppression. How much do we know, actually, about the ability of teachers, or of children of various ages and social backgrounds, to make sense of ironic discourse? I have taught this book with pleasure to hundreds of college students, but I'm not at all confident about my ability to persuade a class of inner-city adolescents—or any literal-minded adolescents, for that matter—that a book can say, or seem to say, one thing and mean another; or that in this case we should not be troubled by the fact that the hero calls black people "niggers" because, after all, that's what all white Southerners called them back then, and anyway, look, in the end he is loyal to Jim.

And besides, what does one say about Jim? There can be no doubt that Mark Twain wants us to admire him; he is a sympathetic, loving, self-abnegating, even saintly, "Christ-like" man. But what does one tell black children about his extreme passivity, his childlike credulity, his cloying deference toward the white boy? Aren't these the traits of a derisory racial stereotype, the fawning black male? To overcome objections on that score, one would have to stress Jim's cunning and occasional refusal to play the minstrel darkie, especially the great episode in which he drops his habitual pose of docility, if it is a pose, and angrily denounces Huck for making him the victim of a cruel joke. "It was fifteen minutes," Huck says about his reluctant apology, "before I could work myself up to go and humble myself to a nigger—but I done it, and I warn't ever sorry for it afterwards, neither." It is a splendid moment, but is it splendid enough to offset the inescapable doubts of black readers about Jim's customary pliancy? Is it enough that Jim, the only black male of any significance in the novel, asserts his dignity in this one moving episode?

To raise these complex issues, it need hardly be said, is not to condone the denunciation of the novel as racist trash. But even if that opinion is as wrongheaded as I believe it to be, it does not follow that those who hold it are necessarily wrong about the inappropriateness of requiring high-school teachers to teach, and students to read, the *Adventures of Huckleberry Finn*. The point at issue, then, is the justification for that requirement. To claim that it should be required reading because it is a great American book is unconvincing: we don't require students to read most great books. Objections to the requirement become more understandable if we recognize the unique character of the niche Twain's novel tends to occupy in the high-school English course. It often is the only book that is centrally concerned with racial oppression.

All of which suggests that educators could take a large step toward resolving the current controversy simply by eliminating the requirement. This would open the way for the ideal solution: allow each teacher to decide whether his or her students should be asked to read *Huckleberry Finn*. It is the teachers, after all, who are best qualified to make a sensible and informed decision, one that would rest on their confidence in their own ability to convey, and their students' ability to grasp, the irony that informs every word of this matchless comic novel.

FURTHER ADVENTURES OF HUCKLEBERRY FINN

DAVID HEIM

The Widow Douglas she took me for her son, and allowed she would sivilize me; but it was rough living in the house all the time, considering how dismal regular and decent the widow was in all her ways; and so when I couldn't stand it no longer, I lit out. I got into my old rags and sugar-hogshead again, and was free and satisfied.[1]

Americans were rather shocked when they first encountered these words. They were used to bits of local color, pleasing samples of folk life that confirmed their sense of cultural superiority. But here was a book written wholly in the vernacular. It wasn't just a book about an adolescent boy named Huckleberry Finn; it was Huck's book—thoughts, feelings, diction and all. Genteel readers condemned it as vulgar, coarse and irreverent. In Concord, Massachusetts, the library committee had this "veriest trash" removed from the shelves.

It has been 100 years since the publication of *Adventures of Huckleberry Finn*, and November 30 marks the 150th anniversary of the birth of Mark Twain (under the name Samuel Clemens). It would be hard today to name a book or author more firmly lodged in both critical regard and popular imagination.

We've recently been reminded, however, that Twain's narrative experiment still has power to offend, though for reasons Twain would not have expected. More and more black Americans are complaining about a book in which characters casually utter racist remarks and use the word "nigger." In Waukegan, Illinois, black parents succeeded in having the book taken off the schools' list of required reading. And John Wallace, a Chicago schoolteacher, has been encouraging his colleagues across the nation to rid their classrooms of the "most grotesque piece of racist trash ever written."

Literary scholars have jumped to Twain's defense. Yale's Shelley Fisher Fishkin cites a recently discovered letter in which Twain agreed to pay a black student's law school tuition. "We have ground the manhood out of . . . [black men] and the shame is ours, not theirs," Twain explained, revealing, at least to some, his enlightened views on race. Thus, in this double anniversary year, Twain has become the subject of an unusual debate involving history and literary criticism.

The charge of racism is likely to sound harsh to readers who recall the book's climax when Huck rejects conventional morality of the day, and decides that he won't turn in Jim, the runaway slave. "I'd got to decide, forever, betwixt two things," Huck reflects before making up his mind. "All right, then, I'll *go* to hell." Huck has neither the language nor the mental capacity to launch a moral critique of slavery. Only by going against his "conscience" can Huck perform what the reader recognizes to be a moral act. Twain does not announce this irony, but simply allows the reader to feel it—one reason the book is so powerful.

This account does not impress Wallace, however, and to some extent it misses the point. "There are lots of interpretations of the book," he says. "The point is, this is not a book for children." In Wallace's experience, *Huck* does not prompt students to ponder the culture of slavery or the depths of racism. It only serves to legitimate the word "nigger" and humiliate students, both black and white, who are forced to read passages aloud.

One may quarrel with Wallace's dismissal of the book as "racist trash" while recognizing the practical import of his argument. Surely it is wise to listen to what teachers tell us students can absorb from books, even if there is more to

glean. We may (to take another example) all agree that the literature of the
Bible is eminently worth teaching to children, while also agreeing that the book
of Judges, say, with its chronicles of violence, is not the best introduction to
that literature. To require Twain's book to be read as one of the great books of
American literature without considering the capacities of particular students to
understand it in its context and to distinguish Twain from his characters is
surely to side with the forces of "sivilization."

It is helpful, in observing the Twain anniversaries, to be reminded that his
greatest book is not, indeed, a book for children. Rather, it exhibits a nostalgia
for youth and a discontent with the demands of civilization that are reserved for
grownups both to feel and to ponder. In writing *Huck*, the middle-aged Twain
returned in his imagination to the Mississippi River towns of his youth. In doing
so, he dramatized a conflict that has the status of myth in the American mind:
the conflict between a naturally sound heart and a corrupt civilization.

Nothing is more radical in Twain—nor, if it comes to that, more open to
parental objection—than the fierceness with which he conceived of this
conflict. Huck's goodness derives from the fact that, as an outcast, he has not
totally absorbed what the Marxists would call his society's "false consciousness." Huck escapes the grip of civilization by

> thinking about our trip down river; and I see Jim before me all the time, in the day, and in the
> night-time, sometimes moonlight, sometimes storms, and we a floating along, talking, and singing,
> and laughing. But somehow I couldn't seem to strike no places to harden me against him, but only
> the other kind (pp. 243-44).

By this spontaneous re-creation of his experience on the raft with Jim, and by
recovering the natural rhythms of life and speech, Huck remains responsive to
his naïve affection for Jim and the natural world.

By linking Huck to Jim's quest for freedom, Twain gives his nostalgia a
political meaning. He suggests that we can find the basis for a truly human
community in natural feeling and honest perception. But Twain's book also
serves as a warning about the appeal of the natural life. To remember Twain
together with his brilliant creation, Huck, is to recall that Huck is just that, a
creation—not "natural" at all, but the projection of a man sitting in his Hartford
study responding to the tensions of his own life and culture.

This distinction is worth remembering when we are tempted to project our
own vision of the natural on others, especially on particular agents of political
change—whether peasants, youth, farmers, proletarians or natives of the Third
World—whom we imagine to possess a natural virtue and authenticity, and thus
to be inoculated against the false consciousness of a corrupt civilization. Especially in light of the recent controversy, it is important to note that
Twain is most vulnerable to charges of racism in the way he attributes to Jim
a certain childlike receptivity to experience—a trait which, in the context of the
novel, is largely positive. Such a portrayal uses a stereotype of a black man,
not a fully imagined character.

Huck also reminds us that "natural" insights are by themselves impotent.
Having made Huck and Jim the moral center of his novel, Twain did not know
what to do with them. He allowed their raft to float downstream, further into
slave territory; and even more disturbing, he let Jim and Huck forget about
their shared quest for freedom. And the book ends with Huck taking orders
from Tom Sawyer, who stages a faked liberation of Jim, knowing all the while
that Jim has already been freed by his master's deathbed wish. Twain could

not imagine any approximation of the natural life within society. Thus it is not surprising that his later work loses the vision of the natural life altogether, and becomes instead a strident attack on all authorities and a mordant contemplation of the "damned human race."

Huck displays the energy and depth of feeling that can come from acknowledging, as Twain did, his deepest longings for a natural life, outside the constraints of society. It urges us to be attentive to the voice of the outcast and to the childlike in ourselves as well as others. But Twain's life and work also remind us that we can escape the futility of nostalgia and self-projection only by trying, tentatively and critically, to embody those voices not only in language but in life. Then we can change the face of "sivilization."

NOTES

1. *Adventures of Huckleberry Finn* (Bobbs-Merrill, 1967), p. 11.

A HARD BOOK TO TAKE

JAMES M. COX

My title may seem at first glance all wrong. If any book has been easy to take for the last hundred years, surely it is *Adventures of Huckleberry Finn*. Read by people of all ages, loved throughout the nation, it finally made its way into the academy so that professors of literature—at least a good number of them—have come to take both confidence and pleasure in deeming it a masterpiece of American literature. Yet if Huck's story seems to tell itself upon a current of ease, he says at the end that it was a hard book to write. And it was from the beginning a hard book to take in some quarters. For example, the Public Library Committee of Concord, Massachusetts—home of Emerson, Thoreau, and Hawthorne—banned it. The *Boston Transcript* approvingly reported the committee's judgment that the book was rough, coarse, and inelegant, "the whole book being more suited to the slums than to intelligent, respectable people." The *Springfield Republican* condemned the book on the ground that it was trashy and vicious. Recalling that, eight years earlier, Mark Twain had shown a singular lack of propriety at the Whittier birthday dinner, the *Republican* averred that the book degenerated into "a gross trifling with every fine feeling."

It became so easy to flog those dear old genteel custodians of New England culture for their utter failure of taste, that a generation of academic custodians of literary culture could forget how long it took for Mark Twain to displace the New England worthies in the schools. They could forget, for instance, that Jim's observation about Frenchmen and the French language is not quite so hilarious to Frenchmen (so I have been told) as it is to us; they could forget that the jokes on religion might not be so funny to a devoutly Primitive Baptist; or that the exposures of village cruelty and Southern mores, pursued with the zeal characteristic of so many published interpretations of the novel, might prove a trial to the humor of rural conservative Southerners. These could be forgotten because the enlightened audience of today does not have to worry about any of these groups. The French, who are far away in their own language, will just have to take the little joke (it is really quite a big one), or, if they cannot, somehow mute the joke in translation; the primitively religious do not really count any more than the Southern rural conservatives. They can stay in their communities, for one thing; for another, they can probably find other books to ban since by nature they distrust the literary imagination. Such was the essentially complacent attitude of the academic establishment that put Mark Twain among the major American writers.

I am part of that establishment, and I have helped put to rout the last traces of the genteel remnant in the academy. Even those professors, refined in taste or devoted to the art of real artists (artists like Henry James or Dante), who used to dismay us with their scorn of the ending of *Huckleberry Finn*, have now been worn down or fatigued by our adroit defenses of the ending. And so they are silenced, as they should have been silenced in 1950 when T. S. Eliot, the very embodiment of high art, affirmed that the book—the whole book, ending and all—was incontrovertibly a work of art. But then we who subsequently went on defending the ending should have also rested, at once silent and content in the knowledge of Eliot's magisterial affirmation. But how could we have known that Eliot's judgment, like so many of his decisions, was to be the literary law of the land, making our subsequent interpretations nothing more than glosses on an approved text.

Despite our confident assurance about the book's quality, there has been, in the last fifteen years, another group—steadily increasing in numbers—that finds the book hard to take. I mean of course black Americans. Since they do, our complacency is, or should be, shattered. We used to be able to assure them—when they were little more than token presences in what we are pleased to call the world of higher education—that they could surely see that the book was in no way really prejudiced against Jim or the Negro (as we used to say before Malcolm X sought to set us free). The presence of the word *nigger* throughout the book, we would go on to say, merely reflected the time and place of the novel and was a manifestation of Mark Twain's celebrated realism. To take the term personally or negatively was to fly in the face of the whole intention of the novel. Editions of the novel that took up the matter at all did what they could to defend Mark Twain, or, in one instance that I remember, to declare complaints about Mark Twain's usage irrelevant, since the author's good racial intentions were manifestly visible.

However much we may recognize those good intentions, we nonetheless know, both historically and personally, that racial objection to that word is not irrelevant. If Mark Twain could use the word in the nineteenth century with a certain freedom and could not use all the four-letter words we have lately allowed to pass the censor, we feel a greater inhibition about that word than we can quite believe Mark Twain ever felt and certainly more hesitation about it than about the four-letter words we are using more easily. Let me come closer home. Almost every student of Mark Twain has felt that he exaggerated the matter of social censorship on writers. To be sure, we know that the Gilded Age had overrefined standards of taste and usage. But even Brooks and DeVoto, both of whom lamented the stifling pressures of New England gentility, ultimately concluded that Mark Twain, more than his society, was primarily responsible for the censorship against which he railed.

The fact remains, however, that *Huckleberry Finn*, alone among the masterpieces of nineteenth-century American literature, remains to this day threatened with censorship. School boards in New York and Pennsylvania have recently considered removing it from assigned reading lists; and recently the Mark Twain High School (of all names!) in Fairfax County, Virginia, within a stone's throw of the nation's capital, found itself determined to remove the book from circulation. There were the usual high-minded editorials defending the book and lamenting the bigotry that keeps failing to understand it. Yet for all the familiar defenses and for all my belief in freedom of the press and my love for the book, I know in my heart that, if I were teaching an American literature course in Bedford Stuyvesant or Watts or North Philadelphia, I might well find myself choosing *Tom Sawyer* or *A Connecticut Yankee* rather than *Huckleberry Finn* to represent Mark Twain.

Such a decision would not necessarily be reprehensible. After all, Huck himself often acted precisely along such lines. He had learned from Pap that the best way to get along with scoundrels like the King and the Duke (and Pap, too, for that matter) was to avoid trouble with them. Even to remember the novel is to remember that Pap had something to teach Huck by precept as well as by forceful presence. He taught Huck to "take a chicken when you get a chance, because if you don't want him yourself you can easily find somebody that does, and a good deed ain't ever forgot" (p. 95). Those who find such wisdom immoral would do well to remember that Thoreau thought the wood he stole made the sweetest fire.

To say a word for Pap may seem to many readers of the book—and good readers—nothing short of sacrilege. Yet entertainment of Pap's humanity—which is, after all, immensely entertaining—can provide an avenue for comprehending as well as acknowledging the power and wisdom of the book. On the one hand he is fiercely cruel, and his cruelty runs directly athwart two of the sacred values the book exploits. First of all, his treatment of Huck convicts him of child abuse; but more important, he is a classic exemplification of racial bigotry. Set against the values the book seems so clearly to uphold, these two forms of behavior characterize Pap as a reprobate.

At the same time, Pap is truly a performer. His speech against the government *is* hilarious as long as we can bring ourselves to laugh at it. But the matter of that speech crosses our sense of humane and rational ideals enough to make us displace our humorous response with a harsh moral judgment when we are writing criticism approved for publication in the journals. Even so, the humor is undeniably present right through Pap's performance. For if Pap is a miscreant, he is also helplessly humorous. Listen to his lament:

"A man can't get his rights in a govment like this. Sometimes I've a mighty notion just to leave the country for good and all. Yes, and I *told* 'em so; I told old Thatcher so to his face. Lots of 'em heard me, and can tell what I said. Says I, for two cents I'd leave the blamed country and never come anear it agin. Them's the very words. I says, look at my hat—if you call it a hat—but the lid raises up and the rest of it goes down till it's below my chin, and then it ain't rightly a hat at all, but more like my head was shoved up through a jint o' stove-pipe. Look at it, says I—such a hat for me to wear—one of the wealthiest men in this town, if I could get my rights." (P. 49)

For all its irony, the passage discloses Pap's incomparable stage presence. In playing, or rather replaying, his public speech before Huck, Pap is in all probability exaggerating, yet the exaggeration is an integral part of his histrionic sense of himself. His unforgettable description of his hat brings him to the edge of a self-consciously humorous grasp of his own image that all but betrays the limitations of illiteracy and cruelty in which his character is conceived. At such a moment the performer is at the brink of eluding the ideational constraint upon his character.

When, in his next breath, Pap launches into his matter of the free Negro professor whose presence in his memory outrages him, we are at the true threshold of the novel. The measure to which the humor—continuing throughout the passage—will be drowned out depends on the indignation the critical audience feels in relation to the matter of the speech. Since that matter is directly racist, it possesses both the volatility and the simplicity to reduce as well as to define its audience. Listen again:

"Thinks I, what is the country a-coming to! It was 'lection day, and I was just about to go and vote, myself, if I warn't too drunk to get there; but when they told me there was a State in this country where they'd let that nigger vote, I drawed out. I says I'll never vote agin. Them's the very words I said; they all heard me; and the country may rot for all me—I'll never vote agin as long as I live. And to see the cool way of that nigger—why, he wouldn't a give me the road if I hadn't shoved him out o' the way." (P. 50)

In the public and social terms of the novel—let us say in its relation to the national conscience—the irony is sufficiently savage to cut athwart the irrepressible humor that continues to ripple the current of Pap's speech. Though the humor reinforces, it nonetheless qualifies the irony of the performance. Thus when Pap says he was about to vote if he "warn't too drunk to get there," his acknowledgment of his condition is at once in character yet again brings him to the threshold of a self-consciousness that belies his relentless hostility to blacks. I don't mean at all that Pap himself is any freer from his bigotry by virtue of his humor; I do mean that in his act of performance—and in Mark Twain's management of that performance—his admission (or is it his boast?) of his drunkenness is very much designed to draw a laugh. It is surely so designed by Mark Twain; even Pap, who remains throughout his replay of his speech insistently aware of his own performance, is all but masterfully producing one of his effects. When he subsequently tumbles over the tub of salt pork, barking his shins, and then, rising and cursing, proceeds to give the tub an unfortunate kick with the foot that has two toes "leaking out the front end" of its boot, he bursts forth with an agonized string of curses that he later says "laid over anything he done previous." Consciously casting himself in the role of a master performer, Pap sees himself as an actor in the great tradition of Sowberry Hagan.

I begin with Pap because his presence and identity are characteristic of a central aspect of the novel. The more seriously we take the matter of the book—I mean the matter of race and slavery—the less we are likely to want the humor to rise to the surface of this passage. If we refuse the rise of humor, in the system of emotional exchange that runs through the book the indignation at Pap's brutality and racism has freer play. Acknowledging the humor—which is to say *experiencing* it—involves an instinctive recognition of Pap's humanity. For if Pap is fierce in being, he is a delight in performance. The delight comes first of all from the exposed ironic relationship between his attitudes and his behavior. Equally important, it comes from the economy of pity we enjoy upon seeing him so justly and so visibly in pain. We are, by virtue of the irony, spared the expenditure of sympathizing with him.

The pity we save at Pap's expense we fairly lavish on Jim as the novel proceeds. Seeing the terms of this emotional exchange is to see Pap's vital function and placement in the book. In terms of affect, he is the figure who opens the way for Jim to be a center of sympathy; in terms of theme, his behavior and his departure make it possible for Jim to displace him as Huck's loving father. Even more important, Pap's inimitable performance literally initiates the racial theme just as Pap himself literally drives Huck out of the childhood world of Tom Sawyer and into the arms of the escaped Jim. The two fugitives—the one from Pap, the other from Miss Watson—find in each other the resources that lift their journey into mythic significance. Borne southward on the great river into the very heart of slavery, they nonetheless embody in their relationship what is probably the most powerful expression of our national dream of freedom.

Yet the fact that the direction of this dream of freedom is into the land of slavery should keep us in touch with the profound contradictions of the book. The novel generates a wish for both freedom and brotherhood embodied in a magically simplified image of human relationship between a black man and a redneck boy. But that simplification, as Pap's presence already indicates, is built upon a series of remarkably complex trades and exchanges. Thus, we can see that, although Pap's speech exposes his viciousness, the matter of that speech would or could still offend a particular audience. That very speech is one I could easily imagine *not* reading to a high-school class in Harlem. Yet if I can imagine such self-censorship in the face of external social pressure, I can just as easily imagine a self-indulgent public emphasis on the negative character of Pap in order to expose his bigotry to the lash of criticism—censoring in the process the humor that is so irrepressibly present in the speech. To censor the humor is to deny Pap the humanity he ineffably possesses.

Even more important, failure to recognize his humanity results in a corresponding reduction of Jim's humanity. For if Pap is often reduced to his racism, Jim is just as often simplistically elevated into sainthood. Here again the simplification results from a refusal to see the humor of Jim's performance. For Jim, like all the characters in this novel, is in the business of humorous performance. If Pap's humor threatens to redeem him from simple racism, Jim's humor threatens him with a minstrel identity. It is just this identity that makes modern audiences—whether black or liberal white—uncomfortable. Thus it is not only the word *nigger*, so liberally distributed throughout Huck's narrative, that publicly troubles us. It is the role Jim plays, or is forced to play. Yet diminishing that aspect of Jim's character results in an emphasis on his goodness, generosity, and essential humility. To be sure, Jim manifestly possesses these qualities in abundance, but they come to the fore almost inevitably at the expense of his intelligence. In other words, the more Jim is made a saint the more he is likely to be the humble victim lacking any semblance of the shrewd humanity Huck so amply possesses.

Yet surely Jim is shrewd, as shrewd as Huck. If we take the incident in Chapter 2, in which Tom lifts the sleeping Jim's hat and hangs it on a tree above his head, we cannot be quite sure, in this world where everyone is involved in tricks, deceit, and confidence games, that Jim is even asleep. If we see in Pap's racism the traces of a humorous consciousness of his own performance, we should be able to detect in Jim's gullible account of being bewitched the apparition of a master of the tall tale. To exclude such a "superstitious" presence is to settle for Huck's complacent feeling of superiority to Jim's gullible belief in superstition. Using this episode as the most genial and disarming initiation into Jim's relation of narrative and relation to the narrative, we can go much further. We know and admire Huck as a liar but are prone never to realize that Jim lies to Huck about Pap's death. He does not elaborate a lie about it; he simply conceals his knowledge from Huck. Though one of his motives for evading Huck's query about the dead man in the floating house may be his tender wish to spare Huck the knowledge of being an orphan, Jim has good reason to suspect that a Huck free of his Pap might leave him high and dry.

The possibility that Huck will abandon or betray Jim is, after all, at the very center of the whole journey—and the two fugitives can never believe in each other sufficiently to annihilate it. That possibility is, after all, nothing less than the likelihood that the social reality from which they both are fugitive will intrude at any time to split asunder their precarious pastoral on the raft. Given this reality, Jim and Huck have confidence in each other at the same time they con each other. There is no better revelation of their relationship than the sequence extending from Huck's apology to Jim after deceiving him about the fog (in Chapter 15) to his wonderful lie to the slave-hunters in the very next chapter.

The fact that two pages after he humbles himself to Jim—that action for which Huck has received so much critical praise—he begins to think about turning Jim in should give us considerable pause. Is Huck's reversal merely a reflection of Mark Twain's carelessness, or is it Huck's own inconsistency of character? Or, more likely, is his rising social conscience integrally related to his sense of guilt at having mistreated Jim about the fog? It is hardly accidental that at the very moment Huck has "matured" in our own eyes by having recognized Jim's humanity he should begin to think about being a good boy in relation to the authority of his own society.

The problem, of course, is that if Huck's determination to be kind to Jim makes him a good boy in our eyes, his wish to be a good boy in his own society puts Jim in great jeopardy. But the paradox runs much deeper. For the fact of the novel is that the passage in which Huck apologizes to Jim literally marks Huck and Jim's passage by Cairo, the Ohio, and freedom. Put another way, the good feeling evoked by Huck's sincere apology literally masks the fact that Jim has irrevocably passed his chance for freedom. As if this were not enough, Huck no sooner ends Chapter 15 asserting that he was glad to have apologized to Jim and "didn't do him no more mean tricks" than he is inwardly planning to turn Jim in. Surely this would be the meanest trick of all. Yet Huck himself betrays no consciousness of his contradiction. Fearing immediately after his apology that they might miss Cairo, Huck proposes to go ashore to discover their exact whereabouts. As he prepares for this excursion, he becomes uncomfortably conscious of Jim's bold anticipation of being free. Troubled by his complicity in Jim's determination to be free, he accuses himself of ingratitude to the respectable people who have tried to help him. His sense of wrong is sufficiently acute to repress for the moment the moral enormity of turning Jim over to the authorities. And so, just as our serious approval of Huck's apology to Jim keeps us from seeing that freedom was being lost at precisely that moment, Huck's serious recognition of his own criminal activity is sufficient to keep him from seeing that he is about to do Jim the meanest of mean tricks. Mean tricks are of course in the world of Tom Sawyer and childhood; and Huck, doubtless feeling and even liking his own maturity as much as we feel and applaud it, cannot see this adult effort to be socially responsible as a mean trick. Besides, Jim is talking bolder, and why shouldn't he? Not only does he think freedom is around the bend; he has also just put Huck in his place. As for Huck, if he has humbled himself to Jim, small wonder that from his new perspective Jim suddenly seems proud.

These observations in no way denigrate the nobility of Huck's apology, but they do gauge the emotional exchange in the book. The smoothness, swiftness, and disarming flow of Huck's narration conceal the snags, reefs, and channel crossings that the narrative is constantly negotiating. Moreover, our tentative scrutiny of this particular sequence in the novel prepares us for the wonderful exchange Huck has with the slave-hunters he is about to meet. Even before he can shove off in the canoe with the ostensible mission of finding out just where he and Jim are on the river—and with the secret intention of reforming himself by turning Jim over to society—Jim just may have divined what we might call a honky in the woodpile. Listen to his heartfelt farewell to Huck and to the response it arouses in Huck:

"Pooty soon I'll be a-shout'n for joy, en I'll say It's all on accounts o' Huck; I's a free man, en I couldn't ever ben free ef it hadn't ben for Huck; Huck done it. Jim won't ever forget you, Huck; you's de bes' fren' Jim's ever had; en you's de *only* fren' ole Jim's got now."

I was paddling off, all in a sweat to tell on him; but when he says this, it seemed to kind of take the tuck all out of me. I went along slow then, and I warn't right down certain whether I was glad I started or whether I warn't. When I was fifty yards off, Jim says:

"Dah you goes, de ole true Huck; de on'y white genlman dat ever kep' his promise to ole Jim." (P. 124)

In this exchange we have the full force of the idyllic myth: Huck the good-hearted boy possessing an innocence tied to irony and cunning; and Jim, the long-suffering man who is equally innocent, but whose innocence is expressed in terms of gullibility and humility. At the same time, we have a Huck with bad intentions and a Jim voicing praise sufficiently intense to betray an intelligence that knows betrayal may be at hand. Such an analysis of their exchange does not deny so much as it qualifies their affection for each other. That is why both language and drama are profoundly in harmony. Jim's speech, with an auditory trace of confidence in its performance, is penetrating Huck's vulnerable psyche precisely because the speech is penetrating and the psyche vulnerable.

Huck has no sooner heard Jim's farewell praise than he is confronted by the very society to which he has intended to hand over Jim. It comes in the form of two men hunting not one but five fugitive slaves. With Jim's affectionate voice still sounding in his ears, Huck, unable to tell the two men the truth, helplessly drops into one of his best lies. When he lied to Judith Loftus, he had been caught in the lie (or did he let himself be caught?) and then, in the teeth of her pleasurable self-congratulation at having caught him, he told her a bigger and bolder lie. This time he lies by implication and withdrawal. Asked whether the man on his raft is black, Huck hesitantly replies that he is white. And to the series of questions that follows, Huck says that the man is his father and is sick. When he adds blubberingly that his mam and Mary Ann are also sick and that no one will help them, the men themselves begin to fill in the blanks, concluding that the whole family has small pox. If Judith Loftus had helped Huck out when, realizing he was not a girl, she supplied him with the details of the identity (an apprentice who had been badly treated) on which he in turn built his second lie to her, the slave-hunters do even better. Keeping their distance to avoid the disease, they are nonetheless so touched by Huck's narrative (which they themselves have fearfully concluded) that they give Huck forty dollars. And Huck takes it. When he returns to the raft so near at hand, Jim is there to praise Huck's performance as much as he had earlier praised his character:

> "I was a-listenin' to all de talk, en I slips into de river en was gwyne to shove for sho' if dey come aboard. Den I was gwyne to swim to de raf' agin when dey was gone. But lawsy, how you did fool 'em, Huck! Dat *wuz* de smartes' dodge! I tell you, chile, I 'speck it save' ole Jim—ole Jim ain't gwyne to forgit you for dat, honey." (P. 128)

They take the money and share it in a moment worthy of the King and the Duke, yet you may be sure that there has been little criticism directed toward pointing up that analogy. As for the two slave-hunters, they have never to my knowledge been given their share of moral credit for their all but spontaneous and certainly heartfelt contribution to Huck's welfare.

Of course they do not know, as we do, that Huck is concealing Jim. Yet they are charged with their intention of hunting runaway slaves at the same time that they are robbed of the moral credit they deserve for sympathizing with what they believe to be Huck's stricken plight. Reflection on the slave-hunters and their fate at our hands, and further reflection on this whole episode, affords an opportunity to ask some genuine moral questions about *Huckleberry Finn*. Having already seen the humor in Pap's racism, the confidence in Jim's gullibility and in his loyalty, the abrupt reversal between the Huck of the apology and the Huck intending to betray Jim to the authorities, and the way in which the emotion of Huck's apology literally displaces the fact that these two travelers have forever passed by Cairo and freedom—having seen so much, we are faced with the forty-dollar charity display of the slave-hunters. We cannot help applauding Huck's dodge as much as Jim applauds it. Yet even allowing for the fact that the men are slave-hunters and that their charity has about it a strong element of payoff in order to avoid the plague they have imagined, they still seem to me a wonderful snag in the moral current of the narrative. Aren't they really as good as anyone in the book? Is there anyone else's charity that is really superior to theirs? And aren't Huck and Jim, by taking their money, just as bad as the King and the Duke, who are waiting in the wings? Of course these questions go against our feelings—they go against the master current of the fiction. Yet not to ask them is to settle for a far tamer stream than the shifting, magnificent Mississippi that absolutely underlies the book.

These questions point us back to a particular kind of moral and emotional exchange that is always going on in the book. The value we are holding to as if it were the measure of all others is, of course, Jim—Huck's relation to and involvement in Jim's freedom lift him out of the childhood world and lift his lies from what we might call the world of low picaresque into what we want to see as the realm of higher humanity. The antislavery sentiment affixed to Jim and his freedom functions as an absolute moral yardstick by which to measure other values. Thus our sense of Pap's anguish is crowded out by our indignation at his racism; thus the slave-hunters' sympathy for Huck's fictive family is set at naught because they *are* slave-hunters; and thus the King and Duke cease to be amusing once they go beyond fleecing the rural, evangelical, and illiterate white communities strung out along the river and take up the business of trading off the Wilks slaves. And Huck himself ultimately loses value when he goes along with Tom's travesty of freeing Jim according to the rules.

Yet Huck has always done all he could to go along with the more powerful forces he confronts—and so many of those forces are more powerful than he, a mere orphan adrift upon the mighty river. His great value lies precisely in his negative relation to the banks of both right and wrong between which both his narrative and his life so beautifully and powerfully run. Look at his own appraisal of the incident involving the slave-hunters:

They went off, and I got aboard the raft, feeling bad and low, because I knowed very well I had done wrong, and I see it warn't no use for me to try to learn to do right; a body that don't get *started* right when he's little, ain't got no show—when the pinch comes there ain't nothing to back him up and keep him to his work, and so he gets beat. Then I thought a minute, and says to myself, hold on,—s'pose you'd a done right and give Jim up; would you felt better than what you do now? No, says I, I'd feel bad—I'd feel just the same way I do now. Well, then, says I, what's the use you learning to do right, when it's troublesome to do right and ain't no trouble to do wrong, and the wages is just the same? I was stuck. I couldn't answer that. So I reckoned I wouldn't bother no more about it, but after this always do whichever come handiest at the time. (Pp. 127-28)

This, it should be emphasized, is his reflection on the action he has all but helplessly had to take—an action which, *negative* in its nature, leaves him feeling *bad* and *low*. Out of that depression and regret he would like to think that had he done the opposite he would have felt better, but he knows that he would have felt no better (he does not say he would have felt worse); and so he concludes with the determination to do in the future only what is handiest or easiest. Thus the essential pleasure principle of ease and handiness that he affirms arises out of a helpless action—and the minute we pursue the origins of that action we are led back to Huck's bad intention of betraying Jim, back from that to his apology for having lied to Jim about the fog, and on back to the encompassing narrative fact that the fog itself along with Huck's apology constitute Mark Twain's own dodge for eliminating the possibility of an Ohio ending for his novel. Yet if the episode of the fog, Huck's lie to Jim, and his subsequent apology literally displace their loss of freedom, this narrative sequence just as surely constitutes Huck's much approved "moral growth" that forms the basis for the serious sentiment on which the novel depends.

There, it seems to me, is a fairly clear analysis of the sequence leading to Huck's affirmation of his pleasure principle. His pleasure principle, of course, involves a bold program, so bold that he himself cannot keep it up, and no reader of the novel should have to be told where he fails. The failure is, as a matter of fact, at the heart of his greatest success—the moment when he determines to set Jim free. That moment is a remarkable variation on both the action and reflection we have just examined. This time, however, Huck is alone, the King and the Duke having "stolen" and sold Jim for "forty dirty dollars," to use Huck's description of the transaction when he learns of it. Realizing Jim's plight, Huck thinks at first of writing Miss Watson, on the premise that Jim will be treated better upriver than where he now is. He decides on second thought not to write because he fears that Miss Watson might vengefully sell Jim back downriver. But then the greatest fear of what people will think of *him* for abetting a fugitive slave gets the better of him—and out of that fear emerges his conscience to upbraid and shame him for his wickedness until he finally decides to write Miss Watson of Jim's whereabouts. In the midst of the flush or self-approval that follows hard upon the completion of his letter, the image of Jim looms in Huck's mind as a rebuke to his first act of writing. Benignly presiding over and pervading Huck's highly compressed mental rehearsal of the journey, Jim stands as the figure against whom Huck, remembering incident after incident of their journey, cannot harden his heart:

and at last I struck the time I saved him by telling the men we had small-pox aboard, and he was so grateful, and said I was the best friend old Jim ever had in the world, and the *only* one he's got now; and then I happened to look around, and see that paper.

It was a close place. I took it up, and held it in my hand. I was a trembling, because I'd got to decide, forever, betwixt two things, and I knowed it. I studied a minute, sort of holding my breath, and then says to myself:

"All right, then, I'll *go* to hell"—and tore it up. (Pp. 271-72)

No attentive reader of the novel can ever wish that Huck had concluded otherwise. Yet his choice, if we take it seriously—and if anything in the novel is to be taken seriously, surely this decision is—seems to run directly athwart his prior determination to do whatever came easiest and handiest. The more seriously the decision is taken—the more it is seen as Huck's "crisis of conscience"—the more disappointing the ending of the novel will be. For instead of living solemnly by his decision, Huck merely submits to Tom Sawyer's extravaganza of freeing Jim. Moreover, Tom's farce is predicated on his concealed knowledge that Jim is already free—and freed by Miss Watson, of all people! She, the moralist of the old order, who has been advertised in the fiction as the person who would sell Jim down the river, turns out to make the will that legally sets him free. How could Mark Twain play such a mean trick?

The least he could have done was to plot his novel better and make Jim the property of the Widow Douglas.

Of course he had given us this authorial warning through a G. G., Chief of Ordnance (could those initials stand for General Grant?):

Persons attempting to find a motive in this narrative will be prosecuted; persons attempting to find a moral in it will be banished; persons attempting to find a plot in it will be shot.

Given such a series of threats, we had perhaps better not even wish for a plot, let alone seek one. Here again, it is worth noting that Mark Twain is not denying the presence of motive, moral, or plot but asserting the danger of seeking for them. We do not wish to take this warning seriously, yet all the criticism written about this narrative, including this essay, is testimony to the book's resistance to motive, moral, and plot.

What, after all, is the almost universal disturbance about the abortive ending but a complaint about Mark Twain's rather high-handed (or was it his casual, or worse, his unwitting?) dismissal of whatever motive, moral, or plot his narrative had generated? And the ending does indeed seem to abort the motive (Huck and Jim's wish for freedom), the moral (the triumph of the natural good intentions of a sound heart over a deformed conscience), and the plot (a young picaro's account of his discovery of a slave's humanity and his subsequent attempt to steal the slave out of slavery). In those last ten chapters Huck and Jim no longer visibly wish for freedom but become passive slaves to Tom Sawyer's "plot"; Huck's sound heart is so still that he seems as heartless as Tom Sawyer; and the act of stealing a slave becomes Tom's charade of enslaving a free man.

No wonder such an ending has driven critics of sound mind to distraction. If it has never really bothered children, there is not all that much evidence that so many of them actually read it. It bothered Leo Marx enough to make him mount an attack on Lionel Trilling and T. S. Eliot, who he felt had not been bothered enough by it. And it has more recently motivated John Seelye to rewrite the book under title of *The True Adventures of Huckleberry Finn*. Putting in all the four-letter words that Mark Twain left out, Seelye, obeying liberal and even radical intentions, has Jim killed so that Huck, speaking in the dark, can conclude the narrative with these words: "I didn't care whether the goddamn sun ever come up again."

The happy effect of Seelye's tour de force, giving us a dead rather than a free Jim, should enable us to realize that such a substitute ending, though it may satisfy those who long for something more serious than Tom's farce and something more real than his fantasy, is little better than a conventional happy ending would have been—an ending that would have had Huck, not Tom, free Jim—and not a *free* Jim either, and certainly not according to the rules. To have accomplished that, Mark Twain would have needed to put the fog and apology far enough upstream (since no one would want them removed) to leave Huck time and space to have his crises of conscience above Cairo. Or, if he had them pass it in order to have his great Arkansas scenes, he would have needed to have them use that forty dollars they got from the slave-hunters to buy passage on a steamboat (as Jim suggests at one point) and come to freedom in style. But we couldn't stand that ending either, because then the slave-hunters would have provided Huck and Jim's passage to freedom. The more anyone thinks about such substitutions, the more Mark Twain's mean trick of an ending seems as good as we are likely to get. He had Tom give Jim forty dollars for being such a good prisoner, and Tom even hoped to take Jim back on a steamboat and have a circuslike celebration in St. Petersburg.

Mean trick though Mark Twain's ending may be, it is probably the best ending we shall ever have. By making us wish for something else, it remains its own discordant reality principle. If we want Huck to have freed Jim, we just want Huck to be a charitable good little abolitionist. Mark Twain might just as well have sent him across the yard in Hartford to Harriet Beecher Stowe's house to ask for Eva, the good little Christian. If, however, we continue to look at the novel in terms of emotional exchange, we can see that Mark Twain determined to save both Huck and Jim at the expense of Tom Sawyer. In the world of literary interpretation, poor old Tom never has got over that decision, and he never will. In the light of those interpretations, we have to see that Mark Twain so loved Huck and Jim that he sacrificed Tom Sawyer for them.

To review Mark Twain's mean trick and his sacrifice of Tom is to be taken back once more to Huck's mean trick and his apology. Remembering just how that remarkable sequence displaced the actual passage by Cairo and the irrevocable loss of freedom ought to instruct us about the implicit vision behind the mean trick of the ending. Surely this second trick discloses that, far from being free, humanity is in slavery. The travesty of Jim's "freedom" in the closing narrative movement reveals in a way that no other ending could that he is not free and will not be. Why else and how else could we, after one hundred years of the book's life, keep being drawn into the splendid lie of a young boy deciding to steal a slave out of slavery? Let me offer three tentative reasons for our being sold by as well as sold on the book. First, deep down we know and know socially every day that neither we nor Jim is free despite the fictions of history and the Thirteenth Amendment; second, we do not even want Jim to be free, in order that we can continue to enjoy the perennial self-approval of freeing him; and third, we tell ourselves he is free because we, like all the characters in the book, want to be lied to. If that last is what the King and Duke know so well, it is also what Huck knows. The lie is, in a world of lies, what comes easiest and handiest to mind and mouth. Knowing so much, Huck, like the King and the Duke, can easily enlist the help of his interlocutors. As he says of Aunt Sally and Uncle Silas when he lies to them about having been on a steamboat that blew its cylinder head, "If I'd a called it a bolt-head it would a done just as well" (p. 283).

The truth we most deeply need to believe in a free country is that we are free—and freedom in this country, first defined as freedom from tyranny, came to be defined as freedom from slavery. Freeing the slaves—emancipation—was the great international and political movement in the West in the nineteenth century. Predicated on the twin humanitarian emotions of indignation at the cruelty to the downtrodden of the earth and sympathy for their plight, emancipation volatilized the American dream of freedom into the war that freed the slaves. Having lived on the great Mississippi that had run directly between freedom and slavery and having come across that river to take up residence next door to Harriet Beecher Stowe—the very embodiment of Christian indignation and sympathy—Mark Twain knew that the current of that emotion was as powerful and deceptive in history as the current of the river. But beyond that he knew that official religions, national claims to truth, moral interpretations of history, the Christian conscience, and even God himself were lies. If he himself had a great sympathetic heart, he had also seen every form of fraud and was himself, as he well knew, hardly exempt from greed and mendacity.

Nietzsche, it is well to remember, during the very years in which Mark Twain was writing *Life on the Mississippi, Huckleberry Finn*, and *A Connecticut Yankee*, was projecting a whole long series of notes, aphorisms, and speculations for a book to be called *The Will to Power*. He saw and felt, with perhaps more clarity and intensity than Mark Twain could see, the lie of the nineteenth century. Indeed his book in every respect constitutes fine parallel reading with *Huckleberry Finn*. One quote from it will suffice to show how Nietzsche defined the lie:

The holy lie therefore invented (1) a *God* who punishes and rewards, who strictly observes the law-book of the priests and is strict about sending them into the world as his mouthpieces and plenipotentiaries; (2) an *afterlife* in which the great punishment machine is first thought to become effective—to this end the *immortality of the soul*; (3) *conscience* in man as the consciousness that good and evil are permanent—that God himself speaks through it when it advises conformity with priestly precepts; (4) *morality* as a denial of all natural processes, as reduction of all events to a morally conditioned event, moral effects (i.e., the idea of punishment and reward) as effects permeating all things, as the sole power, as the creator of all transformation; (5) *truth* as given, as revealed, as identical with the teaching of the priests: as the condition for all salvation and happiness in this life and the next.

Nietzsche concluded that the origin of this holy lie was nothing more or less than the *will to power*. That will was at once the motive and the end of the institutions of knowledge, morality, imagination, and society, which is to say that it was the motive of schools, churches, literature, and nations. He longed for a great human being who lacked "the virtues that accompany respect and 'respectability' and altogether everything that is part of the 'virtue of the herd,'" who "when not speaking to himself wears a mask," who "rather lies than tells the truth," and whose strength of will is "the freedom from any kind of conviction."

Surely anyone familiar with Mark Twain's overt attitudes and expressed observations knows how much he shared Nietzsche's premises. Indeed, Huck Finn is in an uncanny way Mark Twain's expression or version of Nietzsche's great human being. For Mark Twain recognized that the holy American nation, having fought out the battle of good and evil along the lines and under the terms of freedom against slavery, was itself moving toward the goal of imperial power. And if we survey our progress in the one hundred years since the publication of *Huckleberry Finn*, we see how much we are at the threshold of George Orwell's *1984*, in which the Ministry of Truth projected the following slogans:

WAR IS PEACE
FREEDOM IS SLAVERY
IGNORANCE IS STRENGTH

In Orwell's world, Winston Smith, under the vigilant electronic eye of Big Brother, is commissioned to rewrite history each day, first by removing every aspect of it that fails to conform to the originating policy changes of the Ministry of Truth, and second by translating the narrative into Newspeak—a language designed to purge ambiguity, to eliminate irregular verbs, and to use nouns, verbs, adjectives, and adverbs interchangeably so as to annihilate as much as possible the distinctions between act and thing, and between individual and class. In addition, Newspeak built up a vocabulary of compound words with the design of making the political component the absolute dominant power of language. Here good and evil, as defined by the state, could instantaneously be communicated into conceptual linguistic designations such as *goodthink* and *crimethink*, *crimesex*, and *goodsex*, all for the purpose of regulating the lives of the citizens of Oceania.

Having lived through 1984, we may feel sufficiently unthreatened by Orwell's book to contend that history is not corroborating his dystopic vision. Yet each day the paranoid camera eye is projected through an electronic image of a world where an incredible array of missile clusters, called densepacks, are being projected into a projectile called the Peacemaker; where the way to arms reduction lies in the production of more arms; and where the institution for waging absolute destructive war is called the Department of Defense. And all this defense is being stockpiled to keep our national freedom secure from the slavery of rival political ideologies.

The discordant reality principle of Mark Twain's ending in its very act of travesty exposes an implicit vision profoundly related to Nietzsche's holy lie and Orwell's Big Lie. Mark Twain, who had lived across the division of his own nation, could see the holy lie of religion as well as the big national lie of freedom. Yet however much we might see Mark Twain's relation to Nietzsche and Orwell, we unfailingly know that neither the narrative nor the narrator of *Huckleberry Finn* can quite be subordinated to that relationship. By way of pointing up the difference that qualifies the relationship, we can take another passage of the book which, appearing only five pages after Huck's much heralded crisis of conscience, records an exchange between Huck and Aunt Sally just after he lies to her about being on a steamboat that blew its cylinder head. Showing immediate concern, she asks,

"Good gracious! anybody hurt?"
"No'm. Killed a nigger."
"Well, it's lucky; because sometimes people do get hurt." (P. 280)

That brief exchange, surely one of the most universally approved passages in the book, is usually quoted to illustrate the instinctive heartlessness of a slaveholding society. Yet the exchange raises all the moral questions of earlier passages we have examined. How, after all, *are* we to take Huck in the exchange? In light of his long experience with Jim and his recent declaration of love for him, is Huck consciously going along with the value system he knows Aunt Sally to believe in? Is he deliberately or merely instinctively withholding that part of himself that is dedicated to freeing Jim? Or is he impervious to an awareness beyond his individual experience with Jim that "niggers" count as people? Or has he literally forgotten his relation to Jim in this new tight place in which he finds himself? If he continues to refer to Jim as a nigger—which he does right through to the end—can he really think that Jim counts as a person? All these questions point to vital aspects of Huck's character that assume negative relations to a positive and principled desire for Jim's freedom, leaving only our wish that Huck remember his knowledge of and experience with Jim—for if Huck remembers he does not show it. As for Aunt Sally, her earnest remark that people sometimes do get hurt all but convicts her of the cruelty from which we might wish to exempt Huck. Yet the fact remains that both she and Huck are unquestionably kindhearted characters, and *both are momentarily sacrificed in order to produce the vividly savage satire upon the society in which both helplessly exist*. Both, in other words, are made by Mark Twain to perform the little drama intended to expose the cruelty of a benighted society.

To subject this passage to the scrutiny that we have directed upon other memorable and much-approved passages is to come full circle back to the fact that this is a hard book to take. For we see once more that directing satiric scorn harshly upon the slaveholding society robs Aunt Sally of her good intentions and even throws Huck's good heart into question. Moreover, the satiric irony of the passage, no matter how manifest, cannot really make up for the *matter* of the passage—the fatal word—to a black audience. To the audience content to feel a pleasurable thrill at seeing the slaveholding society of the old South or the segregated society of the intermediate South flogged once more, we should be able to say, in the presence of the new South, that they are taking pleasure in flogging a dead horse. Rather than continuing to do that, such an audience ought to be glad that a new black audience is rising in force to object to the book. Such objection is assurance that the book is alive in a living, shifting society and cannot be complacently approved by the new academic tradition that has replaced the old genteel tradition.

Is there a way out of these mean tricks that begin to bare themselves wherever the book is indulgently approved? Just possibly. If we go on to read the lines directly and happily following that famous passage, we find Aunt Sally going on to say,

"Two years ago last Christmas, your Uncle Silas was coming up from Newrleans on the old *Lally Rook*, and she blowed out a cylinder-head and crippled a man. And I think he died afterwards. He was a Babtist. Your Uncle Silas knowed a family in Baton Rouge that knowed his people very well. Yes, I remember now, he *did* die. Mortification set in, and they had to amputate him. But it didn't save him. Yes, it was mortification—that was it. He turned blue all over, and died in the hope of a glorious resurrection. They say he was a sight to look at." (P. 280)

There again is the beautiful principle of emotional exchange at work. If we are indulgently indignant at the cruelty of the slave society, we do not even want to remember the poor Baptist. Certainly we are not meant to sympathize with his fate. But if we care about the humor of the book we cannot do without him. Aunt Sally in this instance is made a little more stupid than she really is, but her sentimentality and kind-heartedness are somehow retained in Mark Twain's determination to move from the savage irony of satire into the dissolution of helpless humor. There is no sign that Huck laughs at this turn of events. He is as silent on the subject as he is about his knowledge of Jim, but the humor of his narrative is undeniably there. If we do not helplessly laugh it is only because we have been unduly arrested by our pleasure in the satiric cruelty that initiates the exchange.

Huck's apparent lack of memory about Jim and his deadpan about the humor are surely the great redemptive facts about this book. Like Nietzsche's great human being, Huck retains a true freedom from all conviction. He truly does belong on the current of the Great Mississippi running between the banks of good and evil, between freedom and slavery, and still running in its lower reaches, between banks where slavery is on both its sides, toward an open sea. We have to recognize, or surely would want to, that even when he chooses to go to hell, he is even then somehow, like the running river, taking the path of least resistance. It is surely easier and handier for him to betray Miss Watson than to betray Jim. His lies are, in their final analysis, better than the truth that our own socially and morally approving conscience would confer upon him. If the people in the black audience find the fatal word and the stereotypical minstrel characterization of Jim hard to take, they are only telling us that we ought to find its manifest and indulgent good intentions as well as its implicit nihilism—nihilism utterly but oh so humorously explicit in its final sentences—harder to take than we do.

It would not be so bad if the book were banned in the public schools. Then we might read it anew and find another passage as central as the much-quoted passages I have cited. When Huck first embarks upon the river after his escape from Pap and before he meets Jim, he writes (for he is a *writer*, we must remember):

I didn't lose no time. The next minute I was a-spinning down stream soft but quick in the shade of the bank. I made two mile and a half, and then struck out a quarter of a mile or more towards the middle of the river, because pretty soon I would be passing the ferry landing and people might see me and hail me. I got out amongst the drift-wood and then laid down in the bottom of the canoe and let her float. I laid there and had a good rest and a smoke out of my pipe, looking away into the sky, not a cloud in it. The sky looks ever so deep when you lay down on your back in the moonshine; I never knowed it before. And how far a body can hear on the water such nights! I heard people talking at the ferry landing. I heard what they said, too, every word of it. One man said it was getting towards the long days and the short nights, now. 'Tother one said *this* warn't one of the short ones—and then they laughed, and he said it over again and they laughed again; then they waked up another fellow and told him, and laughed, but he didn't laugh; he ripped out something brisk and said let him alone. The first fellow said he 'lowed to tell it to his old woman—she would think it was pretty good; but he said that warn't nothing to some things he had said in his time. I heard one man say it was nearly three o'clock, and he hoped the daylight wouldn't wait more than about a week longer. After that, the talk got further and further away, and I couldn't make out the words any more, but I could hear the mumble; and now and then a laugh, too, but it seemed a long ways off. (Pp. 58-59)

How much is beautifully there. The fugitive boy in the stolen canoe running away upon the running river with no time to lose, yet time enough in the idle moment to see the depth of the heavens above him, and ears acute enough to hear the conversation far across the water. And then the wonderful conversation itself with the stupid jokes—showing that for every two people who share a joke there is likely to be a third who finds nothing funny, and showing too humanity's inveterate need to repeat itself in an act of performance. And the stupidity and the corny jokes made incredibly humorous as Huck's written rehearsal redeems those dear old yokels. And finally the voices fading, leaving the mumble and the laughter trailing in the wake of the passage. With no time to lose, how much is gained!

On a great muddy river where, unlike the blue stillness of Walden Pond, the water's action makes reflection impossible just as its color hides its depth, the instinct of both Huck's deviant language and deviant character is equal to the mulatto solution of the current. That is why Huck's being and language are magically and mysteriously identical with the current, and also why the humor he both evokes and records keeps him free from the principle of freedom, the principle that in the economy of moral exchange always threatens to create two rednecks for every slave it frees. Mark Twain knew as well as we know how utterly necessary that principle is for American society. It was the principle we believe we believed in enough to fight the one war when God was truly on our side. Yet the war was bloody and divisive, involving catastrophic loss of life. The humor of *Huckleberry Finn* literally displaces that loss with a gain of helpless and overt pleasure. Such pleasure, a manifest and true expression of the pleasure principle at the heart of all life, serves to disarm the pleasure of principle that is the armor of adult society. The point is that it disarms it but does not overtly attack it. No adult society can do without the pleasure of principle, which, after all, is at once the purpose and conscience of civilization.

Mark Twain believed in it enough to sacrifice Tom Sawyer to it—and we cannot forget that Tom was the character through whom he had discovered Huck Finn. Yet he would not sacrifice Huck to it. Instead he let Huck reject civilization and the adult conscience in the very last pages of his book—an ending that is, as Eliot so rightly realized, as perfect as any in literature.

Holding to the beauty of this humor, yet remembering always that humor involves an exchange that threatens somebody, we should be able not only to stand but to understand civilization's impulse to ban the book. The banning would express society's discomfort with the book just as Huck's rejection of civilization is an expression of his discomfort with adult society. Even if the book were banned in all the schools, we would only be reminded that its very language was proof from the beginning that it never was for the schools. When the book was banned in Concord, Mark Twain applauded the action on the grounds that it would sell thirty-five thousand copies. As both inventor and publisher of *Huckleberry Finn*, he lived in a world where abrupt exchanges were conducted in as well as between the realm of moral indignation and the arena of the marketplace. Huck observes at the outset of the novel that he doesn't like the widow's food because everything is cooked by itself. He likes things cooked together, as if in a barrel of odds and ends, where "things get mixed up, and the juice kind of swaps around, and the things go better" (p. 18). Later, observing the early morning sun shining through the forest leaves on Jackson's Island, he notes the freckled places in the gloom, which "swapped about a little, showing there was a little breeze up there." Lost in the fog on the river and calling out to Jim, he cannot place Jim's answering whoops because he "never knowed a sound dodge around so, and swap places so quick and so much." Finally at Aunt Sally's, when he discovers that he is supposed to be Tom Sawyer and almost slumps through the floor in relief, he regrets that "there warn't no time to swap knives" as Uncle Silas forcibly hustles him into his new identity with a barrage of questions that he happily *can* answer. Swapping, it turns out in this humorous and devious world of moral relativity, leads to possibilities of taste, beauty, anxiety, and pleasure.

Having experienced the manipulative, shifty, shrewd, and humorous exchanges constantly taking place both on and beside the moving Mississippi, we should be able to contemplate with a degree of equanimity the possibility of widespread removal of *Huckleberry Finn* from school and library shelves. In the face of such censorship, we would still be left with the happy choice of pursuing the pleasure of principle with a serious—even outraged—public defense of the book against those who found it hard to take, or indulging the pleasure principle by reading the book in private where we could blessedly take it easy.

NOTES

1. Friedrich Nietzsche, *The Will to Power*, trans. Walter Kaufmann and R.J. Hollingdale (New York: Random House, 1967), pp. 90-91. For the quotes that immediately follow concerning the Great Man, see p. 505.

CONTEMPORARY CRITICISM

RUN, NIGGER, RUN

HAROLD BEAVER

"Ain't them old crippled picks and things in there good enough to dig a nigger out with?" (ch. 35)

Say, an abolitionist *had* taken an interest in Jim's story. It was strange enough, after all, in its flight downstream into cotton territory, protected by a 14-year-old boy. The account might have been published under some such title as "The Narrative of James Watson of Missouri, Formerly a Slave."[1] What would such a narrative have revealed?

At the end of *Adventures of Huckleberry Finn*, Jim is a free man. "Chapter the Last" Huck calls that final chapter. But for Jim, of course, it was only a beginning. Jim was now free to purchase his wife from off that neighboring plantation, as he had planned all along, "saying how the first thing he would do when he got to a free State he would go to saving up money and never spend a single cent" (73/124).[2] But cash might have proved the least of his problems. As a "free Negro" he was barred from re-entering Missouri.[3] In any case he did not yet have his freedom papers. Should he boldly risk a return, he would be in constant danger from "the pater-rollers" as well as bloody-minded busybodies like Old Finn. A sworn statement by any predatory White would "*prove*" ownership; and he'd be clapped back in chains. Huck and Tom could afford to ignore all this. But it was clear enough to Jim. That is why even attempting to *buy* his wife and two children was no easy matter. Their master might refuse to sell. He might (as he foolishly let slip) have to "get an Ab'litionist to go and steal them." Or sneak back himself on the Underground Railway. If Harriet Tubman could do it, why not Jim?

The answer depends on a much wider question. Was Jim capable of taking *any* decisive action? Or was he merely the tool of white men's machinations, a passive focus for others rather than the controlling factor of his own escape? To what extent was Twain, in other words, aware of the social and intellectual identity of the black man whose career his hero had so ambiguously espoused? To what extent was he aware that his link between black man and white boy was rather less than idyllic? Certainly, if it *was* less idyllic, those final chapters

on the Phelps farm might seem less of a betrayal. Since it is Huck's story, not
Jim's, among all other rebounding ironies this question of Jim's truth, as
revealed by Huck's self-centered and often self-deluding monologue, needs
very careful scrutiny.

Jim enters the drama ready-made. Despite his "Missouri negro dialect," that
is, he is wholly stereotyped, a walking cliché, what Elizabethans might have
called a "humor."[4] So the point for Twain, as for Marlowe or Shakespeare,
can hardly have been the stereotype in itself so much as how that stereotype
is handled and developed in the context of the drama. Furthermore the
stereotype is highly selective. It is deliberately detached from that of the idle
chatterbox in *Tom Sawyer*.[5] To use the cant phrases of the period, Jim is neither
"fervent" exactly, nor "gossipy," nor "vain," nor "dishonest," nor "idle," nor
"lying." He fulfills none of those truisms once dear to a Southern heart: that
a Negro lacks mental energy; that a Negro loves finery; that a Negro has a
distaste for bodily labor; that a Negro is prey to transient passions; that a Negro
is overpowered by animal lust. He is detached, too, from the nigger minstrel
tradition. For, though he is recalled as "singing," none of his songs is quoted;
he merely carries around a jew's harp.

Jim is the good nigger: "good-humored," "simple" (with the king and duke),
"improvident" (with his financial investments), "kind-hearted" (to Huck),
displaying a "contented African patience" with a physical endurance that might
have "proved fatal to anyone except an African."[6] The stress throughout is not
on his trances or voodoo potency so much as on his ability to preserve an
equilibrium between "true Negro optimism," as a Southerner would have put
it, and "African fatalism."[7] So much Huck could observe. The inherent
shrewdness was not so conspicuous. For Jim rarely speaks out.

He must be 30 years old at least and a giant of a man with "hairy arms en
a hairy breas'." Weigh him down with chains and he can still wheel a
grindstone "along like nothing!" Tall and muscular, he was a field-hand, a
cattle-herder, going "off wid de cattle 'bout daylight," and not returning "tell
arter dark."[8] On all questions of field-lore—such as bee-keeping, or chickens,
or laying out fish-lines—he holds forth like an expert; and he is practical, too,
building a wigwam on the raft as readily as a raised fireplace. He must have
grown up on a farm; like any rural Black, he sleeps with "a blanket around his
head, and his head . . . nearly in the fire" (37/50).[9] He is illiterate, of course.
Superstitions and ritual knowledge are, by their very nature, oral: how *not* to
cook dinners, or shake out tablecloths, or touch snakeskins, or look at a new
moon over one's left shoulder. "Jim knowed all kinds of signs. He said he
knowed most everything." He even has a smattering of Bible knowledge—however garbled—picked up no doubt at the Widow's and Miss Watson's evening
prayers when "they fetched the niggers in." In his wife's cabin he clearly
played boss, shouting orders at his 4-year-old daughter and sending her
sprawling. A *kind* of family man, then, and a *kind* of Christian, too—but closer
at heart to some atavistic African rites, a religion of the dead—his whole
person, as he well realized, represented a guaranteed emotional and economic
and psychological investment for Whites (with interest paid), while valueless for
his own black needs.

This is the presence for which Huck opts. But Jim as decisively opts for
Huck. He was certainly glad of his company after that snake bite. Now he had
a buddy who supplied him with whiskey. He was looked after until the fever
abated and the swelling went down. That the accident was no *accident* he never

realized. He never suspected a thing. Huck just tossed both snakes into the bushes and never confessed. Even when the guilt weighs heavier and heavier on him, all he can blurt out is, "I wish I'd never seen that snake-skin, Jim—I do wish I'd never laid eyes on it." To which Jim, in all innocence, replies, "It ain't yo' fault, Huck; you didn' know. Don't you blame yo'self 'bout it" (77/129).

But, if Huck nurses a dirty secret, so does Jim. If Huck can keep mum, so can Jim. There was a wall of reticence—of truths suppressed and secrets withheld—by now between them. For Jim had immediately recognized that corpse in the floating house:

"It's a dead man. Yes, indeedy; naked, too. He's ben shot in de back. I reck'n he's ben dead two er three days. Come in, Huck, but doan' look at his face—it's too gashly."

I didn't look at him at all. Jim throwed some old rags over him, but he needn't done it; I didn't want to see him.

He had covered that face instinctively, no doubt, to spare Huck's feelings. But, quick as a flash, it struck him: what if the white boy ditched him? What was to prevent him, once he knew his father was dead, from sloping off to his friends (and cash deposit) in St. Petersburg? "Well, he was right," as Huck more than once was to observe; "he was most always right; he had an uncommon level head, for a nigger" (64/93).

Postwar critics now seem astonishingly naïve. James M. Cox wholeheartedly cherished the mammy image. It is Jim, he explains, "who, knowing secretly that Huck's Pap is dead forever, takes Huck to his own bosom to nourish him through the ordeal of being lost."[11] Daniel G. Hoffman is equally sentimental: "But now it is Jim who comprehends the degradation of Pap's death and protects Huck from that cruel knowledge. Jim is now free to take the place that Pap was never worthy to hold as Huck's spiritual father."[12] Jim *free*? How blinkered could one be! Jim was on the run. He was a fugitive slave. Now at last he held a trump card and he kept it face down. It was a ruthless exercise of power. Huck was now his unconscious hostage. Throughout the length of that 1,000-mile-long journey he clung to that image.

It was not until 1967 that it first dawned on critics that Jim, too, might be capable of double-dealing. "Should not Jim have told him that?" Louis D. Rubin wondered. "Is not the fact that he did not tell him partly attributable to the fact that Jim knows that he will need Huck's help if he is ever to make his way to freedom?"[13] Spencer Brown forthrightly answered these questions: "Huck is really free (free of his father, and thus no longer in danger, he can go back home, or wherever he pleases); but Jim needs Huck for his flight to freedom."[14] So White and Black, from the start, were mutual pawns, utilizing each other, manipulating each other as *objects* of romance or *tools* of escape. Affection—human needs—intervened, but in a slave-holding republic, where human labor was bought and sold, human relations, too, were inevitably turned to strategic devices and men to things. Only Jim's final words reveal his infinite wariness: "you k'n git yo' money when you wants it; kase dat wuz him."

In the light of such power-play, it might be wise to look again at Jim's interventions elsewhere. His room for manoeuvre was slim. But this was his third decisive act. This first had been his escape. He was used to keeping his eyes open. He had noticed the slave-trader sniffing after him. He crept round the house at night. He snooped. He eavesdropped. He knew what was up. As soon as he heard Miss Watson he made a dash, hiding out for twenty-four hours by the river until, on the second night, he plunged in. His plan did not come off. But he had a plan. As Huck was soon to observe, "Jim could most always start a good plan when you wanted one."[15]

I'd made up my mine 'bout what I's agwyne to do. You see ef I kep' on tryin' to git away afoot, de dogs 'ud track me; ef I stole a skift to cross over, dey'd miss dat skift you see, en dey'd know 'bout whah I'd lan' on de yuther side en whah to pick up my track. So I says, a raff is what I's arter; it doan' *make* no track.[16]

He is a strong swimmer and makes it more than halfway across the Mississippi, in the dark, dodging driftwood, struggling against the current until a raft comes along. He can judge the exact speed of a raft:

De river wuz arisin' en dey wuz a good current; so I reck'n'd 'at by fo' in the mawnin' I'd be twenty-five mile down de river, en den I'd slip in, jis' b'fo' daylight, en swim asho' en take to de woods on de Illinoi side.

In five or six hours, that is, from around 10:30 p.m. to 4 a.m., at a speed of 4½—5 miles per hour, he would be twenty-five miles downstream. His maths, too, is pretty good; better than Huck's. But luck was against him as it was to be throughout his bid for freedom—what with snake bites and fog, a collision and finally betrayal.

Still, he made it to Jackson's Island. That was Jim's first decisive act. Next he accepted this white 14-year-old boy when he might easily have throttled him. Huck was already "killed' (as he knew) as far as St. Petersburg was concerned. So why not do away with this awkward interloper and potential witness? But he decided to stick with him. That was his second decisive act. The third was to make sure the boy didn't run off, didn't leave him in the lurch, didn't turn the tables against him by doubling back to St. Petersburg. So he withheld Pap's death. Quick-witted Huck, who can fool almost everybody, turns out to be everybody's fool.

So their special relationship begins. Jim takes control in the privacy of their cave; Huck must take over on the river, making "Jim lay down in the canoe and cover up with the quilt" (45/62). For a white boy is free to come and go as he likes. It is Jim who is in hiding. It is Jim who has committed his life to Huck. With the greatest reluctance he submits to boarding the *Walter Scott*. This gives rise to an appalling dilemma which Huck, even in retrospect, seems barely able to acknowledge. For once Jim speaks out. Usually he kept a tight rein on his tongue. But the closer they get to Cairo, the more he opens up. Until, exhausted after their separation in the fog, he momentarily drops his guard. On Huck's return he calls,

"It's too good for true, honey, it's too good for true. Lemme look at you, chile, lemme feel o' you. No, you ain' dead! you's back again, 'live en soun', jis de same ole Huck—de same ole Huck, thanks to goodness!"[17]

But it is not the "same ole Huck." Suspiciously Jim starts backing off. But when the fog in his brain finally lifts and it dawns on him that Huck had been intent on making him look the traditional "tangle-headed old fool," with a pack of cool lies about nigger drinking and nigger dreaming, he is furious. He is contemptuous, dismissing Huck as "*trash.*" He carries it off with dignity, but the scene should have been avoided. A black man should *never*, under any circumstances, tell a white man to his face exactly what he thinks. For this was not just another piece of tomfoolery, like boarding the *Walter Scott*. This was part of the emotionally distorted white psychology with which a Black must keep on chuckling good terms and somehow try to control for his own ends. It is exactly this head-on racial conflict—of Jim's dignified stand and Huck's abject surrender—that rouses the Southern conscience of caste loyalty in the Missouri boy.

Jim withdraws in a huff. But he had overreached himself; his candor almost proves his undoing. Every White, he well knew, was a potential sneak. Every White, however friendly, needed incessant homage as "genlman" and "boss." Jim had momentarily stepped out of the masonic code of signs and double-talk. That was asking for trouble. As W. J. Cash observed, in "common whites" virtually unlimited power

bred a savage and ignoble hate for the Negro, which required only opportunity to break forth in relentless ferocity; for all their rage against the "white-trash" epithet concentrated itself on him rather than on the planters.[18]

But Jim by now is beyond caring. He talks out loud of *buying* his wife, maybe *stealing* his children. He fidgets up and down, "all over trembly and feverish to be so close to freedom." Not a trace of the old Sambo about him. But even in his euphoria he remains alert. There's a change in the atmosphere: Huck gone curiously quiet suddenly, curiously aloof. Jim feels so vulnerable, so tense, that he senses it instantly. He doesn't let on, though. He gets the canoe ready and puts his old coat in the bottom for luck. Only at the very last minute, when Huck is already shoving off, does he say it:

"Jim won't ever forgit you, Huck; you's de bes' fren' Jim's ever had; en you's de *only* fren' ole Jim's got now."

I was paddling off, all in a sweat to tell on him; but when he says this, it seemed to kind of take the tuck all out of me. I went along slow then, and I warn't right down certain whether I was glad I started or whether I warn't. When I was fifty yards off, Jim says,

"Dah you goes, de ole true Huck; de on'y white genlman dat ever kep' his promise to ole Jim."[19]

In less than four pages he elevates Huck to "white genlman' from white "trash." He successfully confuses and defuses him. That burst of flattery is Jim's fourth decisive act.[20] But it is already too late. They had passed Cairo, it turns out. A steamboat confirms Huck's vision of doom. Mechanical culture, that is, decisively splits them in two.

In a divided world color alone was tell-tale. Only a White was free to masquerade; only Huck could always adopt a new role. At the Grangerfords', Young Finn is unquestioningly confirmed in his white status: allotted a personal nigger and addressed as "Mars Jawge." Jim is salvaged and hidden by his fellow-Blacks. Huck, alias George, is instinctively carried away by the escapades and elopements of the Big House; Jim alone looks after their *things*, patching the raft at night, buying pots and pans, laying in supplies (corn and buttermilk, pork and greens). Huck becomes the willing tool of this whole swashbuckling fiction as surely as he soon becomes the willing tool of the king and duke.

But from here on Jim's hands are tied—literally tied with a rope. He is degraded and can do nothing to fight his degradation. First he is reduced by the duke to a neutered madman in a "long curtain-calico gown" (126/203); then Huck seconds the duke's triumph by dolling him up in Aunt Sally's calico gown. Against Tom, Jim is resourceless; but *not* against the king and duke. It is his fifth decisive act. Once out of their clutches—once they have informed on him—he seizes the initiative. Jim, in his turn, informs on them. He betrays their shoddy swindle. In the duke's phrase, he blows on them. The lovable mask is dropped as soon as he feels secure in his revenge. Just this once Jim has the satisfaction of degrading his persecutors as *he* had been degraded. Huck predictably fails to ponder Jim's share in the event, but rushes off to alert the king and duke. For the white boy is the white men's natural ally; Huck *even now* has a soft spot for that ruthless couple.

But that is positively Jim's last intervention. As Huck truckles to Tom, so Tom dominates over Jim. He is totally at Tom's mercy. He simply has to accept the whole Messianic parody imposed on him, as Huck himself dimly seems to realize: "and as for me, I wished I was in Jerusalem or somewheres" (199/315). But that is exactly where he is. For Pikesville read Jerusalem, with Huck taking the part of St. Peter with his denials. "Who nailed him?"—Huck's own question—opens a long and tedious mock-Calvary. Matthew, 27:28-31, supplies the text:

And they stripped him, and put on him a scarlet robe. And when they had platted a crown of thorns, they put it upon his head, and a reed in his right hand. . . . And after that they had mocked him, they took the robe off from him and put his own raiment on him, and led him away to crucify him.[21]

With "his hands tied behind him," *Ecce Homo*:

They cussed Jim considerble . . . and give him a cuff or two, side the head, once in a while, but Jim never said nothing, and he never let on to know me, and they took him to the same cabin, and put his own clothes on him, and chained him again . . . to a big staple drove into the bottom log, and chained his hands, too, and both legs.[22]

The Gethsemane scene occurs at dawn on the banks of the Mississippi:

then some men in a skiff come by, and as good luck would have it, the nigger was setting by the pallet with his head propped on his knees, sound asleep; so I motioned them in, quiet, and they slipped up on him and grabbed him and tied him before he knowed what he was about, and we never had no trouble . . . and the nigger never made the least row nor said a word, from the start.[23]

To this Calvary Jim has to carry his own cross—rolling the grindstone, hacking the hole with his pick, blessing his persecutors:

"You got any spiders in here, Jim?"
    "No, sah, thanks to goodness I hain't, Mars Tom."
    "All right, we'll get you some."
    "But bless you, honey, I doan' *want* none. I's afeard un um. I jis' 's soon have rattlesnakes aroun'."[24]

Until by sacrificing himself for his persecutor's sake Jim at last achieves resurrection.

That resurrection, unlike Huck's, is a wholly contrived affair; and the final horror is that the victim himself is cast as literary critic. It is Jim's task, as he is well aware, to appreciate the whole fiasco as an *aesthetic* production. "It 'uz planned beautiful," he duly pronounces, "en it 'uz *done* beautiful; en dey ain't *nobody* kin git up a plan dat's mo' mixed-up en splendid den what dat one wuz" (215/340). Jim simply had no choice. Even now he had to prove himself the Grateful Nigger, cajoling the boys, flattering the boys, allowing they "was white folks and knowed better than him" (196/309). A white, he knew, must always take the initiative. A White accepts a nigger's gratitude, that is, as his due. Just as Huck had accepted Jim's gratitude as his due.[25] That was the mark of the South's fatal, self-indulgent delusion.[26]

Jim was trapped. Even now he had to live with these Southerners. Twain should surely be given some credit for drawing this close to black strategies of survival. In the words of one recent study: "the Jim who emerges from our reading is nobody's simple companion. He is a crafty, calculating student of human behavior, a confidence man with an ability to deceive that equals Huck's or Tom's."[27] Jim was trapped from without; Twain remained trapped within, going round and round in tortuous circles. For *Adventures of Huckleberry Finn* was never intended, of course, as a fugitive-slave narrative. If anything, it developed into a wide-ranging survey of this very trap closing in from St. Petersburg to Bricksville, Bricksville to Pikesville. The violent South gives way to the sentimental South of the Wilks girls and their niggers; the sentimental South to the paranoiac South of the Pikesville vigilantes. But the drama comes to rest at the ambiguous heart of Huck's confusion: the smug South of the Phelps plantation, where "Southern hospitality" for Whites is counterbalanced by kind looks and prayers for the Blacks. The doctor is "kind" as old Silas is "mighty nice" and both the Phelpses are "kind as they could be" and "where the people's all so kind and good." For precisely here, on that "little one-horse cotton plantation" (evoking memories of his uncle John Quarles's farm), the unresolved crux of Twain's own Southern heritage and education was painstakingly reached.

NOTES

1. Twain owned a copy of Charles Ball, *Slavery in the United States: A Narrative of the Life and Adventures of Charles Ball, A Black Man, Who Lived Forty Years in Maryland, South Carolina and Georgia, as a Slave* (1837, republished 1859), which he used as a source for *A Connecticut Yankee in King Arthur's Court.*
2. All quotations are double-keyed to the *Norton Critical Edition* (second edition, 1977) and the *Mark Twain Library Edition* (University of California, 1985).
3. Increasingly stringent laws had been passed since 1835, and by 1847 free Negroes and mulattos were prohibited from entering Missouri under any conditions. To know the precise date between 1835 and 1845, in which the novel is so casually set, would be of crucial importance in determining Jim's legal position.
4. See Chadwick Hansen, "The Character of Jim and the Ending of *Huckleberry Finn,*" *Massachusetts Review,* vol. 5 (Autumn 1963), p. 55.
5. cf. his first entrance, *en route* to the town pump: "Jim came skipping out at the gate with a tin pail, and singing 'Buffalo Gals.' Though "the pump was only a hundred and fifty yards off, Jim never got back with a bucket of water under an hour—and even then somebody generally had to go after him" (*Tom Sawyer,* ch. 2).
6. All adjectives and phrases in qoutes are drawn from George R. Lamplugh's study of the *Atlantic Monthly, Harper's Monthly, Scribner's Monthly/The Century* and *Scribner's Magazine* in the closing decades of the nineteenth century: "The Image of the Negro in Popular Magazine Fiction, 1875-1900," *Journal of Negro History,* vol. 57 (April 1972), pp. 177-89.
7. Daniel G. Hoffman has traced the European origins of all Jim's beliefs. Only his divination with the hairball from the stomach of an ox appears to be of voodoo origin. See "Jim's Magic: Black or White?" *American Literature,* vol. 32 (March 1960), pp. 47-54.
8. Miss Watson was offered $800 to sell him down to New Orleans, which was close to the prime rate of $1,000 for a strong working male in his twenties; cf. the doctor: "I tell you, gentlemen, a nigger like that is worth a thousand dollars—and kind treatment, too" (223/353).
9. Unlike Indians, who turn the bottom of their feet towards the blaze.

10. *Huckleberry Finn*, ch. 9, pp. 44-5/61. At this key moment Huck-as-narrator is as duplicitous as Jim. He withholds from the reader the same information withheld from him, in the narrative past, by Jim. The text is poker-faced. Twain deliberately rubs it in: "After breakfast I wanted to talk about the dead man and guess out how he come to be killed, but Jim didn't want to . . ." (45/63). This enigma (as Roland Barthes would call it) remains dormant. The text is nowhere engaged in unravelling it. Even on the final page it is only partly resolved.

11. James M. Cox, "Remarks on the Sad Initiation of Huckleberry Finn," *Sewanee Review*, vol. 62 (Summer 1954), pp. 389-405.

12. Daniel G. Hoffman, "Black Magic—and White—in *Huckleberry Finn*," in his *Form and Fable in American Fiction* (New York: Oxford University Press, 1961), ch. 15, p. 333.

13. Louis D. Rubin, Jr., *The Teller in the Tale* (Seattle, Wash.: University of Washington Press, 1967), ch. 3, p. 65.

14. Spencer Brown, "*Huckleberry Finn* for Our Time," *Michigan Quarterly Review*, vol. 6 (Winter 1967), p. 45.

15. Opening of the Raftsmen's Passage, now *Life on the Mississippi*, ch. 3.

16. *Huckleberry Finn*, ch. 8, p. 40/53.

17. ibid., ch. 15, p. 70/103.

18. Cash, *The Mind of the South*, bk. 1, ch. 3, sect. 9.

19. *Huckleberry Finn*, ch. 16, p. 74/125.

20. For a subtly different reading, see Neil Schmitz, "The Paradox of Liberation in *Huckleberry Finn*," *Texas Studies in Literature and Language*, vol. 13 (Spring 1971), p. 133.

21. cf. also "Acts Seventeen" (199/316), which Uncle Silas was studying before breakfast. It opens in the Thessalonika synagogue: "alleging that Christ must needs have suffered, and risen again from the dead; and this Jesus, whom I preach unto you, is Christ" (Acts 17:3). It closes with Paul's sermon on the Areopagus: God "hath made of one blood all nations of men for to dwell on all the face of the earth, and hath determined . . . the bounds of their habitation" (Acts, 17:26).

22. *Huckleberry Finn*, ch. 42, p. 223/352; cf. the spiritual: "An' he never said a mumbalin' word."

23. ibid., ch. 42, pp. 223-4/353-4.

24. ibid., ch. 38, pp. 205/324.

25. For Huck's involuntary transposition of memory, see *Huckleberry Finn*, ch. 31, p. 169/270.

26. As Tom puts it: "Every animal is grateful for kindness and petting, and they wouldn't *think* of hurting a person that pets them. Any book will tell you that" (205/325).

27. Thomas Weaver and Merline A. Williams, "Mark Twain's Jim: Identity as an Index to Cultural Attitudes," *American Literary Realism*, vol. 13 (Spring 1980), pp. 19-30.

THE RECOMPOSITION OF *ADVENTURES OF HUCKLEBERRY FINN*

LOUIS J. BUDD

Ten years ago my title might have been catchy or at least puzzling. These days, anyone who keeps up with the trends in criticism assumes that I will somehow play upon the principle—most commonly associated with Stanley Fish—that the meaning of a text "has no effective existence outside of its realization in the mind of a reader," that each reader creates the text during the process of absorbing the words that an author has strung together. Furthermore, anyone on the cutting edge expects that my own deep content will reveal that a definitive interpretation of *Adventures of Huckleberry Finn* is not defensible, not even for a truly self-analytic critic who constructed it. The recomposition of *Huckleberry Finn* I much more simply propose, however, involves examining some versions held by various constituencies or interpretive communities.

Those constituencies are various indeed. For example, *Reader's Digest* played up the centennial of *Huckleberry Finn*. In turn, its story quoted Charles Kuralt as speaking for "the feelings of millions of the book's admirers" when he declared on TV: "If I had to say as much about America as I possibly could in only two words, I would say these two words: 'Huck Finn.'" Rising beyond provinciality, John Barth recently proclaimed *Huckleberry Finn* one of "the most profound, transcendent literary images the human imagination has ever come up with." A supposedly scientific poll showed that 96% of college faculty now put *Huckleberry Finn* at the very head of the list of reading for entering freshmen, 68% of whom claim to have already done their duty, that is, to have recomposed the novel in their minds—with some large degree of reverence if they had seen, for instance, a feature article in the *Washington Post* of January 1986. After comparing Huck and Elvis Presley as our national "bad boys," it decides that *Huckleberry Finn* is "the greatest work of art by an American, the Sistine Chapel of our civilization." That's a tall order for a story told by a boy who tries to convince the doctor that Tom Sawyer "had a dream and it shot him" in the leg or who thinks that the trick riders in a circus are performing in their "drawers and undershirt."

Obviously there are now many worshipful, sometimes astonishing interpretations of *Huckleberry Finn*.[1] But even with those readers who may take the novel more calmly or humorously, the concept of recomposition can raise a gamut of problems. Least exciting but perhaps the most important in the long run is the problem of a definitively edited text. In 1986 we will get the long awaited, fully documented text of *Huckleberry Finn* from the Mark Twain Project at the University of California in Berkeley. From being able better to follow Twain's revisions, we will then recompose, that is, will read *Huckleberry Finn* more insightfully, in some passages at least. Actually, the more spartan edition that the Mark Twain Library released in 1985 suggests new points for analysis. As a distorted doppelgänger to that text, Charles Neider has persuaded Doubleday to publish his edition that cuts nine thousand words, mainly from the late chapters. Obviously, his constituency—may it never grow into even a lunatic fringe!—will experience a somewhat different novel.

Any complete survey of recomposition must consider the side-effects of the many versions reshaped for movies, television, and the current Broadway musical *Big River*. Presumably the fallout has ended from the comic strip entitled *Tom Sawyer and Huck Finn* that prospered during the 1920s. Far more important, then and now, because they have a kind of official authority are the shortened or simplified editions handed out in some of our secondary schools. I'm too simple-minded to comprehend what needs simplifying in *Huckleberry Finn*. But some folks are quick to decide that they must streamline mental life for the rest of us. If they had got to the Rosetta stone with a chisel and hammer we still might not be able to decipher hieroglyphics. Anybody who looks into the pre-college curriculum will be startled to find out what publishers have done, deliberately as well as carelessly, to the texts of the classic novels.

As a third and still more disturbing kind of recomposition, especially active in recent years, *Huckleberry Finn* has suffered a long though not crowded history of proposed bannings, seldom successful, and of pious bowdlerizing. In 1931, Harper and Brothers published a selective text to serve better the cause of "wholesome happiness for boys and girls." Some members of the PTA's still get uneasy about Huck's contempt for Sunday school, his flair for lying, and his decision to "*go* to Hell." They can often get their way simply by complaining to the school librarian, who wields more power of censorship through choice of editions than we may realize. Still, we can usually make Twain's own best weapon—laughter—triumph over such complaints if they make the mistake of fighting in the open.

But the charges of racism, when pressed by PTA-committed moderates in the black community, trouble me deeply. For 1885 *Huckleberry Finn* clearly gave heart to the anti-racists, I would argue anywhere. However, we have marched a good way toward racial equality since then, and the novel now may reinforce, in many touches, attitudes that we would like to overcome completely. But what's to be done? I'm not satisfied by the black publisher whose edition substitutes "slave" for the admittedly overdone use of the word "nigger," which Huck would naturally both hear and write. The crux is really the portrayal of Jim, that is, of his character, emotions, motives, and intelligence, and nobody can fundamentally recompose Jim without pretty much wrecking the novel. In conscience the least that we can do is to resist the idea that because we have enshrined *Huckleberry Finn* as a classic, it just cannot be racist at times. Incidentally, what is the unintended effect of bannings or rewritings? Does such publicity encourage the young to get hold of *Huckleberry Finn* on their own or else to make sure that they get what used to be called the unexpurgated, unabridged version of, say, *Lady Chatterley's Lover*? At least it's clear that all those who hear about a proposed censorship come to the novel with different attitudes than they would have had otherwise.

From a fourth kind of recomposition the problem of Jim will soon get more insistent because the original illustrations by E. W. Kemble will become familiar again. In ten years, I expect, most college editions will carry them. There's a puzzle here for Marshall McLuhan or Father Walter Ong. Why have we ignored the illustrations that were common for later nineteenth-century fiction, especially as serialized in the quality magazines, and that in fact appeared in many a novel up until World War I, when they somewhat bafflingly disappeared? Why are we just as suddenly rediscovering them along with the obvious fact that they conditioned the responses of the readers who saw them? The Kemble illustrations have already made a comeback in the facsimile edition that Harper & Row is tying to its new college anthology of American literature. Likewise, all editions, in boards or paperback, from the Mark Twain Project will reproduce all the original illustrations. As yet, nobody has cared to tangle with the fact that when Twain himself hired Kemble he was actually a broad-stroke cartoonist distant by many degrees of achievement from illustrators like Howard Pyle or Joseph Pennell.

Kemble's drawings will heighten our awareness toward the effect of illustrations by other artists with varying talent and literary taste. Some of the Norman Rockwell set, first published in 1940, have had wide circulation apart from the novel itself; Thomas Hart Benton created another prestigious set in 1942. Recently, a scholar interested in pointing out Rockwell's subtly heavy hand has quoted, in basic agreement, the claim of the Heritage Club that "you will never again think of Mark Twain's book without thinking" of its Rockwell illustrations. Nevertheless, far more influential collectively have been the workaday artists who decorated the scores of editions that have kept multiplying since *Huckleberry Finn* passed out of copyright into the public domain. These drawings, often hired casually by the editor of some reprint house, have had as much influence on the engrossed reader as the movie or television images though—to cloud my argument—one edition of *Huckleberry Finn* used still photographs from the film of 1920. On a different level and in a mood far from Kemble, Barry Moser's woodcuts for the luxurious Pennyroyal edition (1985) will make any reader slow down to ponder them.

A fifth kind of recomposition that mostly baffles me occurs through the translations of *Huckleberry Finn*. As of 1982 a scholar could list translations into at least fifty-three languages of forty-seven countries. Once we get over our national pride we start recognizing that these translations present, to some degree, a different novel. Japanese scholars report that *Huckleberry Finn* was especially hard to recreate before their language was modernized. Even now, we hear that *Huckleberry Finn* carries along three difficult problems on its trans-Pacific flight: 1) how to replicate transculturally a colloquial first-person narration, that is, to give it the correct ease within a literature still not used to such a viewpoint; 2) "how to show the sense of time going slowly like the Mississippi"—a problem I don't even comprehend since I'm more ignorant about Japanese than Twain's Jim is about French; and 3) "how to translate the word 'sivilize' when it starts with an 's'." The dean of Russian translators, using *Huckleberry Finn* as a prime example, argues that it's impossible to transmute the vernacular of one people into that of another and therefore advises against even trying.[2] Startlingly to those of us who treasure Bernard DeVoto's rhapsodies about Huck's language or Henry Nash Smith's analysis of its social thrust, he asserts that Soviet readers are fully enchanted by a version that aims at a colorless style. Foreign-language editions tend toward vivid and domesticated drawings, however, which surely distort how their audiences visualize and therefore react to Twain's characters.

Rather than pursue any of those five kinds of recomposition further I will center on a more fundamental, larger one that has a smaller problem embedded in it. The larger problem is: when, how and even why was *Huckleberry Finn* acclaimed as a classic and what effect has this canonization had on the readings of the novel? The smaller problem asks: what was the relationship in 1884-1885 between *The Adventures of Tom Sawyer* and *Adventures of Huckleberry Finn*? This last question primarily concerns not Twain's intentions but the responses of his readership. More specifically, when and how, and to what extent and by whom (that is, holding common readers distinct from professional critics) has *Huckleberry Finn* become separated from the earlier novel and what results has this had for readings of it?

Of course the separation has usually had the purpose of elevating *Huckleberry Finn* above *Tom Sawyer*, and by now most critics imply a hopelessly lower status and even a parasitic future for the earlier novel. But as literary historians we need to understand that *Tom Sawyer* has suffered not only from invidious comparisons by modern critics but from guilt by association now and then, ever since 1885. When the *Springfield Republican* condemned both novels, it really was attacking the new arrival as sweepingly as it could. In 1910 when Arnold Bennett, after praising both novels as "episodically . . . magnificent," then called Twain "always a divine amateur" and thus launched a cliché that would sound intelligent for the next fifty years, he surely had *Huckleberry Finn* more in mind than *Tom Sawyer*.

At the start anyway, in 1885, the pattern was fairly clear.[3] Comparison was natural, inevitable. While reviewers could have groaned, of course, about a falling off, they mostly proclaimed *Huckleberry Finn* better than *Tom Sawyer*. Notice: not of a much brighter magnitude, just better. Twain himself clearly expected his readers to have known about and liked *Tom Sawyer*. Many reviewers assumed that the new novel was a direct sequel, as signaled by the echoing of titles, the subtitle, and Huck's opening sentence. Consistently, so professional a critic as William Dean Howells, partial both to Twain and to plebeian-democratic values, would discuss the two novels together or else switch between them without quite seeming to notice that he had done so. However, a few critics made the linkage in order to belabor both books, as when the *Springfield Republican* complained that "they are no better in tone than the dime-novels which flood the blood-and-thunder reading population." The verdict of joint "dime-novel sensationalism" was reaffirmed by a textbook as late as 1913. Actually, the point had more substance than we care to learn from today.

Up until Twain's death in 1910, the two books were bracketed much more often than one of them was elevated far beyond the other. The continued linkage had the effect of keeping *Huckleberry Finn* within the genre of the juvenile book, that is, of seeing Huck as an eternal boy rather than an adolescent who is growing up fast while we watch. Today, most interpretations assume that Huck acquires some adult values beyond Tom's or even crosses over into maturity alone. But I don't mean to segregate the two novels misleadingly. Besides other Twain books, *The Prince and the Pauper* (1882) and *Life on the Mississippi* (1883) arrived between them. Well into the 1920s a few critics perceived some sort of trilogy—based either on the boy's book or the Mississippi Valley. In the latter case these critics encouraged readers to approach *Huckleberry Finn* not as entertainment or palatable didacticism for the young but as genre realism or what we now call social history. After *Pudd'nhead Wilson* arrived, the Mississippi Writings looked still firmer as a unit, and the first Twain volume in the Library of America has lately reinforced that pattern.

Twain's death in 1910, Albert Bigelow Paine's worshipful three-volume biography in 1912, and the diligence of Harper's at pushing its collected editions kept the commentary expanding until it becomes manageable best by a mind that grasps pattern boldly or has a gift for style. Under the charm of eloquent subtlety we can even admire some critic instead of Twain without quite realizing it. Overall, at least through the 1920s, I still perceive more linkage than separation between *Tom Sawyer* and *Huckleberry Finn* though the most sophisticated instances of such criticism did see the later novel as intensifying—not transcending—the finest qualities of its forerunner. Stuart P.

Sherman's once-famous chapter in the *Cambridge History of American Literature* (1920) did proclaim an ascent yet still respected the lower range. In his judgment, Twain "wrote his second masterpiece of Mississippi fiction with a desire to express what in *Tom Sawyer* he had hardly attempted." If a different gloss of that passage encourages a charge that I am resisting the facts, let me warn that the contributors to the *Cambridge History* often disagreed as sharply as the football fans at ole state university and the newer "aggie" or "tech" college. The *CHAL* chapter on "Books for Children" bracketed *Tom Sawyer* and *Huckleberry Finn* as "stories of the American boy," equally suspect by some libraries for their "general unimprovingness." Relentlessly the chapter also bracketed Tom and Huck with "the author's third book for young people," *The Prince and the Pauper*.

The future grew clearer throughout the 1920s, especially after Van Wyck Brooks exempted *Huckleberry Finn* from his scathing indictment of Twain's character and writings. But, before turning to the effects on *Huckleberry Finn* of its becoming an adult classic in a category by itself among Twain's books, I should post the warning that the gap between it and *Tom Sawyer* has not grown impassable for everybody. The critics who address the college-graduate, general readers have continued to mix scenes and ideas from both novels. In 1942 Bernard DeVoto complained about a book "rather violently created" when thirty-seven out of forty-two ballots for the ten leading American novels merged *Tom Sawyer* and *Huckleberry Finn*. Curiously, in a fused analysis the quotations usually dip into Huck's vernacular but the scenes singled out will usually come from *Tom Sawyer*, with the fence-painting episode well in the lead. In fact, it's the only Mark Twain tableau honored with a U.S. postage stamp, in turn modeled on Norman Rockwell's painting.

As a steady, almost unnoticed influence on recomposition, American publishers have continued to find that a joint edition is highly marketable. Any preface or blurb will of course emphasize the reasons for the pairing, and any illustrations will of course use the same boys for both novels. That pattern applies still more firmly to foreign editions.[4] Given the inevitable sequence in any such editions, all but their most independent-minded readers enter *Huckleberry Finn* after *Tom Sawyer* has shaped their sensibilities. Even Norman Mailer, somewhere between the age of eleven and thirteen, followed that sequence and was "disappointed": "The character of Tom Sawyer whom I had liked so much in the first book was altered, and did not seem nice any more." The readers of a combined translation usually prefer *Tom Sawyer*, but such a comparison is unfair because they miss some of Huck's humor, surely. Likewise, the Hollywood versions of *Huckleberry Finn* have usually followed soon after one of *Tom Sawyer* and have continued much of its tone and its aim at a children's audience. The recent, three-part, color film entitled *The Adventures of Tom Sawyer and Huckleberry Finn*, which reportedly scored a big hit on Soviet television, presents Tom and Huck as three or four years younger than American critics would expect. Surprisingly, the four-hour version that ran on PBS stations here in 1986 treats Tom and Huck definitely as boys, not yet clearly adolescent.

Twain himself was glaringly slow to identify *Huckleberry Finn* as his greatest work. Of course, his reasons may be tangential. Writers are reluctant to belittle their other books by identifying one as the isolated summit or a proof that they had peaked early. Furthermore, Twain had notorious conflicts of ambition. Once, confessing to a reporter that his choice wavered, he explained that "it just depends on the mood I'm in." Eventually he groaned at how interviewers kept asking such questions as, "What is your favorite book?" That question was more and more often posed leadingly, with *Huckleberry Finn* expected as the answer, thereby implying that his touch had kept slipping since 1885. One of his neighbors would recall that Twain in 1908 instructed him as a ten-year-old "to be sure to remember when I was grown up that he had told me himself" that *Personal Recollections of Joan of Arc* was "his best book."

It's easy to imagine a tinge of defeatism in Twain's voice, especially about the candidacy of *Joan of Arc* (1896). For a number of reasons such as the rising tide of immigration and, conversely, the movement of the United States toward world power, the 1890s had brought a new urgency at trying to define the American spirit. Among living writers Twain was soon elevated as its finest exemplar, and among his books *Huckleberry Finn* was increasingly nominated as the long awaited "great American Novel." Before his death in 1910 he had to recognize that *Huckleberry Finn* was gathering a distinctive aura of acclaim.

In the early 1920s William Lyon Phelps of Yale broke the old praise barrier as the first—so far as I know—to declare that *Huckleberry Finn* "is not only the great American novel. It is America." Perhaps quoting from prefaces for hire is unfair, yet I can't help exhuming Clifton Fadiman's salute in 1940 to Twain as "our Chaucer, our Homer, our Dante, our Virgil" because *Huckleberry Finn* "is the nearest thing we have to a national epic." "Just as the Declaration of Independence . . . contains in embryo our whole future history as a nation, so the language of *Huckleberry Finn* (another declaration of independence) expresses our popular character, our humor, our slant."

Phelps, conscious of his mission as an apostle of literature, was always more cautious; he had soared to a record altitude only after much encouragement. Still, without polls to back me up, I propose that the decade of full canonization for *Huckleberry Finn* ran from 1932, when Bernard DeVoto published *Mark Twain's America*, to 1942, when he published *Mark Twain at Work*. In 1932 he made a passionate case for its humor, poetry, authenticity, irreverence, and egalitarianism. Then his long essay in *Mark Twain at Work* gave it the dignity both of a complex gestation and of the dark themes needed under emerging criteria to qualify it as a masterpiece.

After World War II, as the American Century finally started according to some, the stature of *Huckleberry Finn* grew self-evident. If a crowning touch was needed, it descended in 1950 from the reigning emperor of taste with T.S. Eliot's introduction for a reprint: "So we come to see Huck himself in the end as one of the permanent symbolic figures of fiction; not unworthy to take a place with Ulysses, Faust, Don Quixote, Hamlet and other great discoveries that man has made about himself." Though Eliot's list of Huck's peers may startle more than it enlightens us, its impact is imposing, even menacing: if you don't grasp *Huckleberry Finn* as a profoundly adult work of literature, then you are a childish, inadequate reader. DeVoto, disdaining such languid phrases as "not unworthy," had boiled with scorn toward dissenters. Also, he threatened them with the suspicion of lacking robustness or else a sense of humor, more grievous sins in his catechism than falling short of high culture. Actually, the very mention of a "classic" or "masterpiece" carries an undertone of intimidation. Fortunately for our self-respect, the most blatant example that I know comes from mainland China. A visiting teacher of American literature describes how her class got "incredibly excited" at a member "for daring to question" Twain's grammar. Persisting, he had to be squelched with, "Comrade! We've been over this! Remember, this is a masterpiece! Mark Twain doesn't make mistakes!"[5]

We now value the novel so keenly as innovative, lyrical, and rebellious that we like to believe that not only the Victorians, early or lingering, failed to appreciate it but so has every generation before our very own. Collectively, we now admire it so much that we take some of the credit for its existence and even feel some reassurance because of it. The lead editorial in the *New York Times* on New Year's day for 1984 tried to exorcise the long-dreaded Age of Orwell by invoking 1884 as "an epochal year for American culture" because it produced *Huckleberry Finn*. In fact, an impressive range of events celebrated its centennial which, taking advantage of a technicality for dating the first edition, stretched the festivities through both 1984 and 1985.[6]

I had promised to discuss when, how, and why *Huckleberry Finn* attained the status of a classic. Though settling the exact "when" is shaky enough, the "how" is a slippery enterprise because analyzing the levels of audience or the psychology of the marketplace—commercial or academic—has proved rudimentary so far and, in my opinion, will always remain so. Therefore I focus on a single area of the how by arguing that for *Huckleberry Finn* to soar majestically as a classic it first had to be divorced from *Tom Sawyer*. Most crucially, it had to live down its rumored past as a children's book.[7] The most graceful way out that can still honor the facts is to argue that *Huckleberry Finn* belongs to those rare books written for children, like *Alice's Adventures in Wonderland* or *The Hobbit*, that have transcended their genre. That allows a reasonably dignified divorce though we should recognize that *Tom Sawyer*, going strong on the backlist, soon caught up with *Huckleberry Finn* and then stayed ahead during Twain's final years of triumph as an elder statesman, both literary and social. Still, to block any chance of reconciliation, Alfred Kazin, in his much praised *An American Procession* (1984), dishonors the facts in asserting that while "it is impossible to imagine Tom Sawyer as anything but a boy, [a] sassy brat, imagination in America has often indulged itself in the fantasy of Huck Finn grown old."

Another aspect related to or following after "how" reminds me of a get-rich manual entitled "Making Your First Million Is the Hardest." Once a text not only lands within the canon but gets certified as a classic, it plugs into rich sources of energy. It becomes part of a reciprocating process; society uses it for serious rites of passage and also a marker, a blip on the SAT's, or a shared point of reference and allusion, of images and archetypes. Two summers ago I saw a play of local fame about a counterfeiter who keeps his handcrafted thousand-dollar bills in a copy of *Huckleberry Finn*; we can either explicate that detail or just consider it a touch of what the social psychologists call "bonding conversation." However, an accepted classic also gets woven into the highest culture, into the discourse of the intellectual elite who keep validating their status with each other, and even into the web of intertextuality that modernist writing has increasingly developed. In short, a classic gets institutionalized at all levels of literacy, and its status tends to keep rising, earning those next millions more and more easily.

By now *Huckleberry Finn* has sold about twenty million copies. Of course, a classic can eventually fade away. But, with luck from time and place, it can reach a gravity-free orbit above the clinging mass of new attempts to win our attention. Quite simply a classic "has got it made." As for *Huckleberry Finn*, a scholar recently assured the *Los Angeles Times* that it is the "most common

American reading experience, except for the Bible." When Twain, heady over
his first big triumph, bragged that *The Innocents Abroad* "sells right along just
like the Bible," he was almost prophetic. In fact, when William J. Bennett, as
director of the National Endowment for the Humanities, totted up a poll asking
which books "all students should read in high school," *Huckleberry Finn* ranked
third after the Shakespeare tragedies and the founding American documents but
ahead of the Bible.[8] These are evidently the four front-runners that change
rankings depending on the pollster or else the constituency.

In asking "why" *Huckleberry Finn* did in fact climb toward such company
I may sound feeble-minded when the answer is obvious, that is, its merits
infused by a genius. But Frank Kermode's brilliant analysis in *The Classic*
(1975) demonstrates that, for the typical case, the why is tricky. In discussing
the trials that a classic text must pass through, he surprisingly ignores any
criteria of profundity and also of formalist perfection. To the contrary, he
argues that the text must be loosejointed enough to allow posterity to slide over
the dull or anti-humanistic passages. Few of us find prolonged patches of
dullness in *Huckleberry Finn*. But if we dare to run the danger of being called
owlish, we start finding holes in Huck's armor as a natural gentleman. To keep
the raft supplied he sometimes "lifted a chicken that warn't roosting comfortable, and took him along. Pap always said, take a chicken when you get a
chance, because if you don't want him yourself you can easy find somebody
that does, and a good deed ain't ever forgot" (chap. 12). "Before daylight," to
balance the menu, Huck "borrowed a watermelon, or a mushmelon, or a
punkin, or some new corn, or things of that kind." However, Huck and Jim,
to ease their consciences, decide not to steal crabapples and persimmons. "We
warn't feeling just right, before that, but it was all comfortable now. I was glad
the way it come out, too, because crabapples an't ever good, and the p'simmons
wouldn't be ripe for two or three months yet." All that is funny enough, but it
won't stand up to serious ethical questioning and it would grate on the owner
of those chickens.

If we dare to sound like kneejerk humanitarians, we can likewise find a few
breaks in Huck's reputedly endless flow of sympathy. Notice, for instance, how
he bullies and even ridicules the younger Wilks girl who has a hare-lip. More
important, several social-minded critics have puzzled at how calmly Huck
assumes the fact of Jim's death when a steamboat smashes their raft. Huck
comes off still worse in the famous passage when he lies to Aunt Sally that his
steamboat was delayed by an accident, which "killed a nigger" (chap. 32). We
jeer at Aunt Sally, but actually Huck had cast the first stone of racism.

Kermode also argues that the text of a classic must be "naive," that is, it
must be generalized enough to allow successive generations to read into it a
meaning adapted to their own time or, in effect, to recompose it. Groaning
slightly, we can agree that *Huckleberry Finn* meets this criterion. It now holds
the position of the most heavily discussed novel in American literature. Among
the many hundred articles and the twenty or so entire books or pamphlets
devoted to it, the opposing interpretations glare at each other so fiercely that its
text starts to look like merely a pretext for our own originality or else
pugnaciousness. Justin Kaplan quips that the "lettered classes" have turned it
into a "sort of fresh-water *Moby-Dick*."

I don't propose to reserve *Huckleberry Finn* for those who would pay it
homage decorously. The quarrels attract still more readers who admire it
hugely; for most of them it radiates good spirits, perhaps into a personal or

cosmic void. Likewise, its reputation as a classic keeps attracting its share of those mini-Fausts who, like Thomas Wolfe's persona in the stacks of the Harvard Library, choose pell-mell among more books than anybody can find time for. Desperate, some of them become professional students of literature who may get to read *Huckleberry Finn* many times. They then perceive and share among themselves the nuances that no single mind could pick up by itself.

Unfortunately, after absorbing the nuances they may start harping on the flaws, especially because too many critics assume that a classic has somehow laid claim to perfection. I don't mean to sound ungrateful. The intense, quizzical scrutiny sensitizes us to passages that we had overlooked. Several years ago a capable Twainian asked me what Jim means in telling Huck's fortune: "you wants to keep 'way fum de water as much as you kin, en don't run no resk, 'kase it's down in de bills dat you's gwyne to git hung" (chap. 4). Since then I have wondered if that's a portentous touch or a minstrel-show level of joke at Jim's expense. Because I can't decide, I'm tempted, however, to turn querulous toward the text.

To refocus on the point toward which I had started, *Huckleberry Finn* is being read quite differently now than in 1885. More specifically, its achieved status is having enough influence to justify the term "recomposition." In recomposing, however, we may do a much poorer job than Twain. Above all, we may be making *Huckleberry Finn* too solemn. Though Russell Baker proves almost daily that his sense of humor is sharp, he has decided—reacting against the charges that *Huckleberry Finn* can confirm racism in children or adolescents—that readers must reach the age of thirty-five before they are mature enough for it and, besides, must have qualified themselves by a spread of experiences. One learned critic has concluded that it is "certainly a very sad book."

Comedy, to be sure, is more idiosyncratic than tragedy and entails a cruel paradox: the harder we try to explain or just insist on humor, the sillier we look. So I am embarrassed to confess uncertainty whether T.S. Eliot, in his elderly reverence toward *Huckleberry Finn*, misses a joke or else disposes others to do so. Huck, in itemizing the haul from an abandoned shanty, rounds off with: " . . . just as we was leaving I found a tolerable good curry-comb, and Jim he found a ratty old fiddle-bow, and a wooden leg. The straps was broke off of it, but barring that, it was a good enough leg, though it was too long for me and not long enough for Jim, and we couldn't find the other one, though we hunted all around." Eliot judges that the "grim precision" about the contents of the shanty and "especially the wooden leg, and the fruitless search for its mate . . . reminds us at the right moment of the kinship of mind and the sympathy between the boy outcast from society and the negro fugitive from the injustice of society."[9] Eliot reminds me in turn of the anecdote about the man who complained that it had been hard not to laugh right out loud during Twain's lecture in the basement of a church. The thickening dignity of *Huckleberry Finn* has dampened our reactions. We are afraid that by enjoying Jim's prophecy of Huck's fate as a ragged non-sequitur we will overlook a multiple warhead of profundities; we start rummaging for the symbolisms of that matching wooden leg. Underneath such worries hides the assumption that tragedy is far superior to comedy. To the extent that we want to venerate *Huckleberry Finn* as a tragedy, we have to start bending the text to project Huck as a rounded character rather than a chain of often inconsistent though handy attitudes.

Another worrisome way in which prestige as a classic shapes our reading is that we assume that *Huckleberry Finn* needs to be restated abstractly because the "discovery of meaning is the goal of the critical enterprise," because first-rate criticism is "synonymous with interpretation." Furthermore, that interpretation operates from supposedly self-evident principles. "The first requirement of a work of art in the twentieth century is that it should *do* nothing" and especially that it must avoid serving any social purpose. Some critics now hold that literature must be cut off from common experience in order to save it. Such a surgical strike is deadly to Twain, who interacted with his audiences much more intimately, in fact more physically than the high-culture authors in his time or today; from his apprenticeship onward, he stayed alert to responses as conditioned by and conditioning the daily life of his readers. Any distancing through abstractions does greatest harm of all to the stunningly vivid, concrete world of *Huckleberry Finn*. When we elevate its values above gritty place and time we are trying to "sivilize" Huck as mechanically as Miss Watson did and are muffling its post-bellum topicalities as well as its continuing impact on sociocultural discourse.

More basically, by making *Huckleberry Finn* an official masterpiece we may have turned the book against its best qualities. It once challenged—and then, by forcing its way in, changed—the canon of American literature. By doing so it undermined the authority of canon-making itself, the designating of a set of classic texts. A decade after *Huckleberry Finn* was published, Thorstein Veblen argued that the academics' insistence on the idea of classics laid out merely another path of wasteful, conspicuous consumption for the leisure class. Within the last decade of our times, analysis of canon-building, which makes the classic its keystone, has grown much grimmer. We now have to consider seriously the argument that the officially sanctioned, elite culture functions as one of the ways by which the economically and politically dominant maintain their power through peaceful assent from the populace rather than naked coercion. Though I cannot read Twain as quasi-Marxist I can insist that *Huckleberry Finn* should stick as a bone in the throat to dull conservatism.

At times anyway, such as in *Huckleberry Finn*, Twain was subversive toward peaceful, unexamined assent. Later he insisted that he had learned long ago to question any consensus: "I tremble and the goose-flesh rises on my skin every time I encounter one. . . . ten to one there's a trap under that thing somewhere." A consensus may deny more truth than it affirms. As Barbara Herrnstein Smith warns regarding classics, "when the value of a work is seen as unquestionable," then "humanistic scholars and academic critics" tend to "'save the text' by transferring the locus of its interest to more formal or structural features and/or allegorizing its potentially alienating ideology to some more general ('universal') level where it becomes more tolerable and also more readily interpretable in terms of contemporary ideologies."[10] To state her point bluntly, a classic tends to get co-opted, to get neutered. Furthermore, if we keep insisting that a text is a classic, we encourage this suspicion that it cannot attract readers entirely on its own.

To its peril, *Huckleberry Finn* is now absorbed into the canon, which once again looks solidly fixed to the young or to the instinctively reverential. Ironically, Twain's break-in has made the canon more attractive and therefore more defensible against the new heretics who always prowl outside the temple. Compounding the irony, science fiction is trying to get respect from departments of English these days, and there's an overstated drive to certify Twain as one of its founders. However, that drive could instead lower his standing among those academics who want to keep sci-fi in the outer darkness, which sci-fi reminds us is really out there.

I don't want to end with my eyes fixed on outer space, cosmic or intellectual. Close to home, I am worried about keeping the undergraduate major in literature a vibrant and challenging yet sometimes immediately pleasurable experience. Specifically, I worry that the canonical recomposition of *Huckleberry Finn* will make new readers approach it too cautiously, even timidly, contrary to Twain's predominant mood, which could joke that "I am glad that the old masters [of painting] are all dead, and I only wish they had died sooner," which could say that "a very good library may be started just by leaving" Jane Austen's novels out of it, which would "rather be damned to John Bunyan's heaven" than read Henry James's *Bostonians*, which could have Huck in a "sweat to find out all about" Moses until he hears that Moses "had been dead a considerable long time; so then I didn't care no more about him; because I don't take no stock in dead people."

Professional insistence that some text is a classic may not be so much intimidating as simply dispiriting. Norman Mailer believes that "secretly we expect less reward" from a classic than from a "good contemporary novel." Maybe that's why he waited almost fifty years before reading *Huckleberry Finn* again, until he was paid to do so. Of course, Mailer is one of a kind and can't be used to prove Frank Kermode's observation that "it is only when we see some intelligent non-professional confronted by a critical essay from our side of the fence that we see how esoteric we are."[11] Since Kermode feels "moderate rejoicing" because criticism has grown into a formidable expertise, he qualifies as a friendly spokesman for the idea that we academics "have to think of ourselves as exponents of various kinds of secondary interpretation—spiritual understandings, as it were, compared with carnal, and available only to those who, in second-century terms, have circumcised ears, that is, are trained by us."

I don't mean to pose an either-or choice or, much less, to fan the anti-intellectualism that has been getting warm again, lately. But I hope that readers will always feel free to approach, to recompose *Huckleberry Finn* for themselves with the freshness and zest promised by a small California newspaper in 1885:

The adventures of "Huckleberry Finn" . . . will amuse and interest you, where other books prove insipid. . . . Mark Twain is certainly in his element; for this book, while intensely interesting as a narrative—holding the reader's attention with a tenacity that admits of no economy in the midnight oil—is also at the top of the list as a humorous work. Interwoven in its text are side-splitting stories, sly hints at different weaknesses of society, and adventures of the most humorous description.[12]

How many critics have done much better since then in less than a hundred words?

Still, with or without their help and whether or not the future will recompose the novel to their satisfaction, *Huckleberry Finn* will continue to contradict Twain's own definition of a classic as a book that everybody praises and nobody reads.

NOTES

1. To document this essay closely would pile up the citations, as can be seen from Thomas A. Tenney's definitive "An Annotated Checklist of Criticism on *Adventures of Huckleberry Finn, 1884-1984*," in *Huck Finn among the Critics: A Centennial Selection*, ed. M. Thomas Inge (Frederick, Md.: University Publications of America, 1985). That volume also contains an excellent sampling of criticism, old and new. The diversity of current approaches appears fully in *One Hundred Years of "Huckleberry Finn": The Boy, His Book and American Culture*, ed. Robert Sattelmeyer and J. Donald Crowley (Columbia: Univ. of Missouri Press, 1985).

2. *The Art of Translation: Kornei Chukovsky's "A High Art,"* trans. and ed. Lauren G. Leighton (Knoxville: Univ. of Tennessee Press, 1984), 126-29. Jan B. Gordon's essay in *One Hundred Years of "Huckleberry Finn"* analyzes the problems not of language but of underlying mores for Japanese readers.

3. See the precise, impressive study by Victor Fischer, "Huck Finn Reviewed: The Reception of *Huckleberry Finn* in the United States, 1885-1897," *American Literary Realism, 1870-1910*, 16 (1983), 1-57. My introduction for *New Essays on "Adventures of Huckleberry Finn"* (Cambridge Univ. Press, 1985) tries to survey its critical history up to the present.

4. Alexei Zverev, "Mark Twain/Why We Love Him, Too," *Soviet Life*, No. 11 (350), November 1985, 63, asserts that "these two best-known of Mark Twain's books have merged into one for the contemporary Soviet reader."

5. Marilyn Krysl, "Under the Jade Vault: Lei Feng Salutes Mark Twain," *Journal of Higher Education*, 55 (1984), 556-57. Actually, it's not clear to me which passage in the Tom-Huck novels is being discussed.

6. I try to record the highlights and the most typical comments in "How Old Is Huck Finn?" in *Dictionary of Literary Biography Yearbook 1985*, ed. Jean Ross (Detroit: Gale, 1986).

7. In "*Huck Finn's* First Century: A Bibliographical Survey," *American Studies International*, 22, ii (1984), 90, Carl Dolmetsch concludes that "before the 1940's, *Huck Finn's* well-established popularity was principally as a book for children, like *Tom Sawyer*, with the result that most readers came to it too early to see more than its adventure-story surface." In *One Hundred Years of "Huckleberry Finn"* see pp. 166-67 of Alan Gribben's insightful essay on the shared "boy-book elements."

8. See *Washington Post*, 12 August 1984, A12. However, the "church-state issue" evidently handicapped the Bible.

9. "Introduction," *Adventures of Huckleberry Finn* (New York: Cresset, 1950).

10. "Contingencies of Value," *Critical Inquiry*, 10 (1983), 28-30.

11. "Institutional Control of Interpretation," in *The Salmagundi Reader*, eds. Robert Boyers and Peggy Boyers (Bloomington: Indiana Univ. Press, 1983), 364.

12. *Napa Register*, 8 May 1885. I thank Victor Fischer (of the Mark Twain Project) for sharing this item with me. Though plagiarized from a promotional flyer for the novel, it ran as a review.

THE CHARACTERIZATION OF JIM IN *HUCKLEBERRY FINN*

FORREST G. ROBINSON

The London *Saturday Review* for 31 January 1885 carried a review of *Huckleberry Finn* by Brander Matthews, an American who would in later years become a professor at Columbia University. In the midst of much that is apt and insightful, Matthews observes that Jim, the escaped slave who accompanies Huck down river on the raft, displays "the essential simplicity and kindliness and generosity of the Southern negro."[1] This general impression of Jim has been challenged only very rarely in the century since the novel fist appeared. But in place of Matthews's obvious approval of Mark Twain's treatment of Jim, more recent critics have been strongly inclined to contrast the submissive slave who appears in the closing chapters with the more complete human being who moves through the central sections of the narrative. Modern observers are in broad agreement that this simpler, more passive Jim is radically out of character. He is a mere fragment of his former self, a two-dimensional parody, a racial stereotype with roots in the minstrel tradition, and one symptom among many others of Mark Twain's failure of moral vision and artistic integrity in the complex evasion that closes the action. Among the more prominent voices in this critical litany are those of Leo Marx, who finds that Jim "has been made over in the image of a flat stereotype: the submissive stage-Negro," and Henry Nash Smith, who writes that "Jim is reduced to the level of farce." More recently, Joseph Sawicki has observed that the Jim of the final chapters is "reduced to a stock character."[2] In much greater detail, and with much greater moral energy, Neil Schmitz has argued that the conclusion of *Huckleberry Finn* "is an affront . . . because the humanity of its prime character [Jim] is patently, systematically ignored." That Jim should offer "to sacrifice his life (and the family he professes to love) for Tom's sake," he insists, is absurd. He is equally incredulous when "Jim's native goodness negates the crushing burden of his past" and "transcends the pain that has been inflicted on him." In the upshot, Schmitz faults Mark Twain for his surrender to the racial stereotypes of the Reconstruction era. The result, he concludes, is a Jim who is "shorn of his subjective reality, no longer actively engaged in the process of living . . . trapped in the prison of the white man's mind."[3]

It is not my intention to take issue with the view that the submissive, all-suffering Jim of the conclusion "evasion" chapters contrasts rather sharply with the forthright, assertive, essentially good but fully rounded human being who appears in the central sections of the novel. Jim does seem to change, from a plausibly complete man to an apparently incomplete, two-dimensional racial stereotype. At the same time, however, I want to raise the possibility that this major transformation in Jim's appearance can be brought into clear alignment with a coherent analysis of his characterization. Jim changes, I want to argue, because he sees that he must. I find that Jim's characterization is profoundly true to the realities of his experience in the novel; but it is culturally true as well in the apparent inconsistency that it has seemed, in the eyes of the audience, to betray. In this latter, cultural framework, it is not Jim's character that finally requires explanation; rather, it is the general failure to recognize the necessity and significance of his retreat to passivity that we must attend to.

◆

I was first prompted to reflect on the deeper coherence of Jim's transformation by Frederick Douglass's *Narrative*. Douglass makes it clear that the masters had persuaded themselves, against overwhelming evidence to the contrary, that slavery was a benign and morally defensible institution. As one sadly ironic consequence of this delusion, slaves were cruelly punished for the open expression of their feelings about their condition. The dark truth was too much for the master to bear. Thus the slave was obliged, for his or her survival, to retreat behind the mask of a docile, gullible, pliant "darky" who suffers all manner of indignity with silence and a simpleminded smile.[4] As Lawrence W. Levine has shown, this strategy is clearly exemplified in the slaves' didactic tales, which illustrate that silence and dissimulation are the keys to survival.[5] To deceive the master afforded the slave a taste of triumph, and it gave oblique expression to his contempt for the immorality and hypocrisy of the system; but first and foremost the self-conscious resort to a pose of docile simplicity was designed to appease the oppressor, and thus to minimize suffering.

It requires no more than a few moments of reflection to begin to glimpse the ways in which this historical material might be applied to Jim. But while Douglass and the larger slave culture may serve as a valuable heuristic, suggesting an alternative to the view that Jim is no more than a figure of farce, a flat, utterly conventional stereotype, they cannot define in advance what the close study of *Huckleberry Finn* will yield. Others have been moved, as I am, to read the novel, paying special attention to Jim, with this cultural background in mind. Nearly thirty years ago, in his crispy insightful and challenging essay, "Change the Joke and Slip the Yoke," Ralph Ellison argued that there is more to Jim than first meets the eye.

Writing at a time when the blackfaced minstrel was still popular, and shortly after a war which left even the abolitionists weary of those problems associated with the Negro, Twain fitted Jim into the outlines of the minstrel tradition, and it is from behind this stereotype mask that we see Jim's dignity and human capacity—and Twain's complexity—emerge. Yet it is his source in this same tradition which creates that ambivalence between his identification as an adult and parent and his "boyish" naivete, and which by contrast makes Huck, with his street-sparrow sophistication, seem more adult.[6]

While Ellison shares the view that there are at least two dimensions to the characterization of Jim, he makes it clear that the two identities are not incompatible, but merely superimposed, the "stereotype mask" upon the figure of "dignity and human capacity." This doubleness in Jim is testimony to "Twain's complexity," and to the complexity of the tradition of representation within which he worked. For quite in spite of the fact that Mark Twain bowed to "the white dictum that Negro males must be treated either as boys or 'uncles'—never as men,"[7] his novel is deeply subversive of that prejudiced convention, and permits us to "see" a complex, complete human being "emerge" from behind the mask. Thus the doubleness is also integral to Jim's "character," and accounts for what Ellison describes as "that ambivalence" in him.

If Ralph Ellison anticipates and in some measure informs the thesis that I want to develop here, then James M. Cox provides a model for the kind of detailed textual analysis requisite to the elaboration of that argument. Cox's example is everywhere illuminating, but I prefer in this instance to his most recent ruminations on *Huckleberry Finn*, an essay entitled "A Hard Book to Take." Cox's remarks center on "the system of emotional exchange" into which the novel seduces most readers, inviting the indulgence of moral indignation at the evils of slavery, but at the same time obscuring the humorous humanity of numerous major actors. Here as elsewhere in his work, Cox applies genial but firm resistance to this critical loss of balance, urging us too laugh more, condemn less, and offering surrender to the path of least resistance, the path of the great river itself, as the way to a proper equilibrium. Huck, who embodies for Cox "the essential pleasure principle of ease and handiness," and who thus "retains a true freedom from all conviction," is necessarily the focus of critical attention.[8] But along the way, in his deft elaboration of "the system of emotional exchange," Cox pauses at some length over Jim. For most readers, he observes, emphasis on Jim's goodness and generosity and humility has the result of making him seem too gullible and simpleminded to recognize or defend his own best interests: "the more Jim is made a saint the more he is likely to be the humble victim lacking any semblance of the shrewd humanity Huck so amply possesses" (pp. 390-91). Cox responds by insisting that "surely Jim is shrewd, as shrewd as Huck," and then advancing through the analysis of a selection of episodes to confirm his position. From the beginning of the novel, he notes, there is evidence that Jim is involved, along with everyone else, in pervasive "tricks, deceit, and confidence games" (p. 391). Jim conceals from Huck the fact that the corpse in the house of death is Pap, and he does so out of mixed, to some extent selfish, motives. Just so, when Jim makes his farewell to Huck in chapter 16, he seems to sense that Huck is about to betray him, and thus offers an oblique but quite moving and effective appeal to Huck's loyalty.

In Cox's view, then, Jim is no more simple or gullible than Huck; but he is shrewd enough to recognize that the greater wisdom for a slave resides in the simulation of a simplicity "boyish" and comprehensive enough to ease the combined fear and guilt and suspicion of the white oppressor. This is the lesson that his experience in *Huckleberry Finn* serves to reinforce; and his increasing adherence to this hard truth is chiefly accountable for what are perceived to be the untoward shifts in his characterization. Cox does not develop this line of analysis; but in observing that this is "the role Jim plays, or is forced to play," he clearly points the way to it (p. 390). In what follows I want to move much more systematically in this direction, focusing as narrowly as possible on Jim, and on what we may observe and plausibly surmise about his point of view. This avenue of investigation will lead to the general confirmation and very substantial expansion of the insights provided by Ellison and Cox, and it will form the background to some concluding observations on the dynamics of American reader response.[9]

♦

"The possibility that Huck will abandon or betray Jim," Cox observes, "is . . . at the very center of the whole journey—and the two fugitives can never believe in each other sufficiently to annihilate it."[10] Jim's circumstances could hardly be more perilous. He is a runaway slave in slave territory; and he is a leading suspect in what is perceived to be Huck's murder. For white people who know him, he is the object of angry pursuit; for those who do not—as subsequent episodes demonstrate—he is an object of suspicion and heartless grasping after quick profits. So bereft, Jim must run by night, hide by day, and through it all endure loneliness, fear verging toward panic, and a crippling lack of information. He reveals his sense of predicament best when he reports to Huck how it felt too be stranded on the *Walter Scott*.

He said that when I went in the texas and he crawled back to get on the raft and found her gone, he nearly died; because he judged it was all up with *him*, anyway it could be fixed; for if he didn't get saved he would get drownded; and if he did get saved whoever saved him would send him back home so as to get the reward, and then Miss Watson would sell him south, sure.[11]

Saved or not saved, Jim feels doom closing down on him. Little wonder, then, that he is always gratified to see Huck. Jim may in time come to love the white boy; but from the beginning he needs him desperately. Huck is the living proof that Jim is not a murderer. And Huck gives him eyes and ears, information, an alibi, and some small leverage when the inevitable disaster strikes. On those subsequent occasions when Jim welcomes Huck back to the raft, this desperate need, and the sense of breathless relief, provide the warmth in what usually passes for unmingled outbursts of affection. The boy is Jim's best chance for survival; naturally, he is pleased to have him back.

Huck's is one of very few faces that Jim can be happy to see. But in order to get a proper hold on the deep mutuality of the relationship between the man and child, we must recognize that the generalization works equally well in reverse. When Huck discovers that his companion on Jackson's Island is Miss Watson's Jim, his enthusiasm is immediately manifest: "I bet I was glad to see him," he reflects (p. 50). Huck's remarks are often taken to express his respect and friendship for Jim. There may be some of this in his attitude, but in larger part his pleasure has its foundation in relief—and unlooked for relief at that. Upon first discovering Jim's camp, Huck recoils in fear. He is afraid that he will be recognized, and that his desperate scheme to get away from his father will be revealed, leaving him more perilously vulnerable than ever to Pap's really pathological violence. "My heart jumped up amongst my lungs," he says (p. 48). He retreats in haste, first up a tree, and then from the island altogether. But the danger of discovery is even greater ashore; he sleeps fitfully, "and every time I waked up I thought somebody had me by the neck" (p. 50). Feeling, no doubt, as Jim did on the *Walter Scott*—that "it was all up with *him*, anyway it could be fixed"—Huck returns to the island, and with gun at the ready, he passes the night waiting for the mysterious camper to emerge from his blankets.

We do not know for sure what Huck anticipates as he waits, unblinking, in the dark. But he cannot be very sanguine about his immediate prospects. There are obvious difficulties if the face that emerges from the blankets is a familiar one; and there will be suspicion, and questions, and the threat of just as much danger, if it is a stranger's. Thus when it is Jim who emerges, an enormous weight of doubt and fear is lifted. Huck knows Jim. And he seems to recognize almost immediately that Jim has run away. "I warn't afraid of *him* telling the people where I was," he declares (p. 51). Huck seems to think of Jim in a friendly sort of way; and there can be no doubt that his relief has some foundation in grateful release from the nightmares that always pursue him into solitude.[12] "I warn't lonesome, now," he says (p. 51). But at bottom Jim is a source of relief to Huck, in a way that almost no one else could be, because as a runaway slave he is as much Huck's hostage as Huck is his. Huck is "glad" to see Jim, as Jim is pleased to join Huck, not primarily because of their friendship, or because of incipient prompting toward community or family,[13] but because they find themselves, quite by surprise, bound together in mutual desperation. Huck and Jim need each other long before they learn to respect or love one another; and once their needs are satisfied—when Jim is freed from slavery, and Huck is freed from fear of Pap—they separate, immediately. They stay together because it appears that they can use one another in relative safety—a safety to be matched by neither of them with any other companion. And this is so because there is between them, arising out of their desperate secrets from a hostile, encroaching world, a balance of the power to betray, an equality in suspicion and fear, and therefore a tenuous bond of mutual protection.

The tension and uncertainty between the fugitives appear first as ripples of ambiguity in gestures of ostensible reassurance. "I ain't agoing to tell, and I ain't agoing back there anyways," says Huck; "I 'uz powerful sorry you's killed, Huck," Jim replies, "but I ain't no mo', now" (p. 53). They are much more boldly evident in the series of practical jokes that Huck feels compelled to spring on his companion, and in Jim's decision to conceal the identity of the corpse in the house of death. As several scholars have observed, Jim's seeming generosity, by veiling the truth about Pap's death, artificially preserves Huck's principal motive for flight. So long as Jim controls this information, he maintains the balance of power, and thus retains a substantial measure of control over Huck.[14] This carefully guarded illusion of bondage of course anticipates Tom's cruel "evasion" at the Phelps plantation. And it is significant that when Jim, free at last, finally reveals the truth about Pap, Huck proceeds, without comment, to his decision "to light out for the Territory" (p. 362).

I have argued elsewhere that Huck's impulse to play mean tricks on Jim, and his decision to turn him over to the authorities, arise out of an ambivalence about Jim, and about black people generally, that is in turn rooted in the racist ideology of white society. Huck is free enough of the dominant culture to respond to Jim as a human being; but he is also prone to sudden reversals of feeling that betray his deep immersion in the mentality of the white majority. This dividedness in Huck is conspicuously at work in his cruel joke with the "trash" (after he and Jim have been separated in the fog), his prompt apology, his equally sudden decision to betray Jim, and the brilliant, spontaneous deception of the predatory slave hunters that immediately follows. These abrupt, radical reversals are evidence of the boy's wavering marginality, and speak clearly to his restlessness in the ambiguous ties that bind him to Jim.[15]

Jim cannot fail to observe this ambivalence in Huck, and he must recognize it as a leading threat to his survival. His management of the discovery of Pap's corpse is an index to his penetration on this score, and serves to reinforce the impression that his characteristic response to the threat of betrayal is oblique rather than direct, dissimulation and manipulation rather that open confrontation. Jim quite shrewdly takes the measure of Huck's uncertain moods and wavering loyalty. He knows that direct appeals to justice and good faith will backfire by highlighting the cruel truth that such considerations are irrelevant in dealings with slaves, except as incitements to turn them in. Instead, Jim does what he must do to survive: he resorts to all varieties of deception. His mastery in this line is first and most vitally manifest in his seeming incapacity to deceive. Without that simulated two-dimensional face, that happy, carefree, gullible fraud that he retreats to more and more as the hostile world closes in,

Jim would be helpless to defend himself. Naturally enough, in entering this
perilous but virtually obligatory game of cat and mouse, he exploits all the
resources available to him. Not least among these is the deep cultural
investment among white people in the conception of slaves as happy children—gullible, harmless, essentially good. It is profoundly to Jim's advantage
that in retreating to this preposterous stereotype he satisfies an urgent need—the
issue of guilt and fear—in the culture of the oppressors. There is safety, he
knows, in their readiness to be deceived.

Almost from the moment of Jim's first appearance in the novel we are
witness to hints and glancing suggestions that there may be an artful and
self-interested deceiver at work behind the face of the gullible "darky" that
Jim presents to the world. Tom and Huck do not doubt that Jim is completely
deceived by their little prank in chapter 2. So persuaded are they of the slave's
superstitious gullibility that they do not pause to reflect on the numerous
advantages he derives from being so readily taken in. Building on the pretext
provided by the joke, Jim erects an elaborate narrative in which he figures as
hero. His pride swells as other slaves come from miles around to hear his story,
and to admire the charmed nickel that he wears around his neck. In all of this,
of course, Jim's behavior and its consequences anticipate in striking detail the
subsequent exploits of Tom Sawyer, who cultivates adventures that make
crowd-pleasing narratives, and who wears a talismanic bullet around his
neck. The joke on Jim has surely turned to his advantage, and to the advantage
of his slave audience, who gather for fun that may only begin with simulated
credulity in Jim's preposterous story, and that finds its climax in the spectacle
of white, and not black, gullibility. Thus the delicious, perfectly unconscious
irony, submerged in Huck's concluding observation that "Jim was most ruined,
for a servant, because he got so stuck up on account of having seen the devil
and been rode by witches" (p. 8).

A cognate irony runs through the account of the hairball. It is Huck who
seeks the advice of the oracle; Jim simply provides what the boy seeks, and in
the process relieves him of a counterfeit quarter. The irony is compounded by
the fact that Huck regards the quarter as worthless, but offers it to Jim anyway,
referring to "say nothing about the dollar I got from the judge." This rather
minor moment of selfish deception, which takes rise from assumptions about
Jim's gullibility and genial willingness to be exploited, is abruptly reversed
when Jim reveals his plan to use a potato to fix the quarter "so anybody in
town would take it in a minute, let alone a hair-ball." The irony grows even
deeper when Huck refuses to acknowledge that he has been fooled. "Well, I
knowed a potato would do that, before," he insists, quite lamely, "but I had
forgot it" (p. 21). We suspect that what Jim has to say about potatoes, true or
false, is news to Huck. But by insisting that he forgot what in fact he never
knew, the boy submerges the awkward revelation that the tables have been
turned on him. Such an acknowledgement so conflicts with the racist prepos-
sessions manifest in his attempt to deceive Jim that he cannot rise to it. Instead,
as if to seal the slave's triumph, and to invite its repetition, he clings to the
flimsy delusion that Jim has been the easy mark, and not the other way round.

These early episodes may be viewed as opening gambits in a very serious
game whose leading dynamics are racist self-deception rooted in cruel prejudice
but replete with openings for manipulation by the seemingly hapless, in fact
shrewdly resourceful, victims. Of course, the cruelest joke is always at the
slave's expense; but *Huckleberry Finn* offers us a window on the ways and

means employed by the victims in their attempt to retrieve such shreds of power and dignity and laughter as are available to them. To this end, all varieties of deception are fully justified—not least by the example of the master class—in the struggle to maintain morale, and in the larger business of survival. The slave's relish for such duplicity we can only surmise; but having opened our eyes to that possibility, we may begin to glimpse a deeper dimension to Jim's delight in well-made schemes. When Huck reveals the truth about the bloody scene at Pap's cabin, Jim "said it was smart. He said Tom Sawyer couldn't get up no better plan than what I had" (p. 52). But Jim is equally impressed with the shrewdness and style of his own escape, and he is ready with good ideas when it comes to disguises. Not at all surprisingly, when Jack, one of the Grangerford slaves, leads Huck to Jim's hiding place on the pretext that he wants to show him a nest of water-moccasins, Jim observes: "Dat Jack's a good nigger, en pooty smart." "Yes, he is," Huck agrees, readily grasping the point. "He ain't ever told me you was here. . . . If anything happens, *he* ain't mixed up in it. He can say he never seen us together, and it'll be the truth" (p. 151). But Jim reserves his most effusive approval for Huck's magnificent deception of the slave hunters: "lawsy, how you did fool 'em, Huck! Dat *wuz* de smartes' dodge!" (p. 128).

The ultimate objective in all of these admirable schemes is deception, always of white people, and almost always by slaves. What Jim admires most in such ruses is the ability to act on the spur of the moment with resourcefulness and cool, the intuitive knack for anticipating the next move, and the skillful concealment of tracks. In a nutshell, he admires the masterful manipulation of appearances. Such mastery has its counterpart in the ability to interpret appearances, to penetrate beneath shifting surfaces to the truth of things, the drift of circumstance, the hidden designs of others. Thus at the same time that the slave contrives to deceive even to the extent of seeming without guile, he must also be undeceived even while appearing incorrigibly gullible.

From the point of view of whites, the slave's habit of "reading into things" is irresistible evidence of the addiction of racial inferiors to irrational mumbo jumbo. It is to this leading feature of Jim's "racial" makeup that Tom and Huck appeal in their first trick. Jim responds by exploiting the trick in a way that confirms the prejudice that first gave it rise. Thus he has his way, and at the same time reinforces white illusions, thereby concealing the reversal that has occurred, and assuring that he will have opportunities to get his way again in the future. Early in his first meeting with Huck on Jackson's Island, Jim is equally inclined to the indulgence in what appears to be run away superstition. Everything that passes before his eyes or through his mind seems fair game for interpretation. His excess at this early interval is conspicuous and thoroughly untoward. But it plays to Huck's prejudice, draws out his skepticism, and thus works to reinforce his assumption that his black companion is gullible, naively overconfident, harmlessly if rather annoyingly voluble in the matter of signs. This, I am inclined to suspect, is precisely what Jim wants. He knows from the start that some of his shrewdness and subtlety and delight in manipulation are bound to come to view if he is to succeed in his desperate flight. So he is careful at the outset to seal Huck in his quite conventionally prejudiced expectations. Thereafter the boy is so fixed in his conception of Jim as a superstitious slave that he is blind to the deeper coherence and purpose of his friend's words and gestures.

This tendency is clear almost from the start, when Huck's gathering doubts about Jim's interpretation, and his impatience with Jim's claims that "he knowed most everything," move him to pose a broadly ironic question: "It looked to me like all the signs was about bad luck, and so I asked him if there warn't any good-luck signs." But Jim's response—that there are "mighty few" (p. 55) good-luck signs—though laden with the hard won wisdom of slavery, and though a telling revelation of the dark watchfulness behind his carefree exterior, does nothing to catch Huck's attention, or to arrest his mounting incredulity. We are witness to more of the same when Jim betrays his sense of desperation aboard the *Walter Scott*. Huck responds with blithe nonchalance that suggests that he has missed Jim's deeper drift. "Well," he reflects, "he was right; he was most always right; he had an uncommon level head, for a nigger" (p. 93). And the same language—we are tempted to say "formula"—freighted with the same racial condescension, surfaces in Huck's reaction to Jim's scheme for learning the truth abut Cairo. "Jim had a wonderful level head, for a nigger: he could most always start a good plan when you wanted one" (p. 107). The acknowledgement of Jim's intelligence, even when forthcoming, is accompanied by the inevitable racial qualifier, suggesting that Huck cannot, or will not, see the simple truth about Jim that his works of praise point to.

While we may wince at Huck's racist condescension, we should also reflect on the clear suggestion that Jim nourishes this attitude in order that he may exploit the blindness that accompanies it. Jim's maneuvering bears the further suggestion that he is from the very outset uneasy with Huck, alert to his acquiescence in the ideology of the slave system, and aware that the boy's best intentions are only half of a perilously divided sensibility. It is hardly surprising that Jim should feel this way; events certainly bear him out. Indeed, it would be surprising if he did not observe all due caution in his dealings with the boy whose good-heartedness does nothing to conceal his acculturation to white ways of thinking. When Jim reluctantly admits the truth to Huck—"I—I *run off*"—he cannot fail to perceive the shock of disapproval in Huck's response: "Jim!" (p. 52). And that is why he is so cautious with Huck, so careful to confirm the boy's prejudiced expectations before moving carefully, imperceptibly beyond them.

But not carefully and imperceptibly enough. For if Huck's initial response to Jim's penchant for interpretation is more or less tolerant skepticism, not much time has passed before his resistance develops a sharper edge. Huck takes pride in his won acuity when it comes to reading signs, and he reacts with gathering resentment to Jim's implicit challenge. This response is clear in a discussion of Judith Loftus, the kindly woman who penetrates Huck's disguise, but who also alerts him to the danger approaching Jackson's Island.

I told Jim all about the time I had jabbering with that woman; and Jim said she was a smart one, and if *she* was to start after us herself *she* wouldn't set down and watch a camp fire—no, sir, she'd fetch a dog. Well, then, I said, why couldn't she tell her husband to fetch a dog? Jim said he bet she did think of it by the time the men was ready to start, and he believed they must a gone up town to get a dog and so they lost all that time, or else we wouldn't be here on a tow-head sixteen or seventeen mile below the village—no, indeedy, we would be in that same old town again. So I said I didn't care what the reason they didn't get us, as long as they didn't. (pp. 77-78)

The boy's delight in his narrative of adventure and shrewd detection suffers a setback when Jim begins to supplement the story with his own inferences. Huck's resentment is immediately audible in the direct, challenging question that follows his brusque "Well, then." Jim, in turn, seems deaf to Huck's tone. Perhaps the momentum of his insight propels him, all heedless, past the warning; perhaps he credits Huck with a capacity to absorb this challenge. In either case, he forges ahead confidently ("no, indeedy") and plausibly, clearly overpowering Huck with the force of his interpretation, but in the process backing the boy into a mood of silent, sullen defiance ("I didn't care"). In a world where blacks are expected to be amiably dull, Jim has been too obviously smart for his own good.

It may be that conflict between the fugitives in this matter of interpretation is inevitable. Huck and Jim are remarkably alike in their intelligence and articulateness, and in the pleasure they take from testing their wits against the riddling surface of the world. But they are utterly, fatally divided against each other by Huck's incapacity to recognize, let alone acknowledge, Jim's intelligence. This barrier to respect and understanding arises from the heart of the slave ideology, and we should not be surprised when all of Jim's provident diplomatic maneuvering fails to avert a breakdown. Viewed in this light, it is entirely appropriate that a snake should first lead Huck to Jim, and that the continuing struggle for supremacy in the reading of signs should come to focus on what to make of snakeskins. It is equally appropriate, and mordantly ironic, that the old betrayer should reappear in the narrative immediately in the wake of the house of death. Huck wants "to talk about the dead man and guess out how he come to be killed, but Jim didn't want to" (p. 63). Preferring for obvious reasons to avoid this dangerously compromised subject, Jim retreats to what passes for superstition, but what is—like the rest of what he offers up as superstition—a strategic gesture, in this case an evasion. Such speculation "would fetch bad luck," he insists, and Huck draws back momentarily. But when they find eight dollars hidden in the lining of a coat taken off the wreck, Huck's native relish for reading signs, given an added edge perhaps by Jim's uncharacteristic reluctance to try his hand, prompts a direct assault on the foundation of Jim's position.

"Now you think it's bad luck; but what did you say when I fetched in the snake-skin that I found on the top of the ridge day before yesterday? You said it was the worst bad luck in the world to touch a snake-skin with my hands. Well, here's your bad luck! We've raked in all this truck and eight dollars besides. I wish we could have some bad luck like this every day, Jim."

"Never you mind, honey, never you mind. Don't you git too peart. It's a-comin'. Mind I tell you, it's a-comin'." (p. 63)

Perhaps Jim's response is no more that a retreat into dogmatism; more likely, it records a glimpse of the trouble beginning to emerge, inevitably, irresistibly, from his dissimulation about Pap, and ultimately from the cruelly alienating slave system itself, which makes that concealment necessary, makes escape virtually impossible, and hopelessly undermines the movements of goodness between black people and white. Perhaps he sees that the snake is with them on the raft, hidden, but at large now, and coiled to strike.

The first strike follows almost immediately, when Huck plants a dead rattlesnake at the foot of Jim's bed, "thinking there'd be some fun when Jim found him there" (p. 64). The joke backfires when the snake's mate arrives and nearly kills poor Jim. This "mistake" springs directly from Huck's incapacity to sit comfortably with Jim's accomplishments in the reading of signs. Rather than acknowledge what is obvious, the boy resorts to spiteful jokes designed to betray the gullibility and superstition of racial inferior. Instead, and quite ironically, the joke's outcome is testimony to Jim's stunning clairvoyance, and serves to underscore Huck's credulous attachment to empty racial stereotypes. It also illustrates what I have elsewhere described as "bad faith," the deception of self and others in the denial of violations of public ideals of truth and justice. Such departures are frequently group phenomena, collaborative denials, and bear with them the clear implication that people will sometimes permit or acquiesce in what they cannot approve, so long as their complicity is submerged in a larger, tacit consensus. It is a telling feature of acts of bad faith that they incorporate silent prohibitions against the acknowledgement that they have occurred—denial is itself denied. I recognize that bad faith may in some forms be socially beneficial, working to mitigate rigid customs and laws; but I emphasize that in Mark Twain's America the most conspicuous brand of bad faith is race-slavery, a glaring, almost unbearable contradiction in a Christian democracy. Against this background, I argue that *Huckleberry Finn* illustrates, at several levels, the desperate problems that issue from bad faith acquiescence in racism and slavery. Huck's practical joke is obviously one such violation of truth and justice. And his bad faith is even more graphically manifest in his decision, once Jim is through the worst of the pain and danger, to slip out and throw "the snakes clear away amongst the bushes; for I warn't going to let Jim find out it was my fault, not if I could help it" (p. 65). Huck inwardly acknowledges that he is directly at "fault" for Jim's suffering. Quite as clearly, he is ashamed of himself, for he gets rid of the dead snakes with the intent of hiding his moral lapse from Jim. As subsequent developments show, however, he is also hiding from himself. Before long, on those numerous occasions when he is reminded of the snakes, Huck notes that they have been the source of much bad luck, but neglects to acknowledge his own agency in the shifts of fortune. This denial is at the dark center of Huck's bad faith, and confirms his acculturation to the twisted logic of race-slavery. He never tells the truth about the snakes; and he appears to succeed in forgetting the painful truth about himself, and about his relationship to Jim, that the episode betrays. Of course, the denial of the deed is more potent for harm than the deed itself; the deed is done, but its denial is the next thing to a guarantee that it will be repeated. And it is repeated, again and again, right through to the novel's end, when Huck runs one more time, quite hopelessly I think, from the bad faith civilization in himself.

◆

Working against this larger cultural background, it remains to complete the analysis of Jim's maneuvering for survival, as we may glimpse it, most often obliquely, within the web of deception and concealment that the culture—and the narrative—casts around him. Most crucially, we have determined that he is neither as gullible nor as passive nor as stupidly good-natured as the stereotype of the slave would have him. On the contrary, it is one measure of his estimable resourcefulness that he contrives to turn this stereotype to his own advantage. He maneuvers behind the mask that the white oppressors, in bad faith denial of their fear and guilt, have thrust upon him. He is, we have seen, a master of self-interested simulation and dissimulation, though it is clear as well—most especially in his ultimate disclosure about Pap—that he is not deceived by his own acts of deception. We may now advance a step further in this line of analysis, to observe that while Jim is not the fool of his own acts of deception, he is not blind to the fact that other people—most often white people—are. Indeed, there is evidence that this insight into the dynamics of the culture of race-slavery serves him as the basis for subtle, often very effective manipulation. But it is also clear that Jim's penetration, especially as it applies to Huck, is won at a considerable price in humiliation and danger.

This developing dimension in Jim's perspective may be glimpsed in his periodic references to the bad luck brought on by Huck's handling of the snakeskin. Rather than expel this painful episode from memory, Jim clings to it, drawing upon it to raise the specter of imminent disaster, and to assign the disaster a specific cause. Thus a few days after the nearly fatal "joke," Huck vows that he "wouldn't ever take aholt of a snake-skin again with my hands, now that I see what had come of it. Jim said he reckoned I would believe him next time. And he said that handling a snake-skin was such awful bad luck that maybe we hadn't got to the end of it yet" (p. 65). At one level, such remarks are persistent reminders of Jim's apparently superstitious investment in the interpretation of signs. But they also serve to remind Huck in a most direct and painful way of his hand in Jim's suffering. In effect, Jim's remarks interpose an obstacle to Huck's bad faith denial. How conscious is Jim of this dimension to their exchange? To what extent is he consciously playing along with Huck's bad faith denial in order that he may, in a self-interested way, manipulate the guilt behind it? The answer to this question hangs on our assessment of Jim's penetration into Huck's responsibility for the snakes; and the evidence on this score is hardly adequate to a confident response. For myself, I suspect that Jim has had intimations of the dark truth behind his suffering. He may have been stirred to a vague uneasiness by the coincidence of the snake's advent with Huck's resolute views on bad luck; and the sudden, unexplained disappearance of the dead snakes may not have escaped his notice. In short, there may be a trace of suspicion in Jim's remarks, and even some preliminary testing of the hidden leverage that this dawning insight affords.

But if there is a hint of suspicion here, it is a rather faint one. The best evidence in this score is Jim's subsequent failure to behave in a manner compatible with anything even approaching a clear awareness of the truth about the snakes. This truth will be difficult for him to bear, and therefore to see, in part perhaps because he cares for Huck, but much more vitally because he has staked his life and freedom on Huck's wavering fidelity. Whatever the case, Jim does not draw back from the nearly fatal snakebite into deep suspicion of his companion. On the contrary, he is confident, not to say incautious, in his reading of Judith Loftus, and perfectly foolhardy in aggressively advancing his views on King Solomon, and on the propriety of human beings speaking French. Jim cannot know that Huck reacts by withdrawing to a sullen rehearsal of the familiar, self-indulgent lie about Jim's racial inferiority. "You can't learn a nigger to argue," Huck reflects, "so I quit" (p. 98). Equally familiar, of course, is the irony that undercuts Huck's angry conclusion. For the intelligence that he spitefully denies to Jim has in fact been manifest in the foregoing argument; indeed, it is Jim's quite impressive display of intellect that prompts the retreat to sullen, silent denial. It is Huck, obviously, and not Jim, who fails in the business of argument.

In what must seem an entirely appropriate manifestation of the gathering but unspoken trouble between them, Huck and Jim are next separated in a fog that carries them past Cairo and the junction with the Ohio River. Jim cannot know that his argumentative agility has dangerously rekindled his companion's resentment. Thus he is unprepared for the trick that Huck springs when he finds Jim asleep in the midst of the "leaves and branches and dirt" (p. 102) that have collected on deck during the long night's passage. Jim awakens in a mood of delight and gratitude over his friend's safe return; Huck responds by persuading Jim that his memory of the fog is no more than a dream—and a dream in need of interpretation. Quite clearly, of course, the trick is yet another designed to expose the gullibility and superstition that are, Huck assumes, the expression of Jim's imagined racial inferiority. This time, though, once the cruel joke has been played, Jim recognizes the snake for what it is. You are trash he tells Huck, a person "dat puts dirt on de head er dey fren's en makes 'em ashamed." Huck continues, contritely:

It was fifteen minutes before I could work myself up to go and humble myself to a nigger—but I done it, and I warn't ever sorry for it afterwards, neither. I didn't do him no more mean tricks, and I wouldn't done that one if I'd a knowed it would make him feel that way. (p. 105)

Huck is terribly self-deceived in his assessment of the situation. His apology, though appropriate, is woefully inadequate as a stay against his ambivalent feelings toward Jim. The trouble is writ large in his sense that he has humbled himself not to his friend, but "to a nigger." And it is transparent bad faith denial to insist that he would have forgone the trick had he properly anticipated Jim's reaction. Huck knew the trick would humiliate Jim; that was the point in playing it. What he did not anticipate was that Jim would respond to the offense with a sharp, dignified rebuke. Huck was unprepared to hear the truth about his cruel joking. But his bad faith is most graphically evident in his declaration that "I didn't do him no more mean tricks." This characterization of what follows overlooks a great deal, not least the decision, in the next chapter, to break his promise to keep Jim's secret.

Much critical comment to the contrary notwithstanding, this episode does not mark a decisive shift in Huck's attitude toward Jim. The "trash" joke is pretty much business as usual; and the strain of bad faith running through his apology is clearly reminiscent of his concealment of the responsibility for the snakes. But the episode *is* decisive in Jim's development, for it is the first and perhaps the only time that he gives direct expression to his feelings. He approaches this moment with great circumspection, reflecting in silence for five minutes before offering his interpretation, and then setting forth a reading of the "dream" that gives clues to the considerations that initially gave him pause.

Jim feels obligated to "terpret" the "dream" because, he says, "it was sent for a warning." Such warnings surface constantly, he insists, and "if we didn't try hard to make out to understand them they'd just take us into bad luck, 'stead of keeping us out of it." And what do the signs say to Jim? They speak to him of the "troubles we was going to get into with quarrelsome people and all kinds of mean folks." But, he goes on, "if we minded our business and didn't talk back and aggravate them, we would pull through and get out of the fog and into the big clear river, which was the free States, and wouldn't have no more trouble" (p. 104). There are few if any god signs, and the "troubles" that Jim sees all attach to "quarrelsome people" and "mean folks," which is to say, to white people in general, those potential and real enemies who must be avoided whenever possible, and agreed with and coddled when necessary, if he is to have any chance of success.

Clearly, these are not the sentiments of a deeply superstitious man. Bad luck for Jim is not blind; rather it is blindness to signs—signs that yield to interpretation—that gives the turn to fortune. Jim's interpretation is a shrewd assessment of the hostile white majority who stand everywhere in his way, and an equally shrewd program for avoiding and evading them. In the service of this objective, Jim will be invisible, or else two-dimensional, a gullible, docile, goodnatured "darky." Quite on purpose, quite by design, Jim takes refuge in the stereotype, in the mask, of the smiling, superstitious, utterly harmless black "yes-man."

Jim pauses at length before venturing his interpretation because he is undecided whether or not he has in fact had a dream. In the mist of other thoughts that may run through his head, this uncertainty about Huck must assume a prominent place. Jim may also give attention to the possible consequences of calling Huck's bluff; and he may find righteous interpretation of righteous indignation, the likely alternative outcomes of going along, more attractive than the small but equally perilous pleasures of flatly declaring Huck a liar. Whatever the case may be, doubt of Huck is at the bottom of Jim's long pause, just as doubt, more broadly of white people, forms the bedrock of his reading of the "dream."

Jim is certainly on the right track in his interpretation, though as subsequent developments strongly suggest, he does not go nearly far enough toward complete skepticism. Willy-nilly, he is virtually forced to call Huck a liar (Huck blithely admits as much); and he is too stung by the revelation of Huck's betrayal, his own blindness, and the cruelty of his fate, to check the overflow of pain and anger. His recoil from the joke, we must suppose, is a moment when deep, genuine feeling breaks through; but we must also recognize, as Jim must in time, that his surrender to authenticity is a grave mistake. For if his words work as a lash to Huck's conscience, then the pain of guilt, subtly transformed by bad faith denial, leads directly to the decision to turn Jim in.

When Jim calls Huck "trash," he indicates that his doubts about his young companion have moved to a new level of resolution. Jim is now the possessor of irresistible evidence that while Huck is at times a great boon, he is equally a part of the terrible trouble. It is quite conceivable that Jim looks back, in the light of this episode, at the encounter with the snakes, and finds ample confirmation for earlier suspicions. Jim may now perceive that the snake has been with him on the raft all along. Most clearly of all, he now sees that Huck must be numbered with the snags and towheads, with all those "troubles" leading ineluctably back to all those mean, quarrelsome white people who stand in his way.

Not surprisingly, in Jim's next appearance in the narrative he is totally preoccupied with Cairo and the Ohio River and the prospect of freedom. No doubt he is buoyed up by his recent moral victory; but his almost frantic animation suggests that a measure of panic, the issue of freshly confirmed fears, is also at large in his mood. Huck, meanwhile, just as borne down by his abrupt, crushing humiliation, has displaced his misery in spasms of conscience over Jim's behavior, and in a cozy commitment to do right by poor Miss Watson. Buoyed up in turn and feeling "light as a feather" in his evasion of guilt, and in the pious rationalization of his urge to put the uppity slave back in his place, Huck prepares to leave the raft, ostensibly to inquire about Cairo, in fact to betray his friend. Jim senses that something is amiss. Huck's departure, which may remind him of their ill-fated separation in the fog, seems to stir the fears submerged in his rather fervid elation. Suddenly his levitating assertions

of independent initiative give way to declarations of absolute dependence on
Huck and undying gratitude for his faithful friendship.

"Pooty soon I'll be a-shout'n for joy, en I'll say, it's al on accounts o'Huck; I's a free man, en
I couldn't ever ben free ef it hadn' ben for Huck; Huck done it. Jim won't ever forgit you, Huck;
you's de bes' fren' Jim's ever had; en you's de *only* fren' ole Jim's got now." (p. 125)

Not only do these remarks break with the mood of exultant self-assertion that
precedes them, but they sit rather oddly with Jim's recent observations on
"trash." There is, in short, something false about Jim's outpouring of gratitude
and friendship. But such falseness is true in a deeper sense to the features of the
mask of the gullible, optimistic, grateful slave that Jim is obliged to wear. This
simulated identity, he knows, is his best defense against white cruelty and
infidelity. And, of course, it works. Huck fails entirely to perceive the
inaccuracy of Jim's characterization of their relationship, and he fails because
Jim's servile gratitude conforms perfectly to the contours of his bad faith
denial. Huck is comfortable betraying an uppity Jim; but this fawning man-child
so satisfies his fond expectations that (he says) "it seemed to kind of take the
tuck all out of me." His resolution slips even further when Jim continues, "Dah
you goes, de ole true Huck; de on'y white genlman dat ever kep' his promise
to old Jim" (p. 125). It is remarkable that Huck is so ready to accept this
characterization of himself, so proof, in his bad faith, against the powerful
ironies poised in full view on the face of Jim's words. Characteristically, one
of the broadest of these ironies turns on the fact that the innocence, the
gullibility, the hapless surrender to false but grateful illusions, is hardly Jim's.
It is also remarkable that Jim is willing to range so far from the truth in
maneuvering for his safety. Such boldness is a tribute to his acuity in measur-
ing Huck's self-deception, but it is also a mark of desperation. His fear is of
course well founded. He can hardly know that his appeal to Huck's bad faith,
while shrewdly orchestrated, is finally not enough to stop the boy, who goes
reluctantly forward, muttering "I *got* to do it—I can't get *out* of it." But he
must suspect and fear the worst. And he is a witness in terror to the sudden
arrival of the slave hunters, who intercept Huck; he sees, and waits in fear as
Huck pauses, obviously weighing the alternatives, when asked: "Is your man
white or black?" (p. 125). If we imagine that all the drama here is in Huck's
mind, then we miss the even greater tension, the terror verging on blind panic,
that Jim must endure as the boy wavers over an answer. He is of course
perfectly alive to the brilliance of Huck's subsequent evasion of the encroaching predators. But his gratitude must pale before the much darker emotions
that attach to this spectacle of white cruelty and greed. We must imagine that
he is inwardly numb and quivering, a deeply shaken man. He cannot fail to
have noticed the ease and skill with which Huck moves in the terribly fallen
adult world. Huck knows his way around; indeed, were he not much more
adept than the slave hunters at the darkly cynical game, Jim would pay a heavy
price. But Jim sees that the obvious correlative to Huck's intuitive mastery of
adult strategies of deception is an impulse, here only barely restrained, to join
the enemy. Now more clearly than ever Jim perceives that the snakes on
Jackson's Island, and the other serpentine tricks that have pursued him down
the river, are akin in important ways to the varieties of evil manifest in the
slave hunters. As they drift downriver away from this near disaster, but ever
deeper into even graver potential dangers, Jim begins to face the fact that Cairo,

and the slender hope that Cairo holds out, are now behind him. "Maybe we went by Cairo in the fog that night," Huck ventures. Jim replies:

> "Doan' less talk about it, Huck. Po' niggers can't have no luck. I awluz 'spected dat rattle-snake skin warn't done wid its work."
> "I wish I'd never seen dat snake-skin, Jim—I do wish I's never laid eyes on it."
> "It ain't yo' fault, Huck; you didn't know. Don't you blame yo'self 'bout it." (p. 129)

The ironies here are multiple, and quite appropriately, not fully penetrable. Does Huck's regret at having seen the snakeskin bear with it the unspoken acknowledgement of his carefully concealed moral responsibility for the troubles that the snakes brought with them? If so, then Huck suffers exquisitely as Jim tenders his emphatic absolution. Or, alternatively, has Huck's bad faith denial advanced to the point that he is no longer conscious of the guilt that the snakes formerly stirred in him? If this is the case, then the irony is just as painfully at his expense, and equally an index to his immersion in bad faith. In either case, there is a quite extraordinary over-arching irony to be observed—namely, that whether he is conscious of it or not, Huck's bad faith denial leads him into the adoption of precisely that superstitious view of snakes that his original practical joke was designed to expose and ridicule.

Turning to Jim's role in the dialogue, we come upon another, even sharper edge to the irony. For while Huck retreats to transparent bad faith credulousness, Jim maneuvers, in full self-consciousness, behind a mask of simulated superstition. He knows and conceals what Huck does not want to know, and conceals. Jim does this because he is aware that anything approaching a full disclosure of Huck's actual role would threaten a break in the slender thread of hope that their troubled friendship holds out. Thus he opts for the appearance of tenacious gullibility because it confirms the white stereotype of the slave mentality, and thus plausibly stands in place of the truth—about Jim's humanity and suffering and rage, and about his young friend's spiteful racist malice—none of which Huck can bear to acknowledge, least of all to Jim, and at Jim's bidding. Huck denies the truth about the snakes because he cannot bear it; Jim is denying it too, because he recognizes that for a slave in the twisted moral world of race-slavery, the truth can only exacerbate the already terrible trouble. Meanwhile, if it gives him some consolation to look on as Huck squirms in bad faith, it is, we must suppose, a slender, bitter reward. For in assuring Huck that "it ain't yo' fault," he is telling the boy exactly what he wants to hear, and to believe.

Huck's subsequent observations on the snakes do not clearly resolve the question of the level of his consciousness in bad faith. But it is telling that the words are not shared with Jim. Rather, they are a silent resolution, advanced in the name of necessity and rooted in superstition, to keep silence on the score of snakeskins. "We both knowed well enough," he reports, when the raft and canoe disappear during the night, that "it was some more work of the rattle-snake skin; so what was the use to talk about it? It would only look like we was finding fault, and that would be bound to fetch more bad luck—and keep on fetching it, too, till we knowed enough to keep still" (p. 130). This ostensible surrender to superstitious necessity imperfectly conceals Huck's deep, desperate wish to be free of bad faith as it twists and tears in him. His outward submission is in fact a blind plea. But so long as he continues to deny in bad faith the truth about his treatment of Jim, that truth will continue to haunt him and to elude him. For that long he will continue to violate Jim without fully

knowing it, he will continue to run without getting anywhere, and, if he is
Mark Twain, he will continue to write this dark story without ever being able
to finish it. For Jim, meanwhile, bound as he is to a kind of silent complicity
in this accelerating cycle, there is no obvious way to avert almost inevitable
disaster.

It is over this complex spectacle of errant human suffering that the monstrous steamboat sweeps at the end of chapter 16. It comes clearly, if rather
obliquely, in judgment of the godforsaken raft; but it comes as well as an
agency of relief—of brief, bad faith oblivion to the terrible trouble at the heart
of Mark Twain's story. Here the teller set his masterpiece aside for several
years. And here Jim is separated from Huck. For awhile at least, they can go
no further.

◆

The reunion of the fugitives after the feud section in chapters 17-18 is clear
evidence that Jim feels more secure with Huck's company on the raft than he
does without it. Huck may be trouble, but he is also intermittently a vital
resource. At the same time, Jim is chastened and cautious in rejoining Huck,
and displays a resolve to retreat behind a mask of silence and unquestioning
compliance. We see and hear much less of Jim in the remainder of the
novel. To an extent, of course, this is because the action turns away from him;
but he is also quite markedly inclined to turn away from the action when it
comes his way. Jim has tried being "visible" and frank, opinionated, assertive,
even argumentative with Huck, and the invariable result has been trouble. He
has come to see that Huck, for all of his good nature, is quite unprepared to
tolerate the full unfolding of the human being emergent from behind the mask
of the happy, gullible, rather childlike slave. At no little price in suffering and
danger, Jim finally learns to apply to Huck the formula that he earlier advocated
for relations with all mean and quarrelsome white people: "if we minded our
business and didn't talk back and aggravate them, we would pull through"
(p. 104).

The evidence for this shift in Jim's behavior, and in the modified perspective to which it gives rise, is generally so clear and consistent that it requires
little comment. When there is another occasion (in chapter 19) to disagree about
the interpretation of signs in the fog, Jim withdraws into silence. When Huck
conceals the truth about the king and the duke, Jim is not fooled, but he is
careful to test the evidence without betraying his own suspicions.[16] Of course,
Jim has good reason to be wary of the charlatans. From the very beginning it
is clear that they have in mind to turn a quick profit by selling him into
captivity. Jim knows this; and he tries to draw Huck more fully to his side,
suggesting that the aristocrats are really frauds, and then by dramatizing in an
oblique way the terrible injustice and pathos of his circumstances.[17] But Huck
cannot, or will not, hear, primarily because his own secrets make him hostage
to the confidence-men. Jim is certainly well aware of Huck's reluctance to
abandon the king and the duke, and he seems to have glimpsed the furtive
self-interest upon which it rests. Thus he endures without protest the increasingly dangerous conditions that the scheming frauds impose upon him. His terror
and hopeless frustration must be extreme.[18]

Later on, as the Wilks episode unfolds, Huck has so much "on" the king
and the duke that he feels unthreatened by them, and is thus prepared to lay

plans for getting "rid of the frauds." Unfortunately, and as the heartless sale
of the Wilks's slaves serves to suggest, it is too little too late.[19] This can
scarcely surprise Jim. He has seen the trouble coming, just as he sees it coming
again in Tom Sawyer's self-indulgent parody of race-slavery. Jim is of course
much more alert to the danger of Tom's "evasion" than either of his saviors,
but he is also by now seasoned to the extremes of white mindlessness and
cruelty, as he is no doubt prepared for Huck's passive acquiescence in the
really dangerous game. Through it all, his resistance is carefully restrained; if
there is any hope at all, he knows, it is in silent, smiling compliance with the
oppressors. This is quite evidently the strategy behind his decision to stay and
seek help rather than run away when Tom is wounded. He knows too well that
running with Huck will do no good; so he adopts the only course of action
open to him, and behaves as the white people expect him to. Jim is so masterful
in taking his part that the doctor is moved to declare, "he ain't a bad nigger,"
and Huck reflects to himself that "he was white inside" (pp. 352, 341).

The irony in these absurd concessions will strike us as more or less gross
depending on our penetration into Jim's point of view. If we recognize that he
is perfectly self-conscious in adopting the selfless role that Huck and the doctor
so admire, then we will have a window not only on Jim's characterization, but
also on the deep trouble that Mark Twain raised in his novel and then
evaded. If we imagine, on the other hand, that Jim is internally as self-effacing
and compliant as Huck and the doctor take him to be—and expect him to
be—then we will miss this irony, along with many others, and join Jim's
enormous audience of unreflecting admirers in the dark web of the problem.

Jim's virtual invisibility is the correlative, at the level of audience response,
of the fact that his small triumphs as a simulated "darky" have no positive
impact on his final liberation, and may in fact work against it. Though his
calculated retreats into compliance with white expectations earn him brief
reprieves, they bring him no closer to freedom. To be sure, his earlier appeals
to the "white genlman" Huck, his "*only* fren'," seem to pay off in chapter 31,
when the boy gratefully remembers Jim's words as he moves toward his
decision to steal him out of slavery. But this apparent advance in Jim's fortunes
is entirely illusory. Huck's heroic resolve quickly dissipates into passive
compliance with Tom's selfish and very dangerous exploitation of the
opportunity for adventure that his old friend casts in his way. Thanks to the
grand "evasion," Jim is nearly killed before he has the chance to enjoy the
freedom that Tom neglects to mention, and that Huck seems only half-heartedly
interested in pursuing. Jim is finally free not because he successfully out-
maneuvers his enemies, but as the result of an utterly implausible circumstance
of plot. Indeed, we may go even further in this direction to observe that while
Jim is forced for his survival into the role of a happy, harmless "darky," this
necessary retreat yields short range dividends only at the heavy price of
confirming the stereotype that his white oppressors first enforce and then prey
upon. It is the cruelest irony of all that Jim's obligatory denial of the injustice
he endures contributes to the continued life and increasing weight of that same
intolerable offense. Bad faith thus imposes a bitterly knowing version of itself
upon its victims.

This grimly ironic pattern is recapitulated in an audience response that fails
to look past Jim's docile exterior, that construes his smiling compliance as
evidence that he is either flawed as a character or "white inside," and that
regards his freedom as a reward, conferred somehow by Huck, for exemplary

deportment. Such a response—far and away the most common response—fails entirely to recognize that Jim's characterization, his behavior as it is represented in the novel, makes perfectly good sense as the adaptation of a runaway slave to the special circumstances he encounters on board the raft and along the river.[20] The failure to get and keep a hold on this perfectly plausible human being is symptomatic of the much broader cultural evasion that the novel so brilliantly dramatizes. If we fail to follow Jim behind the mask, if we fault Mark Twain for the inconsistency of his portrait, and for inserting a two-dimensional stick figure in the place of a man, then we have failed to recognize the really awesome authority of our culture as it informs the racist conventions governing the representation of blacks in Mark Twain's time and since, and the conventions governing the reception of such figures during the same period. This response marks us as bearers of the culture, rooted deeply in the bad faith contradictions of race-slavery, that has found its premier agent in Mark Twain, and its leading popular expression in *Huckleberry Finn*, the nation's favorite book about its most painful and enduring dilemma.

We return again and again to *Huckleberry Finn* not only because it permits us to ignore as much of the truth about race-slavery as we cannot bear to see, but also because in enabling our bad faith denial—a brand of denial clearly cognate with those dramatized in the novel itself—*Huckleberry Finn* leaves us with the uneasy feeling that we have missed something, and thereby ensures that we well return for another look. One such perpetual oversight—and surely a kind of key to all the others—is the character Jim I have labored to reach in this essay. But the image of the happy, gullible, superstitious "darky" can never be fully separated from its background in injustice and cruelty and suffering, and from the pressure of resistance behind the bland, smiling face. That separation cannot occur in spite of the fact—and perhaps finally because of the fact—that such a separation is the urgent cultural objective toward which the formation and wide reception of that image move. The stereotype that informs Jim was conceived in the unconscious wish that it might draw attention away from the disagreeable tendency of its human model to suffer pain and to resent it; but the trace of that submerged dimension is present, at the very least by conspicuous absence, in the bland, selfless, almost mindless figure who appears at intervals toward the end of Mark Twain's novel. Prima facie the stereotype is incomplete. If we are willing to press against our first impressions of the text, we find that a fuller, much more plausible human figure is present by nearly palpable implication in the two-dimensional mask. But the character also gives us more than we are initially prepared to see; and if we are willing to move further in this direction, we find that the two-dimensional figure has roots, submerged but within reach of recovery, in the bad faith cultural dynamics of our own response. Thus by becoming more attentive to the curve of Jim's development, from a kind of tentative candor and completeness to virtual submergence in the minstrel figure, we are well positioned to learn something about the complex dynamics of his apparent transformation, and about the cultural construction of the role he retreats to.

NOTES

1. As quoted in Sculley Bradley et al., eds., *Adventures of Huckleberry Finn* (New York: Norton, 1977), p. 294.

2. Marx, "Mr. Eliot, Mr. Trilling, and *Huckleberry Finn*," *The American Scholar*, 22 (1953), 430; Smith, *Mark Twain: The Development of a Writer* (Cambridge, Mass.: Harvard Univ. Press, 1962), p. 134; Sawicki, "Authority/Author-ity: Representation and Fictionality in *Huckleberry Finn*," *Modern Fiction Studies*, 31 (1985), 698.

3. "Twain, *Huckleberry Finn*, and the Reconstruction." *American Studies*, 12 (1971), 61, 64, 60.

4. *Narrative of the Life of Frederick Douglass* (New York: Signet, 1968), pp. 35-37.

5. *Black Culture and Black Consciousness: Afro-American Folk Thought from Slavery to Freedom* (New York: Oxford Univ. Press, 1977), pp. 97-101.

6. "Change the Joke and Slip the Yoke," *Partisan Review*, 25 (1958), 215-16.

7. Ellison, "Change the Joke," p. 216.

8. "A Hard Book to Take," in *One Hundred Years of "Huckleberry Finn": The Boy, His Book, and American Culture*, ed. Robert Sattelmeyer and J. Donald Crowley (Columbia: Univ. of Missouri Press, 1985), pp. 389, 395, 401.

9. Several other critics offer insights into Jim's characterization that overlap with some of the points advanced here. Neil Schmitz, in his often brilliant *Of Huck and Alice: Humorous Writing in American Literature* (Minneapolis: Univ. of Minnesota Press, 1983), observes that Huck and Jim are each "other's alibi"; he adds that Jim's "childishness . . . is largely the product of Huck's childish point of view, which requires Jim's genial sufferance of pranks and abuse." Most crisply of all, he insists that "there is another Jim beside Huck's Jim in the ample scan of Huck's writing" (p. 114). I should add that Schmitz and I move from very different points of critical departure, and make different general sense of *Huckleberry Finn*. As a result, the similarities in our perspectives almost always appear in combination with significant differences. Thus, for example, I can agree that Jim's "childishness" is to an extent "the product of . . . Huck's point of view"; but I do not find that this is "largely" the case, nor would I characterize Huck's point of view as "childish." Rhett S. Jones's "Nigger and Knowledge: White Double-Consciousness in *Adventures of Huckleberry Finn*" is one of the many very valuable contributions in the special issue of the *Mark Twain Journal*, 22 (1984), devoted to critical commentary by black scholars. Jones is concerned, as I am, with the complex relationships between culture, characterization, and the novel's reception. At points his argument anticipates mine; at others we agree on the questions to be asked, but differ, in varying degrees, in answering them. Several of the essays in this special issue address themselves to the ironies and ambiguities that attach to *Huckleberry Finn*, and in this their commentary often intersects with that advanced here. I am also aware of Harold Beaver's bold, intermittently stimulating essay, "Run Nigger, Run: *Adventures of Huckleberry Finn* as a Fugitive Slave Narrative," *Journal of American Studies*, 8 (1974), 339-61. Beaver is possessed of numerous insights and hunches, many of them springing from the connection that informs his title. But his essay is so impressionistic and unsystematic, so loose in its movement back and forth between literature and history, and so prone to exaggeration and fanciful analogy, that its value is very substantially compromised.

10. Cox, "A Hard Book to Take," p. 391.

11. *Adventures of Huckleberry Finn*, ed. Walter Blair and Victor Fischer (Berkeley: Univ. of California Press, 1985), p. 93. Hereafter references to this edition are cited parenthetically in the text.

12. Huck's susceptibility to loneliness and his fear of solitude are familiar enough. For one analysis among many, see my essay, "The Silences in *Huckleberry Finn*," *Nineteenth-Century Fiction*, 37 (1982), 50-74.

13. Robert Shulman, following Kenneth Lynn, offers the most recent version of this position in "Fathers, Brothers, and 'the Diseased': The Family, Individualism, and American society in *Huck Finn*," in *One Hundred Years of "Huckleberry Finn*," ed. Sattelmeyer and Crowley, pp. 325-40.

14. Spencer Brown seems to have been the first to make this point. See his "Huckleberry Finn for Our Time," *The Michigan Quarterly Review*, 6 (1967), 45.

15. *In Bad Faith: The Dynamics of Deception in Mark Twain's America* (Cambridge, Mass.: Harvard Univ. Press, 1986), pp. 111-211.

16. Jim asks the king to speak French, and finds—as he must have expected to find—that the old fraud cannot (p. 176).

17. See my analysis of Jim's indirect appeal in chapter 23 (*In Bad Faith*, pp. 167-71).

18. In chapter 24 Jim describes his solitary condition on board the raft as "laying tied a couple of years every day and trembling all over every time there was a sound" (p. 204).

19. It is noteworthy that Jim turns the charlatans in before Huck is able to stop him. We are impressed, of course, with the boy's subsequent dismay at the spectacle of their suffering on the rail. But we should be mindful that Huck wants to constrain Jim not in order to spare the king and the duke suffering, but because he is afraid that they will take revenge by betraying his presence and illegitimate claim to Jim. As he puts it, "I wanted to stop Jim's mouth till these fellows could get away. I didn't want no trouble with their kind. I'd seen all I wanted to of them, and wanted to get entirely shut of them" (p. 275).

20. It fails as well to recognize that Jim, once free, is restored to the mood of confident assertiveness and candor that we witness earlier in chapters 8-16.

ADVENTURES OF HUCKLEBERRY FINN

TOM QUIRK

In 1988, CSE approved editions of *Moby-Dick* and *Adventures of Huckleberry Finn* were published. If these novels stand as monuments of our literature, these editions of them serve as massive, even bulky, evidence of cooperative and exhaustive scholarly effort—of the some two thousand pages of these two editions, more than half are devoted to the textual commentary. In the case of *Huckleberry Finn*, we have, in addition to the novel itself, a treasure trove of supplementary documentary material—accurate and instructive maps of that portion of the Mississippi River related to the novel; a glossary (we learn at last the meanings of "allycumpain" and "pat juba"); ample and illuminating explanatory notes (particularly instructive on the sources of folklore in the novel and the objects of Twain's satire); a meticulous list of alterations in the manuscript; photographic facsimiles of his working notes and of the revised proofs he used for public readings; and reproductions of publisher's advertisements for *Huckleberry Finn*. We have reproduced as well the obscene illustration of Uncle Silas that caused Twain so much aggravation (and cost him time and money as well) and no doubt caused the culprit who defaced the plate an equal glee.

The general introduction sets forth the stages of composition of the book. Twain began Huck's "Autobiography" the summer of 1876. That summer he wrote the first sixteen chapters (minus half of chapter 12 and all of chapters 13 and 14), then, in evident frustration with the way his story was developing, pigeonholed the manuscript. He returned to it in 1879-80 and completed chapters 17 and 18, and he appears to have worked intermittently on chapters 19-21 in 1881 or 1882. In any event, by the late spring of 1883 he had completed those chapters and in a final, eruptive burst of composition wrote the remaining twenty-two chapters as well as the interpolated portion of chapter 12 and chapters 13 and 14 in only a few months. Thanks to Walter Blair's earlier sleuthing, we have known the general contours of the genesis for some time. Nothing substantial is added to the account he gave in his 1958 essay or his much fuller treatment in *Mark Twain and Huck Finn* (1960), though a forthcoming article by Victor Fischer will evidently show that Twain wrote chapters 19-21 in more of a piecemeal fashion than was once thought. The textual introduction, on the other hand, gives a fresh accounting of the circuitous and complex paths the ms. took before it was eventually published, in the American edition, on 18 February 1885. It discusses, among other things, Twain's on again off again thoughts about serializing *Huckleberry Finn*, his plans to publish it in a matched set with *Tom Sawyer*, his irritations with Charlie Webster over canvassing arrangements and promotion, his dissatisfactions with E. W. Kemble's early drawings for the novel, and his acquiescence in the editing of those portions that were published in the *Century Magazine* (he fully expected such editing for a magazine audience and gave his full consent to it).

The only controversial aspect of this authorized edition is the editors' decision to restore the "raft episode," first published in *Life on the Mississippi*. When Twain was contemplating selling *Huckleberry Finn* and *Tom Sawyer* as a matched set, and partly in response to the urgings of Webster and Howells, he decided it best to leave the raft episode out of the novel due to the substantial difference in the lengths of the two books. This plan eventually proved unprofitable and was abandoned, but by that time *Huckleberry Finn* was well along in production and no illustrations were drawn for the raft episode, and no type was set for it. Nor did Twain consider making the chapter divisions that would have been necessary to include it in the novel—as it stands in the present edition chapter 16 is more than twice as long as any other chapter and the John Harley illustrations from *Life on the Mississippi* used for that part of the book interrupt the quality and continuity of the Kemble drawings in the remaining text. Apart from these distractions, however, the inclusion of the raft episode ought not be too disturbing. We may, if we choose, teach the episode out of the book, just as, before, some of us taught it into the book. A more interesting and amusingly ironic implication of the now definitive edition of *Huckleberry Finn* is that the text that has been canonized is not the same text that has now been sanctioned. Unless they happened to read *Huckleberry Finn* in DeVoto's Viking Portable edition of Mark Twain (which also included the raft episode), our cultural literati have likely not yet read the book that has become so securely enshrined in the American canon. In any event, the determinations of textual editors and the speculations of literary theorists are often likely to find themselves in conflict or, more surprisingly, in agreement, and this new edition may spark renewed interest in a book which is perpetually interesting. Meantime, the volume at hand is remarkably satisfying not only because it is handsome and superbly edited, but because it gives us that much more of a book of which, it seems, we can never have enough, and about which we always want to know more.

MARK TWAIN AND THE FIRES OF CONTROVERSY: TEACHING RACIALLY-SENSITIVE LITERATURE: OR, "SAY THAT 'N' WORD AND OUT YOU GO!"

JOCELYN CHADWICK-JOSHUA

I do not believe I would very cheerfully help a white student who would ask benevolence of a stranger, but I do not feel so about the other color. We have ground the manhood out of them, & the shame is ours, not theirs; & we should pay for it. (Mark Twain)

The Problem:

If this novel [*The Adventures of Huckleberry Finn*] is so good for our children and is supposed to make them more aware of racial injustice, then why are we here? This book has done nothing but make my children uncomfortable and embarrassed (a concerned parent during the Plano ISD board hearing on the issue of banning Twain's book from the required reading list).
　　Twain's books punctured some of the pretenses of the romantic Old South. The character Jim in *Huckleberry Finn*, which was published in 1884, is considered one of the best portraits in American fiction of an unlettered slave clinging to the hope of freedom.[1]

　　The controversy in Plano ISD (December 1990) reflects a national concern that causes students, parents, administrators, and even educators themselves to wrestle with accusations of racial insensitivity and outright racism. Even scholars have begun to re-examine not their academic support of works like Twain's *Huck Finn* but their ethical and academic responsibility and accountability for teaching this and other works like it. Scholars such as Wayne C. Booth in his *The Company We Keep: An Ethics of Fiction*, Bernard Bell's "Twain's 'Nigger' Jim: The Tragic Face Behind the Minstrel Mask," Leslie Fiedler's "*Huckleberry Finn*: The Book We Love to Hate," and Stephen Railton's "Jim and Mark Twain," reflect this dialectical process. But while the analysis progresses onward on a scholarly level, the students and parents and even classroom teachers are left in a lurch, trying to discover meaning, direction, and quality learning experiences for their children and students.
　　This paper proposes to examine these two disparate perspectives of Mark Twain's *The Adventures of Huckleberry Finn* as racially sensitive literature. And indeed, one must ask is this work as well as others like it racially sensitive, racist, or simply ambivalent to racial issues. Since its publication in 1884 *The Adventures of Huckleberry Finn* has been the catalyst for debates on racism. Twain's use of the pejorative *nigger* over two hundred times, his usage of Negro dialect, his depiction of Jim as an uneducated, superstitious, and pliable slave who "appears" to place a significant portion of his fate in the hands of an uneducated white adolescent have contributed to multitudinous complaints made against the novel. These complaints, emanating most often today from middle class African-American students and their parents, reflect a growing concern about how to teach not just this novel but about how to teach other literary pieces that also contain racially-sensitive literature.
　　This issue of teaching racially-sensitive literature is indeed a serious one that heretofore has been overlooked *not* because teachers, who are mostly Euro-American, are insensitive to their student population but because

◆ student populations, themselves, have significantly changed since World War II

♦ America has become an even more ethnically diverse culture with each culture demanding *representative ethnic equity* along with its "American" heritage

♦ high school textbooks have begun on a larger scale to reflect this ethnic trend

♦ the diverse economic class structure of students juxtaposes them with diametrically opposed classes in pieces of fiction, such as the typical suburban middle class African-American adolescent with an uneducated, unlettered, 19th-century slave like Twain's Jim
and

♦ Euro-American and other ethnicities are *historically anemic* and need intellectual prostheses prior to their exposure to any literature that requires students to think critically and problematically

Consequently, some traditionally classic works and artists have over a period of time *proven* themselves to be controversial because of an audience's perception of racist overtones. Works such as *To Kill a Mockingbird*, Twain's *The Adventures of Huckleberry Finn*, Wright's *Native Son*, Hughes' "Dream," and Baldwin's "The Creation" and writers such as Lorraine Hansberry, William Faulkner, and Ralph Ellison, for example, are now being read with the belief that the works foster racial insensitivity or racial stereotyping. Their verisimilitude that has always seemed so undeniably apparent before now at times appear murky, their once relevant and societal themes now racially divisive. How and why could such a metamorphosis occur? When did it occur? And perhaps more importantly, should we continue to argue for the inclusion of such controversial works on high school reading lists?

We must, of course, remember that Twain's *Huck Finn* was controversial from its publication. Even Harriet Beecher Stowe's *Uncle Tom's Cabin: or Life Among the Lowly* was controversial among the African-American population. So what is a teacher to do with students who may or may not be offended by the literature that the state and indeed scholars all over the world identify as "academically approved and societally relevant?"

This paper suggests one approach that will enable teachers and students to:

♦ access literature that may have been considered too sensitive to explore in an open classroom environment

♦ experience the attitudes and reactions of the literary milieu

♦ experience the attitudes and reactions of the actual historical setting into which the work unfolds

♦ learn more about themselves, their American culture, and their ethnic culture

♦ engage in critical inquiry as to a work's literary and historical validity

Being an African-American feminist who has required and would yet require the exploration of works such as *The Adventures of Huckleberry Finn* to high school students, I realized that I bring to the controversy a unique position and perhaps controversial perspective. As I mentioned earlier Wayne C. Booth in his *Ethics of Fiction* has re-evaluated his fervor in requiring Twain's *Huck Finn*. Booth based the necessity for such a reassessment on an African-American colleague's reaction. According to Booth Professor Paul Moses, a respected faculty member said of *Huck Finn*:

It's hard for me to say this, but I have to say it anyway. I simply can't teach *Huckleberry Finn* again. The way Mark Twain portrays Jim is so offensive to me that I get angry in class, and I can't get all those liberal white kids to understand why I am angry. What's more, I don't think it's right to subject students, black or white, to the many distorted views of race on which that book is based. No, it's not the word *nigger* I'm objecting to, it's the whole range of assumptions about slavery and its consequences, and about how whites should deal with liberated slaves, and how liberated slaves should behave or will behave toward whites, good ones and bad ones. That book is just bad education, and the fact that it is so cleverly written makes it even more troublesome to me.

Although Booth yet requires this "great American epic" (Eliot), he asserts, and I must add that I heartily concur, that had Twain realized the moral and ethnical dilemma *Huck Finn* was destined to have caused that Twain himself would have been surprised and " . . . no doubt dismayed, at the floods of moral criticism. . . ."[3] What Twain provides for us as audience is a literary historical paradigm of nineteenth-century slavery and the period immediately following—Reconstruction and the establishment of Jim Crow laws. This paradigm though on the one hand can be understood on a black vs. white level can *not* be understood as such in a 1990's high school setting. This same dichotomous pairing assumes a multi-dimensional framework, and instruction, then, must reflect this metamorphosis. Twain's audience has become Jim's and Huck's and Tom's and Pap's and the lettered professor's great-great-great grandchildren whose parents have quite comfortably "removed" them from those troublesome, unhappy times. Unlike his audience in 1884, as Bernard Bell asserts in "Twain's 'Nigger' Jim: The Tragic Face Behind the Minstrel Mask," who reflects through adolescent Huck a nation confused and vacillating between its moral and ethical responsibilities concerning reconstruction,[4] Twain's contemporary audience, the high school adolescent, views life in general as immediate, microwaveable, faxable, and intensely visual. This audience possesses an inherent "right" to the very educational process that Jim was denied, an inherent "right" to say, go, pursue, and envision whatever it chooses. This audience views actions and their consequences as relative with little or no moral considerations. For example, during one lecture about *Huck Finn* to an advanced junior English class, I asked students how they'd feel if they, like the free Professor whom Pap meets in Chapter 6, had to carry their "papers" on them, documenting their free status. I also added that they needed to realize that under the Missouri Compromise of 1820, a freed slave could remain in this area for up to six months, after paying a fee, or deposit.

[According to Pap Finn] "Call this a govment! why just look at it and see what it's like. . . . Oh, yes, this is a wonderful govment, wonderful. Why, looky here. There was a free nigger there from Ohio—a mulatter, most as white as a white man. He had the whitest shirt on you ever see, too, and the shiniest hat; and there ain't a man in that town that's got as fine clothes as what he had; and he had a gold watch and chain, and a silver-headed cane—the awfulest old gray-headed nabob in the state. And what do you think? They said he was a p'fessor in a college, and could talk all kinds of languages, and knowed everything. And that ain't the wust. They said he could *vote* when he was at home. Well, that let me out. Thinks I, what is this country a-coming to? It was 'lection day, and I was just about to go and vote myself if I warn't too drunk to get there; but when they told me there was a state in this country where they'd let a nigger vote, I drawed out. . . . I says to the people, why ain't this nigger out up at auction and sold? . . . Why, they said he couldn't be sold till he'd been in the state six months, and he hadn't been there that long yet. . . ."[5]

I told students that like the professor they risked recapture at the discretion of unscrupulous slave catchers. If you lost your papers, or if they were taken away from you, I posed, what would you do? What could you do?

True to their nineties milieu and mindset student responses ranged from just simply calling home to mom and dad, to xeroxing a duplicate copy, to having someone fax a copy to them, to responding much like Melville's Bartleby, "I prefer not to," thank you very much. Needless to say these students did not stop at any one time to consider prohibited accessibility, prohibited filial support, prohibited mobility, and just simple slave-state mandated-illiteracy. It is only after students envision this kind of role-playing scenario that they begin to differentiate between the definition of *slavery* and *freedom* from a *nineteenth-century* perspective and their twentieth-century one. Prior to this type of preparatory orientation, a typical 1990's high school audience views institutions like slavery not as plagues of madness, injustice, and economic greed and rights of freedom not as an insatiable dream or hope for which to die in order to achieve it for oneself or children, but they view slavery as some gray, amorphous, historical event that occurred in America some time back that culminated with the Emancipation Proclamation, Abraham Lincoln's death, and "complete equity" for all. Freedom for these students, then, is "a given," an inherent right with which they are born that parents try to deny for periods of time when they are attempting to make a point.

With an initial audience such as the one I have described that Twain's novel as well as any other piece of racially-sensitive literature would experience bouts of rejection and misinterpretation seems inevitable. A National Endowment for the Humanities Grant, entitled *Roots of Individualism in American Literary Classics: A Study in Ambiguities* enabled me to research just how today's students respond to and feel about the racial issues in *The Adventures of Huckleberry Finn*. The grant also enabled me to interact with teachers and school districts so that I could develop discussion, written, and participatory activities to facilitate more effective teaching and learning experiences. Interestingly, through a survey administered to most of the students to whom I lectured, I have found that none of the students initially appreciate the realism of the southern dialect spoken by most of the characters. African-American students initially do not appreciate the use of the word *nigger*, and they also take issue with the overall depiction of Jim as an uneducated slave. It is interesting to note here that African-American students and their parents sometimes only notice Jim's speaking in dialect and no one else. Mexican-American students initially take issue with the idea of denied freedom and discrimination experienced "just by African-Americans." And, ironically yet understandably, Asian-American students initially identify with Huck's and Jim's sense of always being told what to do and how to think. They also identify with Jim's and Huck's longing for and embarking on their journey to freedom.

What all of this means for the teacher is that a multi-dimensional strategy must be used, if contemporary students are to experience the novel's intended message. In reality, the teacher must become literary historian, researcher, and rhetorician so that not only students but parents, too, can comprehend the full meaning of these works.

The following annotated construct for teaching racially-sensitive literature is one that reflects the needs of high school students of diverse cultures and ethnicities who desire, according to my research findings, preparatory activities and discussions as well as outside speakers.

Construct for Teaching Racially Sensitive Literature

Generic Construct:

I.   Know your audience.

Generally, today's high school audience reflects society's multi-ethnicity and cultural diversity. This variety, however, is often cloaked in class and economic constraints and peer expectations. The hazard here, of course, is that the teacher may be seduced into a false sense of security and identity. Overall, my research yielded that suburban districts generally have ethnic breakdowns of

> 80% Euro-American
> 9% Hispanic-American
> 8% African-American
> 1% Asian-American

Needless to say, urban districts reverse this generic breakdown according to location within the cities: i.e. the Lincoln Magnet High School in Dallas ISD has higher percentages of African and Hispanic-Americans than Euro and Asian-Americans.

Interestingly, whether urban or suburban, 85% is college-bound; 85% read books (favorite authors listed were Danielle Steel, Stephen King, C.S. Lewis, Isaac Asimov, Evelyn Waugh, Ray Bradbury, and Harlequin); 80% read magazines/newspaper (*Seventeen, Teen, Elle, Popular Mechanics, Newsweek, Discover*); 90% use or hear at home racial slurs (*nigger, honky, boy, chink, wetback, chigger, jap, hebe, women as inferior, feminoids, halfbreed, foreigner, pansy, wuss, kraut, kike, poor white trash*); and most interestingly, 100% detested the use of racial slurs unless they were used in a literary context for "good reason" and not for just shock value.

II.   Avoid allowing students to see or perceive your personal prejudices and/or biases.

Too often in a sincere effort to appear fair and "liberal" teachers paint themselves into the "proverbial corner" because they falsely assume that their minority students, particularly African and Hispanic-Americans, *all* either come from or are intimately connected with someone from an inner-city environment. Teachers sometimes also assume that once the class has participated in a class discussion of *dialect*, they all completely understand the variety of dialects Twain incorporates in *Huck Finn*. To the contrary, students yet do not associate Twain's use of dialect with their own speech patterns, if students are southern, or with those patterns they have heard. Further, African-American students will need extra instruction here because they only see and hear Jim, without the knowledge that teachers have regarding Jim's inability to access the educational system and his ability to assimilate the language aurally.

III.   Avoid social stereotyping.

Teachers should avoid any predisposition to assume that their students will unquestioningly accept their pronouncements about such controversial works like *Huck Finn*. They should also exert caution when discussing characters like Jim, assuming that like they, African-American and other students will see and understand distinctly not only Jim's nobility, courage, and fatherly disposition toward Huck but also Huck's monumental sacrifice, courage and loyalty toward Jim. And finally, teachers must remember that students *are not* aware of America's history, its literary history, or its ethnic history other than in the grossest sense. So understanding Jim's feeling of enclosure and sublimation are emotions not easily comprehended by contemporary high school students.

IV.   Research the work prior to its presentation.

100% of the students polled expressed a desire for some kind of "pre-preparation" before works like *Huck Finn* are formally introduced to the class. This kind of preparation, of course, means taking advantage of a variety of programs—such as the NEH program in which I am currently involved—enlisting the aid of guest lecturers from area universities, and making use of many scholarly books, articles, and videos.

V.   Explore legitimate cultural and ethnic situations confidently, competently, and comfortably.

To my surprise, many teachers in trying to express sensitivity toward *all* of their students actually single out the particular ethnic group being discussed or examined in any given piece of literature, in this case, *Huck Finn*. For example, they avoid asking minority groups what their experiences have or have not been; they do not inquire if students have family or friends who may have had or know other family stories about incidents discussed in the literary piece. The unfortunate result of this kind of circumvention often creates high anxiety and what I call *silent mental festering*. Robert H. Woodward in his "Teaching *Huckleberry Finn* to Foreign Students" identifies these same problems and results with ESL students, and concludes that unless teachers engage themselves and their students into a cultural and ethnic exchange intense frustration often results.[6]

VI.   Encourage discussions about feelings and perceptions.

VII.   Allow for and encourage scholarly disagreement and even adamant refusal to decode "correct" textual meaning, characterization, or authorial style because this kind of dialoguing produces plausible, student-deduced conclusions.

VIII. Refuse to allow non-interaction among students, particularly among your minority students.

IX.   Allow students to evaluate characters' actions and reactions within the framework of the fictional milieu. More importantly, allow them to engage in an investigatory exploration conjecturing how they would respond to identical circumstances then and now.

X.   Encourage students to interview individuals who remind them of the characters about whom they are reading and encourage them to share their research findings with the class.

XI.   Utilize a variety of teaching approaches that require students to engage critical thinking and problem-solving scenarios.

    A. Experiential Learning Labs
    B. Guest Lecturers
    C. Group Discussions
    D. Interviews
    E. Show and Tells
    F. Micro-writing Assignments
    G. Discovery Journals
    H. "Traditional" Writing Assignments: persuasive and expository

I began this discussion with two quotations—one from a concerned African-American parent who could not see that his very presence at an open forum to debate the inclusion or exclusion of Mark Twain's *The Adventures of Huckleberry Finn* was testament to Twain and his artistic desire of making a difference among the common man. As he wrote to a friend Andrew Lang in 1890:

The thin top crust of humanity—the cultivated—are worth pacifying, worth pleasing, worth coddling, worth nourishing and preserving with dainties and delicacies, it is true; but to be caterer to that little faction is no very dignified or valuable occupation, it seems to me; it is merely feeding the over-fed and there must be small satisfaction in that. It is not that little minority who are already saved that are best worth lifting at, I should think, but the mighty mass of the uncultivated who are underneath. . . . (*The Portable Mark Twain*, pp. 722-231)

The opportunity to debate in open forum, to agree to explore other options and ideas, to feel free, *regardless of race, ethnicity, class, and gender*, to accept, reject, and compromise with this issue, or with any issue is one pivotal lesson taught and hopefully learned when students are allowed the privilege of reading this fire of controversy, this *The Adventures of Huckleberry Finn.*
    What follows is a recommended pedagogical approach to the teaching of this novel to high school students.

A Huck Finn Lecture/Discussion/Activity Model

Although the model is not complete, it is designed to suggest additional information instructors might include when teaching *The Adventures of Huckleberry Finn*, or any other literary works that reflect this time period.

I. Historical Perspectives
    A. Pre-Civil War
       1. North
          a. African-American
During the years preceding the first shot fired at Fort Sumter on 12 April 1861, northern African-Americans participated actively in the north's political, economic, and social agenda. Republicans in their politics, these African-Americans, some born free, some born into slavery and paid their way out of it along with those escaped from slavery to Indian territory or the north's non-agricultural scene, championed openly and tirelessly for equality for all humankind. Needless to say these individuals usually confronted animosity from

those in the south who saw not their contributions but only their own economic losses. African-Americans like

Prince Sanders—an ardent and outspoken abolitionist orator

Jarena Lee—activist and 1st female preacher in the African Methodist Episcopal Church

Charles B. Lane—leader of the American and Foreign Anti-Slavery Society

Nancy Gardner Prince—teacher, author, humanitarian

Charles L. Reason—a professor of belles lettres at New York Central College

Frances Ellen Watkins Harper—poet, essayist, novelist

David Walker—leader in the Boston Colored Association who published the now famous *Appeal In Four Articles with A Preamble to the Colored Citizens of the World* and who acted as agent for the first Negro newspaper, *Freedom's Journal*, edited by the Reverend Samuel E. Cornish, pastor of the African Presbyterian Church in New York and John Russwurm, a Bowdoin graduate and first Negro in America to receive a college degree

Lewis Temple—blacksmith and inventor of the toggle harpoon

William Leidesdorff—seaman who launched the first steamboat on San Francisco Bay in 1847 and who built the first hotel in that city

worked to modify the behavior of a still young and emerging nation, the United States. Although some civil rights were withheld such as voting, occupying a cabin aboard a steamship, and other benefits of full enfranchisement, free African-Americans participated in a variety of occupations that would eventually lead to their full enfranchisement and civil rights: seaman, farmers, sailmakers, street-cleaners, seamstresses, artists, barbers, shopkeepers, grocers, druggists, physicians, lithographers, educators, and hairdressers such as Pierre Toussaint (1776-1853).

Interestingly, what many twentieth-century audiences are unaware of is not only these politically active individuals but also the many middle-class entrepreneurs who contributed their own unique talents and ideas to eradicating forever the unjust specter of slavery in the South. Suffragists like Sojourner Truth, Harriet Tubman and Charlotte Forten Grimke helped in the Underground Railroad, a complex escape system that eventually enabled over 75,000 slaves to gain their freedom. African-American politicians such as Frederick Douglass fought for the retraction of the Fugitive Slave Law with its rewards to slave traders and trackers.

b. Euro-American

Many Euro-Americans believed that slavery was an unconstitutional and morally unjust law that inevitably would result in civil war. Euro-Americans sympathetic with the slaves became known as abolitionists and Black Republicans (1854). Many of these individuals fought openly and even died for this cause.

(1) Social

Social activists viewed slavery as a cancer on a young, growing nation. Female suffragists saw the abolitionist movement as a parallel to the subjugation of women, women such as Susan B. Anthony and Elizabeth Cady Stanton.

(2) Religious

Religious leaders sought the freeing of slaves, too.

        (3) Education
        (4) Political
        (5) Cultural
    2. South
      a. African-American

Life for the slave in the South was difficult, harsh, brutal, and allowed for little or no socialization. Transported on over-crowded slave ships, sold, as one slave reported "like horses," separated from family, culture, and country, the African-American has endured. Many sought freedom in a variety of ways:

the Underground Railroad
the nearest river and/or swamp to avoid detection of dogs and to seek Canada
the purchase of freedom, approximately $1200.00
the lawsuit, i.e., Dred Scot
the shipping box (Henry "Box" Brown)
the institution of marriage, Ellen and William Craft
the riot and revolt, i.e., John Brown, Nat Turner

If a runaway slave were caught, punishment was always harsh: whipping, raping, maiming, even amputation. No one was executed, of course, because the value of the slave would be forever lost. Some captured slaves, consequently would die to avoid being returned to slavery: Margaret Garner killed two of her children and drowned herself in the Ohio River; Bill Denby caused his overseer, named Gore, to shoot him when he refused to be beaten anymore.

      b. Euro-American

Southerners capitalized on the increased capital generated by slavery. They used slaves to triple cotton production as a result of Eli Whitney's cotton gin and thereby increased their economic superiority. Northerners, while they did not politically support slavery, quietly felt the increased pressure of job competition and the desire to expand the union westward.

        (1) Social

Socially, African-Americans and Euro-Americans did not socialize, even in the north. Northerners *did*, however, promote separate but equal institutions for African-Americans.

        (2) Religious
        (3) Educational
        (4) Political
        (5) Cultural
  B. Civil War and Reconstruction
    1. North
      a. African-American
      b. Euro-American
        (1) Social
        (2) Religious
        (3) Educational
        (4) Political

            (5) Cultural
        2. South
            a. African-American
            b. Euro-American
                (1) Social
                (2) Religious
                (3) Educational
                (4) Political
                (5) Cultural
II. Mark Twain
    A. The Man and His Society
    B. The Man and *The Adventures of Huckleberry Finn*

NOTES

1. Langston Hughes, Milton Meltzer, and C. Eric Lincoln, *A Pictorial History of Black Americans* (New York: Crown, 1983), p. 235.

2. Wayne C. Booth, *The Company We Keep: An Ethics of Fiction* (Los Angeles: University of California Press, 1988), p. 3.

3. Booth, p. 459.

4. Bernard Bell, "Twain's 'Nigger' Jim: The Tragic Face Behind the Minstrel Mask," *Mark Twain Journal*, 23, No. 1 (Spring 1985), p. 13.

5. Mark Twain, *The Annotated Huckleberry Finn*, ed. Michael Patrick Hearn (New York: Clarckson N. Potter, 1981), pp. 89-90.

6. Robert H. Woodward, "Teaching *Huckleberry Finn* to Foreign Students," *Mark Twain Journal*, 13, No. 1 (Spring 1985), p. 6.

CRITICAL VIEWS ON ADAPTATIONS OF *HUCKLEBERRY FINN*

LAURIE CHAMPION

Unlike the successful adaptations of some classic novels, few adaptations of *Adventures of Huckleberry Finn* have reached critical achievement; nevertheless, Twain's *Huckleberry Finn* is one of the most popular novels to be adapted. In his review "Adapting and Revising Twain's *Huck Finn*,"[1] Michiko Kakutani gives reasons for the popularity of the adaptations:

It is of course, a classic—a classic not only about a rebellious boy's coming of age (in this sense, Huck can be seen as a precursor of such characters as Holden Caulfield and those disaffected youths portrayed by James Dean in the movies), but also about the promise and betrayals of the most powerful of American dreams, the frontier. Its satiric probing of society—and its portrayal of a young man's search for moral values, independent of those handed down to him by a corrupt civilization. . . .

Kakutani poses the book's first-person narration as one of the reasons for translation difficulties. He says adaptations usually "downplay the book's more disturbing aspects" and treat it like *The Adventures of Tom Sawyer*.

Among the attempts to adapt *Huckleberry Finn* to the screen are at least five American film versions, three American television adaptations, and an Encyclopedia Britannica educational film version. Other screen adaptations such as *Back to Hannibal: The Return of Tom Sawyer and Huckleberry Finn*, the Disney cable movie that portrays the continuation of both *The Adventures of Tom Sawyer* and *Adventures of Huckleberry Finn*, represent indirect adaptations. Huck has made his way to theatres across the country and has even been the subject of an opera. Editions of text adaptations of Twain's classic novel also appear: John Seelye's *The True Adventures of Huckleberry Finn* (Northwestern University Press, 1970) depicts his rewritten version that strives to refute critics' objections to the novel; in *The Adventures of Huckleberry Finn Adapted* (Wallace & Sons Co., 1983), John Wallace replaces the word *nigger* with words such as slave, servant, or fellow, in his attempt to alleviate what he considers is offensive to blacks who read the novel. These adapted editions can become confusing if people mistake them for the authentic work. In her essay "The A B C's of Counterfeit Classics: Adapted, Bowdlerized, and Condensed,"[2] Ruth Stein discusses the publication of abridged and edited classics. In 1966 she cites five of such versions of *Adventures of Huckleberry Finn*. She says "these rewritten versions of *Huckleberry Finn* are unpretentious inexpensive volumes having little or no literary or artistic merit. Their respective editors have, by abridging and revising, taken great liberties with the original" (pp. 1160-1161). She points out that these alterations weaken the novel's social satire and the most important omissions are Huck's feelings toward Jim and his increasing awareness of the evils of slavery. She sums up her evaluation:

After a careful examination of the adaptations of this novel, I must conclude that they present really only the skeletal structure of *Huckleberry Finn*, that the heart and soul are gone. These simplified tales are so watered down and distorted, much of what made them great stories has been lost. How can they teach youngsters a love of books in this vapid style is debatable and unmeasurable. . . . Transmission of our cultural heritage is accomplished partially through the teaching of the classics. Those that have survived have had an intrinsic merit of their own. It should not be snuffed out of existence by precautionary or hygienic measures. So many of our original works are presented in attractive, readable, and inexpensive packages, it is a foolish waste of money, time, and effort to settle for any of the inferior revisions. (p. 1163)

The film versions have yet to create successful adaptations as well. The first film adaptation of *Huckleberry Finn* was produced by Paramount in 1920. It was directed by William Taylor and starred Lewis Sargent as Huck and George Reed as Jim. It generally received good reviews. *Variety*[3] says, "The picture is one that will have a thrill for those who have read the Twain story, whether they be boys of 8 or 80." The *New York Times*[4] review objects to the film's portrayal of Huck at the end of the film. Rather than heading for the territory, he plans to return to Mary Jane Wilks; however, this reviewer says the other deviations from the novel "are relatively unimportant." The review praises the performances of the cast. It sums up its evaluation by saying *Huckleberry Finn* tells "'the truth mainly,' and may easily win unqualified indorsement [*sic*] from those not too familiar with, or devoted to, the book. And no matter what its shortcomings may be it should be a joy to every one."

The first sound version was produced in 1931, again by Paramount. It was directed by Norman Taurog and featured Junior Durkin as Huck and Clarence Muse as Jim. The well-known Jackie Coogan played the role of Tom. Overall, the film was well-received by reviewers. Richard Skinner, writing for *The Commonweal*,[5] praises Durkin and Coogan for their performances. Skinner acknowledges the modifications of the book to the screen but says it "remains an epic of boyhood on the edge of adolescence." Skinner refers to Tom and Huck several times but ignores Jim's role in the film. He says: "I cannot imagine a healthier spiritual dose for the harassed man or woman of today than an hour shared with these boys." He compares this particular adaptation to adaptations of Twain's works in general: "Twain classics are among the happiest contributions to screen literature ever made." *Film Daily*[6] says this film provides "just about as much refreshing entertainment" as *Tom Sawyer*, the first picture in the Paramount Mark Twain series. The *Outlook*[7] reviewer contradicts these somewhat favorable reviews, saying Twain's book has been "changed almost beyond recognition." The review condemns the overly romantic theme and the portrayal of Tom accompanying Huck at all times during the movie. He concludes his assessment: "Those who know Mark Twain will be furious, and those who do not will see a passably entertaining story about children called Huck and Tom."

In 1939, the third film adaptation was released by a different distributor, MGM. It was produced by Joseph Mankiewicz and directed by Richard Thorpe. It featured the star Mickey Rooney as Huck and the young actor Rex Ingram as Jim. The reviews were generally negative, and most reviewers commented on the adaptation as ineffectively capturing the spirit of the novel. Bosley Crowther's review in *The New York Times*[8] says the film "is an average, workmanlike piece of cinematic hokum. Pared down to its melo-dramatic essentials . . . Master Rooney's latest vehicle affords little, if any, insight into the realistic boyhood world of which old Mark wrote with such imperishable humor." Crowther says the film is not Twain, objecting most adamantly to the authority figures of early Mississippi, who "exist merely as comic foils. . . ." *Film Daily*[9] says this production is a good adaptation—the failure stems from Twain, who is a humorist, but "was one of the world's worst plot constructionists." The adaptation fails because Mark Twain is outdated. He says the film adaptation exposes "the bald incidents the immortal story," turning them "very flat and mechanical and uninteresting." *Newsweek*[10] defends the "inevitable omissions," saying they lead to "comparatively few distortions. . . . The most notable departure from the original is the elimination of Tom Sawyer and his fantastic plotting in Jim's behalf." This review is not quite so disapproving, adding, "if the *Adventures of Huckleberry Finn* fails to capture the real flavor of Mark Twain's time on the Mississippi, it does succeed in blending reliable screen ingredients into colorful and palatable entertainment."

MGM distributed its second version of *Adventures of Huckleberry Finn* in 1960. The film was produced by Samuel Goldwyn, Jr. and directed by Michael Curtiz. Eddie Hodges played Huck and Archie Moore played Jim. This production received some favorable reviews; however, Bosley Crowther, writing for *New York Times*,[11] Robert Roman, writing for *Films in Review*,[12] and the *Variety*[13] reviewer all expressed Hodges performance as Huck as inadequate. Bosley Crowther says the film comes across as "'cute'—cheerful, chummy, sentimental and, eventually, monotonous and dull." He warns parents against taking children with expectations of meeting Twain's Huck, then suggests they, "explain that this is but entertainment—a plush one. Then give him a copy of the book." The *Variety* review says, "Mark Twain's 'Huckleberry Finn' is all boy. Eddie Hodges' 'Huck' isn't." The reviewer says this is the basic reason the adaptation is not "all it could, and should, be." He does, however, say that "the role is an extremely demanding one, and that his performance is not without its admirable attributes. . . ." He adds, "some of the more complex developments and relationships, presumably for the benefit of the young audience" have been simplified. He largely blames director Curtiz for the failure: "There is a lot of shock for shock's sake . . . but the intense concern that ordinarily accompanies such passages as Huck's brush with his fiercely drunken father has gone out of the story."

Robert Roman, in *Films in Review*, wonders what punishment Twain would have had for someone like scriptwriter James Lee, who "changes not only the book, but Twain's intention" (p. 364). He says Lee has transformed Twain's classic into "a boyhood adventure yarn in which Huck . . . grows to respect and love the Negro Jim" (p. 365). He says Eddie Hodges "is not my idea of Huck" (p. 366), but praises Randall and Shaunessy as "The King" and "The Duke."

In 1974, *Reader's Digest* funded the United Artists' production of the musical version of *The Adventures of Tom Sawyer* and *Adventures of Huckleberry Finn*. J. Lee Thompson began the direction of *Adventures of Huckleberry Finn* and Robert F. Blumofe completed the direction after Thompson's death. Jeff East played the role of Huck and Paul Winfield the role of Jim. Reviewers did not receive this version favorably. Lawrence Van Gelder, writing for *New York Times*,[14] says, "aside from the all-too-few minutes when Mr. Korman [The King] and Mr. Wayne [The Duke] are on the screen—fleecing yokels and orphans, putting on airs, putting down lynch mobs and putting up with all the dullards around them—"Huckleberry Finn" . . . is a lavish bore." He says that except for the performances of Winfield, Korman, and Wayne, "Mark Twain surely would have reserved for them a hoot of derision." Alexander Stuart, in *Films and Filming*,[15] says the acting is not bad and says Jeff East's performance as Huck is "pretty fair" (p. 49). He comments on the slow pace of the musical version and says the songs often "wail out from time to time . . . " (p. 49). Tom Milne, writing for *Monthly Film Bulletin*,[16] gives a brief summary of the plot of the adaptation, then says the adaptation is "drearily elephantine." He compares this musical to the musical adaptation of *Tom Sawyer*: "It isn't just that the songs are pallid echoes of those in *Tom Sawyer*, flatly orchestrated and not nearly so well dovetailed into the action; or that the characters are altogether cruder and much more sketchily played. . . . The whole tone has changed, very much for the worse." (p. 128). Dorothy Some, in *Films in Review*,[17] calls the version, "a depressing musical," and declares Korman and Wayne embarrassing. *The Variety*[18] review says the production is "slightly embarrassing." It "drives family film advocates up the wall."

Perry Frank's essay "Adventures of *Huckleberry Finn* on Film"[19] outlines all of these films. He also covers the 1978 television production for the Schick-Sunn Classics, the 1975 ABC Circle Films television production, the 1973 Russian version of *Huckleberry Finn* released by Mosfilm Studies in Moscow, and the 1965 Encyclopedia Britannica production. Frank draws the following conclusion concerning an overall appraisal of the film adaptations of *Adventures of Huckleberry Finn*: "Not surprisingly, Hollywood scriptwriters have come up with a less compelling story than Mark Twain; *Huckleberry Finn* on celluloid has neither been the powerful vision of America and moral allegory of the novel, nor an engrossing children's film on its own terms" (p. 306). Frank's essay is the most comprehensive examination of the screen adaptations of Mark Twain's *Huckleberry Finn*, complete with a meticulous filmography.

The American Playhouse television version of *Adventures of Huckleberry Finn* was produced by Jane Iredale and directed by Peter H. Hunt. It premiered on four consecutive Monday nights in March, 1986. The *Variety*[20] reviewer says this adaptation has "sweetened the story most notably in the character of Huck himself. . . . Huck's rascality—the trait that has made him a classic personality in literature—has been subdued." Huck possesses "a sensitivity which is not present in Twain's renderings, and while it may appeal to audience's expectations of child behavior, is unnecessary for this knocked-about, tough kid." He says writer Guy Gallo handles the problem of adaptations of the novel with "agility" and praises him for portraying "Huck's belief that he's committing a great sin by helping Jim escape—but just can't help it." Michiko Kakutani says this version depicts Jim as calling Huck "son," which gives "their relationship a paternal sort of air, and in general he eschews the heavier dialect expressions given to him in the book." He quotes William Perry, executive producer: "The Stepin Fetchit sort of language Twain used would have been difficult for today's audiences to accept. We also saw Jim as having a certain primitive strength of character that would be emphasized if we portrayed him as some sort of surrogate father to Huck."

Critics often give plausible assumptions as to why the film adaptations of *Adventures of Huckleberry Finn* have not been more successful. Perry Frank offers the following suggestions:

No doubt the continuing interest in filming *Huckleberry Finn* relates to the novel's central role in the canon of American literature—a role which has taken on increased dimensions with the passing years. Considered by many to be the first—and perhaps the greatest—modern American novel, its humor, cinematic setting, and adventurous plot make it an obvious film subject. At the same time, its complex moral vision, social criticism which centers on the race issue, and the difficult dialect coupled with a first person point-of-view, present problems for filmmakers if they are interested in rendering a faithful adaptation. The upshot is that Hollywood, like the larger society, has been uncertain about whether to treat *Huckleberry Finn* as a major adult work, or as a children's tale. (p. 305)

Robert Irwin suggests other possible assumptions for ineffective film adaptations:

In synthesizing all that has been said about the film versions of these novels [*The Adventures of Tom Sawyer* and *Adventures of Huckleberry Finn*], one can not avoid asking himself what went wrong. Surely there are script adapters who can read Twain. Surely there are producers who understand Twain. The problem revolves around the self-evident truth that a movie must make money. It must lure us to the box-office. It must not offend the Sunday school superintendents or the Daughters of the American Revolution. It must appease small children and teenagers and little old ladies of both sexes. It must appease an American public that is challenged and frightened by what Mark Twain has to say about us all. (p. 10)[21]

Other adaptations of *Adventures of Huckleberry Finn*, however, have been more successful. The Broadway musical *Big River* won seven Tonys in 1885, including best musical. The music and lyrics were written by Roger Miller, and the musical was directed by Des McAnuff. Daniel Jenkins starred as Huck and Ron Richardson played the role of Jim. Brendan Gill, in *The New Yorker*,[22] praises the lighting, costumes, design, direction and says some of the performances are excellent: "One can scarcely blame "Big River" for failing to encompass this subterranean aspect of Twain's genius; still, it is a felt lack throughout the evening." In *The Hudson Review*,[23] Jill Dolan says, "the thrill of spectacle suffuses *Big River*, and time for the audience to applaud the scenery is built into the conventions of the genre" (p. 450). Dolan says Twain's novel loses some of its connotative meanings, such as the commentary about slavery: "the issue of slavery is trivialized and upstaged by the antics of the supporting cast" (pp. 460-61).

Variety[24] says this adaptation is "a rousingly good show and an intelligent, spiritually faithful adaptation of the book." The play reflects Twain's plot except for a few changes, notably "the character of Jim, who has been given dignity, pride and a tough determination in place of the superstitious servility of the original. . . . Only major plot excision is the chapter in which Huck gets involved in a bloody feud." "Big River" preserves "the heart of a great book while entertaining a modern audience." The reviewer praises the performances of the leading characters: Jenkins performance as Huck "gives an admirable account of a mythologically resonant character," Ron Richardson as Jim "offers a near-operatic performance," and John Short as Tom Sawyer is "captivating . . . a talent to watch."

In May, 1971, Hall Overton's opera of *Huck Finn* premiered at the Juilliard American Opera Center. Hall Overton collaborated with Judah Stampfer in the production, and he says the libretto concentrates on three themes: "the characters and relationship of Huck and Jim; crowd scenes—it was important that they be represented because Twain uses them as a foil for the closed world of Huck and Jim; and the symbolic forces of the river and the raft and the freedom that seems to be there wherever the river takes you."[25] The changes include increasing Huck's age to sixteen and the representation of Jim as older and wiser. The ending was also changed: "Jim is freed, as in the novel, by his former owner, but instead of going back with Huck and Tom Sawyer, he takes off on his own to continue his original mission to free his immediate family." Overton says he tried to preserve Twain's language. Raymond Ericson's *New York Times*[26] review of the opera says, "To a large extent he has preserved the cadences of Twain's vernacular speech. He has frequently kept the orchestra subservient, so that the text comes through clearly." He says the best music is Jim's and praises the stagecraft and costumes. Willard White as Jim and David Hall as Huck are both praised. He criticizes the "long gray stretches that fail to define or illuminate adequately what is happening on stage. The grayness comes from the stockpile of current musical usage and from a lack of melodic profile, which obviously stems from the composer's honorable ideas about setting the language."

Adaptations that indirectly allude to *Adventures of Huckleberry Finn* are even less successful than the direct adaptations. One recent example of a reference to *Adventures of Huckleberry Finn* is the 1990 Disney Channel production of *Back to Hannibal: The Return of Tom Sawyer and Huckleberry Finn*, produced by Hugh Benson, which premiered on cable television on October 21, 1990. This production portrays the reunion of Tom and Huck as adults. Tom, now a defense lawyer, and Huck, now a newspaper reporter, return to Hannibal to defend Jim, who is accused of murdering Becky Thatcher's husband. Ron Miller, writing for *The Dallas Morning News*,[27] says of this dramatization: "The whole movie is an immense letdown from start to finish, which just goes to show that screenwriter Roy Johansen is no Mark Twain. Come to think of it, nobody is, so what did we expect?"

In view of the attempted adaptations, it seems as if maybe we should not expect raving reviews from anyone attempting to adapt Twain's masterpiece. Twain's warning against the search for motives, morals, and plots in *Adventures of Huckleberry Finn* may also appropriately apply to those attempting to embrace these elements through revisions of his masterpiece novel. I suspect we will continue to find adaptations poor substitutes for Twain's classic novel; instead, as Louis Budd poignantly puts it, "whether or not the future will recompose the novel . . . *Huckleberry Finn* will continue to contradict Twain's own definition of a classic as a book that everybody praises and nobody reads."[28]

NOTES

1. Michiko Kakutani, "Adapting and Revising Twain's Huck Finn," *New York Times*, 24 February 1986, p. C11.

2. Ruth Stein, "The A B C's of Counterfeit Classics: Adapted, Bowdlerized, and Condensed," *English Journal*, 55 (December 1966), 1160-1163.

3. "Huckleberry Finn," *Variety*, 27 February 1920, p. 46.

4. "Review of Huckleberry Finn," *New York Times*, 23 February 1920, p. 11:2.

5. Richard Dana Skinner, "Huckleberry Finn," The *Commonweal*, 26 August 1931, p. 406.

6. "Huckleberry Finn," *Film Daily*, 9 August 1931, p. 10.

7. "Huckleberry Finn," *Outlook and Independent*, 26 August 1931, p. 534.

8. Bosley Crowther, "Huckleberry Finn," *New York Times*, 3 March 1939, p. 21:2.

9. "Huckleberry Finn," *Film Daily*, 17 February 1939, p. 6.

10. "Huck Finn's Adventures: Mark Twain's Famed Vagabond in Person of Mickey Rooney," *Newsweek*, 27 February 1931, p. 24.

11. Bosley Crowther, "Eddie Hodges Stars in Huckleberry Finn," *New York Times*, 4 August 1969, p. 17:1.

12. Robert C. Roman, "The Adventures of Huckleberry Finn," *Films in Review*, 11 (June-July 1960), 364-366.

13. "The Adventures of Huckleberry Finn," *Variety*, 11 May 1960.

14. Lawrence Van Gelder, "Screen: A Vapid Huckleberry Finn," *New York Times*, 25 May 1974, p. 16:1.

15. Alexander Stuart. "Huckleberry Finn," *Films and Filming*, 20 (August 1974), 48-49.

16. Tom Milne, "Huckleberry Finn," *Monthly Film Bulletin*, 41 (June 1974), 127-128.

17. Dorothy Some, "Huckleberry Finn," *Films in Review*, 25 (June-July 1974), 374-375.

18. "Huckleberry Finn," *Variety*, 3 April 1974, p. 14.

19. Perry Frank, "*Adventures of Huckleberry Finn* on Film," in *Huck Finn Among the Critics*, ed. Thomas Inge (Frederick, Maryland: University Publications of America, 1985), pp. 293-313.

20. "Adventures of Huckleberry Finn," *Variety*, 12 February 1986.

21. Robert Irwin, "The Failure of *Tom Sawyer* and *Huckleberry Finn* on Film," *Mark Twain Journal*, 13 (Summer 1967), 9-11.

22. Brendan Gill, "Review of Big River," *The New Yorker*, 61 (13 May 1985), 128.

23. Jill Dolan, "Text and Context," *The Hudson Review*, 38 (Autumn 1985), 459-462.

24. "Big River," *Variety*, 318 (1 May 1985), 498, 503.

25. Raymond Ericson, "This Huck Finn is Not for Children," *New York Times*, 16 May 1971, p. 13:1.

26. Raymond Ericson, "Hall Overton Attempts Opera About Huck Finn," *New York Times*, 22 May 1971, p. L19.

27. Ron Miller, "Adult Tom and Huck Need Twain," *The Dallas Morning News*, 20 October 1990, p. C5.

28. Louis Budd, "The Recomposition of *Adventures of Huckleberry Finn*," *The Missouri Review*, 10 (1987), p. 128.

Selected Additional Readings

Adams, Richard P. "The Unity and Coherence of *Huckleberry Finn.*" *Tulane Studies in English*, 6 (1956), 87-103.

Anderson, Douglas. "Reading the Pictures in *Huckleberry Finn.*" *Arizona Quarterly*, 42 (Summer 1986), 101-20.

Anderson, Frederick, ed. With the assistance of Kenneth M. Sanderson. *Mark Twain: The Critical Heritage.* London: Routledge & Kegan Paul, and New York: Barnes & Noble, 1971.

Banta, Martha. "Rebirth or Revenge: The Endings of *Huckleberry Finn* and *The American.*" *Modern Fiction Studies*, 15 (1969), 191-207.

Beaver, Harold. *Huckleberry Finn.* London and Boston: Unwin Hyman, 1987.

Bell, Bernard W. "Twain's 'Nigger' Jim: The Tragic Face Behind the Minstrel Mask." *Mark Twain Journal*, 23, No.1 (1985), 10-17.

Bellamy, Gladys C. *Mark Twain as a Literary Artist.* Norman: University of Oklahoma Press, 1950.

Berrett, Anthony J. "The Influence of *Hamlet* on *Huckleberry Finn.*" *American Literary Realism*, 18 (1985), 196-207.

Besant, Sir Walter. "My Favorite Novelist and His Best Book." *Munsey's Magazine*, 18 (February 1898), 659-54.

Bird, John. "These Leather-Faced People: Huck and the Moral Art of Lying." *Studies in American Fiction*, 15 (Spring 1987), 71-80.

Blair, Walter, and Victor Fischer. eds. With the assistance of Dehlia Armon and Harriet Elinor Smith. *Adventures of Huckleberry Finn.* Berkeley, Los Angeles, and London: University of California Press, 1988.

___. *Mark Twain and Huck Finn.* Berkeley: University of California Press, 1960.

___. *Mark Twain's Hannibal, Huck & Tom.* Berkeley and Los Angeles: University of California Press, 1969.

___. "When Was *Huckleberry Finn* Written?" *American Literature*, 30 (March 1958), 1-25.

Blakemore, Steven. "Huck Finn's Written World." *American Literary Realism*, 20 (Winter 1988), 21-29.

Bloom, Harold, ed. *Mark Twain.* New York: Chelsea House, 1986.

Boggan, J. R. "That Slap Huck, Did it Hurt?" *English Language Notes*, 1 (March 1954), 212-215.

Boland, Sally. "The Seven Dialects in *Huckleberry Finn.*" *North Dakota Quarterly*, 36 (Summer 1968), 30-40.

Bowen, James K., and Richard Van DerBeets, eds. *Adventures of Huckleberry Finn. With Twenty Years of Criticism.* Glenview, Illinois: Scott, Foresman and Company, 1970.

Bradley, Sculley, et al., eds. *Aventures of Huckleberry Finn: An Annotated Text. Backgrounds and Sources. Essays in Criticism.* 2nd ed. A Norton Critical Edition. New York: Norton, 1977.

Branch, Edgar M, et. al. *Mark Twain's Notebooks and Journals.* Vol. I: 1853-1866. Berkeley: University of California Press, 1988.

__. "Mark Twain Scholarship: Two Decades." *Adventures of Huckleberry Finn. With Abstracts of Twenty Years of Criticism.* Ed. James K. Bowen and Richard Van Derbeets. Glenview, Ill.: Foresman & Co., 1970. Pp. 344-49.

__. "The Two Providences: Thematic Form in *Huckleberry Finn.*" *College English,* 11 (January 1950), 188-95.

Brooks, Van Wyck. *The Ordeal of Mark Twain.* New York: Dutton, 1920.

__. *Our Mark Twain: The Making of His Public Personality.* Philadelphia: University of Pennsylvania Press, 1983.

Brown, Spencer. "*Huckleberry Finn* for Our Time: A Re-Reading of the Concluding Chapters." *Michigan Quarterly Review,* 6 (Winter 1967), 41-46.

Browne, Ray B. "Huck's Final Triumph." *Ball State Teachers College Forum,* 6 (Winter 1965), 3-12.

Brownell, Frances V. "The Role of Jim in *Huckleberry Finn.*" *Boston University Studies in English,* 1 (Spring-Summer 1955), 74-83.

Budd, Louis J., ed. *Critical Essays on Mark Twain, 1867-1910.* Boston: G.K. Hall, 1982.

__. "Huck at 100. How Old Is *Huckleberry Finn?*" *Dictionary of Literary Biography Yearbook, 1985.* Ed. Jean W. Ross. Detroit: Gale, 1986. Pp. 12-23.

__. *Mark Twain: Social Philosopher.* Bloomington: Indiana University Press, 1962.

__, and H. Cady, eds. *On Mark Twain: The Best from American Literature.* Durham: Duke University Press, 1987.

__. *Our Mark Twain: The Making of His Public Personality.* Philadelphia: University of Pennsylvania Press, 1983.

__. "The Recomposition of *Adventures of Huckleberry Finn.*" *Missouri Review,* 10 (1987), 113-129.

Burns, Graham. "Time and Pastoral: *The Adventures of Huckleberry Finn.*" *Critical Review,* 15 (1972), 52-63.

Cardwell, Guy A. *Discussions of Mark Twain.* Boston: D.C. Heath, 1963.

Carpenter, Scott. "Demythification in *Adventures of Huckleberry Finn.*" *Studies in American Fiction,* 15 (Autumn 1987), 211-217.

Carrington, George C., Jr. *The Dramatic Unity of Huckleberry Finn.* Columbus: Ohio State University Press, 1976.

Carter, Everett. "The Modernist Ordeal of Huckleberry Finn." *Studies in American Fiction,* 13, No. 2 (Autumn 1985), 169-183.

Cecil, L. Moffitt. "The Historical Ending of *Adventures of Huckleberry Finn*: How Nigger Jim Was Set Free." *American Literary Realism,* 13 (Autumn 1980), 280-283.

Cheesman, Elaine, and Earl French, eds. *Twain-Stowe Sourcebook.* Mark Twain Memorial and Stowe-Day Foundation, 1988.

Cleary, Vincent J. "Odysseus, Aeneas and Huckleberry Finn," *The Augustan Age, Occasional Papers*, 1 (1987), 45-55.

Cohen, Ralph, ed. *The Adventures of Huckleberry Finn*. New York: Bantam Books, 1964.

Covici, Pascal, Jr. *Mark Twain's Humor: The Image of a World*. Dallas: Southern Methodist University Press, 1962.

Cox, James M. *Mark Twain: The Fate of Humor*. Princeton, New Jersey: Princeton University Press, 1966.

___. "Remarks on the Sad Initiation of Huckleberry Finn." *Sewanee Review*, 62 (Summer 1954), 389-405.

Cox, John F. "On the Naming of *Huckleberry Finn*." *Publications of the Modern Language Association*, 86 (October 1971), 1038.

Davis, Chester L. "New York City Schools 'Banning' Huck Finn! Mark Twain and the Negro Race Champion for Organized Labor." *Twainian*, 16 (September-October 1957), 1-4.

DeVoto Bernard. *Mark Twain's America*, Boston: Little, Brown, 1932.

___. *Mark Twain at Work*. Cambridge, Mass.: Harvard University Press, 1942.

Emerson, Everett. *The Authentic Mark Twain: A Literary Biography of Samuel L. Clemens*. Philadelphia: University of Pennsylvania Press, 1984.

Eliot, T. S. "Introduction." The *Adventures of Huckleberry Finn*. New York: Chanticleer Press, 1950. Pp. vii-xvi.

Ensor, Allison. "The Contributions of Charles Webster and Albert Bigelow Paine to *Huckleberry Finn*." *American Literature*, 40 (May 1968), 222-7.

Ferguson, DeLancey. "Huck Finn Aborning." *Colophon*, No. 3 (Spring 1938), 171-80.

Fetterley, Judith. "Disenchantment: Tom Sawyer in *Huckleberry Finn*." *Publications of the Modern Language Association*, 87 (January 1972), 69-74.

Fiedler, Leslie. "'As Free as Any Cretur. . . .'" *New Republic*, 133 (15 August 1955), 17-18; (22 August 1955), 16-18.

___. *Love and Death in the American Novel*. New York: Criterion Books, 1960.

___. *Return of the Vanishing American*. Briarcliff Manor, New York: Stein & Day, 1969.

Fischer, Victor. "Huck Finn Reviewed: The Reception of *Huckleberry Finn* in the United States, 1885-1897." *American Literary Realism*, 16 (Spring 1983), 1-57.

___. "A New Edition of *Huck Finn*." *Dictionary of Literary Biography Yearbook, 1986*, Ed. Jean W. Ross. Detroit: Gale, 1987. Pp. 23-27

Fishkin, Shelley Fisher. "Twain, in '85." *New York Times*, (18 February 1985), A17.

Frantz, Ray W., Jr. "The Role of Folklore in *Huckleberry Finn*." *American Literature*, 28 (November 1956), 314-27.

Fraser, John. "In Defense of Culture: *Huckleberry Finn*." *Oxford Review*, 6 (1967), 5-22.

Furnas, J. C. "The Crowded Raft: *Huckleberry Finn* & Its Critics." *American Scholar*, 54 (Fall 1985), 517-24.

Gabler-Hover, Janet A. "Sympathy Not Empathy: The Intent of Narration in *Huckleberry Finn*." *Journal of Narrative Technique*, 17 (Winter 1987), 67-75.

Gaston, George Meri-Akri. "The Function of Tom Sawyer in *Huckleberry Finn*." *Mississippi Quarterly*, 27 (Winter 1973), 33-39.

Gerber, John C., ed. *Studies in Huckleberry Finn*. Columbus, Ohio: Charles E. Merrill, 1971.
___. *Mark Twain*. Boston: Twayne Publishers, 1988.
Gillman, Susan. *Dark Twins: Imposture and Identity in Mark Twain's America*. Chicago: The University of Chicago Press, 1989.
Gribben, Alan. *Mark Twain's Library: A Reconstruction*. 2 vols. Boston: G.K. Hall & Company, 1980.
___. "Manipulating a Genre: *Huckleberry Finn* as Boy Book." *South Carolina Review*, 5 (Winter 1988), 15-21.
Gross, Seymour L. "Sherwood Anderson's Debt to *Huckleberry Finn*." *Mark Twain Journal*, 11 (Summer 1960), 3-5, 24.
Gullason, Thomas A. "The 'Fatal' Ending of *Huckleberry Finn*." *American Literature*, 29 (March 1957), 86-91.
Hansen, Chadwick. "The Character of Jim and the Ending of *Huckleberry Finn*." *Massachusetts Review*, 5 (Autumn 1963), 45-66.
Hearn, Michael Patrick. *The Annotated Huckleberry Finn*. New York: Clarkson N. Potter, 1982.
Heath, William. "Tears and Flapdoodle: Sentimentality in *Huckleberry Finn*." *South Carolina Review*, 19 (Fall 1986), 60-79.
Hill, Hamlin, ed. *Adventures of Huckleberry Finn*. New York: Harper & Row, 1987.
___, and Walter Blair, eds. *The Art of Huckleberry Finn: Text, Sources, Criticisms*. San Francisco: Chandler, 1962.
___. *Mark Twain: God's Fool*. New York: Harper & Row, 1973.
Hinz, John. "Huck and Pluck: 'Bad' Boys in American Fiction." *South Atlantic Quarterly*, 51 (January 1952), 120-29.
Hoffman, Daniel G. "Jim's Magic: Black or White?" *American Literature*, 32 (March 1960), 45-54.
Inge, M. Thomas, ed. *Huck Finn Among the Critics: A Centennial Selection*. Frederick, MD: University Publications of America, 1985.
Johnson, James William. "The Adolescent Hero: A Trend in Modern Fiction." *Twentieth Century Literature*, 5 (April 1959), 3-11.
Kaplan, Harold. "*Huckleberry Finn*: What it Means to be Civilized." *Democratic Humanism and American Literature*. Kaplan. Chicago: University of Chicago Press, 1972. Pp. 225-252.
Kaplan, Justin. *Mr. Clemens and Mark Twain: a Biography*. New York: Simon and Schuster, 1966.
Kastely, James. "The Ethics of Self-Interest: Narrative Logic in *Huckleberry Finn*." *Nineteenth-Century Fiction*, 40 (1986), 412-37.
Kaufmann, David. "Satiric Deceit in the Ending of *Adventures of Huckleberry Finn*." *Studies in the Novel*, 19 (Spring 1987), 66-78.
Kesterson, David B., ed. *Critics on Mark Twain*. Coral Gables: University of Miami Press, 1973.
Krause, Sydney J. "Huck's First Moral Crisis." *Mississippi Quarterly*, 18 (Spring 1965), 69-73.
Lane, Lauriat, Jr. "Why *Huckleberry Finn* is a Great World Novel." *College English*, 17 (October 1955), 1-5.
Lauber, John. *The Making of Mark Twain: A Biography*. New York: American Heritage Press, 1985.
Leary, Lewis, ed. *A Casebook on Mark Twain's Wound*. New York: Thomas Y. Crowell, 1962.

Leary, Lewis. "Tom and Huck: Innocence on Trial." *Virginia Quarterly Review*, 30 (Summer 1954), 417-30.

Lettis, Richard, Robert F. McDonnell, and William E. Morris, eds. *Huck Finn and His Critics*. New York: Macmillan, 1962.

Levy, Leo B. "Society and Conscience in *Huckleberry Finn*." *Nineteenth-Century Fiction*, 18 (March 1964), 383-91.

Light, James F. "Paradox, Form, and Despair in *Huckleberry Finn*." *Mark Twain Journal*, 21, No. 4 (Fall 1983), 24-25.

Long, E. Hudson, and J.R. McMaster. *The New Mark Twain Handbook*. New York: Garland, 1985.

Lynn, Kenneth S. "Huck and Jim." *Yale Review*, 47 (March 1958), 421-31.

__, ed. *Huckleberry Finn: Text, Sources and Criticism*. New York: Harcourt, Brace & World, 1961.

__. *Mark Twain and Southwestern Humor*. Boston and Toronto: Little, Brown, 1959.

Machan, Tim William. "The Symbolic Narrative of *Huckleberry Finn*." *Arizona Quarterly*, 12 (1986), 131-40.

Machilis Paul, ed. *A Union Catalog of Clemens Letters*. Berkeley, California, 1986.

Macnaughton, William R. *Mark Twain's Last Years as a Writer*. Columbia: University of Mo. Press, 1979.

Manierre, William R. "On Keeing the Raftsmen's Passage in *Huckleberry Finn*." *English Language Notes*, 6 (1968), 118-22.

Marks, Barry A., ed. *Mark Twain's Huckleberry Finn*. Boston: D.C. Heath & Co., 1959.

Marx, Leo. *The Machine in the Garden: Technology and the Pastoral Ideal in America*. New York: Oxford University Press, 1964.

__. "The Pilot and the Passenger: Landscape Conventions and the Style of *Huckleberry Finn*." *American Literature*, 28 (May 1956), 129-46.

Mason, Ernest D. "Attraction and Repulsion: Huck Finn, 'Nigger' Jim, and Black Americans Revisited." *College Language Association Journal*, 33 (Sept. 1989), 36-48.

May, Charles E. "Literary Masters and Masturbators: Sexuality, Fantasy, and Reality in *Huckleberry Finn*." *Literature and Psychology*, 28, No. 2 (1978), 85-92.

McIntyre, James P. "Three Practical Jokes: A Key to Huck's Changing Attitude Toward Jim." *Modern Fiction Studies*, 14 (Spring 1968), 33-37.

McMahan, Elizabeth E. "The Money Motif: Economic Implications in *Huckleberry Finn*." *Mark Twain Journal*, 15 (Summer 1971), 5-10.

Monteiro, George. "Narrative Laws and Narrative Lies in *Adventures of Huckleberry Finn*." *Studies in American Fiction*, 13, No. 2 (Autumn 1985), 227-237

Moses, W. R. "The Pattern of Evil in *Adventures of Huckleberry Finn*." *Georgia Review*, 13 (Summer 1959), 161-66.

Neider, Charles, ed. *The Autobiography of Mark Twain*. New York: Harper, 1959.

O'Connor, William Van. "Why *Huckleberry Finn* Is Not the Great American Novel." *College English*, 17 (October 1955), 6-10.

Paine, Albert Bigelow. *Mark Twain: A Biography*. 4 vols. New York: Harper, 1912.

Pearce, Roy Harvey. "'The End. Yours Truly, Huck Finn': Postscript." *Modern Language Quarterly*, 24, No. 3 (September 1963), 253-256.

Pearce, Roy Harvey. "Huck Finn in His History." *Etudes Anglaises*, 24 (July-September 1971), 283-91.

Percy, Walker. "The Man on the Train: Three Existential Modes." *Partisan Review*, 23 (Fall 1956), 478-94.

Pflug, Raymond J. *The Adventures of Huckleberry Finn: The Evolution of a Classic*. New York: Ginn, 1965.

Podhoretz, Norman. "The Literary Adventures of Huck Finn." *New York Times Book Review*, (6 December 1959), 5, 34.

Pribek, Thomas. "Huckleberry Finn: His Masquerade and His Lessons for Lying." *American Literary Realism*, 19 (Spring 1987), 68-79.

Quirk Thomas. "'Learning a Nigger to Argue': Quitting *Huckleberry Finn*." *American Literary Realism*, 20 (Fall 1987), 18-33.

___. "The Legend of Noah and the Voyage of Huckleberry Finn." *Mark Twain Journal*, 21 (Spring 1982), 21-23.

Railton, Stephen. "Jim and Mark Twain: What Do Dey Stan' For?" *Virginia Quarterly Review*, 63 (Summer 1987), 393-408.

Robinson, Forrest G. *In Bad Faith: The Dynamics of Deception in Mark Twain's America*. Cambridge, Mass.: Harvard University Press, 1986.

Rubenstein, Gilbert M. "The Moral Structure of *Huckleberry Finn*." *College English*, 18 (November 1956), 72-76.

Rubin, Louis D., Jr. "Mark Twain and the Language of Experience." *Sewanee Review*, 71 (Autumn 1963), 664-73.

___. "Mark Twain's South: Tom and Huck." *The American South: Portrait of a Culture*. Ed. Rubin. Baton Rouge: Louisiana State University Press, 1980. Pp. 190-205.

Rule, Henry B. "A Brief History of the Censorship of *The Adventures of Huckleberry Finn*." *Lamar Journal of the Humanities*, 12 (1986), 9-18.

Sawicki, Joseph. "Authority/Author-ity: Representation and Fictionality in *Huckleberry Finn*." *Modern Fiction Studies*, 31 (Winter 1985), 691-702.

Sanborn, Margaret. *Mark Twain: The Bachelor Years*. New York: Doubleday, 1989.

Sattelmeyer, Robert and J. Donald Crowley, eds. *One Hundred Years of Huckleberry Finn: The Boy, His Book, and American Culture: Centennial Essays*. Columbia: University of Missouri Press, 1985.

Schacht, Paul. "The Lonesomeness of *Huckleberry Finn*." *American Literature*, 53 (May 1981), 189-201.

Schmitter, Dean Morgan, ed. *Mark Twain: A Collection of Critical Essays*. New York: McGraw-Hill, 1974.

Schmitz, Neil. "Twain, *Huckleberry Finn*, and the Reconstruction." *American Studies*, 12 (Spring 1971), 59-67.

Scholes, James B., and Walter Harding, eds. *Samuel L. Clemens's The Adventures of Huckleberry Finn: A Study Guide*. Bound Brook, N.J.: Shelley Publishing Co., 1962.

Scott, Arthur L., ed. *Mark Twain: Selected Criticism*. Dallas: Southern Methodist University Press, 1955.

Seelye, John. *The True Adventures of Huckleberry Finn*. Evanston, Illinois: Northwestern University Press, 1970.

Sewell, David R. *Mark Twain's Languages: Discourse, Dialogue, and Linguistic Variety*. Berkeley: University of California Press, 1987.

Sidnell, M. J. "Huck Finn and Jim: Their Abortive Freedom Ride." *Cambridge Quarterly*, 2 (Summer 1967), 203-11.

Simpson, Claud M., Jr. ed. *Twentieth Century Interpretations of Adventures of Huckleberry Finn: A Collection of Critical Essays*. Englewood Cliffs, New Jersey: Prentice-Hall, 1968.

Sloane, David E. *Adventures of Huckleberry Finn: American Comic Vision*. Boston: Twayne, 1988.

Smith, Harriet Elinor, et. al. *Mark Twain's Letters*. Vol II: 1867-1868. Berkeley: University of California Press, 1990.

Smith, Henry Nash, ed. *Mark Twain: A Collection of Critical Essays*. Englewood Cliffs, New Jersey: Prentice-Hall, 1963.

___. *Mark Twain: The Development of a Writer*. Cambridge, MA: The Belknap Press of Harvard University Press, 1962.

___. "Mark Twain's Image of Hannibal: From St. Petersburg to Eseldorf." *Texas Studies in English*, 37 (1958), 3-23.

___. "The Publication of *Huckleberry Finn*: A Centennial Retrospect." *Bulletin of the American Academy of Arts and Sciences*, 37 (February 1984), 18-40.

Solomon, Eric. "*Huckleberry Finn* Once More." *College English*, 22 (December 1960), 172-78.

Stein, Ruth. "The ABC's of Counterfeit Classics: Adapted, Bowdlerized, and Condensed." *English Journal*, 55 (December 1966), 1160-63.

Strickland, Carol Colclough. "Of Love and Loneliness, Society and Self in *Huckleberry Finn*." *Mark Twain Journal*, 21 (Fall 1983), 50-52.

Tenney, Thomas A. *Mark Twain: A Reference Guide*. Boston: G.K. Hall, 1977.

Trilling, Lionel. "Introduction." *The Adventures of Huckleberry Finn*. New York: Rinehart, 1948. Pp. v-xviii.

Vales, Robert L. "Thief and Theft in *Huckleberry Finn*." *American Literature*, 37 (January 1966), 420-29.

Vogelback, Arthur Lawrence. "The Publication and Reception of *Huckleberry Finn* in America." *American Literature*, 11 (November 1939), 260-72.

Warren, Robert Penn. "Mark Twain." *Southern Review*, No. 8 (July 1972), 459-92.

Wecter, Dixon. *Sam Clemens of Hannibal*. Boston: Houghton Mifflin, 1952.

Yates, Norris W. "The 'Counter-Conversion' of Huckleberry Finn." *American Literature*, 32 (March 1960), 1-10.

Index

About the Editor

LAURIE CHAMPION, a graduate student at the University of North Texas, is currently working on a collection of critical essays on Eudora Welty's fiction.